T0305877

PARTISAN INVESTMENT IN THE GLOBAL ECONOMY

This book develops a partisan theory of foreign direct investment (FDI) to explain cross-country and temporal variance in the regulation of foreign investment and in the amount of FDI inflows that countries receive. The author explores the host governments' partisan alignment, whether pro-labor or pro-capital, to determine if they will be more open or closed to FDI.

To reach this determination, the book derives the conditions under which investment flows should be expected to affect the relative demand for the services supplied by economic actors in host countries. Based on these expected distributive consequences, a political economy model of the regulation of FDI and changes in investment performance within countries and over time is developed.

The theory is tested using both cross-national statistical analysis and two case studies exploring the development of the foreign investment regimes and their performance over the past century in Argentina and South Korea.

Pablo M. Pinto is an associate professor in the Department of Political Science at Columbia University. His work has been published or is forthcoming in *International Organization, Review of International Political Economy, State Politics & Policy Quarterly, Economics & Politics,* and *Comparative Political Studies.* In addition to this book, he is co-author of *Politics and Foreign Direct Investment* and of numerous book chapters. He received his PhD from the University of California, San Diego.

Partisan Investment in the Global Economy

*Why the Left Loves Foreign Direct Investment and
FDI Loves the Left*

PABLO M. PINTO

Columbia University

CAMBRIDGE
UNIVERSITY PRESS

University Printing House, Cambridge CB2 8BS, United Kingdom

One Liberty Plaza, 20th Floor, New York, NY 10006, USA

477 Williamstown Road, Port Melbourne, VIC 3207, Australia

314-321, 3rd Floor, Plot 3, Splendor Forum, Jasola District Centre, New Delhi - 110025, India

103 Penang Road, #05-06/07, Visioncrest Commercial, Singapore 238467

Cambridge University Press is part of the University of Cambridge.

It furthers the University's mission by disseminating knowledge in the pursuit of education, learning and research at the highest international levels of excellence.

www.cambridge.org
Information on this title: www.cambridge.org/9781107019102

© Pablo M. Pinto 2013

This publication is in copyright. Subject to statutory exception and to the provisions of relevant collective licensing agreements, no reproduction of any part may take place without the written permission of Cambridge University Press.

First published 2013

A catalogue record for this publication is available from the British Library

Library of Congress Cataloging in Publication data
Pinto, Pablo Martín.
Partisan investment in the global economy : why the left loves foreign direct investment and FDI loves the left / Pablo M. Pinto.
  p.   cm.
Includes bibliographical references and index.
ISBN 978-1-107-01910-2 – ISBN 978-1-107-61736-0 (pbk.)
1. Investments, Foreign.   2. Right and left (Political science)   I. Title.
HG4538.P488   2013
332.67′3–dc23   2012029379

ISBN 978-1-107-01910-2 Hardback
ISBN 978-1-107-61736-0 Paperback

Cambridge University Press has no responsibility for the persistence or accuracy of URLs for external or third-party internet websites referred to in this publication, and does not guarantee that any content on such websites is, or will remain, accurate or appropriate.

To Nico, Palo, Joaco, and Loli

Contents

List of Figures

List of Tables

Acknowledgments

This book is the result of many years of work and the generous support, encouragement, and assistance of numerous professors, colleagues, students, friends, and family. The intellectual lineage of the ideas presented in this book can be traced back to my experience as a corporate lawyer for a multinational firm and was shaped in seminar rooms in Aoyama Gakuin University, the University of California San Diego, Columbia University, and other academic institutions. Growing up in Argentina made me well aware that foreign investment and the activity of multinational corporations are indeed sources of heated controversy. I later learned that the Japanese have always been suspicious of foreign business and would systematically restrict its entry. Yet in both cases the negative disposition toward foreign investors did not seem solely rooted in nationalistic sentiment. In Argentina, the indictment to foreign investment was allegedly made in the name of labor. Multinationals and foreign investors were deemed bad, because they tended to line up with domestic capital to exploit workers under the complicit sponsorship of authoritarian rulers. The complaint in Japan came from potential foreign investors who found it virtually impossible to enter the Japanese marketplace; they claimed that the Japanese government was beholden to a tight web of entrenched local business interests who did not like competition from abroad.

My interest in understanding the determinants of business-government relations intensified while working for Toyota in Argentina. At the weekly production meetings held in the mezzanine of the assembly line of Toyota's Zárate plant, I gained insights into the boundaries of labor-management relations that clashed with traditional accounts of the politics of investment. This special relationship between seemingly odd bedfellows was not limited to Toyota. In the regular meetings of the national business association, I witnessed how the union courted multinational corporations by offering them more favorable labor contracts than those prevailing in the factories controlled by local firms, which operated under licensing agreements. The affiliates setting up shop in the country would hold their part of the bargain by rewarding workers with better wages and working conditions. The government would play an important role supporting this close relationship between labor and management.

The blatant contradiction between the events I observed in Argentina and Japan, and the academic and journalistic explanations of the politics of foreign investment piqued my curiosity. It became apparent to me that nationalism failed as an explanation of the pattern of support and opposition to foreign investment in Argentina and Japan. But so did those theories that portrayed the relationship between foreign capital and labor as inimical. My contribution to this debate is coloring the politics of foreign direct investment in partisan hues. I hope this book opens new avenues of research on the politics of globalization and advances our understanding of the causes and consequences of democratic governance in international economic relations. I also believe that this line of research has real-world applications: identifying the conditions that allow countries and investors to engage each other in less conflictive and more productive ways. From a normative standpoint, the ultimate goal is to allow welfare-enhancing opportunities to materialize under democratic governance.

While writing this book I have benefited from the advice of numerous individuals. I am especially indebted to my professors, committee members, and classmates at the University of California San Diego, where I started my research on the politics of investment. My greatest intellectual debt goes to Peter Gourevitch and Miles Kahler, my dissertation committee co-chairs, who have always been strong believers in this project. Their guidance, mentorship, and support throughout the years were critical in my training, inspired my research, and guided my academic career. I am also indebted to Peter for suggesting the subtitle of the book, which nicely captures my central focus on the role of preferences in the political economy of FDI. I have worked closely with the other members of my dissertation committee, Lawrence Broz, Gordon Hanson, Peter Smith, and Carlos Waisman. They generously offered their time and intellect to develop the argument early on, and later helped me identify which parts of the project had the potential to evolve into this book. I am grateful to David Lake, Steph Haggard, Mike Hiscox, Santiago Pinto, and Jeff Timmons, for their relentless disposition to read and comment on the many draft versions of the manuscript I have sent their way. I am indebted to all of them for their support over the years, and I am confident I will rely on their wisdom in my future endeavors.

The project has evolved theoretically and empirically in response to the generous contributions and interactions with peers, colleagues, and friends. I was fortunate to discuss my research with a number of scholars who provided comments, critiques, suggestions for improvement, and guidance in finding data sources, historical narratives, and developing the technical sections of the manuscript. Among them I would like to sincerely thank Carlos Acuña, Daniel Azpiazu, Neal Beck, Bill Bernhard, Glen Biglaiser, Carles Boix, Roberto Bouzas, Tim Büthe, Daniel Chudnovsky, John Coatsworth, Youssef Cohen, Mark Copelovitch, Peter Cowhey, Bob Erikson, Tanisha Fazal, Seth Fein, Ron Findlay, Al Fishlow, Page Fortna, Robert Franzese, Erik Gartzke, Mike Gilligan, Lucy Goodhart, Jude Hays, Vit Henisz, Shigeo Hirano, John Huber, Llewelyn Hughes, Macartan Humphreys, Nathan Jensen, Bob Jervis, Scott Kastner, Bob Kaufman, David Leblang, Marcelo Leiras, Quan Li, Eric Magar, Eddy Malesky, Ed Mansfield, Isabela Mares, Yotam Margalit, Fiona McGillivray, Tim McKeown, Helen Milner, Layna Mosley, Vicky Murillo, Megumi Naoi, Augusto Nieto, Sharyn O'Halloran, Angel O'Mahony, Sonal Pandya, Pablo Piccato, Karen Poniachik, Dennis Quinn, Chad Rector, Stephanie Rickard, Peter Rosendorff, Nita Rudra, Shanker Satyanath, Sebastian Saiegh, Karl Sauvant, Ken Scheve, Jorge Schiavon, Beth Simmons, David Singer, Alastair Smith, Jack Snyder, Randy Stone, David Stasavage, Mariano Tommasi, Tom Trebat, Rafael Vergara, Jim Vreeland, Robert Walker, Matt Winters, Qiang Zhou, and Boliang Zhu. I am extremely grateful to all of them. I presented different parts and sections of the book at many seminars, conferences, and conventions, including the Pennsylvania State University, Washington University in St. Louis, CIDE, Universidad de San Andres, Princeton, Pittsburgh, Duke, Columbia, UNC, the Columbia-Vale Center for Sustainable Development, IPES, MPSA, APSA, and ISA. I owe a debt of gratitude to participants in all of these events for their excellent comments and suggestions. I am especially thankful to Nate Jensen, Quan Li, and Eddy Malesky for creating an environment for scholarly exchange of ideas about the political economy of FDI.

It was a real pleasure working with Scott Parris at Cambridge University Press. Many thanks go to Scott, Eric Crahan, and Lew Bateman for their enthusiasm about the project and their superb editorial advice. I am grateful to Kristin Purdy, Adam Levine, and all the Cambridge staff for helping me navigate the editing, production, and publication processes. I would also like to acknowledge the three anonymous reviewers of the manuscript whose excellent comments were extremely helpful in improving the quality of the book.

Research and fieldwork for the empirical section of the manuscript were generously funded by a number of institutions. Among these funding sources, I would like to acknowledge a Dissertation Grant awarded by the Center for Iberian and Latin American Studies at UCSD; Faculty Research and Travel Grants from Columbia's Institute of Latin American Studies at Columbia University; a Faculty Research Grant from Columbia's Weatherhead East Asian Institute; two Summer Grant Programs in the Social Sciences from Columbia's School of Arts and Science; and a Faculty seed grant from the Institute for Social and Economic Policy and Research (ISERP) at Columbia. I thank Tomas Bril Mascarenhas, Gustavo de las Casas, Eugenia Giraudy, Patrice Howard, Sung Eun Kim, Matias Mednik, Rayhan Momin, Virginia Oliveros, and Michael Smith for their outstanding assistance. They helped me identify and retrieve original data sources; conducted archival research; classified official resolutions and other relevant documents; cataloged legislative activity and historical news sources; cleaned up data, figures, and graphs; and indexed and proofread the book.

I am grateful to my family and friends for their unconditional encouragement and affection. My parents, Yeyé and Pebe, have encouraged me to explore the world, instilled my interest in politics, and challenged me to think critically. I also learned from them how important it is to have strong family ties. My passion for politics and interest in understanding the complex world we live in has also been influenced by the long discussions at their home with my brothers and sisters, nieces and nephews, aunts, uncles, cousins, and friends. I am grateful to my extended family in Mar del Plata (and Australia), with special thanks to my in-laws, Alicia and José Luis, who are always there for us. I truly appreciate the friendship of Paula Ahets, Natalia Gualco, Gabriela Locatelli, Xochitl Medina, Roxana Rostan, Sergio Abramovich, Fede Bares, Gaston Beato, Diego Capelli, Sergio Cavalli, Cuici Ennis, Mariano Gaut, Sebastian Guerrini, Pablo Piccato, Nicolas Stier, Gerardo Wadel, and Marcelo Zitelli. I sincerely thank them for having stoically endured many of my long-winded presentations on different parts of the book.

Finally, I owe more than I will ever be able to gracefully express to my wife and our three children. Dolores has been by my side throughout this journey that started many years ago in La Plata. I cherish her positive attitude, her relentless energy. Her unconditional support and love have been, and will always be, critical to me. Our children, Joaquín, Paloma, and Nicolás are the most delightful, sensitive, and joyous children I could hope for. My greatest satisfaction is dedicating this book to Nico, Palo, Joaco, and Loli. I appreciate their patience, support, and love. I learn from them the most important lessons in life.

ONE

Domestic Coalitions and the Political Economy
of Foreign Direct Investment

1.1 Globalization of Production and Politics

We live in a world of globalized markets, where goods, services, capital, and workers move across national borders with ease, albeit with different degrees of latitude depending on the type of flow. The transforming effects of this rapid process of global economic integration are subject to heated debates among scholars, pundits, and journalists.

Some argue that technological innovation and changes in the patterns of production at a global level have flattened the world and forced national governments to adjust their regulatory standards to the levels acceptable to multinational businesses and institutional investors (Friedman, 2007; Strange, 1996).[1] Globalization pessimists argue that the forces of market integration have led to a negative form of policy convergence: governments are forced on a race to the bottom and a consequent leveling of national regulatory standards. The territorial state, which dominated the industrial era, is increasingly becoming obsolete, and is gradually being replaced by new forms of global governance (Ohmae, 1995; Strange, 1996, 1998; Rosecrance, 1999). Moreover, the pressure from global markets have blurred the ideological differences among political parties not only in developed countries, but particularly in the developing world: to stay competitive in the global marketplace governments of the left and the right alike have become fanatical advocates of the neoliberal cause (see Edwards, 1995; Williamson, 1990; Garrett, 2000). The conclusion is that when dealing with global market forces, politics does not matter any more, if it ever did.

On the opposing side of the debate we find claims that the incentives and constraints created by global economic forces lead to policy divergence

---

[1] See Garrett (2000) for an excellent review of the academic literature on the subject.

rather than convergence (Tiebout, 1956; Vogel, 1996; Berger and Dore, 1996; Kahler, 1998; Kahler and Lake, 2003). The patterns of divergence are systematic: they depend as much on the preferences of the actors as they react to the constraints and opportunities created by global forces (Cameron, 1978; Rodrik, 1997). Scholars ascribing to this tradition argue that governments have ample room to maneuver and make policy choices that are a clear reflection of their types (Swank, 1998; Hall and Soskice, 2001; Garrett and Mitchell, 2001; Swank and Steinmo, 2002). The heated debate on the consequences of globalization, present in politics, journalism, and academia, is far from settled.

Changes in global production spearheaded by multinational corporations are a central characteristic of the current era of globalization (Bordo et al., 1999). Yet, while there is profuse literature on the political economy of trade and financial flows, research on the politics of direct investment flows and the regulation of multinationals has only recently picked up steam. This book develops a political economy explanation of foreign direct investment (FDI) regulation and performance. The partisan theory of FDI, built around the strategic interaction between investors and host governments, predicts that divergence rather than convergence in regulatory standards is more likely to attain even under the pressure created by competition for foreign investment. An important determinant of this divergence is the partisan orientation of the ruling coalition, which determines the motivation to attract or deter FDI, and the ability of that coalition to effect the policy changes aimed at luring investors in or keeping them out.

The partisan theory of FDI is derived from the intuition that FDI "creates winners and losers domestically," and that these expected distributive consequences inform the politics of FDI. These distributive motivations are, at best, only implicitly accounted for in most of the academic work on the subject. The argument developed throughout the book brings preferences towards FDI to the fore. These preferences are explicitly derived from the differential effect of FDI on the demand for the services offered by different factors of production in the economy where the foreign investor operates. The predictions follow the theoretical and empirical literature on foreign investment, which persuasively shows that workers – both skilled and unskilled – tend to benefit from inflows of FDI (Lipsey and Sjöholm, 2004, 2005; Sjöholm and Lipsey, 2006), whereas the return to capital in the FDI-receiving country tends to fall (Lipsey and Sjöholm, 2005; Haddad and Harrison, 1993; Aitken et al., 1996, 1997; Feenstra and Hanson, 1997; Aitken and Harrison, 1999; Figlio and Blonigen, 2000; Feliciano and Lipsey,

1999).[2] Taken together, the results unveiled by the empirical literature on MNC activity suggest that in the aggregate investment flows result in higher labor demand, and this higher wages and employment; MNCs also create competitive pressure on firms in host countries and have limited spillover effects on indigenous firms. Moreover, the literature suggests that on average a dollar in FDI gets translated into roughly a dollar in domestic investment. Therefore, it has the potential to affect labor and capital productivity in the direction assumed by the model. Moreover the theoretical literature on MNCs and FDI, we believe that direct investment is a combination of capital and technology. Therefore, it is likely that at the extremes workers would prefer investment capital and technology that does not substitute for their service in production, and domestic capital owners would prefer access to labor-saving technology but no investment capital.

From the findings of this literature, I develop a political economy model of the interaction between foreign business and domestic government built on micro-foundations. The modeling strategy aims at capturing the incentives and constraints faced by the different actors involved. Regulatory restrictions on foreign investment would thus be a function of the strategic interaction between governments and investors. The argument is related to the positive political economy literature that has been built around trade politics, but the special nature of FDI makes some of the conditions in that literature inapplicable to this case. In particular, the dichotomy between sectors and factors does not necessarily apply as explained in the following paragraph. What matters is the factor bias of FDI: does foreign investment increase the relative demand for labor services and does it create competition to incumbent firms in product and factor markets? (Brown et al., 2004; Pinto and Pinto, 2008).

---

[2] Brown et al. (2004) and Lipsey (2004) review the empirical literature on the consequences of FDI. Brown et al. (2004, pp. 299–303) present an overview of the different theoretical models from which the distributional effects of the flow of capital on factor returns can be derived. They conclude that the *normal case* is "labor earning a higher wage as a result of an inflow of FDI." The result would be reversed in the case where capital substitutes for labor in production (Brown et al., 2004, p. 303, fn. 35), an intuition that is developed in Pinto and Pinto (2007, 2008, 2011). It is also plausible, in theory, that under special conditions an MNC becomes a monopsonist in factor markets and this negatively affect wage bargaining; historical examples could be found in foreign investment in plantation-style activities. But even when MNCs dominate factor markets they are also likely to enjoy product market power, leading to rents that could be shared with workers, especially when they are unionized, and in result wages would not necessarily drop (Katz and Summers, 1989). Yet, most MNCs face competition in labor markets from domestic and foreign firms suggesting that the negative effect on wages is now but an intellectual curiosity (Brown et al., 2004).

The predictions from the theory seem to be borne out by the evidence produced in the empirical section of the book: governments seek out investors that are likely to contribute to the well-being of the core constituents of their party or coalition; and investors choose forms of production that are tailored to the specific political conditions in host countries, particularly the partisan orientation of the incumbent government. By focusing on the constraints and opportunities created by the explosion of foreign direct investment, I can analyze in a rigorous manner the interaction between global economic forces and politics. The conclusions from this analysis provide stronger support to the divergence school, while shedding some light on central debates in political science on the role of political institutions and preferences in foreign economic policy making.

1.2 Domestic Coalitions and the Political Economy of FDI

Despite the dramatic increase in the flows and stock of direct foreign investment in the last thirty years, there is large variance in the amount of foreign direct investment that individual countries receive.[3] The motivations for engaging in FDI have expanded beyond securing access to natural resources, which had characterized most foreign direct investment in the past; manufacturing and particularly services now comprise the bulk of direct investment flows (Bordo et al., 1999). Host governments have quickly reacted to these new trends in production and investment strategies by multinational firms by changing policies targeted at foreign investors. While many governments adopted pro-investor regulations in the 1990s, the menu of policies toward foreign investment is extensive and not always favorable to foreigners (see Table 1.2). Moreover, within countries, changes in foreign investment regulation over time have been quite dramatic as well (UNCTAD 2000, UNCTAD 2010).

Surprisingly, we lack a convincing explanation for the cross-country and temporal variance in the regulation of foreign investment and in the amount of FDI inflows that countries receive. The specialized literature to date focuses on the role of institutional constraints and the protection of investors' property rights (Jensen, 2003, 2006; Li and Resnick, 2003). When choosing location sites for their projects, investors only care about minimizing their risk exposure; risk is likely to be lower when the ruler is institutionally constrained; and institutional constraints are more prevalent in polities with democratic institutions and limited government

---

[3] See section 1.4, Table 1.1, and UNCTAD (2000, 2010).

Table 1.1. *FDI/GDP (%) – selected countries*[a]

	1980–4	1985–9	1990–4	1995–9	2000–04	2005–07
Developed Countries						
EU	0.40	0.67	0.97	2.17	5.10	4.85
France	0.39	0.67	1.33	1.94	2.87	4.52
Germany	0.10	0.22	0.14	1.00	3.20	1.65
Ireland	1.00	0.28	2.10	8.11	13.59	−1.81
Japan	0.02	0.01	0.04	0.09	0.18	0.23
UK	1.04	2.29	1.84	3.65	3.58	7.04
USA	0.55	0.98	0.60	1.68	1.52	1.49
Developing Countries						
Argentina	0.55	0.76	1.42	3.75	2.11	2.64
Brazil	0.87	0.46	0.37	2.57	3.40	2.03
China	0.23	0.81	3.41	4.43	3.13	3.60
Hungary	0.00	0.00	3.44	8.22	4.94	17.08
India	0.03	0.06	0.14	0.64	0.92	1.56
Korea	0.09	0.42	0.25	0.99	0.98	0.45
Malaysia	4.05	2.31	7.10	4.56	2.75	3.76
Mexico	1.15	1.17	1.48	3.01	3.24	2.31
Poland	...	0.02	1.05	3.33	3.54	4.88
Thailand	0.75	1.19	1.84	3.33	3.41	4.26
World	0.54	0.77	0.85	1.99	2.65	3.17

[a] *Source:* World Bank, World Development Indicators (online resource).

(North and Thomas, 1973; North and Weingast, 1989; North, 1990). There-fore, democracy and FDI inflows should be positively correlated. The prediction that democracy should increase FDI through property rights protection is sensible and seems to find preliminary support in the empirical literature (Jensen, 2003, 2006; Li and Resnick, 2003). However, it overlooks two central elements in the political economy of foreign investment. First, it misses investors' central motivation: the search for higher returns. As much as they care about minimizing risk exposure, investors' main concern is to maximize the return of their investment. Second, these explanations treat host governments as passive actors: either they have the features that investors like or not, but there is nothing they can do about it. The decision on where to invest, however, is more properly characterized as the outcome of a strategic interaction between investors and host governments. Host governments enact policies to regulate economic activity, and in doing so they balance the demands of key political actors with the expected reactions of investors to these policies.

Table 1.2. *Changes in national regulations of FDI[a]*

Year	Number of		Type of Changes	
	Countries	Changes	More favorable	Less favorable
1992	43	77	77	–
1993	56	100	99	1
1994	49	110	108	2
1995	63	112	106	6
1996	66	114	98	16
1997	76	150	134	16
1998	60	145	136	9
1999	65	139	130	9
2000	70	150	147	3
2001	71	207	193	14
2002	72	246	234	12
2003	82	242	218	24
2004	103	270	234	36
2005	92	203	162	41
2006	91	177	142	35
2007	58	98	74	24
2008	54	106	83	23
2009	50	102	71	31

[a] *Source:* UNCTAD (2010), p. 77.

I provide an alternative explanation, one where the interaction between investors, who are motivated by the quest for higher returns, and politically motivated host governments, who are interested in advancing the preferences of their core constituents, takes center stage in the politics of FDI. Combining these two motivations, I argue that host governments' partisan alignment – whether pro-labor or pro-capital – determines whether countries are more open or closed to FDI. Arriving to this conclusion requires deriving the conditions under which we would expect investment flows to affect the relative demand for the services supplied by different economic actors in the host country.[4] Building on the expected distributive consequences of investment, I develop a political economy model of the regulation of FDI. I also derive the response of investors to the regulatory framework offered by governments, reflected in changes in investment performance within countries and over time. The explanation emphasizes the role of

---

[4] Whereas the model is based on the effect of inward FDI in factor markets, i.e., changes in the relative demand for services supplied by businesses and workers, the distributive consequences could be derived from increasing competitive pressure in product markets as well.

partisanship, which is defined in terms of the incumbent coalition's pro-labor or pro-capital orientation. The main corollary derived from this model is that labor-based parties or coalitions are more likely to welcome foreign investment, particularly those investments that would result in higher labor demand; conversely, governments catering to domestic businesses prefer restricting direct investment inflows that compete with domestic businesses in product and factor markets.[5] Therefore, countries governed by pro-labor coalitions adopt policies to promote foreign investment and are likely to be better hosts to foreign investors. Contrary to received wisdom, I find that the argument that the Left loves foreign investors and foreign investors love the Left is plausible, and that the result holds beyond the new era of globalized markets.

The main hypotheses of the partisan theory of FDI parallel the intuition behind the literature on the political economy of trade: flows of direct investment capital, such as flows of goods and services across national borders, can result in aggregate economic benefits to the host economy.[6] Just like trade, foreign investment flows are likely to have stark distributional consequences.[7] Direct investment flows have real effects on the host economy: they have the potential to increase output and affect competition in labor and factor markets. Inflows of capital, of which FDI is one form, affect the relative demand for the services supplied by different economic

---

[5] I build my argument around the *direct* effects of investment on the relative demand for labor services (see footnote 2). It is plausible that there are also indirect effects from FDI, where consumers and firms not directly in competition with the investor would benefit (or hurt) from the spillover effects of inward FDI (or its absence thereof) (Lipsey and Sjöholm, 2005; Lin and Saggi, 2005). The model presented in Chapter 2 accounts for these indirect effects: the degree of complementarity between FDI and domestic factors of production would make some local firms – those not in direct competition with the foreign firm – benefit from the higher economic activity that results from the entry of foreign investors, which they tradeoff for the potentially higher costs of factor services that results from the presence of the MNCs. The net effect on the income of these capital owners could thus be positive, yet not as positive as if the foreign investor enters as a substitute for labor (reducing labor costs), which is usually an exception rather than the rule. These positive spillover effects would mitigate the opposition to FDI, particularly when compared with capital owners in direct competition with the foreign investor in product and factor markets. Yet, they would still be relatively more opposed to inward investment than workers.

[6] The aggregate effects depend on the existence of absorptive capacities in the host; see Blömstrom et al. (1994), Easterly et al. (1994), Borensztein et al. (1998), and Carcovic and Levine (2005). On the effect of foreign investment on technological spillovers, see also Findlay (1978), Kokko (1994), Kokko et al. (1996), Blömstrom and Kokko (1998), Glass and Saggi (1998), Lipsey and Sjöholm (2005), and Lin and Saggi (2005).

[7] See Mundell (1957) and Brown et al. (2004). Mundell's equivalency proposition establishes that factor flows are likely to affect factor returns in the absence of trade, the model developed in Chapter 2 extends the logic for the case where the economy is open to trade.

agents in the host economy, and thus the well-being of these agents.[8] To the extent that collective action costs are not prohibitive, economic agents find that organizing politically in defense of their sources of income usually pays off. Put differently, failure to organize politically in the presence of competing groups with opposing preferences on any issue area is likely to make these agents worse off.[9] I predict that domestic capital will oppose FDI and demand policies aimed at keeping foreign investors out, whereas labor will embrace FDI and promote policies that encourage investors to flow in. Whether those demands get translated into policies and regulations depends on the degree of political influence of these groups, which is likely to vary with their organization and with their links to the ruling party. These predictions run counter to a vast body of literature in political science, which argues that foreign investors are aligned with domestic business owners forming a Triple Alliance aimed at exploiting the popular sectors. See, for example, Oneal (1994), Evans (1979), Evans and Gereffi (1982), and O'Donnell (1988).[10]

The central contribution of the partisan theory of FDI is the emphasis on the expected effects of foreign investment on factor markets, which has been neglected in the literature.[11] The model introduced in Chapter 2 explicitly incorporates the fiscal incentives in the regulation of FDI, which the extant literature makes central to its predictions about the politics of investment.[12] In this model, taxing foreign investors could have an effect on individuals' well-being in the marketplace, which they have to tradeoff for their participation in consuming government services financed with the taxes levied on foreign capital. The relative weights placed on the income derived from participation in the market and the utility from consuming government output, or receiving a direct transfer from the government, is reflected in the choice of policies adopted by host governments of different partisan types. These motivations, discussed in more detail in Section 1.6.6,

---

[8] In Chapter 2, I specify the conditions under which investment flows decrease the return to capital and increase the return to labor in the host. See also Pinto and Pinto (2008).

[9] On the conditions for collective action, see Olson (1971). In the canonical model of trade protection, for instance, political organization determines which groups get their preferred outcome and who is forced to pay for it. See Grossman and Helpman (1994).

[10] The conditions for the triple alliance argument discussed in Section 1.5.1 require very restrictive assumptions about the type of investment and the prevailing political conditions in the host country. Pinto and Pinto (2011) show that it could be considered a special case of the partisan theory of foreign investment where governments are pro-business, redeployment costs are high, foreign investment is a perfect complement in production of domestic capital, and/or a perfect substitute of labor services.

[11] Quinn and Inclan (1997), Alfaro (2004), and Pinto and Pinto (2008, 2011) are exceptions.

[12] See Quinn and Inclan (1997) for a review of this literature.

suggest that there are different shades of left: some parties of the Left prefer lowering taxes on MNCs to magnify labor market effects, whereas for others revenue incentives dominate. For most pro-business governments, on the other hand, regulating FDI is dominated by market effects: if FDI competes with domestic businesses in product and factor markets, these governments are more likely to adopt a *prohibitive tax* that would keep investors out.

Whereas a formal framework sustains the logic of the argument, its plausibility is assessed using a variety of statistical tools and historical evidence. The statistical analyses are conducted using data from developed and democratic countries, and from emerging markets that have received the bulk of foreign investment in the past decades. The historical analyses are based on a structured comparison of the evolution of investment regimes in Argentina and South Korea in the post-war era. The choice of cases and time frame aims at maximizing the cross-sectional and longitudinal variance in the degree of labor and capital influence in politics. This variance occurred as a function of changes in the institutional structure of the two countries, including transitions to democratic and authoritarian rule, and of changes in the orientation of the ruling coalition resulting from institutional changes in addition to electoral turnovers and lobbying.

The quantitative and historical evidence presented in the empirical section of the book provide some preliminary support to the partisan hypothesis: investment regimes and investment outcomes covary with the pro-labor or pro-capital orientation of the incumbent coalition in the host country. The corollary is that countries with labor-based coalitions receive more foreign direct investment than those countries whose ruling coalitions are built around domestic capital owners. The partisan effect on FDI could be mitigated when preferences for social spending are high and investment is highly elastic to taxes, or when access to natural resource and other sources of rents makes governments less dependent on factor market conditions to reward their followers. The theory and subsequent findings capture part of the large variance in the level of foreign investment countries receive that remains unexplained in the extant literature. In the ensuing sections, I introduce the puzzle that motivates this research, define the research problem, and discuss where the issue stands in the literature prior to introducing the partisan theory of FDI. The final section presents the layout of the book.

1.3 Political Alignment and Foreign Investment

Foreign investment and the activity of multinational corporations are controversial political issues. A positive or negative disposition toward foreign investors does not seem to be exclusively the result of political actors' attachment to nationalistic causes. In some cases, the objection to foreign investment is made in the name of labor. Some argue that multinationals and foreign investors are bad because their sole motivation is to exploit host countries; therefore, they line up with domestic capital and authoritarian governments to reap profit at the expense of workers. According to pundits and analysts of multinational activity, this negative sentiment is reciprocal: foreign investors hate places where labor is strong, such as Perón's Argentina. This has been the prevalent position of the *Dependentista* literature in the 1970s.[13] On the other hand, foreign investors usually complain about markets such as Japan or South Korea where they feel unwelcome.[14] The issue is, then, identifying the conditions under which different polities are more or less willing to provide a regulatory environment conducive to foreign investment. The Japanese and Korean cases are less surprising given that the interests of domestic business have been at the center of politics in those countries. But the argument that domestic capital in countries like Argentina, and elsewhere, holds FDI in higher esteem than does domestic labor is debatable at best. A military government that ruled between 1976–83 (the regime was known in Spanish as *"Proceso de Reorganización Nacional"*) repressed labor and was allegedly friendly toward business, yet hardly received any foreign investment. In fact, industrial policies under the military regime actively discriminated against multinational corporations (Azpiazu and Basualdo, 1989). As a result, several of the most prominent multinationals, including automakers such as General Motors, Fiat, and Peugeot, left the country altogether during the military regime. In contrast, the country witnessed what was probably the biggest FDI inflow in history under a Peronist government led by Carlos Menem. These flows remained surprisingly high in manufacturing under the Kirchners, despite the reputation of Perón and his followers of having a negative disposition toward all things foreign.

The prevailing view in Argentina that labor hated FDI also seems questionable, especially in light of survey data that shows otherwise (Dominguez, 1982; Ranis, 1994). Moreover, anecdotal evidence seems to suggest that the depiction of FDI by pundits and analysts is flawed. First, democratic governments, which are usually associated with an erosion of the political influence of propertied interests, seem to attract more FDI than

---

[13] Evans (1979), Evans and Gereffi (1982), and O'Donnell (1988). See Moran (1978) for an excellent discussion of the testable hypotheses that could be derived from the *dependentista* research program.

[14] Kodak and Motorola are the typical case studies on the problems faced by foreign investors when trying to enter the Japanese market.

authoritarian counterparts (Jensen, 2003, 2006). Circumstancial evidence from Argentina's recent history suggests that workers in the auto industry and their representatives in SMATA (Sindicato de Mecánicos y Afines del Transporte Automor) – the union of steel and metal-mechanic workers – were eager to offer favorable shop conditions to foreign investors and lobbied for a change in the regulatory environment to lure them in. Foreign multinationals that had left the country under the pro-business military regime responded favorably to the Peronist, the party with the strongest ties to unions and workers. Unions were willing to offer more flexible and better labor contract conditions to foreign investors than they would to the domestic counterparts that had operated under foreign licenses once foreign investors left. Further, workers and unions gave investors indirect access to Peronist leaders. Foreign companies rewarded workers with better wages and contracts.[15] The Argentine government would play an important role supporting this close relationship between workers and foreign investors: it designed a special regime that rewarded those investing in the sector with tax breaks and trade related investment measures (TRIMS), and negotiated with its Brazilian counterpart that foreign investors operating under this regime in Argentina would have preferential access to the Brazilian market under MERCOSUR rules. This special relationship among foreign investors, unions, and the political party representing workers – groups that were seemingly odd bedfellows according to received wisdom – was not limited to the auto industry; it extended to other manufacturers and services as well.[16] Altogether, the evidence discussed in the empirical section of this book seems to defy received wisdom on the subject, and suggests that more often than not we should expect a positive association between FDI and the Left.

Neither institutional explanations, nor preference-based theories that portray foreign capital and labor as inimical to each other explain the pattern of support and opposition to FDI in Argentina, South Korea, and Japan. We need a different explanation, one that allows for the interests of labor and those of foreign investors to be congruent. The partisan theory

---

[15] These findings are consistent with the cross-national evidence of a wage premium in foreign owned firms (Lipsey and Sjöholm, 2004; Lipsey, 2004; Lipsey and Sjöholm, 2005).

[16] While unions are usually associated with benefits to workers in the formal sector of the economy and labor market insiders (Srinivasan, 1998, p. 239), unionization and collective bargaining can make labor markets more efficient and lead to higher labor productivity, and thus are appealing to investors (Brown et al., 2004, pp. 288–289); see also Moran (2002) and Freeman (1993). Moreover, as Brown et al. (2004, p. 321) persuasively show "there is no solid evidence that countries with poorly protected worker rights attract FDI."

of FDI developed in Chapter 2 provides one such explanation that seems to fit the data quite well. The explanation is based on the assumption that, in general, labor benefits from foreign investment inflows and that capitalists are harmed, which is likely the case for most forms of investment except for the natural resource seeking type.[17] In developing this theory, I prove that the argument that labor hates FDI and that FDI hates labor is theoretically flawed and lacks empirical support. To the extent that FDI inflows change the relative demand for labor, FDI is likely to increase wages and decrease the return to capital, in which case labor would support FDI and capital owners operating in the host economy would oppose it. Moreover, when pro-labor governments are in power, they will enact and commit to pro-FDI policies, and therefore receive more FDI. On the other hand, when pro-capital governments are in power, regulation of FDI is more stringent and restrictive and governments find it harder to commit to foreign investors. Consequently, FDI flows are likely to fall. Assuming that FDI has the potential to increase labor demand as the empirical literature on FDI suggests, or even that foreign investment competes with domestic businesses in product and factor markets, the changing pattern of FDI performance under the pro-business military government and under the pro-labor Menem government in Argentina make more sense. The assumptions allow us to make predictions about the politics of investment that brings the Argentine case closer to the Japanese and South Korean experiences where *pro-business* is usually translated into *anti-foreign* business, and pro-labor would translate into pro-FDI.

The logic behind the model is simple: suppose that there are two factors of production in a country, labor, and capital. Given a certain technology of production that determines the ability of the foreign investor to complement either factor of production, an inflow of direct investment affects the returns to labor and capital in the host country. When this inflow of investment competes wages up and rents down, workers favor foreign investment and owners of capital oppose it. As mentioned earlier, these assumptions run counter to conventional wisdom in the literature that predicts labor opposes capital in general and FDI in particular. In the model presented in Chapter 2, governments have an additional motivation: taxes extracted from foreign capital can be used to produce a government good from which individuals

---

[17] Pinto and Pinto (2008, 2011) extend the analysis by relaxing this assumption. They propose that the expected effect of FDI on the return to workers and capitalists in the host depends on the technology with which investors enter the market. This possibility is probed in Chapters 5 and 6 of the book.

may derive utility. The modeling strategy allows me to identify the scope conditions under which revenue motivations are more likely to dominate the incentives to extract from investors. This is usually in those cases where foreign investment is less likely to affect the well-being of households in the marketplace, where those households weigh more heavily the government-supplied good in their utility function, or where the incumbent government does not internalize the effects of investment in factor markets.

Moreover, I also argue that in a dynamic setting constituency links and partisanship could act as a commitment mechanism that makes host governments more reliable to foreign investors: a partisan government will offer investment conditions preferred by its core constituents, and over time will abide to those conditions. Hence, I predict that foreign investment will be attracted to countries with pro-labor governments, or put differently, will shun countries with pro-business governments. In the empirical section I will produce evidence from statistical analyses and from case studies of post-war Argentina and South Korea that suggest that the argument is, at least, plausible. The following section defines FDI, assesses its importance and describes recent trends in foreign investment and the activity of MNCs.

1.4 Trends in FDI

An investment is considered FDI if it provides the parent firm with a stake – usually 10 percent of voting rights, according to IMF reporting standards – in the control and management of the foreign affiliate (Lipsey, 2001). There is a link between FDI and multinational corporations: Multinational Corporations (MNCs) exist to internalize the transactions costs involved in activities where the property of intangible assets, such as brand names, managerial skills, and production techniques makes arms' length relations risky. In these cases, hierarchical organization of production and internalization of transactions may help to make up for missing markets and imperfect allocation of property rights (Dunning, 1977, 1993a,b; Caves, 1996). FDI usually takes the form of capital that is mobile internationally, but specific to an industry in a host country (Caves, 1996). As such, FDI flows and MNC activity are two sides of one process: MNCs are the driving force of direct investment across national borders.

There are at least two reasons why research on this form of investment is relevant. First, FDI flows have increased dramatically in the last two decades (Figure 1.1), have become an important part of total investment flows, and show more resilience than other forms of private capital flows (Figures 1.2

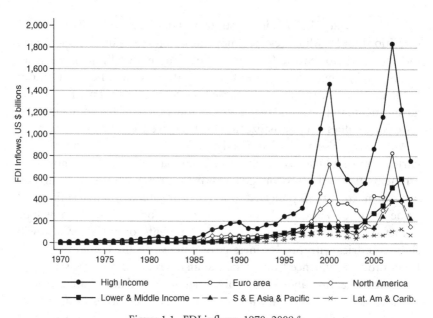

Figure 1.1. FDI inflows, 1970–2009.[a]
[a] *Data Source:* World Bank, World Development Indicators (online resource).

and 1.3). Second, FDI is a vector for the transmission of technology, and thus plays a major role in growth and development (UNCTAD, 1992; Borensztein et al., 1998; UNCTAD, 1999; Przeworski et al., 2000).

Since the late 1970s, FDI has been an important part of total investment flows. In recent years, there has been a massive increase in the scale of FDI flows into emerging markets, which now vastly outstrip portfolio investment and official development assistance (Lipsey, 2001; see Figure 1.2). In the past fifteen years, FDI has grown at a faster pace than output and exports of goods and services, roughly 26 percent to 15 percent annually since the mid-1980s and more so in the second half of the 1990s (see Tables 1.1, and 1.3). Moreover, UNCTAD reports that the foreign market supply of goods and services through FDI has reached U.S.$11 trillion, and was in 2001 larger than the supply of foreign markets through trade which amounts to U.S.$7 trillion (UNCTAD, 2002). Foreign direct investment flows dropped in the 2001 recession, but the pace of internationalization of production regained momentum until the Great Recession of 2008 hit (see Figure 1.1). In 2007, for instance, FDI grew by 36 percent, reaching a record high level of $2.35 trillion, and while it dropped in 2008 and 2009, its contraction was slower than global output. The end result is that the share of value added

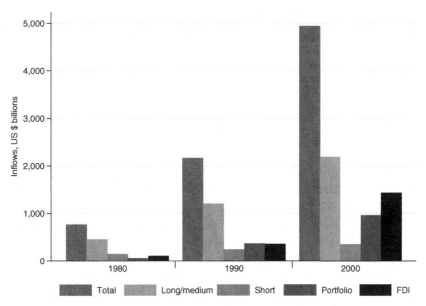

Figure 1.2. Emerging markets: Foreign capital stock.[a]
[a]*Source:* UNCTAD, World Investment Report 2003.

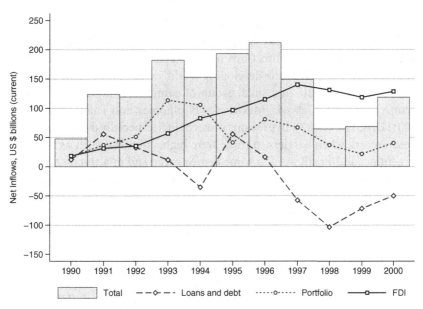

Figure 1.3. Net capital flows to emerging markets, 1990–2000.[a]
[a]*Source:* Dobson et al. (2001), Table A.1, pp. 170–171.

Table 1.3. *World FDI and trade growth*[a]

	Growth rate	
	FDI	Exports
1986–2000	26.2%	15.4%
1995–2000	37.0%	1.9%

[a] *Source:* UNCTAD (2001).

by affiliates of MNCs to world gross domestic product reached 11 percent in 2009 (UNCTAD, 2010).

Historically, developed countries hold the largest share of FDI inflows and outflows, with inflows of up to $1.444 billion dollars in 2007, equivalent to 68.8 percent of world total, and outflows of $1.924 billion of US dollars, representing 84.8 percent of total FDI outflows in the same year. Yet, the share of inflows received by developing and emerging markets has increased dramatically, reaching half of world inflows in 2009. Some developing economies, especially Brazil, Russia, India, and China (BRICs), have become important sources of direct investment outflows, commanding one-fourth of world totals (see Table 1.4).

Among advanced industrialized nations, FDI flows and MNC activity varies significantly. Whereas the United States has been both a source and a destination of foreign direct investment, Japan has been a net exporter of investment capital. In the developing world, on the other hand, FDI has tended to concentrate in a small group of countries comprised of Brazil, China, Indonesia, Malaysia, Mexico, the Philippines, and Thailand (Lipsey, 2001; UNCTAD, 2002). In previous waves of FDI, especially during the early post-war era when barriers to trade were high, countries such as Mexico, Argentina, and Brazil were to some degree successful in attracting foreign investment as they had substantially large and protected domestic markets to offer. Inflows of capital to these countries decreased sharply in the 1980s and did not resume until the 1990s (OECD, 1998a).

Reversals in FDI performance were partly driven by international conditions: in the present period, the world economy has experienced a relentless internationalization of world production, reduction in transportation costs, and the expansion of bilateral and multilateral cooperation aimed at creating an investment climate conducive to transnational activity (UNCTAD, 2003). In 2009 alone, 82 new bilateral investment treaties were signed, and

Table 1.4. *World FDI by regions*[a]

Inflows (billion $)	2007	2008	2009
World	2,100	1,771	1,114
Developed Economies	1,444	1,018	566
Developing Economies	565	630	478
South-East Europe and CIS	91	123	70
Percentage share in world FDI inflows			
Developed Economies	68.8	57.5	50.8
Developing Economies	26.9	35.6	42.9
South-East Europe and CIS	4.3	6.9	6.3
Outflows (billion $)	2007	2008	2009
World	2,268	1,929	1,101
Developed Economies	1,924	1,572	821
Developing Economies	292	296	229
South-East Europe and CIS	52	61	51
Percentage share in world FDI outflows			
Developed Economies	84.8	81.5	74.6
Developing Economies	12.9	15.4	20.8
South-East Europe and CIS	2.3	3.1	4.6

[a] *Data Source:* UNCTAD, World Investment Report 2010.

there were 109 new double taxation treaties concluded.[18] However, changes in domestic regulatory regimes toward foreign investors in those countries have played an important role as well.

In spite of its potential benefits to host countries, FDI is a source of intense political dispute in the real world. In the post-war era, FDI was demonized, particularly by scholars and intellectuals in developing countries. In 1972, revelation of a campaign launched by the American Company ITT in Chile to block the election of Salvador Allende in September 1970 fueled a nationalist reaction against U.S. multinationals. Later, following a gradual conversion from Import Substitution Industrialization (ISI) to export led industrialization, some governments (but not others) became more willing to welcome foreign investors: compare cases such as Thailand with South Korea or Japan with the United Kingdom, as contrasting examples.

[18] According to UNCTAD, at the end of 2008, the cumulative number of BITs signed was 2,750 (UNCTAD, 2010).

More recently, the trend seems to have completely reversed, and it is common practice in the literature to describe governments as entangled in a regulatory race to the bottom in order to attract foreign investment. But, even today, foreign ownership of domestic assets often resonates negatively with the public. Massive layoffs by Spanish-owned Aerolíneas Argentinas in 2001 triggered a widespread campaign in Argentina to boycott Spanish companies and Spanish products.

The debate is not limited to the developing world. The ITT incident in Chile, for instance, was the excuse put forward by the French government in the early 1980s to place ITT on its hit list for nationalization. Moreover, newspapers and magazine articles give testimony of management and capital owners arguing against investment by foreign firms, Japanese and Korean MNCs in particular, in unified Europe. In the United States, public protest against Japanese interests buying a part of America's soul in the early 1990s and negative sentiment against Chinese attempts at purchasing assets in American soil, including the 2005 bid by CNOOC, a Chinese oil company, to buy California based UNOCAL[19] present salient examples.

1.5 FDI in the Literature

As described in the previous sections, we observe that countries receive different amounts of FDI, which do not necessarily correspond to their FDI potential, or the factors that affect countries' attractiveness to FDI (UNCTAD, 2002, 2003). This observation raises several questions: First, can we identify the conditions under which countries open to FDI? Second, and closely related to the previous one, is what determines who gets FDI? Here, we need to look at flows or where FDI goes. Economists have tried to answer this second question indirectly by looking at firms and why they become multinational. However, most of the literature has virtually ignored the link between foreign direct investment and domestic politics.

1.5.1 Determinants of Foreign Direct Investment

There is a vast body of literature in economics on the determinants of capital flows. Explanations can be classified into the following camps: factor proportion explanations and local market supply explanations. Factor proportions explanations state that firms invest where returns are higher, and returns are higher where capital is scarcer (Helpman, 1984; Markusen, 1984;

---

[19] See Frye and Pinto (2009).

Helpman, 1985; Helpman and Krugman, 1985). A variant of this explanation puts emphasis on access to natural resources, human capital, or skills. Foreign investment also takes place in order to supply local markets. This type of investment creates a tradeoff between proximity to consumption and realization of economies of scale (Horstmann and Markusen, 1992; Brainard, 1993b, 1997).

As discussed in the second part of this book, the findings in the empirical literature on FDI are inconclusive: variables traditionally associated with any of the two types of explanations, such as capital, labor, and skill endowments market size, distance, language, and legal systems, are not robust predictors of FDI activity. Further, even those variables with uncontested signs, such as geographical and cultural distance, leave a large part of the variance in FDI performance unexplained (Chakrabarti, 1997; Loungani et al., 2002). In addition, little work explains what countries receive more FDI in the form of aggregate flows. Most importantly, there is a dearth of work on the effects of politics on FDI.

1.5.2 Political Explanations of FDI

Political scientists have looked at the relationship between FDI and politics. One set of explanations link investment outcomes to political institutions. In particular, they focus on regime type, that is, the differences between democracies and autocracies. Some argue that autocracies are better hosts of multinationals because autocratic leaders are more insulated from domestic pressures, particularly those from organized labor, and thus are better able at committing to foreign investors to maintain existing policies after investment has occurred (Oneal and Oneal, 1988; Oneal, 1994). Others assert that democracies should receive more FDI because they offer a more credible environment for investors (Jensen, 2003, 2006; Li and Resnick, 2003). Li and Resnick (2003) add an important nuance to this prediction, which places them in Oneal's camp: democracies place higher burdens on MNC activity through taxation, preferred by the median voter especially in polities with high levels of inequality, and regulation of anti-competitive practices to protect consumers. The controversy is not only theoretical: empirical results are mixed. Li and Resnick (2003) show that the positive correlation between FDI and democracy found by Jensen (2003) turns negative among developing countries once democracy has been purged from the component that measures property rights protection. Both types of explanations assume that the preferences of domestic actors are uniform within democracies and autocracies, completely bracketing the demand side of politics: a movement to and from democracy, for instance, may result in the (dis)enfranchising of actors whose preferences vary over the policy issue dimension at stake (Mayer, 1984). Policy outcomes are not solely the result of changes in the size of the electorate or selectorate in the political marketplace, they also depend on the intersection of the preferences of political principals and agents as mediated by those institutions. A fully specified model of the political economy of FDI needs to account for both demand and supply conditions in policy making.[20]

A second group of institutional explanations looks at political constraints. These explanations are rooted in the transaction costs literature in economics (Williamson, 1979, 1983b, 1985). They argue that investors worry about policy changes, especially after they have deployed their assets abroad. Host governments whose hands are institutionally tied can more credibly commit to these investors. The prediction is that polities with more veto players will provide better reassurance to foreign investors (Henisz and Williamson, 1999; Henisz, 2000b, 2002), because veto players reinforce the status quo, making policies more stable, a condition that investors supposedly prefer.

The institutional environment affects the form of entry of multinationals in different ways, depending on the levels of contractual hazard the firm is exposed to in the host country. When political hazards are high, which occurs when investors face a government that is politically unconstrained and more likely to renege on its contracts, investors may choose to enter in a joint venture with a domestic partner to avert those risks. However, when the nature of the enterprise exposes investors to the potential of being exploited by their local counterparts, majority ownership is the preferred form of entry, exposing foreign investors to political hazard. Therefore, political hazard is not constant across investors types; it can be exacerbated by contractual hazards (Henisz, 2000b).

The emphasis on risk is sensible given the special nature of FDI, but it is subject to two critiques: first, investors care about whether the type of policy that is enacted creates a regulatory environment that is favorable or unfavorable to them. Second, policy stability and rigidity that would result from the existence of higher institutional constraints is but a second best option. Investors would instead prefer policies that covary with changes in the economic environment (Spiller and Tommasi, 2003). Moreover, until the 1980s FDI flowed into countries with institutionalized political systems; however, more recent studies find no negative correlation between indices

---

[20] See Rodrik (1995) for an application of this framework to the literature on endogenous policy formation.

of quality of government and inward FDI (World Bank 1998).[21] Further, anecdotal evidence shows investors flocking to countries where governments do not seem to be institutionally constrained at all, such as Indonesia, Malaysia, China, or even Mexico in the 1990s.

There are other explanations that pay attention to the interests of domestic actors, but their assumptions and predictions differ from those underlying this project. One strand in this literature looks at the link between investment and politics through the prism of class conflict.[22] The *triple alliance* hypothesis – the most prominent exponent of this literature – argues that host governments, domestic businesses, and foreign capital collude to exploit the popular sectors (Evans and Gereffi, 1982). The prediction is, that domestic business owners would welcome foreign investment and labor would oppose it, yet more often than not labor has supported FDI and domestic businesses have opposed it. Further, as Jorge Dominguez demonstrated over thirty years ago, where this alliance between domestic and foreign capital existed it proved to be unstable and short-lived (Dominguez, 1982). The pattern is also found in the specialized literature in international business, where sensitivity to contractual hazard increases the likelihood of entering with control rather than under joint ventures (Henisz, 2000b; Delios et al., 2008).

Other explanations equate FDI with footloose capital, which may harm labor through economic insecurity and volatility of income (Scheve and Slaughter, 2004). The argument is that the sheer threat of moving a production facility abroad would result in an increase in the elasticity of demand of labor services, which would be reflected in a convergence in wages to those of the alternative host countries. Yet the opportunity to engage in FDI results in an upward shift in labor demand in the countries targeted by foreign investors. Moreover, there are different forms of capital flows, which may play out differently in terms of the trade-off between income effects and volatility effects. Given that FDI implies a flow of capital with management responsibility, it is less footloose than portfolio investment and other forms of financial flows. Further, relative to financial capital flows the exit option of FDI is more limited because the markets for realization of the assets that would allow an MNC to leave a country are less developed and liquid than securities markets. It is precisely this frictional factor that makes inflows of FDI preferable to other forms of investment: the income effect associated with an inflow of FDI is not negated by the volatility effect

---

[21] This should not be a surprise for the transaction costs theory of FDI and MNCs: organizing production under control is the natural response to a risky environment.

[22] See Evans (1979), Evans and Gereffi (1982), and Gereffi (1983) among others.

associated with inflows of mobile forms of capital. It also forces investors to look for more reassurance that they are not taken advantage of once they have deployed their assets in a host country.

1.6 A Partisan Theory of FDI

Contrary to the claim that globalizing forces, including the integration of production under the control of multinational corporations, constrains governments' room to maneuver and force political and economic outcomes to converge across countries, I argue that domestic politics plays a major role in shaping countries' regulation of and openness to FDI. Foreign investment inflows provide benefits to the host country but, as in the case of trade of good and services, they are likely to have distributive consequences. Most studies of the determinants of FDI tend to ignore distributive motivations in the regulation of foreign investment. A political economy explanation is therefore required and that is what this book strives to provide. I argue that politics can have a sizable effect on investment decisions given that the conditions for investment are present. FDI activity is affected by the regulatory environment in host countries. Policies regulating economic activities are the output of the political process and political outcomes are strongly affected by government partisanship, which I define as government's pro-labor or pro-capital orientation. In the case of regulating foreign investment, we need to derive the preferences of political actors from the expected distributive consequences of FDI. The political explanation of FDI that I propose starts by identifying the key political actors, their preferences and their interactions, elements that I introduce in the ensuing sections.

1.6.1 Preferences

The partisan theory of FDI is centered on the organization of the interests of domestic political actors around their ownership of factors of production, labor, and capital in the stylized model, a strategy that is common in the literature on the political economy of trade.[23] In order to make predictions about the content of the demands for policy from organized political actors, it is crucial to identify the preferences of those actors. Following the aforementioned literature, I assume that economic agents are rational and forward-looking, and they will try to maximize the present value of their

---

[23] Rodrik (1995) provides an excellent review of this literature.

expected income. In deriving actors' preferences, I follow the literature in international economics that analyzes the determinants and consequences of opening up to trade and allowing factors of production to move across national borders. In this literature the idea that trade and factor flows affect the return of owners of factors of production is fairly uncontroversial (Stolper and Samuelson, 1941; Mundell, 1957). Many authors have used these predictions to analyze the politics of trade.[24] Yet, when analyzing FDI, most of the literature has virtually ignored FDI's distributive consequences: inward foreign investment, just like trade, is likely to affect the reward to different factors of production in the host economy by changing their relative demand.[25]

The claim that outsourcing and outward FDI decreases the demand for labor is fairly uncontroversial. Therefore, we should also expect inward FDI to increase the relative demand for workers leading to higher returns to labor and possibly lower returns to capital owners in the recipient economy under most general conditions.[26] These distributive consequences are likely to create a political cleavage around the issue of regulating FDI. Owners of labor and capital try to exert political influence to protect their sources of income, pushing for policies that would promote or restrict those flows to their advantage.

Preferences toward FDI do not depend on the motivation underlying its entry into the country – whether the investment is resource, market, or efficiency seeking – or whether the recipient industry is labor or capital intensive. The only requirement for the partisan motivation to be at play is that some workers benefit and some business owners are harmed directly from the inflow of FDI. This does not mean that factor intensity or motivation are irrelevant: the inflow might have a larger political impact if it affects a larger number of workers who are able exert greater political

---

[24] See Rogowski (1989), Dutt and Mitra (2005), Milner and Judkins (2004) among others.

[25] MNCs could affect market competition: depending on the political and economic environment MNCs could either crowd out domestic firms leading to concentration, or increase the number of incumbent firms in a specific product market (Pinto and Zhu, 2008). Either way the presence of MNCs also has the potential to affect prices of goods and services produced in the host, which could affect host government preferences. This motivation is partly captured by Li and Resnick (2003) who argue that MNCs lead to concentration, higher prices, and monopoly rents, which the median voter dislikes.

[26] See Moran (1978, 1999) and Kobrin (1987). More recent work on the politics of FDI has linked the differential effect of inward FDI on factor return to whether FDI is a complement or a substitute in production to labor and capital in the host country. Complementarity and substitutability in those accounts depends on the production technology available to investors (see Pinto and Pinto, 2008, 2011, Jensen et al., 2012).

pressure. As has been persuasively shown in the endogenous tariff formation literature that serves as the academic precursor of the argument developed here, however, large numbers of impacted workers and dispersed effects do not necessarily result in political influence. Therefore, what FDI inflows often affect the well-being of workers and pro-labor governments are willing and able to internalize these effects.

It is possible that efficiency seeking FDI might be less controversial to local firms as it results in increased local procurement. Yet, the evidence suggests that more generally foreign investors import their own suppliers, that local procurement by these actors are low, and usually only results from governmental pressure to increase local content. The evolution of regulation of the auto industry in Argentina or Intel's and HP's experiences in Costa Rica provide excellent examples. In the Intel in Costa Rica case, the company's opening of an assembly and test facility resulted in a surge of exports, yet local procurement has remained a tiny proportion of the firm's activity in the country. In the Argentine case, foreign car producers returned to the country in the 1990s pushing out domestic licensees. The industrial regime for the sector included a minimum local content requirement; however, the content was largely produced by relocated foreign subsidiaries, which pushed local parts makers out of the market. There are indeed indirect effects in the local community, but above all, workers seem to have gotten the lion's share of the benefits.

Local businesses would at most tolerate the entry of foreign firms that bring new technology but don't act as competitors. This motivation is at the core of the Korean investment regime discussed in Chapter 6. The chaebols were interested in acquiring technology but worried about foreign firms competing with them in the Korean product and factor markets. Foreign investment was thus limited in form to minority joint ventures followed by divestment after technology had been transferred to the local partner. The net result of the policy was limited entry by foreign firms. In any event, that some firms are likely to be more accepting of foreign investment does not imply opposition by workers. At most, this would mitigate the difference in preferences among workers and businesses, and provide more support for the null hypothesis that partisanship has no bearing on FDI regulation and performance.[27] The country analyses presented in Chapters 5 and 6 substantiate this dynamic in more depth.

[27] Unfortunately, obtaining data that would allow discrimination between FDI of the efficiency, market or resource-seeking types is not readily available even for developed countries. It is plausible that these motivations vary along with the degree of development of the host country, rendering pooling data from developed and developing countries problematic, a point that has been persuasively made by Blonigen and Wang (2005).

1.6.2 Organization and Influence

The partisan theory of FDI advanced in this book is a theory of outcomes, both political and economic. In sharp contrast to Rogowski's work on the effects of trade on political coalitions (Rogowski, 1989), I make predictions that go beyond political alignments. I look not only at how factor flows impact domestic actors' preferences, but also these actors' ability to affect policy outcomes. This framework is similar to that proposed by Rodrik to analyze the demand and supply conditions for commercial policy making: individuals' preferences and their incentives to organize politically constitute the demand side of policy making, whereas politicians' objective functions in interaction with the constraints and incentives created by political institutions – the rules of the game under which politics is played – characterize the supply side of politics (Rodrik, 1995). Those actors potentially harmed by FDI would try to keep foreign investors out, whereas those who benefit would prefer investment to flow in. But preferences alone cannot explain political outcomes. An incumbent who is motivated to effect policy changes needs to be able to pass legislation or enact regulations; in all settings, this ability is a function of the institutions that regulate policy making. Demand and supply conditions need to intersect: those with a motive to change policy need to have access to policy makers to have any impact. The two conditions, motive and opportunity, allow us to predict whether the pro-foreign investment or the anti-FDI coalition is more likely to prevail and be able to enact policies to promote the inflow of FDI or discourage foreign investment. The intersection between the policies enacted by partisan governments and the preferences of foreign investors determines which countries receive more FDI.

1.6.3 Domestic Politics and FDI Performance

Changes in economic flows across borders have been demonstrated to affect political conditions in host countries (Moran, 1974, 1978). More recently, globalization theorists argue that as markets internationalize governments become increasingly constrained to the extent of losing policy autonomy.[28] Although there is evidence to suggest that globalization – understood as increasing internationalization of production and the flow of goods, services, and factors of production across borders – has had significant distributive effects (Wood, 1991, 1994; O'Rourke and Williamson, 1999), there is little evidence to suggest that regulatory standards have been compromised.

---

[28] See Vernon (1971), Moran (1978), and Strange (1996) among others.

What we know for certain is that globalization has played itself out differently in different countries, triggering a variety of political conflicts over distribution and policy (Polanyi, 1957; Katzenstein, 1978; Gourevitch, 1986; Verdier, 1998; Garrett, 1998a,b; Boix, 1997, 1998). Following this line of reasoning, I argue that FDI performance, that is, the level of FDI a host country receives, is ultimately determined by the strategic interaction between host governments and potential foreign investors. The choices available to the host government, however, are constrained by its partisanship, or the host government's responsiveness to labor or capital, and the institutional setting that determines which of these groups are more influential. This interaction between a partisan host government and internationally mobile capital is captured in a simple formal framework whose intuition and main propositions I discuss next.

1.6.4 FDI Performance As a Bargain Between Investors and Governments

For analytical purposes, I make some simplifying assumptions that allow me to make predictions about how investment regulation and FDI flows change with the underlying political conditions in host countries. These assumptions make explicit something that is usually buried in informal derivations of the politics of FDI: the scope conditions under which the predictions of the model are likely to hold.[29] The starting point of the model is setting the choice of policy instruments by a host government as a strategic response to the expected behavior of investors when reacting to those choices. The host government, in turn, has partisan motivations, which are derived from its link to socioeconomic actors in the polity. The first assumption in the model is that these socioeconomic actors want to maximize their utility, which they derive from both the returns received from participating in the market and from consuming goods supplied by the government. In order to bring to the fore the trade-off between the utility economic agents derive from the returns they receive in the marketplace and from social spending, I assume that the host government controls one policy instrument to regulate FDI, which for simplicity is modeled as a tax rate that the host government levies on internationally mobile capital. We may think of this tax rate as comprising all other policy instruments, such as subsidies and regulations that affect the return to investors. Foreign investment has the

---

[29] Several assumptions, including the functional form of production and utility functions are made to simplify the analysis.

potential to affect economic conditions in several ways, including increasing output, returns to domestic factors of production, and government revenue. The host government is assumed to maximize the utility it gets from revenue obtained by taxing capital and therefore seeks to extract as much revenue as possible from regulating economic activity. Starting with a politically unconstrained host government only motivated by the desire to maximize revenue, we would predict that the tax rate on foreign investment would be set as high as possible. The total receipt from taxation, however, depends on the response by investors, who are likely to react negatively to higher taxes. Investors' reactions depend on their elasticity to taxes, which in turn is a function of the opportunity costs of investing in the host country. Therefore, government revenue from taxing foreign investors is increasing at a decreasing rate, after reaching an optimal level revenue falls with higher taxes. For the revenue maximizing government, then, the optimal tariff is never prohibitive.

Inflows of capital can affect the returns to different factors of production in the host economy.[30] The direction and magnitude of this effect depends on whether foreign investment increases (or decreases) the relative demand for the services provided by labor and capital owners in the marketplace. If foreign investment results in higher demand for labor, then we would expect that wages rise and returns to capital owners fall. Yet, foreign investment inflows are also likely to increase government revenue from which actors may derive utility.[31] Host governments who care more about labor or are likely to be held accountable by workers and unions, internalize the effect of taxes on foreign capital on the well-being of workers, that is, the utility of workers weighs more heavily in their decision. Pro-capital incumbents, on the other hand, internalize the preferences of business owners. Thus, the policy adopted by the host government depends on its receptiveness to the demands of business or labor, which is a weighted average of the utility of labor and capital, with two extreme cases where government only

---

[30] See Quinn and Inclan (1997), Alfaro (2004), Pinto and Pinto (2008, 2011), and Pinto et al. (2010).

[31] The weight that actors place on the utility of government spending may vary depending on where they draw their income from: workers, for instance, whose main source of income are wages are more likely to prefer higher government spending. Business owners, however, may prefer lower government spending especially if that spending is used to finance services that they can either provide by themselves or self-insure against or if the spending otherwise results in redistribution through taxation. Hence, when choosing how much to tax investors workers are forced to trade-off wages for social spending. For owners of capital, on the other hand, the choice of taxing foreign investors is likely to be mostly defensive: they would like to set the tax high enough to keep investors out.

cares about capital or where government is pro-labor. A government that only cares about the well being of workers offers the lowest tax to foreign investors. A government that cares about revenue maximization alone will offer an intermediate schedule, whereas the pro-business government will offer the most restrictive conditions, because it prefers keeping foreign investors out. Investors react to these policies by flowing into the country when the pro-labor government is in power, but not when the incumbent is of the pro-business type.

1.6.5 Exchanging Hostages to Support Economic Exchanges

The predictions presented in the previous section capture the relationship between partisanship and foreign investment in a static setup, where investors care about returns to their investment and governments value differently the effect of investment inflows on government revenue and on the returns to their core constituents. These predictions could be interpreted as the long-run equilibrium relationship between foreign investors and host governments. A comparative statics exercise allows us to understand how the relationship changes with changes in partisanship and investors' motivations. Yet, foreign investment is usually a dynamic process with expected benefits that are likely to arise over several periods, forcing investors and governments to be forward looking. In order to incorporate this dynamic component, I extend the intuition of the previous argument to explore how the interaction of partisan governments and foreign investors makes investment possible, even under conditions when the potential for ex-post opportunistic behavior by the host government would make investment risky ex-ante.

As FDI is characterized by intangible proprietary assets (Dunning, 1977; Caves, 1996; Helpman, 2006), it is usually mobile internationally but specific to an activity or use. The existence of these proprietary assets in conjunction with a stream of future benefits exposes foreign investors to opportunistic behavior by host governments. This is the basic insight in the obsolescence bargaining literature: to the extent that redeploying their assets or liquidating their position is costly foreign investors face the risk that their invested interest can be taken hostage by domestic governments (Vernon, 1971; Moran, 1974; Williamson, 1983a,b; Whiting, 1992). Facing a positive probability of being expropriated down the line foreign investors have two options to reduce the risk that governments take advantage of them: they can pay a redeployment cost and leave the country after government intentions become apparent, or they can withhold investment ex-ante in the shadow of opportunistic government behavior. Both conditions are economically inefficient and politically sensitive. The extant literature proposes that adopting an inflexible policy could solve this time-inconsistency problem. Yet, as discussed earlier, the resulting inflexible policy is but a second best option, and could become unsustainable over time as the economic environment changes (Spiller and Tommasi, 2003; Pinto and Pinto, 2011). However, as documented earlier, foreign investment is pervasive whereas expropriation is a rare event, suggesting that foreign businesses and governments are able to commit to each other even in the absence of institutional constraints (Chari and Kehoe, 1990; Klein and Ríos-Rull, 2003).

I propose an alternative commitment mechanism, which is based on the host government's partisanship, not on the institutional constraints it faces. The commitment mechanism provided by investment under governments with partisan motivations is analogous to a mutual exchange of hostages (Williamson, 1983a): investment is secure when a host government's attempt to target investors ex-post may hurt domestic actors that the incumbent cannot afford to ignore. The theory is based on the intuition that governments are able to take hostage the assets owned by foreign investors, as predicted by the obsolescence bargaining literature. However, to the extent that investors are strategic and able to choose an investment strategy tailored to the political conditions in the host, they adopt a production technology that ties their fate to that of other economic agents in the host economy, making them hostage to their performance.

The choice of production technology allows foreign investors to take hostage a domestic political actor whose well-being is affected by the presence of the MNC; investors are thus more likely to choose a production technology that targets a socioeconomic actor who is a core member of the incumbent's coalition. This choice makes investment more secure as the incumbent faces a potential cost if the investor leaves the country and thus a disincentive to renege after entry by foreign investors. For instance, when investors adopt a technology that complements labor in production, workers' interests become congruent with their own, because investors only enter the market if it provides higher profits than those available abroad and workers benefit from inflows of investment and are harmed if investors decide to pack and leave. The corollary is that labor-based coalitions are more likely to be better hosts to foreign direct investment than those coalitions built around domestic capital, especially when investment results in higher wages and employment opportunities for workers. Governments drawing their political power from the support of labor guarantee not only that the investment regime is more favorable to foreign investors, but also that these conditions are sustained over time as long as the coalition stays in power or the investor is able to adapt its production strategy to the changing political conditions. In a dynamic setting, the commitment mechanism linking partisan governments to investors is supported by the potential to inflict harm on each other.[32] This exchange between host governments and investors is secured by the mutual exchange of hostages. It is a form of commitment supported by partisan reputation, rather than by tying the government's hands (Pinto and Pinto, 2011).[33]

The partisan orientation of the incumbent alone is not enough to characterize the orientation of a coalition government, a minority cabinet, or the constraints faced by the executive under divided government. Institutions do play an important role in preference aggregation, and therefore, affect the ability of the government to effect policy changes. In the end, political institutions create the incentive structures that determine whose interests are more likely to be privileged by policy makers. The configuration and alignment of veto points, on which most arguments about institutional constraints are based, are likely to enhance or deny political actors' ability to move policy closer to their preferred outcomes. Thus, a Left or Right-leaning incumbent able to enact and enforce the policies toward FDI demanded by her core constituent when the legislature and other political veto players share her preferences, but are less able to adopt those policies when she is politically and institutionally constrained. The content of the policies adopted ultimately depends on the preferences of those in policy making positions.[34]

---

[32] Pinto and Pinto (2011) show that as long as there are differences in technology that make foreign investment either an imperfect complement or substitute to domestic factors of production the partisan predictions hold even for high levels of redeployment costs: as predicted by the optimal taxation literature, governments have an incentive to tax more heavily the less elastic tax base, yet taxes would still reflect partisan biases in the direction predicted by the partisan theory or investment.

[33] See also Chari and Kehoe (1990) and Klein and Ríos-Rull (2003).

[34] In the empirical section, I develop a more nuanced classification of the partisan orientation of the incumbent by interacting the orientation of the party in government with the measure of political constraints developed by Henisz (2002), which captures the alignment between institutional and political veto players. This interaction can be interpreted as a movement along the left-right dimension (the β parameter in the model presented in Chapter 2). When the chief executive is not constrained institutionally, her preferences and those of other relevant institutional and political veto players are more likely to be aligned. As institutional constraints increase, the preferences of the chief executive and those of other veto players diverge. Therefore, the interaction term allows us to obtain a continuous measure of incumbent partisanship. The expectation is that the sign of the coefficient on the Left dummy will be positive and the

1.6.6 Pro-Labor and the Left

If the partisan theory, in its static or dynamic form, is right, then investment regimes should covary with changes in labor and business influence in politics. Therefore, foreign investment that raises the relative demand for labor are higher when pro-labor coalitions are in power. Throughout the book, I equate pro-labor with the left and pro-business with the political right, but we know that this assumption does not necessarily follow in the real world because there are many shades of left and right. There are two reasons for adopting the assumption that the left is pro-labor and the right is pro-domestic business owners: one is theoretical whereas the other one is driven by the emphasis on within country alternation between parties of different orientations and data constraints in the empirical section of the book. Theoretically I argue that governments adopt and abide by policies that benefit their core constituents. Left-leaning coalitions are more favorable to labor and more receptive to its demands, but right-leaning coalitions instead favor capital. Governments on the left side of the political spectrum tend to cater to labor for political support and place more emphasis on issues such as unemployment and income distribution. Right-leaning parties tend to be more business-oriented, assign high priority to price and stability, and usually clash with labor on issues such as unemployment and income distribution (Hibbs, 1977, 1992; Tufte, 1978). I link the left to labor's material interests because even though labor's preferences in other issue dimensions, including employment, inflation, taxation, and social spending, may be at odds with the interests of business owners, domestic and foreign alike, the expected effect of direct investment inflows on labor demand makes workers' material interests congruent to those of foreign investors. Therefore, I predict that governments of the left receive more FDI than right-leaning governments and that in any given country FDI inflows are higher during years of left-leaning governance. The flip side to the hypothesis about the affinity between the Left and FDI is more intuitive: pro-business governments, usually on the right end of the spectrum, are more willing to shelter domestic firms from foreign competition.

In deriving the partisan hypothesis formally, the relevant parameter is the weight that the incumbent government places on the well-being of different groups in the polity, which I identify with a movement along the pro-labor/pro-capital dimension. In the empirical analyses in Chapter 4,

---

interaction term between Left and political constraints are negative, with a net positive effect at lower levels of the variable, capturing power diffusion. When analyzing the relationship between partisanship and economic performance the presence of institutional constraint is less relevant.

however, I equate pro-labor with the left, which could be problematic in some instances. In practice, the Left and Right are extremely broad categories, especially across polities. The Left includes, but is not limited to, labor-based parties which is the link around which the partisan theory of FDI is built. In Europe, for instance, the Left is traditionally of a social-democratic type and has traditionally been linked to organized labor. In the United States, the link with labor is weaker, but it is apparent that the Democratic Party is more inclined to advance the interests of workers than is the Republican Party. In Latin America, on the other hand, left-leaning parties include the Socialist Party in Chile and the Workers Party (PT) in Brazil, as well as the Movimiento al Socialismo in Bolivia, the Partido Socialista Unido de Venezuela, and the Alianza PAIS in Ecuador. It is apparent that the link between left-leaning parties and workers and organized labor varies dramatically across countries but less so within countries over time.

In the end, within countries, parties on the left are more likely to be pro-labor than their right-leaning counterparts. Irrespective of the different "shades of red" that left-leaning parties represent, it is uncontested that these parties prefer policies that benefit workers and the Right is associated with policies that benefit owners of capital and business managers. Left and Right parties have "different socioeconomic class foundations" (Hibbs, 1977, 1992; Quinn and Shapiro, 1991).[35] The Left draws support from two different groups: those who depend on government spending, especially on social programs, and from unions representing workers who earn wages in the marketplace (Quinn and Inclan, 1997). The first link would create a partisan motivation in regulating FDI that Quinn and Inclan (1997) define as the *macropolicy effect*. This motivation is usually reflected in a preference for increases in social welfare spending and redistributive taxation (Hicks and Swank, 1992). The second partisan motivation, the *factor market effect*, leads governments to choose policy instruments that affect "relative prices," which result in changes in the well-being of different economic actors in the marketplace (Quinn and Inclan, 1997). When it comes to regulating foreign investment, both incentives are likely to be at play; whether the macro-policy motivation or the relative prices effect motivation dominates

---

[35] Following the pioneering work of Hibbs (1977, 1992) and Tufte (1978), a vast body of literature in comparative political economy that analyzes the role of partisan motivations in policy making has emerged. See, for example, Hibbs (1977), Alt (1985), Alesina (1987, 1988), Esping-Andersen (1990), Alvarez et al. (1991), Garrett (1998a,b), Iversen (1999), Boix (1997, 1998), and Franzese (2002b).

or depends on the weight that the incumbent places on the well-being of workers and other groups in the polity, and on the government's ability to collect taxes that can be used to finance public spending.

Although most of the literature has focused on the *macropolicy effect* the partisan theory of FDI emphasizes instead the *factor market effect,* an incentive in the regulation of FDI has been neglected in the extant literature.[36] As discussed in Section 1.6.1, the partisan theory of investment argues that foreign investment can affect the well-being of workers and capital owners in the marketplace. Yet, economic agents hold preferences over other dimensions such as the provision of public goods or government output, which at times could be affected directly or indirectly by the policies enacted to promote or discourage inward FDI. In developing the theory formally, I model the expected effects of foreign investment on product markets and the expected gains from taxing investors that could accrue to individual households through government output. Taxing foreign investment could have an effect on individuals' well-being in the marketplace, which they have to tradeoff for their participation in consuming government services financed with taxes.

I explicitly model this trade-off in Chapter 2. The strategy aims at capturing received wisdom on the alleged preferences of workers for bigger government and the preference of investors for lower taxation. The model suggests that even when workers face this tradeoff between market income and government transfers they would still offer better conditions to mobile capital. Yet, for some parties on the Left of the political spectrum, particularly those representing individuals whose return in the marketplace is less likely to be affected by the presence of MNCs such as Venezuela's PSUV, the fiscal motivation of taxing capital more heavily is likely to dominate. Further, the incentive to tax foreign investors more becomes stronger for investors in sectors that face higher redeployment costs, particularly in extractive industries. The incentives are even stronger when the price of these resources goes up, because higher prices raise the expected benefit of investing in places where the resources are found. The limited effect of foreign investment on the well-being of their followers, who do not benefit directly from an increase in the demand for their services from MNCs, in times of higher resource prices, allow host governments to push for harder

---

[36] Quinn and Inclan (1997) and Alfaro (2004) are exceptions, where relative returns to different agents play an important role in the adoption of capital controls.

bargains, as has been the case in Venezuela under Chavez, Bolivia with Morales, and Ecuador under Correa.[37]

The predictions from the partisan theory of FDI are supported by the quantitative evidence presented in Chapter 4.[38] I find a systematic relationship between government ideology and investment performance in different samples of countries and years: left-leaning governments are associated with larger FDI inflows.[39]

The evidence from the qualitative part of the book, where I compare investment regimes and FDI performance in Argentina from Juan Perón to Néster Kirchner and in South Korea from Park-Chung-hee to Lee Myung-bak, provides additional support for the partisan hypothesis. Argentina and South Korea are good cases to test the relationship between politics and FDI. These two cases were chosen to maximize, within each case and in comparative prespective, variance in levels of political influence of labor and business. The within-country analyses allow me to rely on primary and secondary sources that are not available for the whole samples on which the statistical analyses in Chapter 4 are based. Longitudinal analyses of the two cases allow for the effects of institutional changes to be sorted out from changes in the composition of the ruling coalitions. I am also able to

---

[37] The ability of governments to appropriate rents from exploiting an economy's endowment of natural resources is likely to tilt the balance toward the revenue motivation in regulating foreign investment, and may explain the anti-foreign stand of Chavez, Morales, and Correa. In more diversified economies, like Brazil or even Chile, the tradeoff between market and government effects on the well-being of the support base of the Left are more apparent, especially when the government has a strong presence in natural resource extraction.

[38] Analyzing empirically the link between politics and FDI is marred with data problems. This is a major hurdle for the whole empirical enterprise on this issue: given the nature of the subject of study where most transactions occur within firms with proprietary information which they zealously protect, it is close to impossible to design a single test that would once and for all determine the validity of the hypotheses derived from the partisan theory of FDI or any other politically informed theory of investment. That is why I have tried to produce supportive evidence using different methods and sources. Yet, like in all instances of social science research that relies on observational data, drawing sharp causal claims is problematic because issues of endogeneity, selection, and omitted confounders loom large. Throughout the book, but particularly in Chapters 4–6, I present results using different modeling strategies, samples, and methods which, while not definitive, seem to all point in the same direction. Although I do not have a silver bullet that would settle the issue once and for all, I believe that the evidence is fairly strong.

[39] In the empirical analyses, I identify off of the relative movement between the left and right within countries because I use fixed effect estimators. If most parties on the left in my analysis were not pro-labor, and/or the left were anti-business (foreign and domestic alike), then we would expect to find that the correlation between partisanship and FDI had the opposite sign from the one predicted by my theory. The correlation found in the data would thus be a conservative estimate of the association between pro-labor parties and FDI.

analyze the role of relevant actors including workers, unions, business-people, and their associations under different institutional settings ranging from unconstrained autocracies to electoral democracy.

In the Argentine case, I focus on labor influence in politics as a consequence of changes in political institutions, structural conditions, and partisan alternation in power. From Juan Perón, through the different military regimes and the Radical and Desarrollista governments, to Carlos Menem, Néstor and Cristina Kirchner, the degrees of labor support and the pro-labor stances on the side of government varies greatly. Changes in labor influence have had an effect on investment regimes adopted in each period and on the level of FDI inflows. In Argentina, it is the pro-labor nature of the ruling coalition rather than the governments' ideological placement in the left-right dimension that appears to affect the adoption of more favorable investment conditions and larger FDI inflows.

In contrast, the Korean case is characterized by a pro-business coalition that loses power over time. In the post-war era, Korea adopted a highly restrictive investment regime, and received low levels of FDI, a pattern that is quite similar to that of Japan. The Economic Planning Board acted as the gate-keeper, protecting the chaebols by restricting competition while promoting technology transfers. In times of crisis or savings shortcomings, most foreign capital took the form of loans whose allocation was administered by the government. Conditions reversed in the late 1990s, as the consequence of two processes: democratization, which moved the center of political gravity away from owners of capital and toward owners of labor, and the financial crises of 1997, which eroded the political clout of the chaebols. The end result was a dramatic change in the investment regime, which ultimately led to larger inflows of FDI under the left-leaning governments led by Kim Dae-jung and Roh Moo-hyun. The two administrations have also adopted a more combative attitude toward the domestic business conglomerates. Yet, after receiving a hard blow during the financial crisis, some of the chaebols survived the push prepared to fight back. They found a more receptive ear in power when Lee Myung-bak and the GNP regained office in 2008 and this pro-business coalition is steadily impacting the regulatory process resulting in a less friendly environment for FDI.

1.6.7 Opportunism and Time-Inconsistency

Problems of time-inconsistency that could alter the predictions from the static or longrun predictions presented in Chapter 2. The main concern is that direct investment is usually not a one-shot event. Therefore, even when governments may prefer ex-ante to promote direct investment they have an incentive to act opportunistically ex-post once the investment, has become less elastic to the policy intervention. Irrespective of their orientation, host governments face a typical time inconsistency problem when dealing with investors. Once investment has flown in the host government may reverse the policies originally offered to attract investors. Moreover, governments have an incentive to act opportunistically if and when investors' exit option is relatively costly, which is usually the case for most forms of foreign direct investment. The end result would be that no matter how favorable to foreign investors the policy regimes offered by host governments look ex-ante, these promises become inconsistent ex-post and result in sub-optimal levels of investment. This is the traditional hold-up problem around which the obsolescence bargaining argument is built.[40]

The extant literature on the politics of FDI is built around this time-inconsistency problem, which is usually described as political risk. This form of risk can be mitigated when the government is institutionally constrained and thus cannot change policy at her will. Yet, as much as MNCs worry about the possibility of opportunistic behavior by host governments that would affect the profitability of their affiliates, they also need to worry about other forms of risk that determine the desirability of an investment location that could arise from movements along the business cycle, disruptions of production, and the loss of control over the proprietary assets that characterize FDI.

It is precisely these types of risk that lead firms to choose to invest with control when servicing the host market or tapping onto its resources. Therefore, investment in risky environments is likely to occur under control and is dominated by firms that are better able at coping with risk. Most of these firms would prefer a policy environment that is stable but has some degree of flexibility, particularly when economic shocks negatively affect their profitability. Moreover, the argument that the presence of multiple veto players eliminates the time inconsistency problem is incomplete: veto players' preferences along a policy space are not absolute, but instead depend upon the realization of different parameters that enter into the actors' maximands. In the case of regulating foreign investment, the optimal policy for all actors is a function of the expected effects of investment on aggregate and individual welfare, the opportunity costs faced by investors, and the elasticity of investment to taxes and regulation. In a dynamic setting, as the

---

[40] Henisz (2000b) provides the best example on the application of this problem to the investor's choices of the form of entry.

tax elasticity of investment drops, all governments have an incentive to tax investors more heavily. Institutional constraints indeed restrict the ability of any actor to move the policy away from the status quo as long as the status quo dominates any other option. Yet, the drop in the elasticity of investment to taxation or regulation moves the optimal policy space for all actors alike. Therefore, increasing the number of veto players alone does not prevent a movement toward a new optimal policy that incorporates the change in elasticity. Institutional constraints matter, but in a different fashion that depends upon the preferences of those holding veto power. The corollary is that governments are indeed able to commit to investors in a dynamic setting. The host government's internalization of the well-being of workers or business owners may aggravate or mitigate the time inconsistency problem that governments face when dealing with internationally mobile capital in ways that institutional constraints cannot. The expected consequences of FDI on the well-being of different actors, from which I derive the preferences for higher levels of investment, affect how far veto players are willing to move the policy ex-post. The commitment mechanism is not based on traditional audience costs or institutional constraints logics, but instead on constituency links, which I describe as partisan motivations.[41]

1.7 Conclusion

I have argued that the partisan alignment of host governments help explain the change in foreign, investment regimes which systematically affect the variance in cross-country FDI performance. To the extent that workers benefit from FDI they push for policies that encourage FDI inflows. Domestic business owners are likely to be harmed by these types of foreign investment inflows, in which case capital owners act politically to restrict inflows.[42] The basic findings are that countries where labor is more politically influential are likely to adopt investment regimes that are more favorable to foreign investors. The second finding is that countries where labor is more influential are likely to receive more FDI inflows. The theory and findings capture part of the variance in foreign direct investment that countries receive,

---

[41] See Pinto and Pinto (2011) for a formal presentation of this argument.

[42] The assumption that labor benefits and domestic capital hurts from investment inflows can be relaxed to allow for different types of FDI having different effects on the relative demand for labor and capital, as discussed in Chapter 2. Yet, under most general conditions FDI is likely to increase labor demand as suggested by the positive correlation between inward FDI and wages, particularly under the Left. See Pinto and Pinto (2008, 2011) and Jensen et al. (2012).

which remains unexplained in the extant literature in economics and political science. The combination of the quantitative and within-country analyses provides strong support to the partisan theory of FDI. In sum, this book suggests that there is good reason to believe that the Left loves FDI and FDI loves the Left.

1.7.1 Layout of the Book

As discussed in the previous sections, the extant literature on the politics of investment is rather agnostic on the distributional consequences of FDI and tends to assume that in the eyes of investors most parties look the same. All of the action is on the investor's side, who chooses investment locations that minimize risk; furthermore, risk is a function of institutions, not of preferences. This literature provides the null hypotheses for my argument, namely that there are no partisan differences in FDI regulation and performance. The old dependentista argument, on the other hand, would provide an alternative hypothesis. Another plausible alternative hypothesis that reverses the direction of the partisan link is that pro-business parties create a better environment for economic activity and thus attracts more FDI than their big government, pro-labor counterpart. Throughout the book, I spell out the reasons why I believe that the pro-labor/pro-FDI logic is more likely to hold.

For analytical and narrative purposes, the book is divided into several distinctive parts. Chapters 2 and 3 introduce the partisan theory of foreign investment. They explain why we should expect domestic actors to organize politically to respond to the distributive consequences of FDI inflows. When governments are partisan, they tend to respond to the preferences of the pivotal members of their coalition by adopting regulatory regimes that are more or less favorable to foreign investment. Policy choices depend on the orientation of the incumbent coalitions, that is, whether labor or capital are part of it. The theory explains how government partisanship ultimately affects the level of foreign investment flowing into host countries. Chapters 4 through 6 present quantitative and historical evidence to support the theory, including statistical analyses of a large cross-section of developed economies and emerging markets, and within-country analyses of the evolution of investment regimes in Argentina and South Korea from the post-war era to the end of the twentieth century.

This chapter has introduced the research and lays out the plan for the rest of the book. I explore how exposure to foreign investment mobilizes political cleavages and has potential to affect politics. Therefore, policy choices are likely to reflect the potential consequences of higher exposure to FDI: the content of regulatory regimes adopted toward foreign investment depends on who is in power and economic outcomes. Polities where labor is more influential are more likely to be friendlier to foreign investors, when capital is more influential, the environment turns more hostile to foreign investors. One of the conditions introduced in this chapter is that political motivations can be binding even when institutional constraints are not. The risk of losing the support of core constituents may force partisan governments to hold their promises to foreign investors even when facing a priori incentives to act opportunistically. For this reason, pro-labor governments receive more foreign investment and pro-capital governments receive less.

Chapter 2 presents the partisan theory of FDI. The logic of the theory is supported by a formal model that captures the distributive effects of inflows of FDI. The model explains why we should expect pro-labor governments to welcome foreign investment and business-oriented governments to oppose it. The model is based on simple assumptions about the effect of factor movements on the marginal product of capital and labor, and consequently on changes in their marginal revenue. These assumptions parallel those in the classical Hecksher-Ohlin/Stolper-Samuelson/Mundell framework.[43] The return to labor and capital is determined by their marginal contribution to output. The main effect of this assumption is that an inflow of capital increases the return to labor and decrease the return to capital. I derive two propositions from comparative statics exercises with the formal model. The first proposition links the partisanship of governments to foreign investment regimes. It states that the larger the value that government agents place on the political support of labor, the lower the tax schedule (proxy for investment policy orientation) offered to foreign investors, all else equal. The second proposition links the tax schedule (investment policy orientation) to investment outcomes: the larger the value that government agents place on the political support of labor, the higher the level of foreign investment in the country, all else equal. The assumption is that when constrained by a constituency base that is positively (negatively) affected by investment flows governments are more likely to commit (renege) on the policies that they offer to foreign investors. Therefore, investment regimes and investment outcomes are likely to covary with changes in the institutional setting that empowers different groups in the polity and/or with changes in the partisan orientation of the incumbent coalition.

---

[43] For an extension in a model where at least one factor is sector specific, see Pinto and Pinto (2008).

Chapter 3 extends the predictions of the model introduced in Chapter 2 to explain how partisanship may help overcome the time consistency problem that governments face when regulating foreign investment in a dynamic setting. Chapter 2 identifies the conditions under which we should expect labor to take a position that is pro-foreign capital and domestic capital to oppose. The main prediction is that FDI flows are larger when labor is more influential, and smaller when capital owners call the shots. Chapter 3 analyzes how partisanship can act as a commitment mechanism: it discusses the conditions under which host governments can reassure investors that the conditions offered to them ex-ante are sustained over time. I describe the interaction between foreign investors and host governments as analogous to a mutual exchange of hostages (Williamson, 1983a). The relative influence of labor in domestic politics may work as a reassurance to foreign investors, whereas influence of owners of capital in the host country may dissuade foreign investors.

Chapter 4 presents the results of several statistical tests on the implications of the theory introduced in Chapters 2 and 3, namely that host countries appear to be better hosts of foreign investors when a pro-labor party is in power and is able to effect policy changes. Statistical tests conducted on measures of openness to investment derived from observed FDI flows suggest that partisan effects are indeed at play: left-right orientation of the chief executive in the host country has a positive and statistically significant effect. Additional tests on panel data for samples of fourteen OECD countries and twenty emerging markets over a twenty-two-year span seemingly confirm these predictions: FDI flows are larger in countries and years where the left is in power. The tests find limited support for an alternative hypothesis; institutional constraints indeed limit the ability of governments to enact their preferred policies but seem to have no direct effect on FDI flows as predicted by the literature.

Chapters 5 and 6 contrast the post-war experience of Argentina and South Korea with FDI. The choice of cases allows for within and between country variation in terms of political regimes, institutional design, and degree of labor and capital influence. The Argentine case looks at episodes of waxing and waning labor influence from Juan Perón to Carlos Menem, its effects on investment regimes adopted in each period, and how those changes affected the level of FDI inflows. The South Korean case looks at changes in domestic business influence from Syngman Rhee to Kim Dae-Jung. It discusses the evolution of the foreign investment regime in the country, and compares two economic crises in the country (those of 1980 and 1997).

It shows the joint effect of democratization in the 1990s, which moved the political center of attention toward labor and away from owners of capital, and the erosion of the political clout of the chaebols. In the Korean case, the turning point is political competition and the damaging effect on domestic business of the 1997 financial crisis that effected a dramatic change in the investment regime, and ultimately led to larger inflows of FDI.

TWO

A Political Economy Model of Foreign
Direct Investment

2.1 Introduction

As discussed in Chapter 1, foreign direct investment (FDI) flows have become an important part of total investment flows, and now play a major role in growth and development. National and local governments across the planet have adopted various types of policies to attract or deter inward FDI. Allegedly, developed countries have converged on less discriminatory regimes toward foreign investors. A tally of the number of changes in foreign investment regulation seems to underscore this trend (Table 1.2). However, Table 1.2 also shows that the number of restrictive measures have increased dramatically since 2001, probably as a response to the global recessions of 2001 and 2008, and regional crises in most corners of the world. There is also great variance in the orientation of investment regimes across countries and over time, even among OECD countries. In recent years, discontent toward foreign investors has become rampant not only in crisis-stricken countries, but is expressed in a rhetoric that resonates with the the policy debates of the 1970s.

In this chapter, I present a formal derivation of the logic behind the partisan theory of foreign investment, which aims at explaining the observed variance in regulatory regimes toward foreign investment and the positive association between left-leaning governments and direct investment flows.[1]

---

[1] The evidence suggests that politics in general, and government partisanship in particular, are likely to affect investment performance: aggregate direct investment flows are higher when pro-labor governments are in power and drop when domestic businesses are politically influential. Pinto and Pinto (2008) document the existence of partisan cycles in investment performance at the industry level in OECD countries: when the left is in power, FDI flows tend to be larger to those sectors where FDI is more likely to complement labor and substitute for capital. Pinto et al. (2010) extend the argument to financial capital and corporate governance, and report a strong correlation between the left market capitalization.

Given that the conditions for investment are present, domestic politics is likely to play a major role in shaping how foreign investment is regulated, or how open countries are to FDI. Despite the potential for aggregate gains from inward investment inflows, some actors in the host country may win whereas others may lose: owners of factors into the host country that complement foreign capital in production stand to benefit from inflows of FDI, factors for which FDI substitutes are harmed. As discussed in Chapter 1, most studies tend to ignore these distributive effects.

The logic of the argument is derived from a decision theoretic model aimed at capturing the interaction between foreign investors and host governments. The model allows for different effects of direct investment inflows on the differential demand for the services offered by factors of production in the country that hosts the investment.[2] Yet, in the aggregate there is good reason to believe that the net effect of FDI inflows result in higher relative demand for labor. To simplify the analysis, I add an extra assumption to the model to allow for foreign capital to complement labor in production: as foreign direct investment flows into a host country, labor productivity and wages improve. At the same time, the return on capital is likely to fall, as rents and profits are competed away.[3] Given the differential impact that the allocation of foreign capital has on the return to the factors owned by domestic political actors, it is expected that workers benefit from foreign investment, and governments that cater to workers are inclined to promote policies that stimulate investment inflows. Moreover, as discussed in Chapter 3, I speculate that foreign capital owners feel confident that such policies are not reversed as the policies disproportionately benefit the government's core constituents. Right-leaning governments, on the other hand, tend to act in the opposite way, preventing investment that has the potential to reduce the marginal productivity of capital, and thus its return.

The predictions from this model stand in stark contrast with those in recent literature on FDI, which has focused on the net welfare consequences of direct investment to the host economy, because FDI is valuable,

---

[2] For an extension where the effects of FDI on the marginal product of labor and domestic capital owners varies across sectors, see Pinto and Pinto (2008, 2011).

[3] Formally, this assumption implies that if output in any sector of the economy is $Y_i = f(K_i^D, K^F, L)$, then $f_{LK^F} > 0$ and/or $f_{K_i^D K^F} < 0$, which means that the marginal product of labor (f_L) increase with higher FDI (K^F), whereas the marginal product of capital (f_{K^D}) falls with higher FDI. Note that for foreign inflows to have an effect on factor returns any of the following conditions must attain: at least one factor is sector specific, the economy is specialized, or it is closed to trade.

governments always want more of it. Therefore, the analysis concentrates on the decision of investors who are assumed to be motivated solely by the risk environment in host countries. Entry decisions are, thus, usually assumed to be an optimal response to economic, institutional, and other traits of host countries. Based on these characteristics, some countries are attractive to investors, whereas other locations fail to attract any FDI. Yet, these analyses tend to overlook the investors' incentives to obtain higher returns, and the expected distributive consequences of foreign direct investment. Distributive concerns, just like in trade politics, have the potential to create a cleavage around FDI politics, and therefore affect how governments regulate foreign investment. Furthermore, the restrictiveness of the regulatory environment has the potential to affect investors' decisions to enter the market.

The partisan theory of investment argues that the level of investment is the end result of a strategic interaction between a host government and potential foreign investors as proposed by the bargaining literature on foreign investment. Host governments here, however, are partisan: they are tied to a core constituency whose interests they want to advance.[4] Choices available to the incumbent are indeed constrained by political institutions, as much as they are by partisan links. Irrespective of the aggregate effect of foreign investment on economic activity and government revenues, and provided that labor is a complement of FDI in production, direct investment inflows result in higher labor demand. As such, governments that favor labor adopt policies that promote investment inflows, whereas governments that favor owners of capital try to restrict those flows. Note that this prediction would hold even if workers and capitalists, and the parties that represent them, have different preferences regarding the level of government revenue and spending. If the pro-labor party, on the left side of the political spectrum, values taxation and expenditure more heavily than its pro-business counterpart, as documented in the literature on partisan business cycles, we would still expect it to internalize the effect of FDI on the return to labor. The pro-labor government, for instance, is more sensitive to the elasticity of FDI to taxes because workers are more likely to value the expected positive effect of inward investment on the demand for their services and the potential effect of FDI on government coffers. Therefore, the pro-labor government offers investors a tax schedule that balances incentives to maximize revenue with incentives to increase the return to labor in the market place, whereas

---

[4] For simplicity, I assume that there are two main political actors, owners of labor and owners of capital, and define partisanship as either pro-labor or pro-capital.

the pro-business party is more likely to adopt a prohibitive tax, such as, the one that keeps potential competitors out.

In choosing the investment regime, governments internalize the reaction of foreign investors, but foreign investors also anticipate the host government's decisions. In turn, the interaction between governments and investors determines which countries receive more FDI. This interaction between a partisan host government and internationally mobile capital is captured in a simple formal model, which predicts that pro-labor governments adopt investment regimes that are friendlier to FDI, whereas pro-business governments adopt more restrictive investment regimes. These predictions run counter to the extant literature on the political economy of foreign investment, but are consistent with the broader literature on partisanship and globalization discussed in Chapter 1. Moreover, the emphasis on preferences helps cast the scholarly debate on the role of institutions through a different prism as becomes apparent in the analysis of the evolution of the politics of investment in Argentina and South Korea. Changes in political institutions, like enlargement of the franchise, have the potential to alter the identity of the median voter or lead changes in the ability of different individuals or groups with different policy preferences to become more politically influential.

The problems faced by governments in regulating foreign investment is analogous to those discussed in the literature on optimal taxation. An optimal tax schedule is one that places the burden on those factors least elastic to taxes. An ex-ante optimal tax policy is one that maximizes consumer welfare subject to government and private-sector budget constraints (Eichengreen, 1990). Thus, mobile capital, which is usually relatively elastic to taxes, should be taxed more lightly. Democratic governments find it difficult to commit to an optimal tax schedule, as provided that capital income is more concentrated than labor income – such as how mean and median factor endowments differ – a majority of the population would gain from shifting part of the tax burden to capital despite the resulting loss in efficiency (Persson and Tabellini, 1994). Delegating policy-making authority to conservative agents is usually the prescribed recipe to mitigate this problem, resulting in a lower tax burden on capital (Persson and Tabellini, 1994). The mechanism discussed in the following sections is different: to the extent that labor and capital are complements and governments can discriminate between internationally mobile and immobile capital, a different equilibrium is possible where left-leaning governments are gentler and kinder to foreign investors, and right-leaning governments are more hostile. Pinto and Pinto (2011) extend this argument to a dynamic game where investors vary in terms of their degree of mobility and have access to different types of technology.

This chapter is organized as follows: Section 2.2 places the argument in the context of the extant literature on the politics of investment. In Section 2.3, I introduce the model from which I derive the prediction that left-leaning governments should welcome foreign investment, whereas right-leaning governments should be opposed. The model is based on simple assumptions about the effect of factor movements on the return to domestic factors of production. From this model, I derive two propositions: the first proposition links the partisanship of governments to foreign investment regimes. It states that the larger the value that government agents place on the political support of labor, the lower the tax schedule (a proxy for the foreign investment regime) offered to foreign investors. The second proposition links investment regimes to investment outcomes: the larger the value that government agents place on the political support of labor, the higher the level of foreign investment in the country.

Note that I am not trying to explain taxation of foreign capital here. I use tax as a proxy for the numerous policy instruments that governments use to attract or deter the inflow of FDI, including tax schedules and taxation system, regulatory regimes on sectoral activity and market structure, trade policy, local procurement rules, and differential exchange rate regimes. All these instruments and regulations either affect the cost of doing business or the price that firms can charge for their goods and services, and are hence reflected in a firm's bottom line. For simplicity, the model assumes that the host government controls only one policy instrument to regulate FDI – a tax rate that the host government levies on internationally mobile capital – which must be interpreted as the summation of all government intervention that impact investors' profitability.[5]

2.2 The Politics of Investment

Over the past decade, scholars from diverse backgrounds have churned out numerous articles seeking to explain the relationship between globalization and politics, including globalization's causes and consequences.[6] More

---

[5] On the effect of taxation on the activity of multinational corporations, see Hines (2001) and Desai et al. (2002).

[6] Wood (1991, 1994) and O'Rourke and Williamson (1999) provide excellent accounts of these trends.

recently, globalization theorists have argued, that as markets internationalize governments become increasingly constrained to the extent of losing policy autonomy.[7] There is evidence to suggest that the increasing internationalization of production, and the flows of goods, services, and factors of production across borders has had significant distributive effects.[8] To date, the claim that regulatory standards have been compromised has found little empirical support: governments retain substantial powers in most major policy areas, including public finance and redistribution, trade, financial market regulation, and environmental protection.[9] What we know for certain is that globalization has played itself out differently in different countries, triggering a variety of political conflicts over distribution and policy.[10]

The analysis of FDI is one of the most recent areas of globalization that has piqued the curiosity of scholars and pundits (Henisz, 2000b, 2002; Delios and Henisz, 2003; Li and Resnick, 2003; Jensen, 2003, 2006). A recent body of literature analyzes the determinants of foreign investment flows (Carr et al., 2001, 2003; Markusen and Maskus, 2001a,b,c, 2002). However, most of the scholarly work in this issue area either takes the content of the regulatory framework as given, or analyzes investors' reactions to political characteristics of the host country such as regime type and the presence or absence of institutional constraints.[11] This is problematic for a number of reasons: on one hand, policy regimes adopted by governments are likely to affect investment decisions. On the other hand, foreign investment affects the relative prices paid to owners of capital and labor in the host country, creating incentives for these actors to try to influence government to adopt their preferred policy regime.[12] The main shortcoming in this literature is probably its neglect of the distributive consequences that factor flows

---

[7] See Vernon (1971) and Strange (1996), among others.

[8] The Stolper-Samuelson theorem proves that the flow of goods and services is likely to affect owners of factors of production differently based on their relative scarcity, and thus we have accepted that trade is likely to have distinctive effect on politics (Stolper and Samuelson, 1941; Rogowski, 1987, 1989; Frieden, 1991). Robert Mundell has shown that the effect of factor mobility is equivalent to that of trade (Mundell, 1957). The claim that capital mobility, either across sectors or international, may affect the demand for policy in different issue areas including trade, and monetary, social and fiscal policy is fairly uncontroversial. See Milner (1988), Hiscox (2002), Alt et al. (1999), Boix (2003), and Adserà and Boix (2002), among others.

[9] See Garrett (1998a,b), Vogel (1996), Kahler (1998), Swank (1998), Alvarez et al. (1991), Iversen (1999), Boix (1997, 1998), Hall and Soskice (2001), Garrett and Mitchell (2001), Swank and Steinmo (2002), and Franzese (2002a).

[10] See Polanyi (1957), Katzenstein (1978), Gourevitch (1986), Verdier (1998), Cameron (1978), Rodrik (1997), and Rodrik (1998), among others.

[11] See, Henisz (2000b), Rogowski (2003), Jensen (2003), and Jensen (2006).

[12] The consequences of restricting capital mobility are discussed in Alesina and Tabellini (1989), Quinn and Inclan (1997), Quinn (1997), and Alfaro (2004). These four papers focus on capital controls, but make contradictory predictions. See also Alesina et al. (1994).

may have on factor income. Usually, some domestic actors benefit from the inflow of foreign investment, whereas others are harmed.[13] In order to make predictions about these reciprocal effects, we need to model the strategic interaction between investors and governments.

Among those approaches that actually look at the disparate effects of direct investment flows on different actors in the host country, we find *dependency theory*, which was influential in the 1970s.[14] Yet, these authors make predictions that are radically opposed to those advanced in this book. According to scholars in this tradition, local capital shares the preferences of foreign capital along several policy dimensions, such as the desire to suppress labor organization and to lower work standards, to reduce taxes on capital, and to eliminate environmental regulation.[15] These shared preferences are advanced politically by a *triple alliance* between foreign and domestic capital and authoritarian governments aimed at exploiting the popular sectors in the host country. The predictions of this theory are likely to hold when foreign and domestic capital are complements, not substitutes. In the latter case, this alliance cannot be stable, as Jorge Dominguez persuasively argued more than two decades ago: a shared interest in reducing taxes on capital and suppressing organized labor cannot explain why domestic capital would tolerate foreign capital inflows that are likely to compete their rents away (Dominguez, 1982).

Contrary to the old dependency claim, I argue that in general the preferences of workers, not capital, are more likely to be in line with those of foreign investors.[16] The reason is simple: to the extent that labor and foreign capital are complements in production, inflows of capital change the marginal product of labor and capital, and affect relative returns to owners of domestic factors of production. The effect on capital, whose marginal product is likely to decrease with an inflow of capital that changes the relative labor to capital ratio, is predicted to be negative, whereas the effect

---

[13] These consequences follow from the Stolper-Samuelson theorem and Mundell's equivalence proposition, which states that in the absence of trade factor mobility can affect factor returns (Stolper and Samuelson, 1941; Mundell, 1957). To the extent that factor flows have the potential to affect factor returns, the logic holds for open economies as well. This includes cases of full specialization or restricted factor mobility.

[14] On dependency and multinational activity see Evans (1979), Evans and Gereffi (1982), Gereffi (1983), and Moran (1978), among others.

[15] See Kahler (1998) and Garrett (1998b) for a critical review on this literature.

[16] It is possible to derive conditions under which FDI has positive spillovers, complements domestic capital in production, or enters the host country with labor-saving technologies. There is ample evidence to suggest, however, that in the aggregate inward FDI results in higher wages and possibly greater employment (Brown et al., 2004; Pinto and Pinto, 2008).

on labor is likely to be positive.[17] Section 2.3 discusses a partisan theory of FDI policy orientation constructed around these premises.

2.3 Distributive Concerns, Partisanship, and Regulation of Foreign Investment

I introduce a stylized version of the interaction between host governments and investors. For simplicity, I assume that foreign capital owners care about the net rate of return to investing in a host country. This rate is affected by the conditions offered to investors by host governments and the likelihood that these conditions are enforced.[18] I also assume that, if unconstrained, the host government would like to lure investors in and to extract as much from foreign investors as possible. However, when host governments are partisan they are likely to offer foreign investors a contract that they will abide by, because that contract would serve to minimize the backlash from the domestic actors of whose interests the governments are more responsive.

In order to capture the main characteristics of foreign direct investment, capital, and technology, I allow foreign investment to be more productive than domestic investment and to pay a search cost when investing abroad. For simplicity, I also assume that the production function is homogenous, that there are constant returns to scale, and that factors are paid according to their marginal contribution to output. Whereas labor market institutions and market structure may affect the bargaining position of workers and management, in the long run we would assume that their return is related to their marginal contribution to output. It becomes apparent that inflows of capital affect the return received by domestic labor and domestic capital.[19]

---

[17] There is profuse evidence of instances where labor has opposed outflows of capital (Caves, 1996). Further, anecdotal evidence suggests that management and capital owners oppose foreign investment in Europe: Anthony Rowley, Onto the drawbridge; Japanese and South Korean firms lay siege to "fortress" Europe, *Far Eastern Economic Review*, May 18, 1989, v144 n20 p68(3). Finally, in the case of the United States, public protest against Japanese interests investing in the United States in the early 1990s serves as an example. *Financial Times*, October 4, 1989, Chief of Sony tells why it bought a part of America's soul. See Chapter 1.

[18] After economic shocks, investors would also prefer a policy schedule that automatically adjusted to their advantage such that the contract offered to them would change when the state of the world changed in an unfavorable manner, but not otherwise.

[19] In order to have this effect, investment inflows should have the potential to affect the stock of capital in the host country. I also assume a homogeneous technology and put aside bargaining issues, which may result in returns that differ from those determined by investment's contribution to output. The assumptions are adopted to bring to the front the tradeoff between market returns and consumption of government output in the actors' utility functions. Relaxing these

The prediction from the model is that to the extent that FDI complements labor in production, governments that cater to a domestic coalition built around workers offer conditions that are more favorable to foreign investors, whereas governments that draw their support mostly from capital owners are less favorable. Another result, explored in ensuing sections, is that inflows of foreign direct investment is larger under pro-labor/left-leaning governments than under pro-capital/right-leaning governments, holding all else equal.

2.3.1 Autonomous Government and FDI

The model starts with two actors: a *host government* and a *foreign investor*. These actors receive a payoff from their interaction that takes the form of tax revenue (τ), in the case of *government*, and return to investment in the host country to the *foreign investor*. The foreign investor has two options: she can invest at *home* (rest of the world), an action for which she would receive a return r (net of home taxes), or she can invest in the host country, incurring a cost c and receiving a return to her investment denoted by R.[20] Let K^F be the amount invested by foreign investors in the host country, whereas K^D is the amount invested in this market by domestic capital. The total amount invested in the host country by foreign and domestic investors is K, where:

$$K = h(K^F, K^D) \tag{2.1}$$

The indirect utility function of the host government (U^G) is a function of the taxes levied on capital:

$$U^G = \tau(K) \tag{2.2}$$

Output (Y) is produced according to:

$$Y = F(K, L) \tag{2.3}$$

Also, assume that labor is fixed, and normalize L to unity. Then,

$$y = f(K) \tag{2.4}$$

---

assumptions to allow for a more general functional form, or even for costs of entry and wage bargaining protocols, does not affect the main predictions from the model. The only critical assumption is that the equilibrium return to domestic factors of production is related to the factors' contributions to output.

[20] For simplicity, in the following analysis I assume that r includes the search costs of investing abroad, hence for investment to occur $R > r + t + c$.

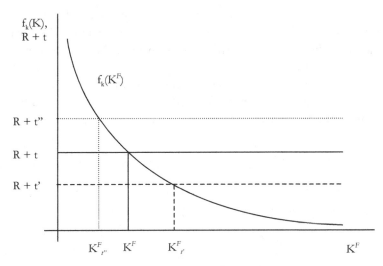

Figure 2.1. Changes in FDI (K^F) with changes in t.

The marginal product of capital is $f_K(K)$. Output increases as capital increases, $f_K > 0$, and the marginal product of capital is diminishing in K, that is: $f_{KK} < 0$. The net return to a *foreign investor* in the host country (R) is:

$$R \equiv f_K \frac{\partial h}{\partial K^F} - t \tag{2.5}$$

R must be at least equal to r (the return abroad) for the *foreign investor* to invest in the host country:

$$R \equiv f_K \frac{\partial h}{\partial K^F} - t = r \tag{2.6}$$

The amount of foreign investment (K^F) that flows into the host country is a function of foreign investors' reservation value (return abroad or r), the rate or return in the host country ($f_K \frac{\partial h}{\partial K^F}$), and the taxes (t) levied by the host government on foreign capital, which as introduced before proxies for the net effects of the regulatory regime on foreign investment. By rearranging equation (2.6), we obtain: $r + t = f_K \frac{\partial h}{\partial K^F}$. To simplify the analysis, assume that the tax (t) is only raised on foreign investment, that domestic capital is (relatively) inelastic to taxes, and fixed in supply, that is: $K^D = \bar{K}$.[21] Figure 2.1 depicts the relationship graphically.

---

[21] The implicit assumption here is that by choosing the regulatory regime on investment, proxied by t, the host government discriminates between domestic and foreign capital. Note that the

The amount of K^F flowing into the host country is marked by the intersection of $f_k(K)$ and the constant $r + t$, which is to say that the return to capital in the host country minus the taxes paid to the host government equals the rate of return abroad. When the host government reduces t to t', K^F rises to $K^F_{t'}$. On the other hand, if the government raised t to t'', the amount of foreign investment flowing into the host country would fall to $K^F_{t''}$. This result can be derived formally from equation (2.6):

$$R \equiv f_K \frac{\partial h}{\partial K^F} - t = r \Rightarrow f_K \frac{\partial K}{\partial K^F} - t = r \tag{2.7}$$

$$\left(f_{KK} \left(\frac{\partial K}{\partial K^F} \right)^2 + f_K \frac{\partial^2 K}{\partial K^{F2}} \right) \frac{dK^F}{dt} - 1 = 0 \tag{2.8}$$

$$\frac{dK^F}{dt} = \frac{1}{f_{KK} \left(\frac{\partial K}{\partial K^F} \right)^2 + f_K \frac{\partial^2 K}{\partial K^{F2}}} \tag{2.9}$$

By assumption, we know that $f_K > 0$, and by concavity of f_K, that $f_{KK} < 0$. The sign of dK^F/dt depends on the functional form of $h(K^F, K^D)$. Suppose that foreign capital is relatively more effective than domestic capital, or $K = h(K^F, K^D) = \theta K^F + K^D$, where $\theta > 1$. In this case, $\partial K/\partial K^F = \theta$ and $\partial^2 K/\partial K^{F2} = 0 \Rightarrow$

$$\frac{dK^F}{dt} = \frac{1}{f_{KK} \theta^2} < 0 \Rightarrow \frac{dK^F}{dt} < 0 \tag{2.10}$$

Next, we return to the host government's utility, defined by equation (2.2). Assume that $\tau(K)$ takes the following functional form: $\tau(K) = t\,K(t)$. The government's maximization problem becomes:

$$\max_t \; t\,K^F(t) \tag{2.11}$$

The First Order Condition (FOC) to this maximization problem is:

$$K^F + t \frac{dK^F}{dt} = 0$$

The Second Order Condition (SOC) is:

$$\frac{dK^F}{dt} + \frac{dK^F}{dt} + t \frac{d^2 K^F}{dt^2} < 0$$

---

effect of t on K is given by: $dK/dt = (\partial K/\partial K^F) \, (dK^F/dt)$. Hence, $dK/dt = dK^F/dt$ because domestic capital is assumed to be constant ($\bar{K}$), and t is levied on foreign capital (K^F) alone.

Table 2.1. *Changes in t**
with changes in r

r	t^*
0.01	0.007
0.02	0.013
0.03	0.020
0.04	0.027
0.05	0.034
0.06	0.040
0.07	0.047
0.08	0.053
0.09	0.060
0.10	0.066
0.20	0.129
0.30	0.181
0.40	0.221
0.50	0.247

From equation 2.10, we know that the first two terms are negative $(dK^F/dt = (f_{kk})^{-1} < 0)$, whereas $d^2 K^F/dt^2$ can be derived by assuming a specific functional form for the production function y.[22] The optimal tax rate (t^*) that maximizes the government's utility function U^G in equation 2.2, provided that the first and second order conditions are fulfilled, is implicitly defined by:

$$t^* = \frac{-K^F}{dK^F/dt} \tag{2.12}$$

We could interpret this result in terms of elasticity, where the host government chooses t^* such that, in equilibrium, the tax elasticity of foreign capital supply equals unity, that is $|(dK^F/dt)/(-K^F/t^*)| = 1$. The intuition behind this result is that a revenue maximizing government internalizes the effect of taxes on inflows and the effect of inflows on the return to capital in the host country, which run in opposite directions. A numerical exercise could help visually portray the predictions from this model. Table 2.1 shows how the optimal tax t^* changes when returns abroad (r) change.

---

[22] When the production takes a Cobb-Douglas functional form, the SOC to the government's maximization problem is $t < K^{-1}(2\alpha(\alpha - 1))/(\alpha - 2)$.

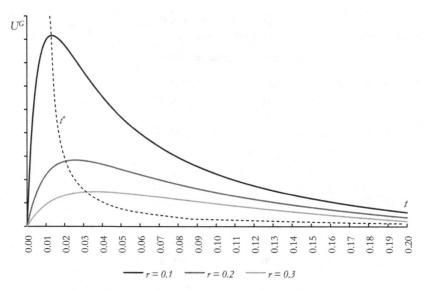

Figure 2.2. Government utility and taxes on foreign capital ($\alpha = 0.6$; $K^D = 0.1$).

Figure 2.2 graphs the utility function of government as t increases, for different levels of return to investment abroad (r), holding constant technology and domestic investment (at $\alpha = 0.6$ and $K = 0.1$, respectively).[23] The corollary is that a revenue, maximizing government is pressed to raise the tax rate on FDI as the opportunity to invest abroad increases. The total revenue raised is lower, as predicted by globalization pessimists, and the host government are worse off than when the opportunities to invest elsewhere are restricted, but the tax rate goes up, not down. Note that these conclusions are driven by the assumptions that the host government's only concern is to maximize revenue, that domestic capital is fixed and does not change with taxes, and that the only source of revenue depends on the level of foreign investment, of which the government would like to receive more, rather than less.

2.3.2 Foreign Investment and Distributive Concerns

What happens when the host government is constrained by the demands of different domestic actors? Following Hillman (1982), I model a *political support function*, where the government not only cares about total revenue but also values the well-being of two groups of domestic actors: workers

---

[23] Values where chosen to yield $K^F > 0$.

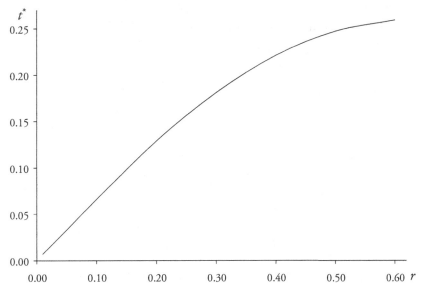

Figure 2.3. Changes in t^* with changes in r ($\alpha = 0.7$; $K^D = 0.5$).

and owners of capital.[24] In the political support function presented in this section, the government's objective function is augmented to capture the indirect utility derived from the weighted average of the welfare of domestic labor and capital, and the direct utility derived from increased revenue through taxes levied on foreign capital, as in the model previously described.[25]

Political support in the case of capital flows results from the value domestic actors place on the distributive effects associated with factor flows. The utility domestic actors derive from their participation in the market, which depends upon their position in the economy, is affected by the investment decision of the foreign investor (K^F).[26] There are two actors that have the

---

[24] The political support function model used by Hillman (1982, 1989) to assess the effects of supporting a declining industry is derived from the Stigler-Peltzman model of regulation; Stigler (1971); Peltzman (1976).

[25] Grossman and Helpman (1994, 2001) adopt a broader form of this political support function originally developed by Hillman, where government's selection of policy outputs result from a trade-off of domestic welfare for political contributions. It also differs from the function used by Dutt and Mitra (2005).

[26] An extension of the model, discussed in Appendix 1, analyzes how direct investment inflows affect actors' income indirectly through redistribution from government activity. Pinto and Pinto (2007) further extend the analysis to multiple sectors, different technologies, and link fiscal motivations to the provision of unemployment insurance.

potential to affect government, owners of labor ($\mathcal{L}$) and owners of capital ($\mathcal{K}$), whose utility functions are (respectively):

$$U^{\mathcal{L}} = U^{\mathcal{L}}(x); \quad U^{\mathcal{K}} = U^{\mathcal{K}}(z)$$

where output (y), return to labor (x), and domestic capital (z) are, respectively:

$$y = f(K) \equiv wL + r^D K^D + r^F K^F$$

$$w \equiv x = f(K) - f_K(K)K$$

$$r^D \equiv z = f_K(K)K^D$$

Recall that $K = h(K^F, K^D)$ in equation (2.1), then:

$$y = wL + f_K \frac{\partial h}{\partial K^D} K^D + f_K \frac{\partial h}{\partial K^F} K^F$$

Given the assumption that L was fixed, and normalized to unity (equation (2.4)), then:

$$w \equiv x = f(K) - f_K \frac{\partial h}{\partial K^D} K^D - f_K \frac{\partial h}{\partial K^F} K^F$$

$$r^D \equiv z = f_K \frac{\partial h}{\partial K^D} K^D$$

Because the utility of labor and capital are increasing functions of w and r^D, respectively:

$$U_x^{\mathcal{L}}, U_z^{\mathcal{K}} > 0; \quad \text{and} \quad U_{xx}^{\mathcal{L}}, U_{zz}^{\mathcal{K}} < 0$$

The host government's utility function is given by:

$$U^{Gp} = t(K^F(t)) + \beta U^{\mathcal{L}}(x) + (1 - \beta)U^{\mathcal{K}}(z) \tag{2.13}$$

In this model, the host government is partisan as it weighs the support of labor and capital differently.

This is captured by the parameter $\beta \in [0, 1]$ in equation (2.13). A higher value of β reflects a government that places higher value on the support of domestic labor, whereas a lower β implies that the government values more heavily the utility derived by owners of domestic capital. In the utility function presented in equation 2.13 β can be interpreted as a change in institutions that empowers different political actors (Mayer, 1984), or as a change in the partisan orientation of the government (Hibbs, 1977 and Tufte, 1978). To simplify the analysis without affecting the thrust of the model, I assume that domestic capital is risk neutral, in which case $U^K = z.$[27]

$$\max_t \ t \ K^F(t) + \beta \ U^{\mathcal{L}}(x) + (1 - \beta)z$$

Replacing x and z, the maximization problem becomes:

$$\max_t \ t \ K^F(t) + \beta \ U^{\mathcal{L}}\left[f(K) - f_K \frac{\partial h}{\partial K^D}K^D - f_K \frac{\partial h}{\partial K^F}K^F \right]$$

$$+ (1 - \beta) f_K \frac{\partial h}{\partial K^D}K^D$$

The first order condition (FOC) to this maximization problem is:

$$K^F + t\frac{dK^F}{dt} + \beta \ U_x^{\mathcal{L}}\frac{dx}{dt} + (1 - \beta)\frac{dz}{dt} = 0 \tag{2.14}$$

This equation can be expanded to:

$$K^F + t \frac{dK^F}{dt} + \beta \ U_x^{\mathcal{L}}\left[f_K \frac{\partial h}{\partial K^F} - f_{KK}\frac{\partial h}{\partial K^F}\frac{\partial h}{\partial K^D}K^D - f_K \frac{\partial^2 h}{\partial K^D \partial K^F}K^D \right.$$

$$\left. - f_{KK}\left(\frac{\partial h}{\partial K^F}\right)^2 K^F - f_K \frac{\partial^2 h}{\partial K^{F2}}K^F - f_K \frac{\partial h}{\partial K^F}\right]\frac{dK^F}{dt}$$

$$+ (1 - \beta)\left[f_{KK}\frac{\partial h}{\partial K^F}\frac{\partial h}{\partial K^D}K^D - f_K\frac{\partial^2 h}{\partial K^{F2}}K^D \right]\frac{dK^F}{dt} = 0 \tag{2.15}$$

This, in turn, can be simplified to:

$$K^F + \frac{dK^F}{dt}\left\{ t + \beta U_x^{\mathcal{L}}\left[K^D \left(-f_{KK}\frac{\partial h}{\partial K^F}\frac{\partial h}{\partial K^D} - f_K\frac{\partial^2 h}{\partial K^D \partial K^F} \right) \right.\right.$$

$$\left. - K^F\left(f_{KK}\left(\frac{\partial h}{\partial K^F}\right)^2 - f_K\frac{\partial^2 h}{\partial K^{F2}} \right) \right]$$

$$\left. + (1 - \beta)K^D \left(f_{KK}\frac{\partial h}{\partial K^F}\frac{\partial h}{\partial K^D} - f_K\frac{\partial^2 h}{\partial K^{F2}} \right) \right\} = 0 \tag{2.16}$$

The second order condition (SOC) is defined by:

$$\frac{dK^F}{dt} + \frac{dK^F}{dt} + t\frac{d^2 K^F}{dt^2} + \beta \ U_{xx}^{\mathcal{L}}\left(\frac{dx}{dt}\right)^2 + \beta \ U_x^{\mathcal{L}}\frac{d^2 x}{dt^2} + (1 - \beta)\frac{d^2 z}{dt^2} < 0 \tag{2.17}$$

[27] To further simplify the analysis we could also assume that labor is risk neutral, leading to $U^{\mathcal{L}}(x) = x$. I make use of this assumption in this section; see equation (2.24).

This gives a solution (as long as the SOC and other parameters of the model are satisfied), which implicitly defines the tax offered by a partisan government, t^{Gp}:

$$
t^{Gp} = -\frac{K^F}{dK^F/dt} - \beta\, U_x^{\mathcal{L}} \left[K^D \left(-f_{KK} \frac{\partial h}{\partial K^F} \frac{\partial h}{\partial K^D} - f_K \frac{\partial^2 h}{\partial K^D \partial K^F} \right) \right.
$$
$$
\left. - K^F \left(f_{KK} \left(\frac{\partial h}{\partial K^F} \right)^2 - f_K \frac{\partial^2 h}{\partial K^{F2}} \right) \right]
$$
$$
- (1-\beta)\, K^D \left(f_{KK} \frac{\partial h}{\partial K^F} \frac{\partial h}{\partial K^D} - f_K \frac{\partial^2 h}{\partial K^{F2}} \right) \tag{2.18}
$$

Again, the solution to the problem depends on the functional form of the production function (2.1). As in section 2.3.1, suppose that capital is relatively more effective than domestic capital, or $K = h(K^F, K^D) = \theta K^F + K^D$. Replacing into equation (2.18), we obtain:

$$
t^{Gp} = -\frac{K^F}{dK^F/dt} - \beta U_x^{\mathcal{L}} \left[K^D(-f_{KK}\,\theta) - K^F\, f_{KK}\,\theta^2 \right] - (1-\beta)K^D \left(f_{KK}\,\theta \right)
$$

This can be further simplified to:

$$
t^{Gp} = -\frac{K^F}{dK^F/dt} + \beta\, U_x^{\mathcal{L}} \left[K^D f_{KK}\,\theta + K^F\, f_{KK}\,\theta^2 \right] - (1-\beta)K^D f_{KK}\,\theta
$$
$$
t^{Gp} = -\frac{K^F}{dK^F/dt} + \beta\, U_x^{\mathcal{L}} \left[f_{KK}\,\theta(K^D + K^F\,\theta) \right] - (1-\beta)K^D f_{KK}\,\theta
$$
$$
t^{Gp} = -\frac{K^F}{dK^F/dt} + f_{KK}\,\theta \left[\beta\, U_x^{\mathcal{L}} K - (1-\beta)K^D \right] \tag{2.19}
$$

Expanding equation (2.19), we obtain:

$$
t^{Gp} = -\frac{K^F}{dK^F/dt} + f_{KK}\,\theta \left[\beta\, U_x^{\mathcal{L}} K^D + \beta\, U_x^{\mathcal{L}}\,\theta K^F - K^D + \beta\, K^D \right] \tag{2.20}
$$

Comparing the solution to the maximization problem obtained in equation (2.19) with the solution obtained in equation (2.12), the case of the non-partisan government, it becomes apparent that the level of the optimal tax varies with β. First, we know that the first term in equation (2.19) is negative; we also know by definition that $f_{KK} < 0$ and $\theta > 1$. The sign of

t^{Gp} therefore depends on the sign of the terms in square brackets in (2.19):

$$\beta \, U_x^{\mathcal{L}} \, K - (1 - \beta)K^D \gtrless 0$$

This term is positive when:

$$\beta \, U_x^{\mathcal{L}} \, K > (1 - \beta) \, K^D$$

$$\frac{\beta}{(1 - \beta)} \, U_x^{\mathcal{L}} > \frac{K^D}{K}$$

If we assume that labor is risk neutral, $U(x) = x$, and $U_x^{\mathcal{l}} = 1$, then:

$$\Rightarrow \frac{\beta}{(1 - \beta)} > \frac{K^D}{K}$$

As the incumbent government becomes pro-labor, the optimal tax goes down ($\tau^{Gp} < 0$).[28] For the pro-labor government $\beta > \frac{1}{2}$, implying that the term in square brackets in equation (2.19) is positive ($\beta \, U_x^{\mathcal{L}} K - (1 - \beta)K^D > 0$), because by definition $K^D \subseteq K$ (i.e.: $K^D/K \leq 1$). This conclusion can be derived analytically from a simple comparative statics exercise. First, take the FOC of the government's maximization problem, equation (2.14), and let $G \equiv d\tau/dt$, so that the first order condition $G = 0$ implicitly defines the relationship between t and the exogenous variables, β in particular. By the implicit function theorem:

$$\frac{dt}{d\beta} = -\frac{(dG/d\beta)}{(dG/dt)} \tag{2.21}$$

Note that $(dG/dt) = (d^2\tau/dt^2) < 0$ if the second order condition is satisfied. In addition:

$$\frac{dG}{d\beta} = U_x^{\mathcal{L}}\frac{dx}{dt} - \frac{dz}{dt} \tag{2.22}$$

which can be expanded to:

$$\frac{dG}{d\beta} = \frac{dK^F}{dt}\left[U_x^{\mathcal{L}}\left(-f_{KK}\frac{\partial h}{\partial K^F}\frac{\partial h}{\partial K^D}K^D - f_K\frac{\partial^2 h}{\partial K^D \partial K^F}K^D - f_{KK}\left(\frac{\partial h}{\partial K^F}\right)^2 K^F \right. \right.$$

$$\left. \left. - f_K\frac{\partial^2 h}{\partial K^{F2}}K^F \right) - \left(f_{KK}\frac{\partial h}{\partial K^F}\frac{\partial h}{\partial K^D}K^D + f_K\frac{\partial^2 h}{\partial K^{F2}}K^D \right) \right] \tag{2.23}$$

---

[28] In reduced form: $t^P = \tau(\beta)$.

The sign of $dG/d\beta$ in (2.23) depends on the relationship between domestic capital (K^D) and foreign capital (K^F), or the functional form of $h(K^F, K^D)$ in equation (2.1), which determines the partial and cross-partial derivatives in equation (2.23). Suppose that foreign capital (K^F) is an *imperfect* substitute of domestic capital (K^D) and that foreign capital is relatively more effective than domestic capital: $K = h(K^F, K^D) = \theta K^F + K^D$, where $\theta > 1$. Let's also assume, for simplicity, that labor owners are risk neutral, in which case $U^{\mathcal{L}}(x) = x$. We obtain:

$$\frac{dG}{d\beta} = \frac{dK^F}{dt}\left(-K^D\, f_{KK}\,\theta - K^F\, f_{KK}\,\theta^2 - K^D f_{KK}\,\theta\right) \quad (2.24)$$

We know that $(dK^F/dt) < 0$ and we can see that the term in parentheses is positive: $(K^D > 0, \ K^F \geq 0, \ \theta > 1,$ and $f_{KK} < 0)$. Therefore, $(dG/d\beta) < 0$.[29] Combining with $(dG/dt) = (d^2\tau/dt^2) < 0$ in equation (2.21), we obtain the following: $(dt/d\beta) < 0$. In sum, as β increases the optimal tax offered by a *partisan* host government decreases.[30]

Thus, we may define $t^p_{\mathcal{L}}$ as the solution to the government's maximization problem when $\beta = 1$, whereas τ^p_K is the optimal tax when $\beta = 0$. The previous results suggest that $\tau^p_K > \tau^p_{\mathcal{L}}$, which is to say that the optimal tax offered by the pro-domestic capital government is larger than the one offered by a government that places higher value on $U^{\mathcal{L}}$ (the utility of workers).

It is fair to state that the tax schedule decreases in β. When foreign capital increases labor productivity, a host government that places more weight on the support of labor (when $\beta > \frac{1}{2}$) would choose a tax on foreign capital that is lower than the tax structure chosen by a government that places more weight on the support of owners of capital (a lower β). Figure 2.4 represents this result graphically.

The behavior by government affects domestic constituents in different ways, in line with the effects that FDI has on different types of individuals in the host country. This section shows that as investment inflows change the relative endowment of labor and capital, owners of capital are hurt, whereas labor benefit. Translating the previous comparative statics exercise into words allows us to derive the following proposition:

---

[29] This result holds for any other form of $U^{\mathcal{L}}(x)$ for which $U^{\mathcal{L}}_x > 0$, if foreign and domestic capital are substitutes.

[30] The exact amount of the change can be determined (through a numerical example) using an explicit production function and an explicit utility function.

Proposition 1: *the larger the value that the government places on the political support of the owners of labor, the lower the tax schedule it offers to foreign investors, all else equal.*

Moreover, combining $dt/d\beta < 0$ with $dK^F/dt < 0$, which we know from equation (2.10), we may derive the following proposition:

Proposition 2: *the larger the value that the government places on the political support of the owners of labor, the higher the level of foreign investment, all else equal.*

Under this scenario, a potential loss of support from pivotal domestic actors may help solve the time consistency problem (see Chapter 3). The host government must now tradeoff the additional tax revenue levied when acting opportunistically with the loss of political support from domestic actors resulting from the expected effect of taxes on inflows of capital on the income of their constituents. Therefore, a *pro-labor* incumbent in the host country discriminates *in favor of* internationally mobile foreign capital and presumably tax domestic capital *more* heavily. A *pro-domestic capital* incumbent, on the other hand, discriminates *against* international capital by levying higher taxes on it.

2.3.3 Intuition and Discussion

In the models previously discussed, the host government is assumed to maximize the utility it gets from the revenue obtained by taxing capital. When the host government is relatively autonomous it only cares about maximizing revenue and prefers a higher tax. Revenue is in turn affected by the decision of foreign investors who compare the net return available in the host country to the opportunities they face abroad. As taxes rise, FDI drops. When the host government is partisan, it internalizes the utility of labor or capital. Therefore, the policy adopted is more restrictive to FDI when domestic capital is part of the ruling coalition and more liberal when the coalition is built around labor. Figure 2.4 presents a simplified representation of the solutions to the maximization problem that government faces: a pro-labor government (that is, when $\beta > \frac{1}{2}$) offers a lower tax to foreign investors, which is the policy most favorable to foreign investors. A pro-business government (when $\beta = 0$) offers the most restrictive conditions, because even though the host government values revenue it would like to please domestic capital by keeping foreign investors out. The theory predicts that conditions

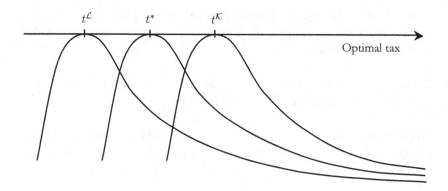

$$t^{\mathcal{L}} < t^* < t^{\mathcal{K}}$$
$t^{\mathcal{L}}$ = optimal tax under pro-labor government ($\beta = 1$)
t^* = revenue maximizing optimal tax ($U^G = t(K)$)
$t^{\mathcal{K}}$ = optimal tax under pro-capital government ($\beta = 0$)

Figure 2.4. Changes in optimal tax (t) with changes in government partisanship (β).

would be more favorable toward foreign investors as governments take a more pro-labor stance. As discussed earlier, the downward sloping curve in Figure 2.5 shows a fall in the optimal tax as governments internalize the material interests of workers (as β approaches 1). The upshot is that FDI increases as governments take a pro-labor position, which is reflected in the upward sloping curve in Figure 2.5.

The model introduced in this chapter is based on simple assumptions about the production function and technology, yet it captures the essential features of FDI and the crux of the interaction between governments and foreign investors.[31] It also relies on very simple assumptions about actors' preferences. The combination of these simplifications results in a rather simple objective function. However, the model allows us to make predictions about the expected sign of the investment regime that host governments would offer to foreign investors, and ultimately about the level of investment in the host country.

The main assumption is that the concern about the distributive consequences of FDI inflows makes labor's interests converge with those of foreign investors, while those of domestic businesses are divergent. Yet it

---

[31] The assumption that the production function is defined by constant returns to scale is perhaps the most problematic one when dealing with multinational activities, especially under the Horstmann and Markusen (1992) and Brainard (1993b) models where the decision to invest abroad is driven by the tradeoff between proximity and economies of scale.

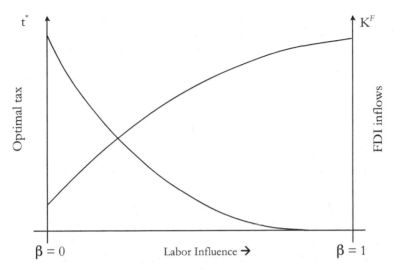

Figure 2.5. Changes in FDI inflows (K^F) with changes in labor influence (β).

is also possible that preferences of labor and foreign capital do not fully converge as is shown in an extension of the model discussed in Appendix 1. There, labor's preferences are mapped onto a two-dimensional space: one dimension represents the value labor places on income received from participation in the market, and following straight from the trade theoretic literature, changes in relative endowment compete wages upward. The other dimension is related to the value labor places on government spending, which acts as a form of social insurance against the potential hardship associated with downturns in economic activity that is beyond the control of labor.[32] Social insurance implies higher taxation, which affects the return to investors. Foreign capital compares the return at Home, net of taxes and subsidies, with the potential return in the host country. Return in the host country is affected by the level of social spending, which implies higher taxes. Increasing labor (capital) influence has a negative (positive) effect on the return on investment in the host country through increasing (decreasing) welfare taxes and transfers, all else equal. Yet, increasing labor (capital) influence could still have a positive (negative) effect on the return to investment in the host country as it reduces uncertainty about the policy environment.

Moreover, this extension to the model suggests that even when workers value higher taxes or government spending, the level of taxes offered to

[32] See Cameron (1978) and Rodrik (1997, 1998) among others.

foreign investors is lower than when capital owners are more influential on government. This prediction holds despite the fact that, by assumption, capital owners do not place any value on the extra revenue obtained from taxing foreign capital.

2.4 Conclusion

In this chapter, I argue that government activity is likely to affect the regulatory environment faced by foreign investors and the activity of multinational corporations. In the end, the nature of the regulatory regime toward FDI can be derived from the incumbent party's alignment with labor or capital. Foreign investors react to the changes in the regulatory environment by deciding to flow into a host country (and a specific sector in that country) if a pro-labor party is in power. Investment regimes are friendlier to foreign investors when FDI complements labor in production, and workers are politically influential and able to change policy. When a pro-business party is in government, investment regimes and conditions are likely to be more stringent and less favorable to foreign investors. The regulatory environment is broadly defined to include all conditions that affect the return to foreign investments. The multiple instruments and regulations that the regulatory environment is comprised of either affect the cost of doing business or the price that firms can charge for their goods and services, and are thus reflected in the firms' bottom line.

A complete political economy model of FDI regulation (and outcomes) must account for the demand and supply conditions in policy making, and should include the preferences of the different actors involved and the incentives faced by politicians when they respond to demands from different groups in the polity. The causal chain becomes more apparent when these different elements are modeled within a system of equations. Such a system identifies the outcomes that are endogenous, which in this case are regulatory policies, investment flows, factor returns and government spending. The first stage characterizes the equilibria: what is the optimal policy from the perspective of the government, how is it the policy linked to other economic outcomes it aims to affect? Next, through comparative statics exercises, I both explore how policy changes when one of the variables of interests changes and how these changes impact flows, factor returns, or even government spending. The main results from the model suggests that pro-labor parties have a motivation to promote investment inflows that increase the demand for labor and that a host country is more open to foreign investment when the pro-labor party is able to enact those investor-friendly policies.

Like any political economy approach, formal or informal, the model here relies on simplifying assumptions that allow us to analyze complex relationships. In my case, the model is built around the following assumptions: 1) investment has the potential to affect the relative demand for factors of production (irrespective of the functional form); 2) changes in relative demand are reflected in factor returns; 3) governments have an objective function that weighs differently the well-being of different groups of economic actors in the polity; 4) the government's choice of policy toward internationally mobile investment anticipates the expected response from investors; and 5) investors react optimally in anticipation to the host government's policy choices, which have the potential to affect the return to their activity in the host.

The first two assumptions are supported by the findings in the empirical literature on MNCs that foreign capital is a complement of labor and an (imperfect) substitute of capital, allowing me to place labor and capital on opposing sides of the issue (see Brown et al., 2004). As discussed in the previous chapter, we could imagine conditions under which the presence of an MNC would increase the demand for services that could be provided by local firms. There is good reason to believe that under fairly broad conditions the entry of foreign firms negatively affects the returns to their domestic counterparts by increasing competition in product and factor markets. Further, the empirical literature demonstrates that irrespective of the sector and form of entry, foreign capital is likely to increase relative labor demand, while the potential for positive spillovers on local firms is more limited, suggesting that the assumption is not too far off the mark. Note that the model does not require there be a sectoral bias in investment such that investment flows into labor intensive sectors; all that is necessary is that investment flows are an (imperfect) complement of labor in production. As such, it does not necessarily fall in the traditional *factor versus industry* divide that characterizes trade policy (Stolper and Samuelson, 1941; Rogowski, 1987, 1989; Alt et al., 1999; Hiscox, 2002).[33] What matters, is that foreign firms entering the market affect factor returns, and that actors are willing

---

[33] It is possible that some group of workers could coalesce with some capital owners, further increasing the difference between the predictions of the links between politics and FDI and traditional arguments about partisan alignments. This could happen when FDI affects both wages and employment, and when the choice of FDI policy has the potential to affect the provision of a public policy such as unemployment insurance. Fairly restrictive conditions can be identified under which some workers and some capital owners would coalesce around a tax schedule offered to FDI but for different reasons (Pinto and Pinto, 2007 and Jensen et al. 2012).

and able to mobilize politically to advance their interests on the issue of regulating foreign investment.

. The modeling strategy also assumes that the government only has one policy instrument: a tax on mobile capital. That tax, which can take positive or negative values, captures the net aggregate effects of different policy instruments that impact foreign investors. All the simplifying assumptions in the theoretical section come at a very low cost. Under certain conditions, foreign investment could benefit capital and possibly harm labor, as explored in Pinto and Pinto (2008), yet in the aggregate FDI inflows seem to be associated with higher wages and labor benefits.[34]

In an extension of the model, I introduce differential preferences for social spending. At one extreme, when there are no revenue considerations factor market effects dominate, implying that pro-labor governments promote FDI inflows and pro-business governments restrict inflows. Adding taxation and spending motivations to the model aims at capturing traditional distinctions between workers' and capitalists' preferences over government output. This extra layer of complexity reinforces the incentives associated with partisan motivations, irrespective of whether the government can discriminate between mobile and immobile capital. Given that domestic capital is relatively more inelastic to taxes, governments and local capital owners have already agreed on the tax on (domestic) capital whereas the treatment of the mobile tax base remains to be bargained over. Even in the case where the government cannot discriminate between different forms of capital, it needs to internalize the effect that higher taxes have on the mobile tax base. Adding a partisan motivation forces governments to trade-off higher taxes and revenue for the indirect effect that taxes on mobile capital have on inflows, and thus on the market return to their constituents. In both cases, we would still find that the pro-labor government offers a relatively lower tax rate on foreign, mobile capital than does its pro-capital counterpart.

Finally, assuming that the left holds a pro-labor stance could be problematic. In many instances, the left has been associated with nationalist stances and has clashed with foreign businesses, for example, Chavez in Venezuela, Kirchner in Argentina in recent years, and Allende in Chile.

---

[34] Domestic business interests would strictly prefer technology transfer agreements to investment capital inflows as is shown in the Korean example discussed in more depth in Chapter 6. The Korean government adopted a highly restrictive investment regime, limiting foreign capital to hold a non-controlling stake in Korean corporations, promoting technology licensing to indigenous firms, and ultimately forcing foreign MNCs to divest from those joint ventures they entered into once the Korean partner firm had mastered the technological innovations furnished by its foreign counterpart (Haggard, 1990; Pinto and Pinto, 2008).

It is plausible, however, that in some cases revenue considerations dominate the utility function of left-leaning governments. This effect would be more apparent when the returns of the constituents of the left are not affected by FDI inflows in factor markets, as is arguably the case in these examples. In any event, it is likely that pro-business parties prefer keeping foreign investors out, especially those investors that raise the costs of their production inputs, including wages in the host country, or those that lower the prices of the goods and services provided by competing domestic firms. These predictions stand in stark contrast to those prevailing in the current theoretical and empirical literature on the politics of FDI. Moreover, the hypotheses derived from the model receive empirical support from the systematic statistical tests presented in Chapter 4 and from the restrictiveness of the foreign investment regimes in post-war South Korea and Japan, two of the most pro-business political regimes in recent history.

APPENDIX 2.1

Partisan Government, Taxes, and Investment

The model discussed previously in the chapter can be trivially modified to incorporate alternative conditions, usually associated with partisan variation in the assessment of higher taxes, as a proxy for government intervention in the economy. For example, domestic actors may accrue benefits (losses) not only from the effect of the inflow of capital on their returns, but from revenue as well: they may receive a share of g.[35] Previously, the model assumed that labor and capital valued the income they obtained from participation in the market, but labor is also likely to prefer to receive a form of social insurance, resulting in higher taxes, all else equal. Higher (lower) taxes lead to lower (higher) foreign (and overall) investment, which reduces (increases) labor's income from the market in this Appendix. I extend the model to account for labor's preference on this dimension. Labor now faces a tradeoff between the utility of income obtained from participation in the market and the utility obtained from goods produced with the extra taxes collected. The government raises taxes but can only keep proportion δ of the revenue obtained, where $\delta \in [0, 1]$, and the rest of the revenue is

---

[35] An alternative would be to change weights on the objective function, making revenue more valuable to the government than the indirect utility of the government's constituents.

used to provide a good g.[36] Assume, also, that only labor values a higher level of government expenditure (g) while capital is indifferent, where: $g = (1 - \delta)tK^F$. The utility functions of labor $(\mathcal{L})$ and domestic capital $(\mathcal{K})$ are, respectively:

$$U^{\mathcal{L}} = U^{\mathcal{L}}(x, g)$$
$$U^{\mathcal{K}} = U^{\mathcal{K}}(z)$$

The host government (G) has the following utility function:

$$U^G = t(K) + \beta U^{\mathcal{L}} + (1 - \beta)U^{\mathcal{K}}(z)$$
$$U^G = \delta\, t(K) + \beta U^{\mathcal{L}} + (1 - \beta)U^{\mathcal{K}}(z)$$
$$U^G = \delta\, t(K) + \beta\{U^{\mathcal{L}} f(K(t)) - f_k(K(t))K(t), (1 - \delta)tK^F(t)\} +$$
$$+ (1 - \beta)U^{\mathcal{K}} f_k(K(t))K^D \qquad (2.25)$$

Thus, the host government's maximization problem becomes:

$$\max_t \; \delta\, t(K) + \beta\{U^{\mathcal{L}} f(K(t)) - f_k(K(t))K(t), (1 - \delta)tK^F(t)\}$$
$$+ (1 - \beta) f_k(K(t))\bar{K}$$

The first order condition (FOC)[37] to this maximization problem is:

$$\delta K^F + \delta\, t\frac{dK^F}{dt} + \beta\, U^{\mathcal{L}}_x\left[f_k\frac{dK^F}{dt} - f_{kk}\frac{dK^F}{dt}K - f_k\frac{dK^F}{dt}\right] +$$
$$+ \beta\, U^{\mathcal{L}}_g\left[(1 - \delta)\, K^F + (1 - \delta)t\frac{dK^F}{dt}\right](1 - \beta)\, f_{kk}\frac{dK^F}{dt}\bar{K} = 0 \Rightarrow$$

$$\Rightarrow \delta\left[K^F + t\frac{dK^F}{dt}\right] + \beta\, U^{\mathcal{L}}_x\left[-f_{kk}\frac{dK^F}{dt}K\right] + \beta\, U^{\mathcal{L}}_g\, (1 - \delta)\left[K^F + t\frac{dK^F}{dt}\right] +$$
$$+ (1 - \beta)\, f_{kk}\frac{dK^F}{dt}\bar{K} = 0$$

---

[36] $1 - \delta$ captures the weight placed on g by different types of government. A decrease in δ would reflect the fact that an extra dollar in revenue is valued more heavily by a left-leaning government. In the model discussed previously in the chapter, $\delta = 1$.

[37] In order to save space the second order condition $(\tau'' < 0)$ is omitted here.

The solution to this maximization problem is an implicit function of β, δ, and the other relevant parameters in the model:

$$t^* = \frac{-\beta\, U_x^{\mathcal{L}}\left(-f_{kk}\frac{\mathrm{d}K^F}{\mathrm{d}t}K\right) - (1-\beta)f_{kk}\frac{\mathrm{d}K^F}{\mathrm{d}t}\bar{K}}{\left(\delta + \beta\, U_g^{\mathcal{L}}(1-\delta)\right)\frac{\mathrm{d}K^F}{\mathrm{d}t}} - \frac{K^F}{\frac{\mathrm{d}K^F}{\mathrm{d}t}} \qquad (2.26)$$

A comparative statics exercise helps understand the effect of changing values of δ. Let $G \equiv \mathrm{d}\tau/\mathrm{d}t$ (from the preceding first order condition), so the FOC $G = 0$ implicitly defines the relationship between t and the exogenous variables, δ in particular. Then, by the implicit function theorem: $(\mathrm{d}t/\mathrm{d}\delta) = -[(\mathrm{d}G/\mathrm{d}\delta)/(\mathrm{d}G/\mathrm{d}t)]$. Note that $(\mathrm{d}G/\mathrm{d}t) = (\mathrm{d}^2\tau/\mathrm{d}t^2) < 0$ if SOC is satisfied (should be satisfied at a maximum). In addition,

$$\frac{\mathrm{d}G}{\mathrm{d}\delta} = \left(K^F + t\frac{\mathrm{d}K^F}{\mathrm{d}t}\right) - \beta U_g^{\mathcal{L}}\left(K^F + t\frac{\mathrm{d}K^F}{\mathrm{d}t}\right) = (1 - \beta U_g^{\mathcal{L}})\left(K^F + t\frac{\mathrm{d}K^F}{\mathrm{d}t}\right)$$

If $K^F, t \geq 0$, $\left(K^F + t\frac{\mathrm{d}K^F}{\mathrm{d}t}\right)$ should always be strictly positive, so that $(\mathrm{d}G/\mathrm{d}\delta) > 0$ if $\beta = 0$. In this case $(\mathrm{d}t/\mathrm{d}\delta) > 0$. If $\beta = 1$, the sign of $(\mathrm{d}G/\mathrm{d}\delta)$ depends on the sign of $(1 - U_g^{\mathcal{L}})$, which can be greater or less than 0.[38] A graphical example of the predictions from this model are presented in the following Table 2.2 and Figure 2.6.

Table 2.2. *Changes in t* with changes in β and δ*

		t^*	
β	$\delta = 1$	$\delta = 0.5$	$\delta = 0$
0.0	0.129	0.151	∞
0.1	0.110	0.106	0.034
0.2	0.092	0.078	0.009
0.3	0.077	0.058	0.004
0.4	0.063	0.043	0.001
0.5	0.050	0.032	0.000
0.6	0.038	0.022	0.000
0.7	0.027	0.015	0.000
0.8	0.016	0.008	0.000
0.9	0.007	0.002	0.000
1.0	0.000	0.000	0.000

[38] To simplify this prediction, we could assume a different functional form for $U^{\mathcal{L}}(x, g)$; assuming that g is an in-cash transfer, then $x = w + g$.

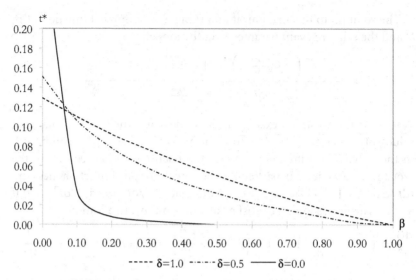

Figure 2.6. Changes in t^* with changes in β and δ ($\alpha = 0.7$; $K^D = 0.5$; $r = 0.3$).

THREE

Tying Hands or Exchanging Hostages: Partisan Governments, Commitment, and FDI Performance

3.1 Introduction

As discussed in previous chapters, foreign direct investment (FDI) has become an important source of revenue and foreign exchange for governments, employment opportunities for workers, and access to technology and markets for host country firms (Graham, 1996; Moran, 1999; Lipsey, 2001, 2004; Carcovic and Levine, 2005; Brown et al., 2004). Moreover, the free flow of investment capital leads to allocative efficiencies that foster growth and aggregate welfare gains for sending and receiving countries, and across the global economy. Despite the potential aggregate gains from cross-border flows of investment capital, Multinational corporations (MNCs) are often highly controversial and are the source of heated political debates. The end result is that significant variation exists in the regulatory environment offered to foreign investors across countries and over time. What explains, variation in policy toward FDI? The theory introduced in this book suggests that changes in the political influence of workers and businesses could help explain this puzzle.

Cross-country comparisons show that governments have chosen very different policies toward foreign investors. Japan and South Korea, for example, both of which are associated with pro-business governments and business-friendly economic policies, have been highly restrictive toward foreign investors, whereas Singapore, The Netherlands, and Belgium have set up foreign investor-friendly regulatory environments. In the liberalizing 1990s, numerous countries abandoned import substitution and command economic policies. Many of those countries have embraced structural adjustment policies that resulted in the liberalization of their trade and investment regimes, and led them to embark on promotional campaigns aimed at attracting FDI by reforming elements of their fiscal systems, including import duty exemptions, tax breaks, and income tax holidays, by granting investors special subsidies and accounting rules, and by building infrastructure to lure investors in (Caves, 1996; UNCTAD, 2003). Yet, the movement toward liberalization has not been monotonic and convergence in regulatory standards is hardly an accomplished fact.

Within countries, the policies offered to investors and investors' responses to local conditions vary over time as well: many economies that had historically looked closed to investors, such as Argentina, Brazil, and even South Korea, have partially liberalized their foreign investment policies in the 1990s, and some had adopted stringent regulations toward foreign investors by the turn of the century. Indices developed by ECLAC, UNCTAD, and the Heritage Foundation reflect this trend: in the aggregate, countries liberalized to foreign investment in the 1990s. The timing and pace of these changes toward regimes that are friendlier to foreign investors varies dramatically across countries, however (OECD, 1998a; UNCTAD, 2002, 2003; Morley et al., 1999; The Heritage Foundation, 2010). The index of investment policy orientation described in Chapter 4 also reflects these changes.

In the 1970s, most developing countries, particularly those in Latin America, placed heavy controls on capital transactions performed by both citizens and foreigners. Many countries limited the sectors that were open to foreign investors and placed ceilings on the repatriation of interest and dividends. Liberalization did not pick up speed until after the debt crisis. Argentina liberalized its investment regime in 1976 and again in 1991. In South Korea, the Foreign Investment Promotion Act of November 1998 and other reforms substantially opened the South Korean economy to foreign investment (Yun, 2003). Yet, several of the erstwhile liberalizers have introduced restrictions on foreign investor activity and many more have adopted policies and practices that directly discriminate against foreign companies, including but not limited to *buy local* provisions in most of the stimulus packages passed in the wake of the Great Recession of 2008.[1]

There is also large variance in terms of the levels of foreign investment flows, which is reflected in the difference between *FDI potential*, or the presence of certain underlying conditions that make countries targets for investment, and *FDI performance*, or the actual amount of investment countries receive, as estimated by UNCTAD (2002, 2003). The large variance in investment performance cannot be fully explained by countries' investment climate or even by traditional variables such as country size or factor endowment, the distance between countries, or common features between

---

[1] "The fragile web of foreign trade," *The Economist*, May 30, 2009. Vol. 391, Iss. 8633; pg. 16.

home and host countries such as language, legal system, or colonial links. The previous chapter presents a theoretical framework where differences in regulations toward foreign investment are a function of changes in the orientation of the ruling coalition in the host country, specifically whether this coalition is built around parties that cater to workers or to domestic owners of capital. The expected distributive consequences of FDI are the driving force behind the propositions derived in the model introduced in Chapter 2.

The framework parallels the literature on the political economy of trade: it is well established in that literature that trade has distributive effects, as discussed extensively in previous chapters (Stolper and Samuelson, 1941).[2] The field of international economics provides a reasonable explanation why factor flows are likely to have distributive effects equivalent to those created by trade in goods and services (Mundell, 1957). Some authors have identified political motivations in the regulation of FDI: "... attracting multinationals may benefit specific constituencies from whom politicians derive support..." (Hanson, 2001, p. 23). The "tariff jumping FDI" literature underscores a similar distributive rationale: labor unions that experience employment gains and local communities that benefit from the location of the foreign affiliates facility are central constituents for pro-FDI policies.[3] Grossman and Helpman (1996) argue that the main cleavage around FDI politics pits "domestic firms wanting investment restrictions" against "workers with industry-specific skills wanting free entry by multinationals" (Grossman and Helpman, 1996). Yet, the source and magnitude of the distributive consequences of FDI remains underdeveloped in that literature.

In theory, the flow of factors of production across national borders, just like the flow of goods and services, can provide benefits to host countries; yet just like trade factor flows have distributive effects as well.[4] FDI is itself a form of capital flow which under most general conditions results in higher labor demand in receiving countries, subsequently increasing wages and employment, and possibly leading to lower returns to domestic capital owners. Relative political influence of labor or capital, in the stylized

---

[2] See Dutt and Mitra (2005) for a review of the literature in economics. In political science, Rogowski (1989) offers an application of the Stolper-Samuelson theorem to political conflict around trade policy.

[3] See Bhagwati et al. (1992, p. 188).

[4] If trade and factor flows are substitutes, factor price equalization occurs through trade, or through factor movement when trade is inhibited. Robert Mundell has developed a formal derivation of this proposition (Mundell, 1957). Scheve and Slaughter (2001a,b) analyze the effect of the presence of MNCs and migration on labor market conditions including factor returns and income volatility.

model introduced in Chapter 2, might therefore determine whether governments adopt policy regimes that are more open or closed to foreign investment.

The predictions from the model presented in Chapter 2 are static, but foreign investment is a dynamic enterprise in so far as its expected benefits are likely to arise over several periods. Thus, irrespective of its partisan orientation, host governments face a typical time inconsistency problem when dealing investors: once investment has flown in the host government may reverse the policies originally offered to attract investors. Moreover, governments have an incentive to act opportunistically if and when investors' exit option is relatively costly, which is usually the case for most forms of foreign direct investment. The end result is that no matter how favorable to foreign investors the policy regimes offered by host governments look ex-ante, these promises become inconsistent ex-post and result in sub-optimal levels of investment. The extant literature on the politics of FDI is built around this time inconsistency logic, which is usually described as political risk. This form of risk can be mitigated when the government is institutionally constrained and hence cannot change policy at will. Yet, as much as MNCs worry about the possibility of opportunistic behavior by host governments that would affect the profitability of their affiliates, they also need to worry about other forms of risk that determine the desirability of an investment location that could be linked to movements along the business cycle, disruptions of production and the loss of control over the proprietary assets that characterize FDI. It is precisely these types of risk that determine the choice of investing with control to service the host market or tap into its resources. Therefore, investment in risky environments is likely to occur under control and is likely to be dominated by firms that are better able at coping with risk. Most of these firms would prefer a policy environment that is stable but that also has some degree of flexibility, particularly when economic shocks could negatively affect their profitability.

In this chapter, I explore how governments' partisanship, or their links to workers and business owners, may work as a source of reassurance to investors even in a dynamic setting, thus helping mitigate the time-inconsistency problem that governments face when dealing with internationally mobile capital. I discuss the sources of commitment available to host governments and show how the relative influence of labor or capital in domestic politics may work as a signal to foreign investors. These investors, concerned with the probability that governments change policies to their disadvantage after they have incurred the cost of deploying their assets abroad, use host governments' partisan attachments to assess the potential risk of opportunistic behavior by their prospective hosts.[5] Partisan connections between the incumbent government and domestic actors – whose interests are congruent with those of the foreign investors – act as a reassurance that these investors not be taken advantage of once they have paid the sunk costs of their investments, as argued by Williamson (1983b). The logic is simple: owners of labor and capital organize politically and can make their voices heard in the political arena, and governments' responses to these demands depends upon their partisan sympathies and allegiances. As workers benefit from inward flows of FDI that result in higher labor demand, left-leaning governments respond with liberal policies toward foreign investment. The reverse outcome occurs when a pro-business coalition is in power, as is shown in Chapter 2.

Received wisdom, formalized in scholarly work in economics and political science, states that international mobility allows firms to circumvent governmental initiatives to regulate their activity. This implies that internationally mobile capital should face few incentives to lobby governments for preferential treatment. The alleged footloose nature of capital is traditionally presented as the driving force behind liberalization. There are good reasons to think that this is not the case for FDI, however. First, there are sizable costs to investing abroad and MNCs usually face non-trivial costs of relocation. Second, affiliates of MNCs devote significant resources to contact and cajole government officials in the countries where they operate (Malesky, 2009). Once established in a host country, MNCs do engage in lobbying activity as frequently as their domestic counterparts and more often than not they favor regulation that would keep competitors out. A sizable share of this lobbying activity is not aimed at liberalizing trade but is instead conducted to receive protection.[6]

In many instances, MNCs do not get their way because government officials find it difficult to justify favoring foreigners over their own nationals. However, foreign investors are able to add voice to their exit option by linking their investment strategy to the well-being of local actors, particularly those who are politically influential (Hirschman, 1970). According to the specialized literature, MNCs opt to choose a domestic partner or to enter a strategic alliance with domestic firms when facing a hostile government.

---

[5] This intuition is formalized in Pinto and Pinto (2011).

[6] A clear example is the auto industry in Argentina: in 1997, the foreign members of the Association of Automobile Manufacturers of Argentina (ADEFA) set up a commission to pressure the government for an extension of the special industrial regime for the sector in MERCOSUR, which was set to expire in 2000 under WTO rules. Interview with Fernando Rodriguez Canedo, Executive Director of ADEFA, August 14, 2006.

For this alliance to pay off, the MNC must be complementary in the production of the services provided by the local partner. When foreign investment has the potential to compete in product and factor markets with local firms, or when FDI crowds out other incumbent firms with political access to the government, such an alliance is unlikely to work. Under more general conditions, FDI is likely to complement labor in production. Under pro-labor governments, or when labor can make its influence felt in politics, the partisan links of workers with the incumbent may reassure foreign investors that the government not act opportunistically against them. These predictions are in sharp contrast to alternative hypotheses in the literature, particularly those that put emphasis on the role of democracy and audience costs in tying the government's hands (Jensen, 2003, 2006).

The institutional solution to the commitment problem that results from the existence of political constraints requires that the policies adopted by a host government before investment occurs remains in place afterwards and does not change even if they are subsequently harmful to investors. The regulatory environment cannot adapt to changes in economic conditions unless there are changes in the partisan alignment of veto players. In any event, the solution provided by the adoption of an inflexible policy that results from tying the government's hand is a second best option (Spiller and Tommasi, 2003). Moreover, Henisz (2000b, 2002) suggests that contractual risk, which arises at the firm level, could be aggravated in the presence of political risk. In the partisan government solution, on the other hand, policies are more likely to adapt in a direction that could benefit investors once economic conditions change, providing a better solution to the time inconsistency problem. The partisan solution to the commitment problem is thus better for investors because it provides them with a degree of flexibility they would like to have in case of changes in the economic environment.

The following section presents a brief review of how the literature on the politics if FDI addresses the role of political risk in the investment decision and the commitment problem. I subsequently introduce the conditions under which partisanship can resolve the commitment problem by transforming the relationship between foreign investors and host governments into a mutual exchange of hostages that mitigates the incentives that governments have to behave opportunistically. Finally, I derive testable hypotheses whose empirical validity is assessed in Chapter 4. Short narratives describing two different episodes when the Argentine government changed policies toward FDI, one during Perón's second presidency in the early 1950s and another one during Eduardo Duhalde's tenure after the 2001 economic crisis. These episodes provide examples of the exchange of hostages analogy at play. The narrative suggests that sudden shocks can upset the equilibrium relationship linking governments to investors and create incentives for governments to behave opportunistically against foreign investors. It is reassuring that under these conditions political actors behave off the equilibrium path as predicted by the partisan theory of FDI.

3.2 Investment Risk, Politics, and Commitment

As discussed in Chapter 1, there is a vast literature on the determinants of capital flows. There is a consensus that these flows result from *push* and *pull* factors, identified, respectively, with conditions that are external and internal to the recipient countries (Calvo et al., 1993, 1996). Political and economic stability, openness, and credibility are usually at the top of the list of factors associated with host country conditions (pull factors). Among the external conditions (push factors), the empirical literature on financial flows point to imperfections in credit markets, interest rates and technological changes affecting international capital mobility (Fernández-Arias, 1996). But foreign direct investment differs from other forms of capital flows as does its causes and consequences. Hymer (1976a,b), the first scholar to identify these differences, highlights the fact that FDI involves the transfer of capital and technology from one country to another. While still a flow of investment capital across national borders, FDI differs in a significant manner as the foreign investor holds a controlling stake over the affiliate in the host. This transfer usually takes place in order to arbitrage differential returns to capital between countries where capital's marginal product differs. Building on Hymer's insight, the literature shows that rate of return differentials do not suffice to explain foreign investment, however, as FDI is not randomly distributed across industries and corporations rather than financial intermediaries conduct most FDI (Hymer, 1976a,b).

The choice of organizing production under a common entity is related to the existence of proprietary intangible assets as discussed by the literature on multiplant-firms. Multinational corporations (MNCs), the driving force of direct investment across national borders, are one form of multiplant-firms (Caves, 1996). MNCs exist to internalize the transaction costs involved in activities where the property of intangible assets, such as brand names, managerial skills, and production techniques, makes arms length relations risky. In these cases, hierarchical organization of production and the internalization of transactions may help to make up for missing markets and the imperfect allocation of property rights (Dunning, 1977, 1993a,b; Caves, 1996).

Transaction costs associated with protecting valuable intangible assets that the firm owns justify the extra expense of setting up a hierarchical structure of control over an affiliate operating abroad (Caves, 1996). As FDI and MNCs are two sides of a single yet complex economic process, explanations of the determinants of FDI need to take into account the fact that multinational corporations are the vector through which foreign investment occurs.[7] Multinational corporations are, thus, heterogeneous entities, just like any other firms within national borders (Hanson et al., 2001). MNCs' choices of the form of entry and activity are tailored to local conditions, and the consequences of these decisions are likely to vary with the firms' types and investment strategies. Furthermore, firm type and investment strategy are in turn likely to be affected by political conditions in host countries.

As discussed in previous chapters the literature has focused on the effect of political regimes on the risk environment faced by foreign investors as the most relevant political condition in host countries (Oneal, 1994; Jensen, 2003, 2006; Li and Resnick, 2003). The explanations are based on the constraints and opportunities granted to host governments to engage in opportunistic behavior at the expense of foreign investors. In some accounts, autocratic regimes are insulated from the political demands made by interest groups and are therefore less likely to tax foreign investors heavily or to restrict their activities (Oneal, 1994; Li and Resnick, 2003). Others assert that democracies should receive more FDI because they offer a more credible environment for investors (Jensen, 2003, 2006). The benefits associated with FDI create audience costs that constrain democratic leaders leading to better protection of property rights and a more propitious environment for FDI (Jensen, 2003, 2006; Li and Resnick, 2003). The interpretation behind the results in this literature could also point at an alternative mechanism at play: a movement to and from democracy, for instance, may result in the (dis)enfranchising of actors whose preferences vary over the policy issue dimension at stake (Mayer, 1984). Policy outcomes would thus reflect a change in the identity of the pivotal member of the electorate or the selectorate in the political marketplace.

In general, the link between regime type, political institutions, and FDI-friendly policies is oversimplified, and more often than not lacks micro-foundations. The literature that develops this link tends to overlook the

---

[7] As discussed in Chapter 1, historically, FDI has been a phenomenon associated with developed countries, which were the main source and recipient of flows of FDI. More recently, the share of developing and emerging markets in inflows has increased dramatically, reaching around half of world inflows in 2009. Moreover, some emerging markets, especially Brazil, Russia, India, and China (BRICs) have become important sources of direct investment, commanding one-fourth of world outflows.

distributive effects created by factor flows. In addition, there is a vast body of literature in comparative politics that suggests that there is a large variance in the incentive structure faced by political actors within democracies and autocracies, further obscuring the interpretation of the already discordant empirical findings of this literature. Alternative explanations point to either varying legal systems or the impact of bilateral treaties that promise national treatment of foreign investors (Sauvant and Sachs, 2009; UNCTAD et al., 2009). However, access to courts or even bilateral treaties rarely provide reliable protection for investors against discrimination and expropriation (Moran, 1998).

Explanations grounded in the transaction costs tradition argue that institutional constraints help governments overcome the time-consistency problems they face when they cannot otherwise commit ex-ante to a policy schedule that is optimal ex-post (Williamson, 1985; Henisz and Williamson, 1999; Henisz, 2000b). Institutional design may provide the type of reassurance demanded by foreign investors: increasing the number of political actors whose acquiescence is required to change the status quo allows governments to credibly commit to not encroach upon investors' property rights and provide policy stability (North and Weingast, 1989; Olson, 1993). Yet, when veto gates are aligned, the only reassurance possible is given by the political preferences of those holding the levers of the policy-making process. Further, investors may prefer policies that adapt to economic shocks over inflexible rules, as policy rigidity is but a second best option. Investors have access to alternative technologies that can help mitigate the effects of political risk. Among them, we find the choice of the form of entry, that is, whether to set up a fully owned subsidiary or a joint venture with a local partner who has better access to the levers of political power (Henisz, 2000b, 2002; Henisz and Zelner, 2003).

Moreover, despite its potential benefits to host countries, FDI is a source of intense political dispute in the real world. In the 1970s and early 1980s, for example, a wave of dependency theorists denounced the triple alliance between governments, domestic capital, and foreign capital aimed at exploiting popular sectors (Evans, 1979; Evans and Gereffi, 1982; Gereffi, 1983). According to this argument, local capital shares similar preferences with foreign capital along several policy dimensions, such as the suppression of labor organization and labor standards, the reduction of taxes on capital, and the elimination of environmental regulations (Evans, 1979; Evans and Gereffi, 1982; Gereffi, 1983; Haggard, 1990). The *Triple Alliance* proposition has major shortcomings. Theoretically, its micro-foundations are weak, as the hypothesis fails to specify the scope conditions under which workers are expected to oppose foreign investment and capitalists are expected to tolerate the entrance of potential competitors. Such a situation requires a very specific type of foreign investment that either introduces labor-saving technologies, commits to transfer technology to local firms, or doesn't introduce competition to local firms in product or factor markets. Under more general conditions, the inflow of foreign capital is likely to negatively affect the return to domestic capital, ultimately trumping the purported shared preferences between foreign and domestic capitalists. Empirically, there have been no good tests of the propositions derived from the Dependentista research agenda (Moran, 1978; Kobrin, 1987). Further, case studies suggest that the alliance between domestic and foreign capital was unstable and short-lived even when it existed (Dominguez, 1982; Ranis, 1994).

This critique is related to accounts of workers' attitudes toward MNCs in recent literature in international business. Guillen (2000), for instance, argues that labor may adopt responses to foreign multinationals that range from hostility to active partnership. According to Guillen, organized labor's attitude toward MNCs is affected by two factors: the relationship between FDI and trade (whether FDI is import substituting or export promoting), and the stance adopted by the state (whether it is permissive or restrictive). In countries with repressive political systems and a populist ideology, organized labor tends to perceive foreign investors as villains, whereas in democratic systems with a modernizing ideology, MNCs are perceived as partners (Guillen 2000). The first condition is sensible as trade regime can affect the effect of factor flows on factor returns. The second condition, however, points to the main shortcoming of the triple alliance literature: the assumption that labor reacts to government behavior but has no direct influence on policy making. As discussed in Chapters 5 and 6, the extent of labor's political influence varies dramatically across political regimes.

An example of this limitation helps to clarify this point. As discussed in Chapter 5, Perón reformed the Argentinian foreign investment regime in 1952, reversing the wave of nationalization started by the previous military regime, of which Perón himself was member. Another Peronist leader, Carlos Menem, established a liberal foreign investment regime in 1991. In both circumstances, scholars and pundits alike tend to conclude that labor was betrayed, trumped, or bought off (Fuchs, 1981; Monteon, 1987; Murillo, 2001). It is uncontested that in both eras organized labor was the backbone of the Peronist movement, yet when trying to explain the policies adopted toward foreign investors by Perón in the early 1950s or Menem in the early 1990s, the literature overlooks workers' preferences. When researchers observe changes in the policy stances by Peronist leaders, they conclude that either labor grudgingly acquiesced for loyalty reasons or that these leaders betrayed their followers (Fuchs, 1981; Monteon, 1987; Rock, 1987). As the conditions under which workers would prefer more or less, FDI are not specified in that literature, however, they cannot be tested.

Setting up joint ventures with domestic business groups is another solution often proposed in the literature. Yet, the historical record suggests that a joint venture relationship with a partner related to the host government does not offer protection against contract renegotiation or subsequent intervention. Local business owners, on the other hand, may use political connections to procure favorable treatment or preference over foreign firms (Wells, 1998). Henisz (2000b) provides an excellent account where the conditions under which foreign investors would choose a joint venture as their entry strategy depend on the type of investment, which determines how sensitive investors are to contractual risk, and political risk, which creates an incentive to hook up with a local partner. On the contrary, in many circumstances these partners have created a hostile environment for their foreign counterpart.[8] In order to predict how labor or capital react, to foreign investment we need a sound theory of the policy preferences of pivotal political actors. The theory presented in the previous chapter, which draws on the expected economic consequences of inward FDI, properly specifies these preferences.

3.3 Partisanship As a Commitment Mechanism

FDI differs from other forms of investment and capital in its ability to move from country to country and in its employment of proprietary assets. The use of these assets create an incentive for foreign investors to organize production in a hierarchic structure under the control of the parent company. Entry of FDI has the potential to affect the relative return to labor and capital, creating a political cleavage around investment. We expect workers to favor FDI that complements labor in production or that leads to higher labor demand and to encourage inward flows of this type of investment. Capital owners try to block inward flows of types of FDI that negatively affect them in product and factor markets. The factor market effects of FDI are mitigated by the possibility that domestic actors may receive compensatory fiscal spending financed by the taxation of foreign capital.

The conditions for these predictions to hold can be construed in terms of the *motive* and the *opportunity* to effect policy changes. Motive to regulate investment flows results from the distributive effects of capital inflows: those

---

[8] In a survey of 66 joint ventures in 27 LDCs, Beamish (1988) found that dissatisfaction and instability to be endemic in these relationships (Moran, 1998).

harmed by it try to keep foreign investors out, while those who benefit try to keep investment flowing in. Opportunity is related to economic actors' access to policy making: when should we expect governments to react to their demands? By combining motive and opportunity, we can predict that polities where labor (capital) is more influential are more likely to be friendlier (more hostile) to foreign investment that increases the relative demand for labor. Therefore, governments are more likely to adopt FDI friendly regimes when labor is more influential, and more restrictive regimes when capital is. However, policy regimes themselves might not be enough to explain investment flows. Countries could have very open and liberal investment regimes yet still attract little FDI (UNCTAD, 2001, 2003).

If mobile capital is highly elastic to taxes, governments might be forced to engage in classic races to the bottom. But direct investment usually becomes inelastic immediately after it occurs and sunk FDI faces high relocation costs. This makes FDI more vulnerable to opportunistic behavior by host governments as persuasively argued by the *obsolescing bargain* literature. This could reduce the incentives to invest and even result in no investment at all. But investment would take place if investors can get some form of reassurance from host governments (Persson and Tabellini, 2000). Policies directed toward foreign investment are likely to become tainted by the classical time consistency problem of optimal economic policy in the absence of commitment constraints discussed in the economic literature (Kydland and Prescott, 1977; Calvo, 1978). Time inconsistency arises when policy sequencing is present (Drazen, 2000), but this sequencing is a necessary but not sufficient condition. Further, time consistency requires ex-post preference heterogeneity, which occurs when the choices made by governments ex-ante become suboptimal ex-post. As becomes clearer in the following paragraphs, these two conditions, policy sequencing and ex-post heterogeneity, are present in the relationship between foreign investors and host governments. There is no external enforcement mechanism that can reassure investors that conditions offered by host governments are honored, resulting in policy sequencing. Changes in the ex-post elasticity of investment creates an incentive for host government to tax it more heavily over time. However, as inflows and outflows of capital have different effects on the return to the factors owned by different actors in the host, the severity of the time inconsistency problem depends on the partisan orientation of the host government.

Recall that according to the transaction costs theory of MNCs (Caves, 1996), though FDI is by definition internationally mobile, the presence of site or project specific assets can affect the costs of relocation. Absent a self-enforcing commitment mechanism, governments usually have an incentive to act opportunistically to the disadvantage of investors in general, and to foreign direct investment in particular. In other words, as bargains become obsolete it is ex-post optimal for host governments to choose the highest possible tax rates on capital, even for governments that promise to maintain tax rates at their ex-ante optimal levels (Kindleberger, 1969; Vernon, 1971, 1977; Moran, 1974; Whiting, 1992). Investors anticipate the government's behavior and likely decide not to enter if relocation costs are high, resulting in missed investment opportunities and suboptimal policy. This is a form of the classical time consistency problem (Kydland and Prescott, 1977; Calvo, 1978; Drazen, 2000). The established view in the obsolescing bargain literature is that whenever redeploying their assets is costly, foreign investors can be taken hostage by domestic governments. Foreign investors' propensity to invest in a given country is reduced by the likelihood that host governments opt to exploit them over time (Vernon, 1971, 1977; Dixit and Pindyck, 1994).

The literature has focused on ex-ante commitment mechanisms in the form of democratic institutions, veto-gates or institutional constraints (Jensen, 2003, 2006; Li and Resnick, 2003; Henisz, 2000b, 2002). Pinto and Pinto (2011) show that these kinds of commitment mechanisms are only optimal under fairly extreme realizations of the parameters that determine how easily investors can relocate and how foreign investment interacts with factors of production in the host. Janeba (2001) offers a similar explanation driven by distributive concerns and voter backlash: initially, governments compete for FDI, offering investors subsidy packages, but later governments retract these policies. Voters disagree over their assessment of the net benefits of attracting multinational corporations because of concerns over their redistributive consequences. Furthermore, economic and political shocks could affect the number of people who support the MNCs.[9]

I argue in this chapter that there is an alternative commitment mechanism related to the partisan orientation of the ruling coalition. As proposed by Williamson (1983a,b, 1985) investment takes place when governments

---

[9] Pinto and Pinto (2011) show that the main predictions from the partisan theory of FDI that investment is likely to covary with the orientation of the ruling coalition holds even in the presence of hight relocation costs: as capital becomes less elastic, governments have an incentive to tax it more heavily, yet the optimal tax depends on the technological parameter that determines whether foreign investment complements or substitutes for the factor of production owned by the core constituent of the party in government. So while high relocation costs increase the incentives to act opportunistically, we should expect the severity of the commitment problem to covary with the type of investment and the orientation of the incumbent even in a dynamic setting.

and investors can mutually exchange hostages. Investment is secure when attempts by the government to target investors hurts domestic actors that the government cannot afford to ignore, and when investors can adopt an investment strategy that intentionally takes hostage an actor that is a pivotal player in the ruling coalition. Foreign investors usually have limited electoral voice in the political system; as a result, they generally seek strategic alliances with domestic counterparts that amplifies their political demands. Henisz proposes that political risk increases the incentives to enter in a joint venture (Henisz, 2000b, 2002). Political contributions may buy foreign investors some influence over policy outcomes as persuasively argued by Malesky (2009), but their political clout is ultimately enhanced by their ability to harm an influential member of the governing coalition when they threaten to exit. What kind of hostages should investors take? As stated earlier, they should choose those who have the motive and opportunity to affect government behavior. The ideal hostage must be influential and it must benefit from FDI inflows. To the extent that foreign capital complements labor in production, workers' interests become congruent with those of foreign capital. Thus, investors become politically influential under pro-labor governments where labor can make its influence felt in the political system.

Therefore, it is not through institutional constraints that tie the hands of the government and provide foreign investors sufficient reassurance that contracts offered to them prior to investment are duly enforced. Foreign investors' ability to take hostage a pivotal political actor in the host country with their investment strategies increases the probability that these contracts are self-enforcing. Preferential treatment to foreign investors is thus ransom that political leaders are willing to pay to prevent pivotal domestic actors from being harmed.

3.3.1 Partisan Investment in a Dynamic Setting

Chapter 2 formally models the relationship between politics and FDI as an interactive bargain between foreign investors and a host government over a regulatory regime for FDI. In this section I, extend predictions derived from this model to a setting where the interaction occurs over more than one period. This extension allows me to derive the conditions under which partisanship may reassure foreign investors that the host government does not act opportunistically and renege on favorable conditions offered to them. The idea of commitment by reputation can be directly linked to the role of partisanship in the model presented in Chapter 2. When investors and governments face each other repeatedly, partisanship may substitute for other forms of commitment and ex-ante optimal tax rates can be sustained in equilibrium (Chari and Kehoe, 1990).[10]

The predictions from the static model presented in Chapter 2 would also hold in a dynamic framework if we assume that foreign investment flows are able to adjust perfectly to the level investors desire after governments change capital tax rates, or, alternatively, if foreign capital completely depreciates before tax rates are changed. Specifically, suppose that there is no foreign capital in the economy. At the beginning of time period τ, a partisan government chooses t^τ and foreign capital decides k^τ. Under the previous assumptions, the government would face in time period $\tau + 1$ the same problem as the one it faced in time period τ. In every period, the equilibrium tax rates would be the ones obtained in Chapter 2. However, investors' reaction to changes in the host government's behavior may take some time.

Alternatively, suppose that the interaction between governments and investors occurs over more than one period. Foreign investors would form expectations about the optimal government response as follows: initially foreign investors assume that partisan governments promise to tax capital at the ex-ante optimal tax rates $\{t_h^{i*}, \ldots, t_h^{n*}\}$ for periods $i = 1, \ldots, n$, the tax rates that solve the maximization problem in Chapter 2 and which depend on the government's type $h = \mathcal{L}, \mathcal{K}$. As soon as capital owners realize that governments have deviated by choosing $\tilde{t}_h^i \neq t_h^{i*}$, they expect that the government will implement confiscatory tax rates $\hat{t}_h^i$ in the future. Therefore, expectations significantly change once investors observe that the government has deviated from the optimal tax t_h^{i*}, in which case they penalize the government by withholding investment. Under these conditions, governments may only benefit in the short run from opportunistic behavior by choosing $\tilde{t}_h^i$. Given that confiscatory tax rates $\hat{t}_h^i$ are expected by capital owners thereafter and that capital consequently not enter in the future, partisan governments face a lower stream of future payoffs relative to those that they could obtain by sticking to the ex-ante optimal policy. Suppose that ρ is the partisan government's discount factor. Then, $\{t_h^{1*}, t_h^{2*}\}$ can be sustained as an equilibrium of the repeated game if ρ is sufficiently large. Note, however, that in the dynamic setting the government faces a tradeoff: the stream of revenue from taxing capital in the future has to be weighed

---

[10] The discussion here draws on Pinto and Pinto (2008) and Pinto and Pinto (2011).

against the benefit of deviating from the tax schedule to opportunistically extract from a foreign investor who cannot relocate in the current period. Yet, while the benefits from opportunistic behavior are likely to be higher for any government that is able to attract foreign investment, in the political economy setup presented in the previous chapter, the willingness to provide better conditions to lure investors in contingent on the expected benefits of factor returns. The pro-labor government's incentive to adopt the one-off opportunistic tax is thus mitigated by the negative effect it has on its constituents' return in factor markets. For the pro-business government, on the other hand, the incentive to act opportunistically, while lower, reinforces the beneficial factor market effect on its constituent.

Therefore, in the presence of relocation (or capital mobility) costs, the incentives to act opportunistically differ for incumbents of different orientations, a theoretical result derived formally in Pinto and Pinto (2011). The predictions are derived from the combination of two basic parameters traditionally associated with the existence of MNCs: variable costs of redeployment and the effect of inward FDI on the relative demand of labor and capital (Caves, 1996; Markusen, 1995). The combination of these parameters can help explain the existence of political and partisan cycles in foreign direct investment, even when the time horizons of governments and investors do not match. Investors internalize the probability of opportunistic behavior by host governments when deciding their investment strategies. Further, governments that by assumption cannot commit themselves to maintaining stable tax rates over time are obligated to internalize the expected reaction of forward-looking investors when they enact policies aimed at luring investors in or keeping them out (Pinto and Pinto, 2011). The main corollary from this model is that the incentive structure presented by the obsolescing bargain hypothesis is either augmented or mitigated by partisan motivations rooted in the expected distributive consequences of foreign investment. In the model presented in Chapter 2, which is derived from FDI's distributive consequences, the predictions of the obsolescing bargain model are a special case. Moreover, it should be noted that the probability that an incumbent is replaced in the future has the potential to increase partisan investment rather than to eliminate it. Alternation in office does not necessarily result in lower investment, but instead in lumpy investment, as governments who want to lure investors in to benefit their constituents have to offer them rates of return that are large enough to compensate for the costs of relocation these investors endure when facing a more hostile incumbent in the future. The implication is that the rate of return offered by a pro-labor government should be high enough to sustain profitability for investors during its tenure when relocation costs are sufficiently high. In the end, as costs of redeployment increase it is optimal for all governments to raise taxes, given that sunk investment turns it into an inelastic tax base. As this change in elasticity moves the optimal policy space in the same direction for all incumbents, it would affect their incentives such that political constraints are ineffectual. Partisan links, however, could still mitigate the incentives to act opportunistically because revenue motivations are affected by factor market motivations as predicted by the partisan model presented in the previous chapter. Still, institutional constraints could play an important role in securing the property rights of domestic investors who do not have an exit option, as these constraints guarantee that investors could appropriate the return to their effort (North and Weingast, 1989).

In sum, with perfect capital mobility, the adjustment of foreign capital stock to changes in policy is immediate. If it is costly to change the stock of capital, only partial adjustments take place and the speed at which foreign capital stocks levels reach the new desired levels are reduced, increasing the incentives governments face to act opportunistically. Yet, as shown in Pinto and Pinto (2011), partisan motivations in the regulation of FDI do not disappear in the presence of higher costs of redeployment. Facing similar types of investors we should expect pro-labor and pro-capital governments to reflect the preferences of their constituents in their choice of investment policies. Whereas the literature on policy convergence predicts that globalization constrains governments' ability to enact their preferred macroeconomic policies, increases in international capital mobility could instead result in incumbent parties on the Left and the Right adopting starkly different investment regimes. As government's ability to tax international capital may decrease when capital becomes more mobile, governments are likely to compete for different types of capital. Further, these differences are likely to result from the differential distributive consequences of the various types of investment flows.

3.4 Political Influence On and Off the Equilibrium Path

In previous sections, I have described the relationship between governments and foreign investors in a dynamic setting as analogous to a mutual hostage situation. The narratives presented in the following section seem to support the assumption that the interests of labor and other socioeconomic actors who benefit from direct investment flows become congruent with those of foreign investors. The first narrative describes the relationship between governments and foreign investors in postwar Argentina. The second narrative discusses the conflict between the Argentine government and foreign investors in the oil industry in the wake of the economic crisis of 2001. Both episodes suggest that this alignment of interests may provide foreign investors with additional leverage even when the original bargain becomes obsolete.

3.4.1 Labor, Business, and Investment Regimes

In the early 1950s, foreign investment returned to Argentina under Perón, a leader who was institutionally unconstrained, had earlier nationalized the railways and public utilities, opportunistically expropriated German interests, and made no effort to tone down his anti-capitalist rhetoric, as reflected in the official Peronist anthem: "to the great Argentine, who beguiled the masses, fighting capital." In 1951, Perón unveiled a new plan aimed at lifting the economy out of a sharp recession. One of the key elements of this plan was to deepen import substitution and to encourage export promotion by courting foreign investors. Chapter 5 describes the statutes enacted in Argentina to regulate foreign investment in the post-war era. In 1948, Perón established a foreign investment statute and created a government agency aimed at overseeing foreign investors' activities in the country. The investment regime, and consequently the agency, would help lure foreign investment into the manufacturing sector (Altamir et al., 1967). This was the first attempt to unambiguously regulate and promote inward foreign investment. As discussed in more depth in Chapter 5, the promotion of FDI occurred at a time when the government restricted imports and threatened to expropriate equipment, machinery, and inputs that the government deemed were not being used in production.[11]

The absence of institutional constraints, the adoption of interventionist policies, and a history of systematic violations of property rights in conjunction with an economic environment characterized by stagnant growth and ever increasing influence of organized labor should not have made the prospect of investing in Perón's Argentina appealing at all. Yet, the foreign investment position of the country remained stable, and by 1953 there

---

[11] In his February 18, 1952, televised speech to the Argentine population, "El Plan Económico para 1952," Perón described the policy package adopted by his government. It aimed to overcome the hard times faced by the country that resulted from domestic conditions, including fiscal and foreign exchange gluts, and external conditions, including the Korean War, a decline in export prices, the exclusion of Argentina from the list of exporting countries to Europe under the Marshall Plan, and Britain declaring the end of the free convertibility of the pound. This document is available at: http://www.depeco.econo.unlp.edu.ar/docpolit/polit1.pdf.

was a net inflow of FDI, reversing the trend of disinvestment and expropriations that had characterized the previous two decades.[12] The change in attitude toward foreign investors occurred as economic activity slowed down, foreign reserves dried up and the government was forced to adjust. It also coincides with a steady estrangement of the urban industrialists by the ruling coalition as it became labor-centered. At the opposite end of the ideological spectrum, the military regime that took power in 1976 adopted an economic liberalization program aimed at controlling inflation and at restructuring the economy in favor of the most internationally competitive sectors, particularly agriculture. The government drastically cut tariffs on imported goods and services, which resulted in a drastic reduction of output by and employment in the manufacturing sector. The regime adopted a foreign investment statute that on paper looked liberal and permissive but led to foreign investors pulling out of the country. The agency in charge of overseeing the investment statute was very selective, limiting access to promotion benefits and encouraging MNCs to associate with domestic firms under non-competitive terms, similar to policies adopted in South Korea in the 1980s.

I argue that it is precisely the links between Perón and organized labor and between the military regime and domestic business interests that made the investment regime more or less credible to MNCs, resulting in starkly different investment outcomes. The relevant counterfactual here is what would have happened had capital been more influential during this time. The closest example is probably found in the South Korean experience. Facing similar external constraints to those of Argentina under Perón in the form of balance-of-payment problems, South Korea adopted policies toward foreign investment that were restrictive. Labor here was repressed, however, and politics dominated by a ruling coalition centered around domestic capital interests. When regulating foreign investment, the Economic Planning Board, the agency in South Korea in charge of economic policy, acted as a gatekeeper. The outcome was that South Korea received hardly any foreign investment at all during this period, especially when compared to other Asian NIEs (Haggard, 1990). More recently, South Korea began to open up

---

[12] While since 1934 net flows of investment had been negative following the nationalization of railways, public utilities, and services, by the early 1950s foreign investment inflows turned positive again, rising to $58 millions in 1953 (Altamir et al., 1967, p. 371). Note that the sharp decrease in foreign capital stock between 1945 and 1949 maps almost directly on to the sums paid by the Argentine government for the formerly British owned railways. All other forms of investment in the country increased in the same period.

to foreign investment, especially after the 1997 crisis (Yun, 2003). Democratization and the collapse of the *chaebols* seem to have opened the door to
investment liberalization as both of these events likely lowered the weight the
South Korean government placed on the well-being of business in its objective function. As the chaebols recovered and the political pendulum moved
back toward the right FDI dropped in Korea, but it never returned to the low
levels of the 1980s. In sum, the regulation of foreign investment in Argentina
and South Korea in the post-war era documented in depth in Chapters 5 and
6 suggests the existence of the partisan cycles as is predicted by the partisan
theory of investment. Pro-labor governments in Argentina tended to promote FDI in manufacturing and encourage investors to reinvest dividends,
while pro-business regimes in both countries discriminated against foreign
firms or promoted joint ventures with limited foreign investor presence.
In the next section, I present anecdotal evidence that illustrate the mutual
exchange of hostages' analogy at play off the equilibrium path.

3.4.2 Investment and Taxation Off the Equilibrium Path

Soon after Eduardo Duhalde took office in January 2002, the Argentine
Congress passed an emergency law that put an end to the currency board
exchange rate system.[13] The currency board, which pegged the local currency (peso) to the U.S. dollar at a one-to-one rate, was a central component
in the economic adjustment program adopted in Argentina in 1991 to fight
hyperinflation under the guidance of Domingo Cavallo, Minister of Finance
of the Menem administration. Ending the peg of the local currency to the
dollar resulted in a sharp devaluation of the peso. The law passed by Congress
also decreed that all dollar denominated loans would be converted to pesos
and authorized the executive branch to levy taxes on exports of oil and other
primary products.[14] The revenue raised from the taxes on exports was used
to compensate banks for the cost of the decreed *pesoification* of loans and
ultimately to finance government expenditure.[15]

---

[13] Duhalde, the Peronist leader and former governor of the province of Buenos Aires who had been
    defeated in the 1999 presidential elections, was appointed president by the Argentine Congress
    on January 2, 2001, becoming the fifth person to hold the chief executive office in less than two
    weeks. A few days earlier, Rodriguez Saa, who was in charge of the chief executive position for
    one week, had declared a unilateral moratorium of the country's foreign debt.

[14] La Nación, January 6, 2002, Privatizadas y petroleras, en alerta (Privatized and oil companies
    on the alert); El Mundo, January 7, 2002, El Parlamento Argentino aprueba un plan muy
    dañino para las Empresas españolas (Argentine Congress approves plan which will hit Spanish
    Companies).

[15] *Pesoification* implies forced conversion of dollar denominated loans and contracts to peso
    denominated obligations.

The crisis gave the government an opportunity to take advantage of foreign investors while benefiting heavily indebted industrialists. Many of these industrialists had taken loans denominated in dollars under the currency board and would profit from either the reduction of imports or the increase of exports brought upon by devaluation, depending on their sector of operation.[16] The government publicly argued that fairness dictated that somebody pay for the compensation provided to the banks that had been forced to take a peso for each dollar they had loaned. Earlier that week, Duhalde had promised representatives of agriculture that his government would suspend the old system of taxes on agricultural exports. Duhalde's administration looked determined to tax exports of oil instead.[17] The rationale for levying export taxes on oil was straightforward and appealed to a broad constituency, particularly in a country where people had taken the streets on December 20, 2001, to demand the resignation of De la Rua and his cabinet, chanting "que se vayan todos" ("send the rascals out"). The country was broke, exporters would benefit from the devaluation of the local currency, and given that foreign firms controlled the oil sector, it seemed unjust that the government would let these firms be the only that profited from the windfall in natural resources.

The oil industry in Argentina had experienced the starkest effects of the economic reforms of the early 1990s. Fiscal motivations led the Menem administration to privatize YPF, the national oil firm. Later Menem liberalized the exploration and exploitation of oil fields and promoted foreign investment in the sector. A following wave of mergers and acquisitions in the sector, part of a trend that was not exclusive to the country, resulted in increased concentration of power in the hands of a decreasing number of, mostly foreign, employers (ILO 2002).

In Argentina, as in other Latin American countries, the relationship between the national oil company and the oil workers' union had been cooperative.[18] The restructuring of the sector following privatization, its liberalization and later its concentration in a handful of firms resulted in

---

[16] Federico de Mendiguren, Duhalde's appointee to the Secretary of Industry, was an outspoken businessman who represented this group of local industrialists in the CGE who had lobbied for devaluation during previous administrations but had taken loans in dollars in the past few years.

[17] Clarín, January 4, 2002, El nuevo gobierno: Temores en el campo. Aseguran que Duhalde no quiere retenciones a productos del agro, by Héctor A. Huergo.

[18] Where the national oil market has been protected, such close relationships have sometimes led to accusations of collusion at the expense of the public (ILO 2002). The exception in the Argentine case was union activism against Frondizi's oil program in 1958; see Chapter 5 for an in-depth discussion.

a massive reduction in direct employment; however, the union's attitude toward management in the industry remained constructive for which it was duly rewarded by Menem's government. At the onset of the privatization process, the labor union (SUPE)[19] was placated by a compensation package that included a sizeable portion of the shares of the formerly state-owned company. Rationalization in the industry involved voluntary retirement and many workers were encouraged to form service companies that were granted YPF contracts (Murillo, 2001). Cooperation between unions and management continued after privatization.

After Eduardo Duhalde made clear the government's intentions to tax the oil industry's exports, representatives of the sector protested, launching a campaign aimed at putting pressure on government officials to stop the initiative.[20] They argued that the tax would reduce their overall profitability and would cause several of their fields to close. Despite the initial protest the government made clear that it was determined to go ahead with the policy. By mid-February 2002, the unfolding events looked as if they had been taken from an old piece in the obsolescing bargain literature: after deploying their assets, foreign investors had lost all their bargaining power vis-à-vis a government whose predecessor had made an enormous effort to lure them in. Moreover, bashing foreign oil producers was quite coherent for a political class that a few weeks earlier had cheerfully celebrated the government's decision to repudiate its foreign debt.[21]

Having failed to curb government officials' determination, oil producers summoned labor leaders and announced that they would cut costs and limit investment in order to reduce their level of exposure in a country that in their view was becoming riskier day after day. Soon after these announcements, the oil workers' union mobilized politically as a reduction in investment would result in massive layoffs in the sector. A labor strike called by the union on February 20, 2002, paralyzed the oil producing provinces.[22] Governors and legislators from these provinces aligned with

---

[19] SUPE is the acronym for the Federación de Sindicatos Unidos de Petroleros del Estado (Federation of Unions of State-Owned Oil Workers).

[20] La Nación, January 10, 2002, Las petroleras presionan para evitar retenciones. Con algunos gobernadores, adoptaron una estrategia común. "Oil companies lobby against export taxes. They have adopted a joint strategy with governors (from oil producing provinces)."

[21] Clarín December 24, 2001, Asumió Rodríguez Saá y dijo que suspenderá el pago de la deuda.

[22] Clarín, February 20, 2002, La Crisis: Preocupación por despidos. Chubut: una marcha contra las retenciones "(Crisis: Chubut, worried about layoffs [workers] march against export taxes)." "La Nación, February 20, 2002, Protestas de los petroleros en el Sur Oil producers and workers protest in the South."

workers and producers in the sector.[23] At this stage, it became clear to the government that it could no longer afford to ignore the demands from trade unions. Ultimately, Duhalde decided to use the export tax as a chip in a larger bargain with foreign investors that included, among other things, looser conditions for the repatriation of profits, and a secure supply of fuel in the domestic market.[24] Moreover, in April, the government reinstated the previously suspended taxes on agricultural exports.[25]

The case suggests that even when governments have a clear incentive to change investment conditions ex-post in order to seize the windfall profits that would have otherwise accrued to foreign investors, they are constrained by domestic politics. Whether Duhalde reacted to labor mobilization alone, or whether he was also concerned with the impact an increase in fuel prices would have on consumers, is debatable. However, it is worth noting that the initiative to tax foreign investors impacted political alignments in a manner that is consistent with the predictions made earlier in this chapter.

Two points are worth noting at this stage: first, although the narrative does not constitute a test of the theory, it is a practical instance of the "mutual exchange of hostages" at play. Similar instances of labor supporting the bargaining strategies of MNCs can be found in the auto industry in Brazil, Argentina, and Venezuela.[26] A similar pattern is observed in Mexico, where unions in the new plants in the border states ultimately behave as local entrepreneurs who cater to foreign businesses; the pro-business behavior of the unions in the border states contrasts with the fierce opposition of unions in the old plants around Mexico City, where militancy and conflict was the rule.

Second, this narrative describes a sequence of actions off the equilibrium path. This is the kind of behavior we would expect to observe if any actor were

---

[23] Governors from oil producing provinces lobbied for a tax on gas sales, and a withholding tax on production, levied at the provincial level to replace the export tax. Clarín March 7, 2002, La Crisis: Reunion de gobernadores con Duhalde para apurar la ley. Las provincias impulsarán un impuesto al petróleo. Son las petroleras. Aplicarán un 8 percent a la producción del crudo y se eliminarán las retenciones.

[24] Export taxes on gas were reduced from 20 percent to 5 percent (La Nación, July 11, 2002, Acuerdo por el precio y el abastecimiento de gas licuado), while export taxes on crude oil were reduced in August 2002 (La Nación August 24, 2002, Acuerdan un subsidio especial para el gasoil).

[25] Clarín, April 4 2002, La Crisis: Retenciones: serían del 20 percent sólo para granos, aceites y harinas. Clarín, November 10 2002, El Impacto de la Crisis: El campo reclama "equilibrio".

[26] The following passage is more than eloquent: "automobile unions in Argentina used their corporatist ties with state actors to pressure the government into promoting change through negotiations and concerted action. Thus, beginning in 1991, representatives from the state, management, and unions signed sectoral and plant-level agreements covering a wide array of issues, including wages, employment, strikes, automobile taxes and tariffs, and so forth" (Tuman and Morris, 1998).

to deviate from the strategies that maximize their well-being conditional on other actors' behavior. The fact that the government and investors reached this part of the game needs additional explanation, which goes beyond the scope of this chapter but is analyzed in the case study of investment regulation in Argentina.

3.5 Testable Implications

Having established the role of distributive motivations in the political economy of FDI, as well as the potential for partisanship to act as a commitment device, I move next to the derivation of an empirical strategy aimed at assessing the plausibility of the argument.

To the extent that labor's interests are congruent with those of foreign capital, labor influence in politics generates the commitment mechanism previously discussed. The influence of domestic capital has the opposite effect, reducing the credibility of the government's commitment. As redeployment costs go up, incentives to act opportunistically increase. The model shows, however, that the partisan orientation of the incumbent can mitigate the commitment problem that arises in the dynamic setting if foreign investment results in a higher demand for the services supplied in the marketplace by the core constituents of the governing coalition. Suppose that foreign capital complements labor in production. In this case, a pro-labor government would maintain a relatively low capital tax rate, or at least taxes would not be raised. Behaving otherwise would provide capital with incentives to leave the country, affecting negatively wages and employment in the host. Therefore, in a dynamic setting where governments have strong links to specific constituents, Proposition 2 in Chapter 2 can be restated in the following terms:

> *Labor Influence:* if FDI complements labor in production, the higher the value that the government places on the political support of labor (capital), the lower (higher) the taxes the government will levy on foreign investment, and the lower (higher) the likelihood that it will renege on the tax offered ex-ante, all else equal.

Note that this claim here is unconditional: no matter what the policy environment looks like, FDI flows into countries where labor is more influential and shuns countries where capital is instead. The null hypothesis is that there is no relationship between foreign direct investment flows and labor influence in politics.[27] An alternative hypothesis is derived from the institutional constraints literature (Henisz, 2000b, 2002; Tsebelis, 1995, 2002): foreign direct investment inflows are higher (lower) in countries where the government is more (less) institutionally constrained. Cox and McCubbins (2001) argue that a polity's ability to commit to policy depends not only on its institutional configuration, but also on the effective number of vetoes in political decision making, which is a function of both the number of political actors that can veto a policy change (institutional veto), and the degree to which the interests of interest these actors conflict (partisan veto).

The statistical analysis presented in Chapter 4 aims to test the empirical content of both sets of hypotheses. To test the labor influence hypothesis on a large-n panel of countries and years, I equate pro-labor with the left and pro-business with the political right. Left-leaning coalitions are more favorable to labor and more receptive to its demands, whereas right-leaning coalitions are instead favor capital. Governments on the left tend to place more emphasis on issues such as unemployment and income distribution. As workers are usually left-leaning governments core constituency, they more often than not adopt the policies they prefer. Right-leaning parties, on the other hand, tend to be more business-oriented. They assign higher priority to prices and economic stability, and collide with labor on issues such as unemployment and income distribution. Note that whether the left- or right-leaning incumbents can effect policy changes depends on the distribution of political power in the polity, that is the number of institutional or partisan veto players whose acquiescence is required to move polices away from the status quo. Therefore, the orientation of the chief executive does not necessarily map onto the β parameter in the model presented in Chapter 2, which captures the weight that the government places on the well-being of workers and capitalists. If a left-leaning executive, for instance, is constrained by a right-leaning legislature, for example in the case of divided, coalition, or minority government, then the incumbent is less likely to move the status quo toward its optimal policy. Instead, the outcome is likely to be policy compromise that weighs all actors' preferences or instead the prevalence of the status quo. In the empirical section, I construct measures of government orientation along the left-right dimension by combining both partisanship of the incumbent and institutional constraints. This interaction is, arguably, a better operationalization of the

---

[27] I later introduce some conditions that enhance or limit the effects of labor influence on foreign investment flows.

β parameters in the model when testing the link between partisanship and investment policy.

3.6 Conclusion

This chapter explores the relationship between domestic governments and foreign investors. Based on simple assumptions about actors' preferences that are derived from the trade theoretic literature, I argue that the relative influence of labor or capital in domestic politics affects the inflow of foreign capital and the activity of MNCs in host countries. To the extent that labor's interests are congruent to those of foreign capital, the influence of labor in domestic political coalitions serves as a commitment mechanism to foreign investors. This mechanism operates as a signal to foreign investors who use the information to assess the risk of opportunistic behavior by the host government after they have incurred the cost of deploying their assets. The influence of domestic capital has the opposite effect, reducing the credibility of the government's commitment.

The chapter establishes the conditions under which the relationship between governments and investors plays out with a simple analytical framework. I derive hypotheses, which are probed in the following chapter with a series of quantitative (cross-sections and time series) analyses to assess their empirical validity.

Finally, factor flows, of which FDI is one form, can be either a complement or a substitute of trade. In addition, trade could mitigate the effect of the change in relative endowments that results from factor flows. In the Hecksher-Ohlin framework, an increase in the capital stock changes factor proportions. When the economy is open to trade, this would affect trade volumes in such a way that factor returns move back to normal. Therefore, if trade and investment are substitutes, countries are open to trade, and countries export goods that use the domestically abundant factor more intensively, then FDI should at most have no effect on factor returns. When these conditions hold, trade would have a mitigating effect on the movement of factors.

In any event, this discussion underscores the need to analyze trade and investment regimes side by side. Whereas labor would benefit from inward foreign investment, the effects of trade depend on factor endowment. The existing work in political science has not adequately accounted for this puzzle, thus opening a new research agenda.

FOUR

Partisan Governments and Foreign Direct Investment: Results from Cross-Country Statistical Analyses

4.1 Introduction

In this chapter, I aim to assess the effect of the partisan alignments of the chief executive in the host country on the levels of inbound foreign direct investment (FDI) flows. I present the results from statistical analyses of the main hypotheses derived in Chapters 2 and 3. The statistical models build on a vast body of empirical literature in economics on the determinants of capital flows. The analysis establishes that when the conditions for investment are present, politics can have a sizable impact on investment flows. The driving political force in the host country reflects the expected distributive consequences of investment inflows. As I argue in Chapters 2 and 3, governments are likely to adopt investment regimes that benefit their core constituents and to abide by these policies over time. Pro-labor governments promote the well-being of workers and pro-business governments promote policies that benefit domestic capital owners. In the first stage of the analysis, I assess the external validity of one of the implications of this partisan hypothesis, namely the effect of partisanship on investment policy.

For this purpose, I develop a measure of investment policy orientation using data from OECD countries. There are numerous policy instruments, or political outcomes, that affect either the returns to capital or its form of entry, which is ultimately what FDI regimes target. Host governments may, among other initiatives, grant tax breaks and subsidies, regulate market structure, adjust trade policy, protect property rights, establish nationality and/or performance requirements, or create differential exchange rates in order to attract or deter the inflow of capital. Empirically, there is no simple way to assess the incidence of these various types of policies.[1] Several

---

[1] As discussed in the next section, there are no standardized measures of FDI policy orientation that can be used for cross-country comparisons.

of these instruments are complements, whereas others have substitutive effects that are difficult to capture in measures suitable for cross-national comparison. Moreover, the theory discussed in the previous chapters predicts that there should be a positive effect of labor influence on foreign investment flows irrespective of the type of political regimes toward foreign investment adopted. In the tests, I explore the correlation between an index of investment policy and the orientation of the ruling coalition.

In the second part of the chapter, I analyze the correlations of investment performance using data for a large panel of countries, replicating results reported in the literature. To the extent that the left is pro-labor, we should expect left-leaning governments to be friendlier to investors as foreign investment raises the relative demand for labor and subsequently wages and employment opportunities; we should also expect larger FDI flows to countries governed by the left.

In the next section, I derive testable hypotheses and discuss the operationalization of concepts and methodological issues associated with these hypotheses in order to assess their empirical validity. The last two sections present the results of the statistical models and discuss the findings, which suggest that at a minimum the partisan theory is plausible despite the limitations that arise due to the dearth of reliable data.

4.2 Partisanship and FDI Regulation

The original prediction from the partisan theory of FDI states that partisanship determines how governments regulate direct investment. Testing this prediction across countries and over time is a daunting task. Investment policy regimes are the combination of numerous policies including restrictions, concessions, and benefits that have the potential to raise or lower the cost of foreign investment. The orientation of these policy regimes can range from friendly to hostile to foreign investors.[2] There is no publicly available measure of FDI policy that covers the numerous instruments that affect FDI that could be used for cross-country comparison.[3]

Constructing an aggregate measure of investment policy orientation is difficult because multiple policies and political conditions have the potential

---

[2] The orientation includes what Golub (2003) terms as hidden "institutional and behavioral restrictions on FDI," such as business organization (i.e., the Japanese keiretsu) and business-government collusion practices (Golub, 2003, pp. 94–5).

[3] Pandya (2008) is an exception. She develops an of ownership restrictions at the industry level. Her index is a measure of formal regulations affecting the form of entry. These regulations do not necessarily map onto FDI activity because it does not cover other policy instruments that are likely to affect the incentives to enter and stay active in a host country.

to affect the form of entry or the returns to foreign capital. Among these instruments, we find protection of property rights, including intellectual policy; rules regulating technology transfers; fiscal policy, subsidies, corporate and other tax rates; tax exemptions and other provisions of the tax system; sector specific regulatory regimes; corporate governance regimes; rules regulating market structure, or lack thereof; the trade regime, tariffs, and non-tariff barriers; local content and origin requirements; openness of the capital account; exchange rate policy and monetary regimes; FDI-specific rules such as national treatment, ownership, notification procedures; and management and operational restrictions. To date, we have no way to assess the incidence of these various types of policies in any general way.[4] Moreover, because many of these policy instruments have substitutive effects, it is difficult to capture their effects in isolation in most of the measures available for cross-national comparison. In this section, I discuss a procedure aimed at trying to fill this void. I create a measure of investment policy orientation that allows for comparison of the aggregate effects of foreign investment regimes across countries and over time.[5]

4.2.1 Estimating a Measure of Investment Restrictions: Methodology

Developing a measure of investment policy orientation presents a similar challenge to that faced by researchers trying to measure trade openness and commercial policy orientation regarding whether to look at policies or instead to concentrate on outcomes. In the trade case, for instance, we have tariff and tariff revenue data and measures of non-tariff barriers coverage, but we know that tariff and NTB data are but incomplete measures of commercial policy because while these instruments have the potential to affect flows of good and services, they are also affected by these flows (Ray, 1981; Marvel and Ray, 1983; Trefler, 1993). In the case of investment policy, credit and risk rating agencies adopt a qualitative approach and rely on surveys of experts that assign governments a position on an ordinal scale of risk. Such subjective measures of policy orientation suffer from several drawbacks, especially those associated with inter-coder reliability and the consistency of the criteria across countries and years.

Using data on bilateral investment flows compiled by the Organization for Economic Cooperation and Development (OECD), I develop an index

---

[4] Of all these instruments that together determine the investment policy orientation of a country, Golub's measure of investment restrictions only covers FDI-specific restrictions (Golub, 2003).

[5] The project is linked to initiatives aimed at the construction of trade policy orientation indices. See Hiscox and Kastner (2002).

of openness to FDI that is derived from objective measures of observed investment activity. The estimated measure of investment policy orientation captures the impact of the the vast array of policy instruments that may affect foreign investment simultaneously once the main determinants of investment in host and home countries have been accounted for. The drawback is that I am only able to derive this index for a limited number of countries with reliable data.[6]

An analogous model also helps us identify abnormal or distorted patterns of investment and estimate the extent to which these patterns are due to the policies of particular nations. Hiscox and Kastner (2002) have derived a measure of trade policy restrictions in similar fashion. A basic form of the gravity model has proven to be an extremely effective framework for gauging what patterns of trade are normal or natural among nations.[7] The gravity specification has also been used to analyze the effect of policy on investment flows.[8] The basic form of the gravity model can be expressed as:

$$FDI_{ij} = f(Endowments_{ij}, Links_{ij}, Distance_{ij}) \qquad (4.1)$$

Where the subscripts i and j represent the recipient/host country and the sender/home country, respectively. Variation over time is reflected by the subscript t. The measure of investment policy restrictions is obtained in two stages. In the first stage, I estimate the model in log-linear form, using different proxies for endowments and other conditions that affect outflows from the home country, including its links with the host country

$$\ln FDI_{ijt}/Y_{it} = \alpha_{it} + \beta_1 \ln distance_{ij} + \beta_2 \ln real\ GDP_{jt}$$
$$+ \beta_3 \ln arable\ land_{jt} +$$
$$+ \beta_4 \ln GDP\ per\ capita_{jt} + \beta_5 \ln average\ school\ years_{jt} +$$
$$+ \beta_6 common\ language_{ij} + \beta_7 colonial\ links_{ij} +$$
$$+ \beta_8 common\ border_{ij} + \varepsilon_{ijt} \qquad (4.2)$$

[6] The data used in deriving this measure includes inflows and outflows to and from 27 OECD countries for 1980–2000. The source of the data on inflows is SourceOECD: International direct investment by country. The 27 OECD countries used in this analysis account for roughly 95 percent of world investment outflows and 90 percent of world inflows. See also Pinto (2004).

[7] The model posits that the volume of trade between two nations is an increasing function of the income of the nations and a decreasing function of the distance between them. See Frankel and Wei (1993), Aitken (1973), Frankel et al. (1995), Baier and Bergstrand (2001), and Anderson and van Wincoop (2004), among others.

[8] Other variables, including whether the countries share a common border, language or legal system, are often added to the model, unpacking the residual or *"resistance term,"* as it is known in the technical jargon of this literature. See Blonigen and Davies (2004).

In the second stage, I regress the country-year fixed effect α_{it} on a vector of regressors aimed at capturing the host country i's relative endowment of capital, labor, skill, and size, which according to the literature are likely to have an important effect on the level of inflows.[9]

$$\alpha_{it} = \gamma_0 + \gamma_1 \ln \textit{real } GDP_{it} + \gamma_2 \ln \textit{ arable land}_{it}$$
$$+ \gamma_3 \ln GDP \textit{ per capita}_{it} +$$
$$+ \gamma_4 \ln \textit{average school years}_{it} + \theta_{it} \quad\quad (4.3)$$

The index of investment policy orientation is derived from the residuals, θ_{it}, obtained from estimating the second stage equation (4.3) where the country-year fixed effect of a gravity model (the average effect vis-à-vis all partners) is regressed on country-year covariates. This measure compares the individual country/year deviation from the sample average measure of openness to investment. A higher (lower) value on the measure implies that a country is more (less) open to FDI after economic, geographic, and cultural determinants of investment flows have been controlled for. The measure thus obtained is used as the dependent variable in the tests on the effects of partisanship on the regulation of foreign direct investment.[10] Because of data availability, I estimate the index for 27 countries in five-year intervals, which are reported in Table 4.6 and Figure 4.10 in the Appendix. Figures 4.7 through 4.9 present scatterplots of this measure of investment policy orientation and a summary measure of FDI-specific restrictions created by Golub (2003), which is available for the years 1980, 1990, and 2000. The negative pattern observed in the scatterplots, particularly in the last two periods, is consistent with the way both measures were constructed: higher values on Golub's index are associated with more restrictions to FDI, whereas the investment policy orientation index takes higher values when investment regimes are more open.[11] The low correlation between the measure based on flows and the measure based on regulations for the earlier period should

---

[9] Carr et al. (2001), Markusen and Maskus (2001b,a, 2002), and Markusen and Maskus (2001c) construct an "unrestricted" empirical model of FDI activity that comprises a number of alternative theories of MNE activity, including the horizontal, vertical, and knowledge-capital models, the last of which integrates the previous two. Years of schooling in the host country is included on the right-hand side of the estimating equation to proxy for the skill/knowledge effects.

[10] Note that the variable used to capture the endowment of human capital, which is a key component of the knowledge-based model of MNCs (see Carr et al. (2001)) is only available in five-year intervals for the years 1980-2000. I have also estimated the index on one-year intervals excluding education (see Appendix 4).

[11] The correlation coefficients of the two measures are: -0.0443, -0.1861, and -0.3596 for the years 1980, 1990, and 2000, respectively.

not be surprising in light of the evidence presented in Chapters 5 and 6, where I analyze the evolution of investment regimes in the Argentine and Korean cases and discuss their relationship with investment activity. The *de jure* measures of restrictions accounts for the policies that are on the book but does not account for their enforcement and for discretionary policies targeted at individual investment initiatives. The index of investment policy orientation, on the other hand, is a rough proxy of the non-economic determinants of FDI. The measure has benefits, because it accounts for conditions that are not related to the receiving country and is not limited to a unique policy dimension, which could be non-binding. The measure also has drawbacks, however, including measurement error.

4.2.2 Empirical Strategy

I argue that the regulation of foreign investment is a function of the preferences of owners of factors of production in the host country, their relative power, their potential to influence the policy-making process, and the receptiveness of the incumbent party to the demands of labor or capital owners. Assuming that FDI complements labor in production, the model presented in prior chapters predict that workers support policies that encourage direct investment inflows, whereas owners of capital support more restrictive policies. It is conceivable that labor would prefer a bigger government, resulting in a level of taxes on capital that is higher overall, which would deter investors from entry. Yet, an extension of the model discussed in the Appendix of Chapter 2 suggests that even when owners of labor prefer higher levels of government spending financed by a tax on capital if possible – defined as δ in the model – they would still prefer to tax mobile capital less heavily in order to lure investors in, whereas domestic business owners would prefer policy regimes that keep investors out. In the tests, we need to find a measure of the parameter β in the model, linking the preferences of labor and capital to policy makers, for which I turn to different measures of government partisanship.

The assumption that governments have partisan (and electoral) incentives in regulating economic activity is pervasive in the literature that explores the links between politics and macroeconomic management. Hibbs (1977, 1992) and Tufte (1978) are the precursors in this tradition.[12] Political

---

[12] More recent models of partisan and electoral business cycles include Alesina (1987, 1988), Alvarez et al. (1991), Alesina and Rosenthal (1995), Boix (1997, 1998), Garrett (1998b), Iversen (1999) and Franzese (2002b), among others. The existence of a partisan business cycle has received more support than its electoral counterpart. See Franzese (2002a) for an excellent

parties build and nurture ties to groups of voters, whether these voters are organized or not, and when in government tend to deliver policies valued by these groups for material (or ideological) reasons. When the government is politically responsive to either of the two domestic actors in the host country, namely labor or capital, it internalizes that actor's utility. For simplicity, I assume that partisanship is of two types, either pro-labor or pro-capital, and that these two type are identified with the left and right, respectively. Left-leaning governments enact policies that favor owners of labor and right-leaning governments adopt policies that favor capital.[13] If these predictions are right, we should find that investment regimes covary with government partisanship. Thus, the main testable hypothesis derived from the propositions derived in Chapters 2 and 3 are:

Partisan Hypothesis: when a party of the left (right) is in government, investment regimes will be more open (restrictive), all else equal.

Accordingly, we would expect governments to adopt investment regimes that are more favorable toward foreign investors when the pro-labor party is in power, or in the model, as β increases. On the contrary, right-leaning governments, which are more likely to cater to domestic owners of capital, adopt policies aimed at keeping investors out.

Even if it is elected, the pro-labor party is unable to adopt the policies preferred by its core constituents if, depending on the institutional setting, policy-making authority rests in the hands of political actors bearing

review of this literature. In recent literature on the relationship between politics and trade, Dutt and Mitra (2005) and Milner and Judkins (2004) show that ideology and partisanship (whether left- or right-leaning) are good predictors of countries' (and parties') trade policy orientation. Right-leaning governments (and parties) are associated with open trade policies in developed (capital abundant) countries, while left-leaning governments are more protectionist in these countries. The outcomes are reversed for capital scarce countries, which is consistent with the predictions derived from the Hecksher-Ohlin model of trade (Stolper and Samuelson, 1941).

[13] As discussed in Chapter 1, equating pro-labor with the left, and pro-business with the political right demands some explanation. There is good reason to believe that left-leaning parties will be more receptive to labor's demands, while right-leaning parties favor owners of domestic capital. Governments on the left side of the political spectrum tend to cater to labor for political support, and place more emphasis on issues such as unemployment and income distribution. Right-leaning parties tend to be more business-oriented, assign high priority to prices and stability, and usually clash with labor on issues such as income distribution (see footnote 12). Parties of the left and right alike may be at odds with the interests of foreign investors for ideological reasons, which I bracket from this analysis because I have no reason to believe that these ideological reasons, usually associated with nationalism, are more likely to prevail at either side of the political spectrum. Therefore, I focus on the material interests of labor and capital alone and analyze how inflows of FDI are likely to affect their returns.

a different ideological orientation. The larger the number of veto-players required to overturn the status quo, the harder it is to shift policy, particularly when the preferences of those in position to veto policy changes are not congruent with those of the chief executive. β should therefore be interpreted as the interaction between the orientation of the partisan incumbent and the institutional constraints it faces. An alternative interpretation is offered by Tufte (1978) where the orientation of the incumbent determines its preferences, or motive, and institutional constraints, or lack thereof, create the opportunity for changing the status quo. Under these conditions the expectation is that left-leaning incumbents facing institutional constraints are associated with higher restrictions on FDI inflows compared to a similar government that is unconstrained. This is because only the unconstrained left-leaning incumbent are able to move the policy to its preferred position where investment is lured into the host country. For the right-leaning incumbent, however, constraints are associated with lower restrictions as it is not able to increase them in order to benefit its business constituents.

4.2.3 Analyses

The plausibility of the argument is assessed with a series of statistical analyses discussed in the following paragraph. The objective is to determine whether governments classified as left-leaning are associated with friendlier investment regimes relative to governments of other ideologies, in particular those classified as right or center and to identify how institutional constraints affect this relationship.

Appendix 4 describes the explanatory variables used and the sources of the data. An important challenge to the empirical strategy is the limitation of available data for the construction of the dependent variable to a subset of countries and years.[14] The ideal design would require a more disaggregated measure of labor influence and of FDI policy at the sectoral level, because there is good reason to believe that the complementarity or substitutability of FDI to capital and/or labor varies across industries (Pinto and Pinto, 2008).[15] To assess the empirical validity of the hypotheses derived in Chapter 2, I fit the following model:

$$FDI\ Policy\ Orientation_{it} = \alpha_0 + \alpha_1 Left_{it} + \beta' X_{it} + \varepsilon_{it} \qquad (4.4)$$

---

[14] The dependent variable used in the statistical tests, investment policy orientation, was introduced earlier. I use Golub's index of FDI restrictions as an additional dependent variable.

[15] The unit of analysis is industry-country-year, in the tradition of the endogenous tariff literature, and industries/sectors within countries should be chosen randomly.

Where the subscripts i and t denote country and time, respectively. FDI Policy Orientation is the measure θ_{it} obtained from the two-stage process discussed in the previous sections. A higher value on the dependent variable indicates a friendlier regime toward foreign investment. Left is a dummy variable that indicates whether a left-wing party is in government in country i at time t and X is a vector of control variables. A value of α_1 significantly different from zero would suggest that the investment regime is more favorable to FDI in years under *left* governance compared to years of governments of a different ideology. The data on political orientation are obtained from the Database of Political Institutions (DPI) (Beck et al., 2000).[16] Yet, the partisan orientation of the incumbent as captured by the DPI does not map directly on to the β parameter in the model presented in Chapter 2. Changes in the orientation of the chief executive as measured by the DPI may not be enough to effect changes in policy: the partisan orientation of the chief executive cannot account for the orientation of a coalition government, a minority cabinet, or the constraints faced by the executive under divided government. The β parameter, on the other hand, aims at capturing the weights that the government places on the well-being of workers and domestic capitalists in the policy maker's objective function, so it depends as much on the orientation of the chief executive as it does on the orientation and preferences of other veto-players whose acquiescence is required. Depending on the institutional design, the acquiescence of other political actors might be needed. We would expect a status quo bias represented by an intermediate value of β in countries where governments are more constrained institutionally. Examples of institutionally constrained governments include cases where the number of institutional veto-gates players is large, such as divided government in Presidential systems, and cases where the government is politically constrained, such as minority or multiparty coalitions in Parliamentary settings.[17] Enacting the preferred

---

[16] I detected several problems in the DPI dataset that are likely to affect the results in systematic ways, especially in the sample of emerging economies. First, the dataset's classification of party on the left-right dimension is based on party names where such distinction is possible. The dataset further makes the classification based on the party's affiliation with international organizations of parties. In the case of Argentina, for instance, there is a change over time in the dataset's classification of the Peronist party, which is initially coded as left leaning in the 1970s and then as right leaning in the 1990s. The purported change in the policy orientation of the party that grants such a reclassification did not affect its relationship with organized labor in the country which still identifies with the party. Second, the dataset codes as 0 those years when military regimes are in power. Even in the Western Hemisphere, where most of the military regimes have leaned towards the right, there are major exceptions such as Velasco Alvarado's tenure in Peru.

[17] Henisz (2002, 2000a) has constructed an index that captures how institutionally and politically constrained the executive is. Relying on a simple spatial model of political interaction Henisz

policies of the core constituents of the party in government is easier when governments are less constrained or when these constraints are less binding. Therefore, we would expect that the coefficient on Left is positive when political constraints are low, or when the executive is able to enact the policies that benefit FDI, but not when political constraints are high, which would be equivalent to a lower β in the model.

To obtain a more nuanced classification of the partisan orientation of the incumbent some of the models interact the Left dummy variable with Polcon, the variable developed by Henisz (2002) to capture political constraints. This interaction term allows for the derivation of a continuous measure of incumbent partisanship, one that arguably better captures the main parameter in the model. Given the way Polcon is constructed, when it takes a value of zero the orientation of the chief executive reflects the orientation of the ruling coalition. Therefore, for Polcon values approaching 0, the preferences of the chief executive and other relevant institutional and political veto players are more likely to be aligned. As Polcon increases, the preferences of the chief executive and those of other veto players diverge. Therefore, the sign of the coefficient on the Left dummy is positive and the interaction term between Left and political constraints is negative, with a net positive effect at lower levels of the variable, capturing power diffusion across parties of different partisan alignments.

$$\theta_{it} = \alpha_0 + \alpha_1 Left_{it} + \alpha_2 Polcon_{it} + \alpha_3 Left_{it} \times Polcon_{it} + \beta' X_{it} + \varepsilon_{it} \quad (4.5)$$

Table 4.1 reports the results from regressing the index of investment policy orientation on political orientation of the chief executive, the existence of institutional constraints and the interaction of these two variables, as described in equation (4.5).[18] Models 1 and 2 return a negative coefficient on the Left dummy variable, which is not significantly different from zero, suggesting that governments coded as left-leaning are associated with

---

derives a measure of how constrained the chief executive is in her choice of policies. It is a measure of the likelihood of a change in policy given the structure of political institutions (the number of veto points) and the preferences of the actors that hold each of these points (the partisan alignment of various veto points and the heterogeneity or homogeneity of the preferences within each branch). Possible scores for the final measure of political constraints range from zero (most least constrained, and arguably a more hazardous environment) to one (most constrained).

[18] I report results from linear regression models, pooling observations from different units. Similar results are obtained with alternative specifications.

Table 4.1. *Partisanship and investment policy*

Independent variables	Dependent variable: Investment policy orientation index				
	Model 1	Model 2	Model 3	Model 4	Model 5[d] (PCSE)
DV t-1	0.515^c	0.515^c	0.487^c	0.513^c	0.789^c
	(0.085)	(0.089)	(0.087)	(0.102)	(0.036)
Left	−0.071	−0.071	1.704^c	1.420^a	0.514^b
	(0.153)	(0.153)	(0.610)	(0.794)	(0.212)
Pol. Constr.		0.022	1.416^a	1.467	0.155
		(0.841)	(0.850)	(1.008)	(0.226)
Left x Pol. Constr.			-3.999^c	-3.491^b	-1.115^b
			(1.373)	(1.733)	(0.451)
Government				−0.003	
Consumption				(0.020)	
Move Left					1.179^a
					(0.653)
Move Left x					-2.386^a
Pol. Constr.					(1.415)
Constant	−0.097	−0.107	-0.740^a	−0.701	−0.111
	(0.110)	(0.389)	(0.392)	(0.509)	(0.111)
Observations	96	96	96	72	478
Groups	24	24	24	18	24
R^2	0.2922	0.2923	0.3408	0.3226	0.6752

Significance levels: $^a p < 0.1$, $^b p < 0.05$, $^c p < 0.01$.
Robust standard errors in parenthesis (PCSEs in model 5).
[d] Model 5 uses a modified version of the Investment Policy Measure, available for 24 countries for 1980–2000.

investment policies that are neither more, nor less open than the regimes adopted by their counterparts of the center or the right.[19] Model 3 provides partial support to the partisan hypothesis discussed earlier: introducing an interaction term between the left dummy and the index of political constraints returns a positive and statistically significant coefficient on the left variable and a positive coefficient on the political constraints variable (capturing the effect of constraints when the left dummy takes a value·of zero), whereas the interactive effect is negative and highly statistically significant. I simulate the expected values of the effect of increasing political constraints

---

[19] To control of temporal dependence, I include a lagged dependent variable on the right-hand side of the estimating equation. The lagged DV is positive and highly significant. The findings are robust to alternative modeling strategies.

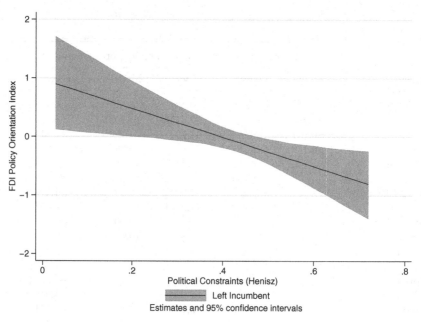

Figure 4.1. FDI policy orientation and political constraints (Left = 1).

when the incumbent party is left-leaning compared to the case where the incumbent party is center or right-leaning.[20]

Figures 4.1 through 4.3 show these effects graphically. Figure 4.1 presents the point prediction and the 95 percent confidence interval around those estimates for the left party; Figure 4.2 shows similar predictions when the left dummy takes a value of zero. Figure 4.3, on the other hand, compares the effect of partisanship and constraints when the government is of the left and when it is not. When political constraints are low and the incumbent is able to alter the status quo, investment policies become more open. The confidence interval when the left dummy takes a value of one does not overlap with the confidence interval when it takes a value of zero where political constraints (Polcon) are low. As constraints increase, the left becomes associated with more restrictive investment policies, whereas governments led by parties of the center or right end of the political spectrum are associated with more open policies. The finding that governments are more likely to adopt the policies predicted by the model when unconstrained

---

[20] Because the parameters in the model are estimated with uncertainty, I use the statistical package clarify developed by King et al. (2003). Clarify generates a thousand simulations of the param eters, allowing for the estimation of quantities of interest such as changes in expected values associated with changes in the explanatory variables (King et al. 2003; Tomz et al. 2003).

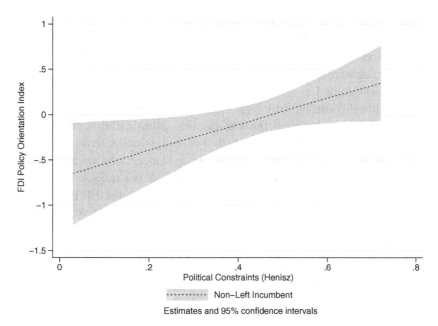

Figure 4.2. FDI policy orientation and political constraints (Left = 0).

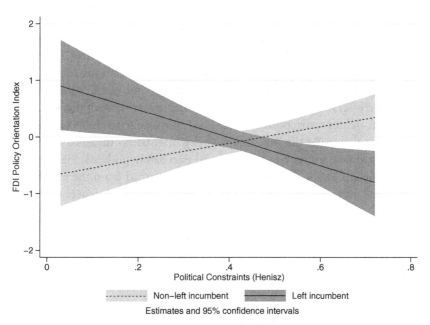

Figure 4.3. FDI restrictions index and political constraints.

suggest that once the institutional characteristics of the polity are controlled for, the partisan hypothesis gains plausibility.

That a constrained government of the left is more restrictive than its right or center counterpart facing similar constraints is not surprising. Note that the policies adopted by left- or right-wing governments tend to converge when political constraints are high, suggesting that policies are locked-in. This conforms to the predictions of the veto-gates literature. When the government is coded as left the joint effect of the level and interaction could be interpreted as a movement along the β axis in Figure 2.5. Model 5 provides partial support for this interpretation.[21] 'Move Left' is a variable that takes a value of one when the chief executive has moved to the left in a given year. The coefficient on this variable is positive and significant, whereas the interaction of the "Move Left" dummy with the political constraints variable is negative and significant.[22]

To control for the market versus government tradeoff faced by owners of labor in the model discussed in the Appendix of Chapter 2 (between the cash transfer g or the return z), Model 4 includes government consumption as a regressor. The effect of this variable on investment policy orientation is negative but not statistically significant. However, note that controlling for government consumption affects the coefficient and significance of the other regressors in the model, although the substantive effects remain.

Table 4.2 reproduces the tests in Table 4.1 using as a dependent variable a measure of investment restrictions developed by Golub (2003). As discussed earlier, this index measures FDI-specific restrictions adopted by governments such as limitations on foreign ownership, notification procedures, and operational restrictions. Note that a higher value of this variable represents tighter restrictions on FDI. The results are remarkably similar to those obtained using the investment policy orientation measure as a DV, providing strong support to the modified partisan hypothesis. Figures 4.4 to 4.6 reproduce graphically the simulations obtained from the estimates in Model 8. In Figure 4.6, take note of the point predictions where political

---

[21] Model 5 uses an alternative measure of the Investment Policy Orientation Index, obtained on a yearly basis for the period 1980–2000. This estimate does not control for education (which is available in five-year intervals) in either of the two stages. The correlation coefficient between both measures is 0.9846 and is significant beyond conventional levels ($p > t$: 0.0000).

[22] The relationship is robust to model specification. Moreover, using Swank's measure of ideological orientation of the incumbent, which is only available for 17 OECD countries, yields identical results. Swank's Comparative Political Parties Dataset is available at http://www.marquette.edu/polisci/faculty_swank.shtml.

Table 4.2. *Partisanship and investment restrictions*

Independent Variables	Dependent variable: FDI restrictions index (Golub 2003)				
	Model 6	Model 7	Model 8	Model 9	Model 10
Left	-0.051^a	-0.055^a	-0.314^c	-0.293^b	-0.297^b
	(0.031)	(0.032)	(0.101)	(0.146)	(0.147)
Pol. Constr.		-0.102	-0.256^a	-0.706^c	-0.274
		(0.138)	(0.131)	(0.246)	(0.211)
Left x			0.586^b	0.580^a	0.593^a
Pol. Constr.			(0.231)	(0.317)	(0.315)
Centralized				0.148^b	
Business Org.				(0.058)	
Government					0.003
Share of GDP					(0.003)
Constant	0.299^c	0.346^c	0.418	0.588^c	0.370^c
	(0.021)	(0.069)	(0.065)	(0.122)	(0.113)
Observations	72	72	72	36	54
Units	27	27	27	18	18
R2	0.0370	0.0441	0.0898	0.0792	0.0719

Significance levels: $^a p < 0.1$, $^b p < 0.05$, $^c p < 0.01$.
Robust standard errors in parenthesis.

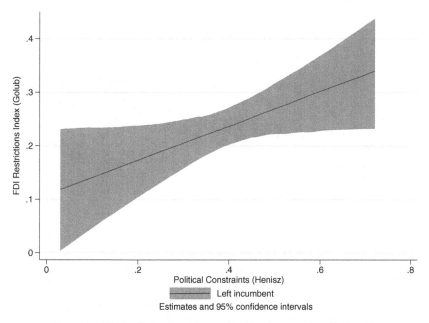

Figure 4.4. FDI policy orientation and political constraints (Left $= 1$).

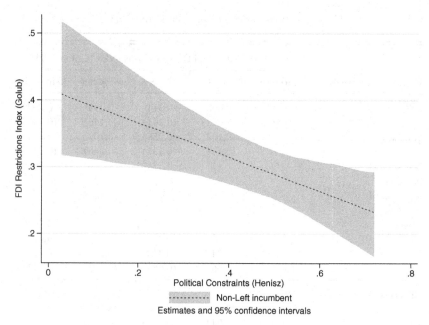

Figure 4.5. FDI restrictions index and political constraints (Left = 0).

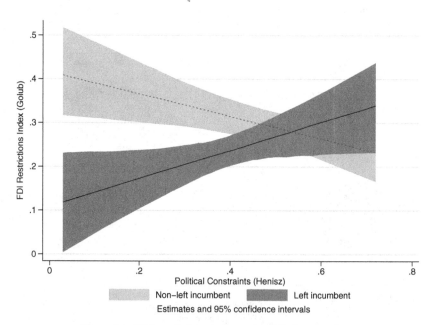

Figure 4.6. FDI restrictions index and political constraints.

constraints are low that show that left-leaning governments are associated with less restrictions on FDI. That the confidence intervals of the estimates produced for left-wing and governments of other political orientations do not overlap in this region underscores the stark difference between governments of the left and those in the center or right of the political spectrum. Also, note that at high levels of political constraints it is difficult to detect significantly different behavior between chief executives of different ideologies which consistent with the prior interpretation of the interactive term.[23] Models 9 and 10 introduce alternative controls, such as the existence of strong and centralized business organizations, which are associated with more restrictive FDI-specific restrictions in Model 8, and government consumption in Model 9, producing results similar to those obtained in Model 4.

As a whole, the statistical results provide strong and robust evidence that partisanship is correlated with the measure of investment policy orientation in the direction predicted by the partisan investment theory presented in Chapters 2 and 3. The results can be interpreted as follows: when a pro-labor party is in power, it is more likely to adopt policies preferred by labor. It would, therefore, regulate foreign investment more favorably because inflows of capital, which are assumed to complement labor in production, are likely to increase the return to labor. The ability of the pro-labor party to advance labor's preferred agenda is institutionally and politically constrained. As constraints increase, the pro-labor government is not able to advance labor's preferred agenda. In fact, there is reason to believe that when these constraints are high, they tend lock in policies that differ from those that are championed by the incumbent. Therefore, a status quo bias resulting from the presence of high political constraints may explain why we frequently see pro-foreign investment policies when the incumbent party is of the right.

In sum, whereas the extant literature provides sensible explanations of how political institutions affect the incentives faced by foreign firms when deciding what form of entry and investment strategy to employ in order to reduce exposure to political risk, I find that government partisanship is a good predictor of the regulatory environment of aggregate investment flows.[24] Parties of the left, particularly those with a more nationalist bent,

---

[23] The highest value of $\beta = 1$ attained when the left is in power and Polcon $= 0$, which occurs when the left controls the chief executive position and political constraints are at their lowest level.

[24] I conduct, but do not report, additional tests using a measure of restrictions at the sectoral level taken from Golub (2003) which is available for a set of 28 OECD countries for the

are likely to find that framing these policies as protecting labor's income is more politically appealing than instead pitching them as benefiting foreign investors.

4.3 Partisanship and Investment Flows

I argued earlier that the responsiveness of government to foreign investors is a function of the relative power of labor or its potential to influence the policy-making process, and the receptiveness of politicians to labor's demands. While it is possible that a government that has internalized the interests of labor would enact a level of taxation on capital that is higher than the level a pro-business government would introduce, potentially deterring investment, the tax rate applied to foreign capital by such a government is likely to be lower than the rate applied by a government that reflects capital's interests. If these predictions are right, we should expect higher levels of foreign direct investment in countries where governments are more responsive to labor. A possible proxy for responsiveness to labor demands is the ideological orientation of the ruling party. Thus, governments on the left of the political spectrum would be better at promoting foreign investment that results in higher labor demand. The main testable hypothesis is the following:

Partisan Hypothesis: foreign direct investment flows will be larger to countries where the left is in power.

An alternative hypothesis derived from the literature on the politics of FDI explores the role of institutions. This hypothesis states that foreign direct investment flows are larger to countries where the government is institutionally constrained.

In order to test these hypotheses using data on direct investment flows, we need first to identify the conditions that determine where FDI goes, which is what I do in the next section.

year 2000. In this cross-sectional setting, the left is associated with lower restrictions across the board, but especially in manufacturing, which seems to confirm the findings reported in Pinto and Pinto (2008) and Jensen et al. (2012). There we find support for the argument that pro-labor governments promote the inflow of FDI into more labor-intensive sectors to the benefit of labor, and owners of foreign capital decide to invest in those sectors. Further, we argue that the likelihood of a policy reversal is reduced as left-leaning governments internalize the positive impact of FDI inflows on the return/welfare of labor, their core constituent.

4.3.1 Determinants of Foreign Investment

As discussed in previous chapters, the literature on FDI and multinational activity is extensive and controversial. In the profuse literature in economics, we can identify two main explanations of the determinants of multinational activity. On the one hand, we find factor proportions explanations, those that stress that investment flows are driven by differences in endowments (Helpman, 1984; Markusen, 1984; Helpman, 1985; Helpman and Krugman, 1985). On the other hand, several authors have pointed to a trade-off between proximity to consumption markets and economies of scale that investors face when deciding to supply consumers located at home and abroad (Horstmann and Markusen, 1992; Brainard, 1993b, 1997).[25] Yet, theories that explain why companies become multinational do not seem to be enough to explain where capital goes. Variables traditionally associated with these explanations, such as capital, labor and skill endowment, market size, distance, language, and legal systems, among others, leave a large part of the variance in FDI performance unexplained. Empirical approaches have adopted different methodologies to analyze the flow of investment capital. The findings of these approaches are difficult to compare because of lack of correspondence in the universe of cases, sample size, model specification, and choice of controls.[26] This results in a lack of consensus about the factors that should be considered as determinants of multinational activity, and/or the sign attributed to them (Chakrabarti, 1997).

From this extensive and diverse literature the main variables that appear to be consistently related with FDI flows are factor endowment, market size, and trade orientation (Carr et al., 2001, 2003; Markusen and Maskus, 2002).[27] Market size usually returns a positive result, which probably reflects the presence of economies of scale (Wheeler and Mody, 1992). Research on the effect of investment on labor costs report mixed results. While previous studies had found a negative correlation between wages and investment flows, Lucas (1993) shows real net FDI to be less elastic with respect to costs of capital than to real wages. Employing an econometric analysis of a single-equation model based on Cobb-Douglas technology using aggregate data

---

[25] Factor proportions relates to horizontal FDI, whereas vertical FDI can be identified with the proximity/scales economy explanation (Markusen, 1995).

[26] The most successful empirical approaches are probably those based on gravity specifications. See Blonigen and Davies (2004). But gravity techniques, which are good at capturing vertical and horizontal models of FDI, cannot account for the knowledge-capital model of multinational activity (Carr et al., 2001; Markusen and Maskus, 2001b, 2002).

[27] Language and distance should be included in the list when estimating gravity models of investment.

on seven South-East Asian economies over the period 1961 to 1987, Lucas failed to find evidence that higher real wages in rival host countries increase inbound FDI. Caves (1974), Kravis and Lipsey (1982), Lipsey and Kravis (1982), and Kravis and Lipsey (1993) also obtained a positive relationship between FDI and real wages. This finding, however, has been typically described as spurious or is attributed to unmeasured labor quality. More recent studies have found a positive effect of FDI activity on wages paid to workers on spillover to local firms and on local average wages (Haddad and Harrison, 1993; Aitken et al., 1996, 1997; Feenstra and Hanson, 1997; Aitken and Harrison, 1999; Figlio and Blonigen, 2000; Feliciano and Lipsey, 1999; Lipsey and Sjöholm, 2004). These studies underscore the potential of FDI to affect relative labor demand.[28]

Regarding the relationship between investment and trade, the results are contested. The theoretical debate is to whether trade and investment are complements or substitutes (Caves, 1996; Markusen, 1995; Ethier and Markusen, 1996; O'Rourke and Williamson, 1999; Markusen and Maskus, 2001b,a; Brainard, 1993b,a, 1997; Blonigen and Feenstra, 1997; Blonigen and Davies, 2004). While Mundell (1957) assumes that the flow of goods and services, and the flow of factors of production are substitutes, recent work by O'Rourke and Williamson (1999) challenges this assumption. In particular, these authors reject the hypothesis that trade and factor flows are substitutes, at least for the pre-WWI period. There is also work done at the firm level. Using cross-sectional data on the activity of affiliates of U.S. multinationals, Brainard (1993a, 1997) finds that the share of affiliate exports and sales is positively related to trade barriers. Blonigen and Feenstra (1997) confirm the relationship between the threat of protection and investment, using data on flows of Japanese FDI in to the United States between 1980 and 1987. On the other hand, Wheeler and Mody (1992) find no significant relationship between trade openness and FDI. Based on this profuse literature and its results, I include in the statistical tests variables that proxy for market size (GDP in constant U.S.$ and in purchasing power parity), relative endowment of capital (GDP per capita in constant U.S.$ and labor share of income), and trade orientation (openness, which measures the ration of exports and imports to output) to control for the determinants that stand out in the literature. One of the main assumptions in Chapter 2 is that domestic and foreign capital are substitutes. In several models, I add savings in the host country as one of the regressors to control for this substitution effect. The cross-sectional models compromised of more heterogeneous units also include variables such as schooling

---

(to control for differences in the human capital endowments) and protection of civil rights.[29]

4.3.2 Methodology

I use a number different of statistical techniques to conduct tests of the previous hypotheses on three different samples of data. The different tests try to overcome problems related to data availability and those related to research design, including the inability to randomly assign observations to treatment (changes in the independent variable) and control groups. The first, large sample comprises all countries for which data is available. The sample includes least-developed, developing, emerging, and developed countries for over twenty-five years. An additional problem with this design is that observations of the units before and after political changes are unavailable. Another important challenge to the empirical tests of the argument is data availability. The Time-Series Cross-Sectoral (TSCS) and the gravity panel designs partially solve the second part of the problem: even though there is still no random assignment, the units are observed over time. The TSCS and the gravity designs are more data-intensive, and the data is only available for a limited set of countries and years.[30] I further discuss issues related to the research design of the tests in the sections that report the results obtained for each model.[31] For the reasons described in the previous paragraphs, it should be noted that the tests performed do not truly establish causality. They should be interpreted as observational studies that simply suggest the plausibility of the argument.

4.3.3 Dependent Variable

Foreign direct investment is a net inflow of investment that acquires a lasting management interest in an enterprise operating in a country other than that

---

[29] Other variables used in the empirical literature include competitiveness, domestic investment, growth, government intervention, infrastructure, privatization, and trade balance (Wheeler and Mody, 1992).

[30] The ideal design would require a more disaggregated measure of labor influence and of FDI policy. The unit of analysis should be industry/year, in the tradition of the endogenous tariff literature, and industries/sectors within countries should be chosen randomly. Yet this data is only available for OECD countries: see Pinto and Pinto (2008). I have conducted sectoral tests for the cases of Argentina and South Korea, presented in Chapters 5 and 6. There I am better able to capture the pro-labor and pro-business orientation of the ruling coalition beyond the crude conventional measures of partisanship used in the cross-country analyses conducted in this chapter.

[31] Appendix 4 describes the variables used and sources of data, whereas Table 4.7 and 4.8 presents summary statistics.

of the investor (Lipsey 2001). Direct investment is the sum of equity capital, reinvestment of earnings, and other long-term and short-term capital as shown in the balance of payments. The variable used in the tests is FDI net inflows in to the host country in U.S. dollars.[32] In the TSCS tests, I use the natural log of FDI net inflows instead, which transforms the variable such that negative values of FDI inflows, which reflect the repatriation of capital, are converted to zero. In order to preserve the information from those observations that are now recorded as zeros and to reduce the risk of bias in the estimates, the log is taken after adding \$1 to the dollar amount of FDI inflows: $ln\ FDI_{it} = ln(FDI_{it} + 1)$. The gravity model specification uses the natural log of the ratio of FDI flows from source to recipient country to the recipient country's GDP in percentage points. This variable is created using bilateral investment data whose transformation is described in Appendix 4.

4.3.4 Explanatory Variables

Labor/Capital influence: The concept to be operationalized is the power of domestic actors to affect policy, or the relative influence of labor versus capital. I have identified several measures that could be used as proxies for this concept, including labor/capital shares of income, union density, centralization of wage bargaining, and the ideological orientation of government. Following Dutt and Mitra (2005), the measure of labor influence used is the ideological position of the party or the ruler in power, as coded in the Database of Political Institutions (Beck et al., 2000).[33] Just like the models previously tested, the ideological position assigned to each country corresponds to the orientation of the chief executive for political systems classified as presidential in the database and to the orientation of the majority or largest government party for systems classified as parliamentary. A higher value on this scale represents a more leftist orientation of the chief executive. I create a dummy variable labeled *Left* that takes the value of 1 if Ideology is "Left" and 0 otherwise. "Left" relies on the coding of the executive if the political system is presidential or semi-presidential. In parliamentary systems, the variable is derived from the partisanship categorization of the largest party in the government. Again, I explore the alternative hypothesis on the role of institutions as proposed by the extant literature on the

---

[32] FDI inflows in current dollars are converted to constant 1996 dollars using a GDP deflator obtained from the World Bank (2010) WDI.

[33] As a robustness check, I use the centralization of wage bargaining as an alternative measure of labor influence. This measure is is available for the subset of 14 OECD countries.

politics of investment. I use a variable developed by Henisz (2002), Political Constraints, obtained from the 2010 version of his dataset.

4.3.5 Controls

Factor endowment: Comparable measures of capital stock and labor endowment across countries are notoriously limited in coverage and suffer from a great deal of measurement error, and thus seriously flawed (Dutt and Mitra, 2005). For practical reasons in the tests reported in the following paragraph, I use per capita GDP instead (Heston et al., 2002, 2011; PWT 6.2, PWT 7.0). Per capita GDP is a coarse proxy for capital endowment. To the extent that it captures relative endowment of capital the coefficient on GDP per capita is expected to return a negative sign. Yet, GDP per capita may also signal a larger consumption potential in the host economy, the similarity of consumption preferences, or complementarities between home and host countries, each of which would lead to higher investment and an expected positive sign.

Natural resources: These variables are constructed as the sum of exports of fuel, mineral ore, and metal to total exports in percentages. The source is World Bank (2010) World Development Indicators. For resource-seeking FDI, the effect should be positive, but the presence of natural resources may also crowd out manufacturing and other activities, therefore keeping out efficiency or market seeking investors. The expected relationship is thus indeterminate.[34]

Arable Land: Includes the percentage of arable land to total land area, in percentages. The source is World Bank (2010) World Development Indicators. As with natural resources, the effect is indeterminate.

Gross Domestic Product: GDP is a proxy for size (Heston et al., 2002, 2011; PWT 6.2, PWT 7.0). Larger countries are likely to attract more FDI. The expected sign is positive.

Domestic Savings: Gross domestic savings are calculated as GDP less final consumption expenditure, including private and public consumption (World Bank, 2010, WDI). To the extent that domestic and foreign investment are substitutes as assumed in Chapter 2, the resulting crowding out effect implies that the expected sign on this variable is negative.

---

[34] Measuring natural resource endowments as exports is also problematic, as these exports might be the product of foreign firms operating in the sector, raising concerns of endogeneity.

Property rights: According to a large body of literature, the protection of property rights is one of the main determinants of investment, both domestic and foreign, and growth (North and Weingast, 1989; North, 1990). Yet, the transaction costs theory of MNCs developed by Caves (1996) argues that firms are more likely to internalize transactions in a hierarchic organization where the existence of proprietary assets make arms' length transactions riskier. I use Freedom House (2010)'s index of civil rights as a proxy for property rights protection (Freedom House 2010). The contradictory implications of these two strands of thought is that an environment where the violation of property rights is pervasive may have two effects on foreign investment flows that run counter to each other: on the one hand, the lack of protection of property rights may inhibit foreign and domestic investment. On the other hand, to the extent that foreign investment takes place in countries where property rights are not protected, it is more likely to take the form of FDI (as opposed to portfolio investment or other forms) as predicted by the transaction costs literature. The expected effect is thus indeterminate.

Schooling: The average years of schooling of the population 25 years old and over. The expected sign for this variable is positive (Barro and Lee, 2001).

Trade/GDP (%): The sum of exports and imports of goods and services measured as a share of gross domestic product. The expected sign is negative if trade and factor flows are substitutes, or positive if they are complements (Heston et al., 2002, 2011; PWT 6.2, PWT 7.0).

Labor Share: Labor's share of income. This variable is constructed as the economy-wide aggregate measure of sectoral share of labor compensation to sectoral output (OECD, 1998b, STAN).

4.3.6 Effect of Partisanship on FDI Openness

In Table 4.3, I present results from pooling time series and cross-sectional data from different samples of countries for different years.[35] Model 1 includes all countries with a population over one million people for which data on FDI and other covariates is available for the period 1970 to 2005.[36]

---

[35] I adopt a conservative strategy, fitting a General Method of Moments specification recommended by Arellano and Bond (1991) for dynamic panel models (Arellano and Bond, 1991; Arellano and Bover, 1995; Arellano, 2003).

[36] Model 2 adds a dummy variable for the center-leaning party, which returns a coefficient that is substantively large but not statistically significant at conventional levels.

Table 4.3. *Arellano-bond generalized method of moments estimator*

	DV: FDI/GPD					
	(1)	(2)	(3)	(4)	(5)	(6)
Δ FDI/GDP$_{t-1}$	0.379^b	0.379^b	-0.162^c	-0.163^c	0.366^c	0.367^c
	(0.153)	(0.153)	(0.033)	(0.033)	(0.107)	(0.107)
FDI/GDP$_{t-1}$	-1.242^c	-1.244^c	-0.460^c	-0.460^c	-0.682^c	-0.684^c
	(0.089)	(0.089)	(0.032)	(0.032)	(0.019)	(0.020)
Left	0.584^a	0.674^a	0.348^b	0.361^b	0.005^b	0.006^b
	(0.347)	(0.375)	(0.173)	(0.173)	(0.003)	(0.003)
Center		1.069		0.221		0.007
		(0.699)		(0.249)		(0.007)
Pol. Constr.	0.998	0.900	0.265	0.239	-4.953^a	-4.998^a
	(0.833)	(0.854)	(0.399)	(0.400)	(2.710)	(2.709)
Real GDP/cap	0.733	0.728	0.423^c	0.422^c	0.245^c	0.256^c
	(0.549)	(0.547)	(0.060)	(0.060)	(0.091)	(0.097)
Trade/GDP	0.062^b	0.062^b	0.004	0.004	0.102^c	0.101^c
	(0.026)	(0.026)	(0.005)	(0.005)	(0.031)	(0.030)
Savings/GDP	-0.033	-0.031	0.007	0.007	0.080	0.080
	(0.032)	(0.031)	(0.014)	(0.014)	(0.051)	(0.051)
GDP	-0.001	-0.001	-0.001	-0.001	-0.001^b	-0.001^b
	(0.001)	(0.001)	(0.001)	(0.001)	(0.0002)	(0.0003)
Govt/GDP	-0.055	-0.052	0.035	0.037	-0.086	-0.076
	(0.055)	(0.055)	(0.026)	(0.026)	(0.130)	(0.133)
Nat. res. exports	-0.007	-0.007	-0.009	-0.009	-0.022	-0.022
	(0.025)	(0.025)	(0.006)	(0.006)	(0.028)	(0.029)
Pol. Rights	-0.239	-0.236	-0.041	-0.039	0.748	0.754
	(0.200)	(0.201)	(0.059)	(0.059)	(0.687)	(0.684)
Constant	-5.165	-5.263	-2.199^c	-2.245^c	-8.020	-8.413
	(5.641)	(5.692)	(0.661)	(0.664)	(5.179)	(5.433)
Sample	All	All	Emerging	Emerging	Developed	Developed
N	2,052	2,052	895	895	548	548
Groups	122	122	32	32	21	21
Wald chi^2	818.8	829.3	414.1	414.4	29693	53005
Arellano-Bond (1)	-2.602	-2.605	-2.979	-2.992	-1.562	-1.564
Pr > z =	0.009	1.087	0.003	0.003	0.118	0.118
Arellano-Bond (2)	1.095	0.009	-1.000	-1.044	-0.692	-0.692
Pr > z =	0.274	0.277	0.318	0.297	0.489	0.489

$^a p < 0.1$, $^b p < 0.05$, $^c p < 0.01$.
Arellano-Bond Dynamic Panel Data; robust std. errors.
Sample: see footnotes 38 and 39.
Left (Center) = Left (Center) share of Cabinet Portfolios in Models 5 and 6.

This model returns a positive association between governments of the Left and openness to FDI; the relationship is statistically significant beyond the 90 percent level of confidence.[37] Yet pooling developed economies with emerging markets and developing countries for purposes of estimating the determinants of FDI is problematic as is persuasively demonstrated by Blonigen and Wang (2005). Model 3 in Table 4.3, repeats the GMM exercise on a subsample of the data for thirty-two emerging markets for which at least twenty years of observations are available.[38] These results show that there is a positive association between the Left and changes in FDI/GDP. The results are relatively small when compared to the variance in the sample, but this should not be a surprise because we are looking at differences. In Model 4, center-leaning incumbents seem to be associated with openness to FDI as well, yet the coefficient does not attain statistical significance. The political constraints index, on the other hand, returned a positive coefficient, but does not attain statistical significance. Finally, Model 5 in Table 4.3 presents the results for a subsample of developed economies.[39] In this sample, I use an alternative measure of partisan orientation of the incumbent: the Left and Center parties' shares of Cabinet portfolios developed by Dwane Swank (see footnote 22). The results provide additional support to the partisan hypothesis: there is a positive association between the change in the left party's share of Cabinet portfolios and changes in the degree of openness to FDI. In Model 6, the Center party's control of portfolios, on the other hand, also seems to have a positive association with FDI openness, but the result is not statistically significant at conventional levels; political constraints, on the other hand, are negatively correlated with openness. Taken together

---

[37] Given that the variables enter in first-differences, there is no need to account for unit specific effects; for this reason, there is no value in interacting the incumbent orientation with political constraints either, because we are already looking at the effect of moving along the political spectrum holding changes of constraints constant. In the interactive models, however, the results remain substantively the same: the Left variable is positively associated with greater openness to FDI, but less so when constraints are high. The right-leaning incumbent, on the other hand, is associated with higher openness when institutionally constrained.

[38] The countries included in this subsample are Algeria, Argentina, Bolivia, Brazil, Chile, Colombia, Costa Rica, Ecuador, Egypt, El Salvador, Guatemala, Honduras, India, Indonesia, Ireland, Jamaica, Jordan, Kenya, Korea, Madagascar, Malaysia, Mexico, Morocco, Pakistan, Peru, Philippines, Sri Lanka, Thailand, Tunisia, Turkey, Uruguay, and Venezuela. During the period of analysis, this group of countries received roughly 95 percent of the FDI inflows outside the developed economies.

[39] The sample includes the following OECD members: Australia, Austria, Belgium, Canada, Denmark, Finland, France, Germany, Greece, Ireland, Italy, Japan, Netherlands, New Zealand, Norway, Portugal, Spain, Sweden, Switzerland, the United Kingdom, and the United States.

these results suggest that there is a positive association between the partisan orientation of the incumbent government and the degree of openness to FDI. These findings are in line with the association between the Left and the investment policy measures presented in previously in Section 4.2.3. In the ensuing sections I further explore the relationship between partisanship and openness within subsamples of developed and emerging markets for which better FDI data is available from the OECD. These tests use alternative transformations of the dependent and explanatory variables, different controls, as well as different modeling strategies to explore the robustness of the link between partisanship and FDI.

4.3.7 Time-Series Cross-Section Data from OECD Countries

I run a series of tests on a subset of OECD countries for the period 1975 to 1996. As units are not randomly selected into the sample, I measure the dependent variable before and after changes in political coalitions and in their influence on the policy-making process. All cases are advanced democratic members of the OECD with relatively similar levels of development. These cases contain changes in the composition of ruling coalitions and in political regimes and partisan cycles, which resulted in variation of the relative influence of labor and capital. There is also variance in political institutions across countries and along time. The sample includes cases from more than one region of the world, allowing for intra- and inter-regional variance. Stratification of the sample and introduction of appropriate controls and econometric techniques allows holding constant the residual variation in terms of development, political institutions, and endowments.

Due to the time-series cross-section structure of the data as repeated observations over fixed units, I run a linear regression model with standard errors corrected for panel effects on a rectangular matrix of 14 countries over 22 years for a total of 308 observations. Beck and Katz (1995) find that the panel corrected standard errors estimator performs well when the data has a time-series cross-section structure, as is the case here. All models include a one-period lag of the dependent variable on the right-hand side to control for serial correlation, as recommended by the same authors (Beck and Katz, 1996).[40] The inclusion of one lag of the dependent variable seems

---

[40] Similar results are obtained using method of generalized estimating equations (GEE) and the Arellano-Bond generalized method of moments (GMM) estimator. Regression results using GEE and GMM are available from the author upon request.

Table 4.4. *Panel of OECD countries (1975–96)*

Independent variables	Dependent variable: Log FDI net inflows						
	Model 1	Model 2	Model 3	Model 4	Model 5	Model 6	Model 7
Log FDI$_{(t-1)}$	0.26^c	0.26^c	0.26^c	0.26^c	0.26^c	0.23^c	0.23^c
	(0.09)	(0.09)	(0.09)	(0.09)	(0.09)	(0.09)	(0.09)
Log GDP per Capita	−1.76^b	−1.98^b	−1.56^a	−1.83^a	−1.85^a	−3.47^c	−2.30^b
	(0.83)	(0.93)	(0.92)	(1.04)	(0.99)	(0.94)	(1.06)
Log GDP (PPP)	1.30^c	1.34^c	1.53^b	1.51^b	1.51^b	1.16^d	2.30^c
	(0.22)	(0.23)	(0.77)	(0.77)	(0.74)	(0.24)	(0.80)
Log Trade/GDP	2.04^c	2.06^c	1.98^c	2.01^c	2.02^d	1.50^d	1.33^d
	(0.37)	(0.37)	(0.38)	(0.38)	(0.39)	(0.32)	(0.31)
Political Constraints		1.73		1.68	1.67	2.58^a	2.15
		(1.25)		(1.28)	(1.34)	(1.48)	(1.33)
Log Savings/GDP			−0.27	−0.20	−0.19		−1.38
			(0.84)	(0.84)	(0.85)	(0.79)	
Left	0.89^c	0.99^c	0.89^b	0.99^c	1.00^c	0.85^b	0.79^b
	(0.35)	(0.38)	(0.35)	(0.38)	(0.37)	(0.35)	(0.36)
Labor Share					0.55	3.95	
					(4.09)	(4.24)	
Constant	−20.08^b	−19.90^b	−21.12^b	−20.68^b	−21.12^b	1.42	−4.94
	(8.88)	(8.97)	(9.16)	(9.31)	(9.62)	(8.21)	(9.05)
Observations	308	308	308	308	306	306	308
Groups	14	14	14	14	14	14	14
R-squared	0.3006	0.3028	0.3009	0.3029	0.3032	0.4142	0.4175
Year Dummies	No	No	No	No	No	No	Yes

Significance levels: $^a p < 0.10$; $^b p < 0.05$; $^c p < 0.01$.
Panel corrected standard errors in parentheses.

to correct for serial correlation in the data.[41] Model 7 also includes year dummies to control for latent temporal breaks in the series.

4.3.8 OECD Panel Results

I run several variants of this model with similar results, which are reproduced in Table 4.4. From these results we see that the coefficient on Left

---

[41] The original dataset comprised 322 observations, but 14 observations are lost due to the inclusion of the lagged dependent variable. The use of panel corrected standard errors in conjunction with ordinary least squares estimates corrects for heteroskedasticity and contemporaneous correlation in the data (Beck and Katz, 1995, 1996).

is positive and significant beyond conventional levels of confidence in all reported models. The effect is not quite substantive, though, when compared to the whole sample: a movement to the left is associated with an increase in the dependent variable (natural log of FDI) of close to one-third of a standard deviation. For example, taking Model 5 as a benchmark, a movement from right to left would result in roughly a $1.5 billion increase in FDI inflows for an average country/year in the sample.[42] Regarding the control variables, the lagged dependent variable is highly significant, suggesting that there is more variance across units than within countries, which is not surprising. GDP is positively associated with inflows, probably indicating the influence of market size.[43] Savings, which enters the equation in log form, returns a negative coefficient, consistent with the crowding out effect. This coefficient is never significantly different from zero, though. In Models 6 and 7, reproduced in Table 4.4, I control for the relative share of factors of production in the economy using a variable labeled as labor share. This variable is constructed as the economy-wide aggregate measure of the sectoral share of labor compensation in manufacturing to sectoral output. The variable is a measure of either relative endowment, if technology is identical across units and time, or, if not, of technological changes that determine a different combination of labor and capital across countries or along time.[44] Labor share is positively related to the log of FDI inflows but its coefficient is never significant.[45] The findings are robust to alternative specifications and controls. The inclusion of the following variables does not affect the relationship found between left orientation of government and the log of FDI flows: arable land, exports of fuel and exports of food as proxies for endowment of natural resources, and international capital mobility

---

[42] For a country like the United States in 1991, for instance, the model would predict that a change from right to left would result in somewhere between $13 billion to $26 billion extra inflows of FDI. But we should be careful when constructing these counterfactuals for several reasons: first, the variance explained by the model is low, as reflected in the R^2 for each model. Second, most of the action is across rather than within countries, as reflected by the coefficient on the lagged dependent variable.

[43] The natural log transformation may also reflect the relationship between foreign investment and growth.

[44] Note that it could also reflect the ability of labor to claim a higher share of output and would therefore measure organized labor's influence in the marketplace. In the Argentine case, the correlation between labor share of income and FDI is positive, implying that the direction of causality might be reversed.

[45] Similar results are obtained when centralization of wage bargaining is entered in place of labor share, as well as Garrett's index of Left/labor power (Garrett, 1995, 1998b). It is worth noting that labor share and the power index are relatively constant within countries; most of the variance comes from cross-country comparisons.

proxied for by the log of world FDI outflows.[46] To ensure that no individual country was driving the relationship found in the models previously discussed, I reran the test on different samples of the data by sequentially dropping observations for individual countries.[47] Results remain robust to these adjustments as well.[48]

4.3.9 Gravity Model: Developing and Emerging Countries (1980–2000)

The use of gravity specifications has long been a tradition in the empirical analysis of trade. The basic gravity model posits that the volume of trade between two nations is an increasing function of the incomes of the nations and a decreasing function of the distance between them, although other variables, including whether the countries share a common border and/or a common language are often added to the model (Aitken, 1973; and Frankel et al., 1995). The model has proved to be an extremely effective framework for gauging what patterns of trade are normal or natural among nations (Frankel and Wei, 1993; Baier and Bergstrand, 2001). Similar models have been used in analyzing variation of FDI activity across countries.

The gravity model is flexible and has allowed authors to ground their analysis of foreign investment on different theories of FDI and multinational activity by tinkering with model specification and the variables included on the right-hand side of the estimating equation. A measure of dyadic FDI inflows are regressed on variables that capture the source and recipient countries' relative endowment of capital, labor, natural resources and skill, size and distance, and variables that are likely to have an important effect on the level of inflows.[49] The basic form of the gravity model can be expressed as:

$$FDI_{ij} = f(Distance_{ij}, Size\ Country_{ij}, Endowments_{ij}, Z_{ij}) \quad (4.6)$$

---

[46] Results are available from the author upon request.

[47] Similar tests were conducted by systematically eliminating years from the sample, with no substantial change in the findings previous reported.

[48] Using data from a sample of 17 sectors in 21 the OECD countries elsewhere I show that while FDI flows are larger under the Left across the board, the relationship is stronger in manufacturing (Jensen et al., 2012, Chapter 4).

[49] Carr et al. (2001, 2003), Markusen and Maskus (2001b,a, 2002), and Markusen and Maskus (2001c) construct an unrestricted empirical model of FDI activity that nests a number of alternative theories of MNE activity: horizontal, vertical, and knowledge-capital model (which integrates the previous two). Earlier I have used the gravity setup to derive a measure of investment policy.

Where the subscript i identifies the recipient/host country and j is the sender/home country. Subscripting the variables by t denotes time variance. Z_{ij} is a vector of variables that together form the *resistance term*. Unpacking the resistance term has been part of recent empirical activity on non-economic determinants of FDI. Blonigen and Davies (2004, 2002), for instance, use a modified version of the Carr, Markusen, & Maskus model to estimate the effect of bilateral trade agreements on FDI.[50] The gravity setup assumes that the relationship between these factors is multiplicative. Using OLS, the gravity model can be estimated in log-linear form. The dependent variable of interest is the amount of FDI from the source country received by the recipient country. These amounts are weighted by the recipient countries' product. Once we have controlled for the fundamental economic determinants of investment flows using the gravity specification, we may proceed to include the political variables of interest, in this case a dummy variable intended at capturing whether the incumbent government is of the left. The models to estimate take the following form:

$$Ln\ FDI_{ijt}/Y_{it} = \beta_0 + \beta_1\ ln\ Real\ GDP_{jt} - \beta_2\ ln\ Distance_{jt} +$$
$$+ \beta_3\ ln\ Arable\ land\ ratio_{jtt}$$
$$+ \beta_4\ ln\ GDP\ per\ capita\ ratio_{ijt} +$$
$$+ \beta_5\ ln\ GDP\ per\ capita_{jt} + \beta_6\ Left_{it} + \epsilon_{ijt} \quad (4.7)$$

$$Ln\ FDI_{ijt}/Y_{it} = \beta_0 + \beta_1\ ln\ Real\ GDP_{jt} - \beta_2\ ln\ Distance_{jt} + +$$
$$+ \beta_3\ ln\ Arable\ land\ ratio_{jtt}$$
$$+ \beta_4\ ln\ GDP\ per\ capita\ ratio_{ijt} +$$
$$+ \beta_5\ ln\ GDP\ per\ capita_{jt} + \beta_6\ ln\ average\ school\ ratio_{ijt} +$$
$$+ \beta_7\ ln\ average\ school\ years_{it} + \beta_8\ Left_{it} + \epsilon_{ijt} \quad (4.8)$$

Alternative specifications of these two models include country (α_i) and time (γ_t) fixed effects.

Gravity Model Results

I fit the previous specifications of the gravity model on dyadic FDI inflows for a set of twenty emerging and developing countries over twenty years. These recipient countries, listed in Appendix 4, account for the bulk of FDI inflows received by developing and emerging markets. The source countries

---

[50] See Blonigen and Davies (2004, 2002) and Carr et al. (2001, 2003).

Table 4.5. *Panel of emerging and developing countries (1980–2000)*

Independent Variables	Dependent variable: Ln FDI$_j i$/GDP$_i$							
	Model 1	Model 2	Model 3	Model 4	Model 5	Model 6	Model 7	Model 8
Ln Distance$_{ij}$	−1.37^c	−1.83^c	−1.35^c	−1.83^c	−1.29^c	−1.75^c	−1.75^c	−1.41^c
	(0.08)	(0.10)	(0.08)	(0.10)	(0.16)	(0.20)	(0.20)	(0.07)
Ln Arable land Ratio	−1.09^c	−1.06^c	−1.08^c	−1.06^c	−1.06^c	−1.03^c	−1.03^c	3.37^c
	(0.04)	(0.04)	(0.04)	(0.04)	(0.08)	(0.08)	(0.08)	(0.90)
Ln GDP capita Ratio	4.08^c	3.80^c	3.82^c	3.80^c	4.04^c	3.79^c	3.81^c	5.39^c
	(0.12)	(0.12)	(0.12)	(0.12)	(0.36)	(0.36)	(0.36)	(1.59)
Ln Real GDP$_i$	2.05^c	3.76^c	1.91^c	1.36^c	1.97^c	4.10^c	−4.23	2.23
	(0.05)	(0.17)	(0.05)	(0.43)	(0.10)	(1.47)	(2.97)	(1.38)
Ln GDP per capita$_i$	6.18^c	4.10	5.59^c	4.83^c	5.69^c	3.54^b	10.22^c	7.44^c
	(0.14)	(0.39)	(0.15)	(0.42)	(0.42)	(1.54)	(2.61)	(1.60)
Ln Arable Land$_i$	−1.15^c	−2.76^c	−1.06^c	3.37^c	−1.18^c			3.32^c
	(0.07)	(0.33)	(0.07)	(1.06)	(0.14)			(0.90)
Ln GDP ratio	1.89^c	1.86^c	1.86^c	1.86^c	1.75^c	1.73^c	1.72^c	2.08
	(0.03)	(0.03)	(0.03)	(0.03)	(0.06)	(0.06)	(0.06)	(1.39)
Left$_i$	0.80^c	0.84^c	0.72^c	0.69^c	0.82^c	1.13^b	0.68	0.76^c
	(0.12)	(0.20)	(0.12)	(0.21)	(0.24)	(0.44)	(0.45)	(0.11)
Ln Av. School$_i$					0.97	1.44	1.12	
					(0.61)	(1.63)	(1.65)	
Ln Av. School ratio					−0.82^a	−0.73	−0.79^a	
					(0.47)	(0.46)	(0.46)	
Constant	−115.47^c	−134.75^c	−106.89^c	−82.78^c	−111.55^c	−145.72^c	12.96	−135.80^c
	(1.94)	(2.42)	(2.16)	(8.72)	(4.22)	(24.64)	(54.60)	(21.86)
Country$_i$ fixed effect	No	Yes	No	Yes	No	Yes	Yes	No
Year fixed effect	No	No	Yes	Yes	No	No	Yes	No
N	10066	10066	10066	10066	2380.00	2380.00	2380.00	10066
R^2	0.4206	0.4731	0.4296	0.5117	0.4141	0.4583	0.4654	0.4949
Adj R^2	0.4201	0.4718	0.4280	0.5094	0.4116	0.4518	0.4581	0.4933

Significance levels: $^a p < 0.10$; $^b p < 0.05$; $^c p < 0.01$
Robust standard errors in parentheses.

are twenty-five OECD countries, which together account for roughly 90 percent of world total FDI outflows in any given year. Table 4.5 reproduces the results obtained from these estimations; the results suggest that the relationship found between the left (our proxy for pro-labor orientation of government) and FDI (weighted by gross domestic product) is positive.[51] As predicted by the partisan theory of FDI, the coefficient associated with the left dummy is positive in all models, and in every case (except for Model 7) the coefficient is significantly different from zero beyond conventional

---

[51] Models 1 through 4 in Table 4.5 use the specification described in equation (4.7), whereas Models 5 through 7 use the specification described in equation (4.8).

levels.[52] This is equivalent to 1/7 of the standard deviation of the dependent variable in the sample. Simulating quantities of interest based on the point estimates and their corresponding standard errors we find that for the average dyad/year in the sample the value of FDI/GDP would increase two-fold if the government orientation were to move from right (pro-capital) to left (pro-labor).[53] The results returned for the controls in the different models are quite intuitive: FDI flows are higher to countries that are closer to foreign investors' home countries. The amount of inflows appears to be negatively related to home and host countries' relative endowment of natural resources, proxied for by the ratio of arable to total land area. This result suggests that access to natural resources could be one of the motives for FDI activity. However, the absolute endowment of the host country is negatively related to FDI. Interpreting the positive coefficient on the income and per capita income variables is also fairly intuitive: the source countries are larger and better endowed with capital. It is also apparent that among the countries in the sample, larger countries and those that are better endowed with capital are likely to receive more FDI. Finally, while FDI inflows do not seem to covary with the average years of education in the host country, the negative coefficient on the years of schooling ratio variable suggests that FDI flows are associated with similar levels of education in the home and host country.

4.4 Conclusion

In this chapter, I have conducted a series of statistical tests on the hypothesis that left-leaning governments are more likely to adopt regimes that are more friendly to foreign investors and to attract higher levels of FDI. The preliminary evidence previously reported supports the core hypotheses derived from the partisan investment model presented in Chapters 2 and 3.

The first tests are run on an original measure of investment policy orientation created from bilateral investment flows after having fitted a

[52] The exception is Model 7 where due to limitations in the data available for education attainment the panel is estimated in 5-year intervals. The simultaneous introduction of country and year-fixed effects appear to wipe out the significance of the coefficient on labor, though the sign remains positive.

[53] I use Clarify to simulate these values. The prediction is that a change in partisanship to the left would cause an increase in the FDI/GDP ratio of 114 percent if we use the mean value of the estimate, or somewhere between 105 percent to 126 percent given the 95 percent confidence interval around this estimate.

gravity model of investment. Preliminary tests using the investment policy orientation index provide partial support for the partisan argument: when in power, pro-labor parties are more likely to adopt policies that favor direct investment inflows. Having found a strong correlation between the left and friendlier investment regimes is worth note, particularly given the low signal to noise ratio. For these reasons, it should be noted that the tests performed do not truly establish causality. Instead, they should be interpreted as observational studies that simply suggest the plausibility of the argument.

Next, I move to a broader sample of countries and years to analyze the correlates of direct investment inflows. The tests suggest that two political conditions are likely to have an effect on the level of FDI flows. The first condition, namely that pro-labor governments are more open to FDI, is consistent with the predictions derived from proposition 2 in Chapter 3. The second condition relates to the institutional constraints hypothesis which returns a positive coefficient when all countries are pooled and in the subsample of emerging markets, but does not stand in the panel of developed countries. This result should not be surprising as these countries tend to be more politically stable and more institutionally constrained. The TSCS tests conducted on the sample of developed countries and the gravity model tests on the sample of developing and emerging countries take advantage of longitudinal variance in the data whereas at the same time both designs control for unit heterogeneity. I find support for the partisan investment hypothesis: in developed and developing countries alike, FDI inflows are larger in countries when a pro-labor party is in power. It is remarkable that the results seem to hold for advanced and developing countries in a similar way. Although these results should not be taken as conclusive evidence, the fact that they capture a direct relationship between the partisan orientation of government and foreign investment using aggregate data, where the ratio of signal to noise is likely to be low, is quite promising.

Moreover, the theory is about the preferences of domestic actors derived from their position in the economy. I use measures of variables that are, but poor proxies do not fully map onto the main concepts in the theory. Preferences and policy outcomes are assumed, whereas influence and several of the relevant political and economic variables are only measured indirectly. Ideology is a coarse measure of the propensity of governments to respond to labor demands on this particular dimension. It places parties on a left-right scale, which usually taps into the party's preferences with respect to the degree of government intervention in the economy or taxation of capital, two variables that at certain values may create a disincentive to invest in the country. It is remarkable, though, that results are found using such a coarse measure to operationalize labor and business influence.

These statistical tests need to be complemented by longitudinal analyses within countries. The within-country studies allow for more disaggregate measures of FDI policy, labor organization, variance in labor market institutions, and labor influence to be employed. All these caveats notwithstanding, the results presented in this chapter suggest that the partisan theory of investment is plausible.

APPENDIX 4.1: DATA SOURCES AND DESCRIPTION

The data employed in the analysis comes from various places. In this Appendix I provide a description of the variables and their corresponding sources. The descriptive statistics for variables used in each test are reproduced here as well.

Dependent Variables

Investment policy orientation index: An index obtained by the two-stage estimation technique discussed in Section 4.2.1. A higher value on this index reflects a more open foreign investment regime. The index is available for twenty-seven OECD countries for the period 1980–2000, in five-year intervals. Countries: Australia, Austria, Belgium, Canada, Denmark, Finland, France, Germany, Greece, Hungary, Iceland, Ireland, Italy, Japan, Korea, Mexico, Netherlands, New Zealand, Norway, Poland, Portugal, Spain, Sweden, Switzerland, Turkey, United Kingdom, and the United States

Investment restrictions index: An index of FDI-specific restrictions, such as limitations on foreign ownership, screening or notification procedures, and management and operational restrictions. Available for the years 1980, 1990, and 2000 for the following countries: Australia, Austria, Belgium, Canada, Denmark, Finland, France, Germany, Greece, Iceland, Ireland, Italy, Japan, Netherlands, New Zealand, Norway, Portugal, Spain, Sweden, Switzerland, Turkey, United Kingdom, and the United States. Source: Golub (2003).

FDI net inflows: Foreign direct investment is net inflows of investment that acquire a lasting management interest (10 percent or more of voting stock) in an enterprise operating in an economy other than that of the investor. It is the sum of equity capital, reinvestment of earnings, other long-term capital, and short-term capital as shown in the balance of payments. This series shows total net, that is, net FDI in the reporting economy less net FDI by the reporting economy. Data are in current U.S. dollars. Source: World Development Indicators (2001).

Foreign Direct Investment: The amount of net direct investment inflows in current U.S. dollars from a home country i to a host country j in year t. The source for this variable is OECD, International Direct Investment Statistics Yearbook (online resource, accessed on: 07/06/05). Data is available for OECD countries for the period 1980–2003.

Log FDI/GDP: Natural log of the ratio of bilateral flows from source country to recipient country to recipient country's GDP. To calculate this variable, I use the value of FDI net outflows from country j to country i. The original Source OECD dataset does not discriminate between missing and 0 values. Where the recipient country is a member of OECD (Ireland, Korea, Mexico, and Turkey), I replace these missing values with FDI net inflows to country i from country j. An analysis of the dataset suggests that for this set of countries it is safe to treat missing values as 0. To allow for a logarithmic transformation of the FDI/GDP values, I arbitrarily add $10 to all observations. Next, I deflated to constant 1996 U.S. dollars. The variable thus obtained, FDI net inflows in constant U.S. dollars, is divided by constant GDP to obtain the FDI/GDP ratio, which is finally converted to its natural log. Source for the original dyadic FDI and exchange rate data is: SourceOECD: International direct investment by country (OECD 2002).

Explanatory Variables

Ideology: The data on political orientation are obtained from the Database of Political Institutions (DPI) (Beck et al., 2000). The authors have created a large cross-country database of political institutions that covers 177 countries over 21 years, 1971–1995. The database lists the political orientation of the chief executive and of the majority party in the legislature as "Left," "Center", or "Right". Alternatively, I use the *Left:* dummy variable that takes the value of 1 if Ideology is "Left" and 0 otherwise.

Center: A dummy variable that takes the value of 1 if Ideology is "Center" and 0 otherwise.

Political Constraints: A proxy for institutional constraints on policy-making (institutional and partisan veto gates).

Left: A dummy variable coded 1 when the party of the chief executive is listed as Left in the Database of Political Institutions (Beck et al., 2000). The ideological position assigned to each country corresponds to the orientation of the chief executive for political systems classified as presidential in the database, and that of the majority or largest government party for systems classified as parliamentary. Source: see Ideology.

Left and Center share of Cabinet: Is the share of cabinet portfolios controlled by the Left or Center parties (Swank 2006).

Controls

Border: Dummy variable that takes a value of 1 if countries share a common border. Source: CIA Factbook.

Common language: Dummy variable that takes a value of 1 if countries speak the same language.

Distance: The direct-line distance in kilometers between the major airports in countries i and j. Source: World Handbook of Political and Social Indicators III (Taylor and Jodice, 1984).

Civil rights: The Freedom House index for civil rights provides a subjective classification of countries on a scale of 1 to 7 on political rights, with higher ratings signifying less freedom. Source: Freedom in the World (Freedom House, 2010).

GDP (current U.S.$): GDP is the sum of gross value added by all resident producers in the economy plus any product taxes and minus any subsidies not included in the value of the products. It is calculated without making deductions for depreciation of fabricated assets or for depletion and degradation of natural resources. Data are in current U.S. dollars. Dollar figures for GDP are converted from domestic currencies using single year official exchange rates. For a few countries where the official exchange rate does not reflect the rate effectively applied to actual foreign exchange transactions, an alternative conversion factor is used. Source: World Development Indicators (World Bank, 2010).

GDP per capita (constant 1995 $): GDP per capita is gross domestic product divided by midyear population. GDP is the sum of gross value added by all resident producers in the economy plus any product taxes and minus any subsidies not included in the value of the products. It is calculated without making deductions for depreciation of fabricated assets or for depletion and degradation of natural resources. Data are in constant U.S. dollars. Source: World Development Indicators (World Bank, 2010).

GDP per capita, PPP (current international $): GDP per capita based on purchasing power parity (PPP). PPP GDP is gross domestic product converted to international dollars using purchasing power parity rates. Source: World Development Indicators (World Bank, 2010).

GDP, PPP (current international $): PPP GDP is gross domestic product converted to international dollars using purchasing power parity rates. An international dollar has the same purchasing power over GDP as the U.S. dollar has in the United States. GDP is the sum of gross value added by all resident producers in the economy plus any product taxes and minus any subsidies not included in the value of the products. It is calculated without making deductions for depreciation of fabricated assets or for depletion and degradation of natural resources. Data are in current international dollars. Source: World Development Indicators (World Bank, 2010).

Government share: Government Share (in %) of real GDP. Source: 6.1 (Heston et al., 2002).

Labor Share: Labor's share of income. This variable is constructed as the economy-wide aggregate measure of sectoral share of labor compensation to sectoral output. Labor Compensation includes all payments made by employers to their employees, in cash and in kind, in the form of salaries and wages, plus contributions to social security, private pensions, and insurance. Source: International Sectoral Database (OECD, 1998b).

Openness: Total trade (exports plus imports) as a percentage of GDP, in constant prices. Openness may affect investors' decision to flow into the host country to jump over trade restrictions to supply local consumers, or cater to foreign consumers using the facility in the host country as an export platform. Source: Heston et al., 2002, 2011; PWT 6.2, PWT 7.0.

Population: Population in the host country, to control for country size. Source: Heston et al., 2002, 2011; PWT 6.2, PWT 7.0.

Real GDP (chain) per worker: The denominator for this variable, worker, is usually a census definition based of economically active population. Source: Heston et al., 2002, 2011; PWT 6.2, PWT 7.0.

Real GDP per capita (chain): A chain index obtained by first applying the component growth rates between each pair of consecutive years, to the current price component shares in the lagged year to obtain the DA growth rate for each year. This DA growth rate for each year t is then applied backward and forward from 1996, and summed to the constant price net foreign balance to obtain the Chain GDP series. Source: Heston et al., 2002, 2011; PWT 6.2, PWT 7.0.

Real GDP per capita (Laspeyres): Obtained by adding up consumption, investment, government and exports, and subtracting imports in any given year. The given year components are obtained by extrapolating the 1996 values in international dollars from the Geary aggregation using national growth rates. It is a fixed base index where the reference year is 1996. Source: Heston et al., 2002, 2011; PWT 6.2, PWT 7.0.

Savings (% of GDP): Gross domestic savings are calculated as GDP less final consumption expenditure (total consumption). Source: World Development Indicators (World Bank, 2010).

Schooling: The average number of schooling years in total population over the age of 25 and over. Source: Barro and Lee, 2001; World Development Indicators (World Bank, 2010).

Real GDP per capita: Gross domestic product divided by total population, proxying for relative endowment of capital. Source: Heston et al., 2002, 2011; PWT 6.2, PWT 7.0.

Real GDP per worker: Gross domestic product divided by total number of workers in the economy (usually a census definition based of economically active population). Source: Heston et al., 2002, 2011; PWT 6.2, PWT 7.0.

Sample for Investment Policy Orientation Index

The index is available for twenty-seven OECD countries for the period 1980–2000, in five-year intervals. *Countries:* Australia, Austria, Belgium, Canada, Denmark, Finland, France, Germany, Greece, Hungary, Iceland, Ireland, Italy, Japan, Korea, Mexico, Netherlands, New Zealand, Norway, Poland, Portugal, Spain, Sweden, Switzerland, Turkey, United Kingdom, and the United States

Samples for GMM Models (1972–2002)

Emerging Economies: Algeria, Argentina, Bolivia, Brazil, Chile, Colombia, Costa Rica, Ecuador, Egypt, El Salvador, Guatemala, Honduras, India, Indonesia, Ireland, Jamaica, Jordan, Kenya, Korea, Madagascar, Malaysia, Mexico, Morocco, Pakistan, Peru, Philippines, Sri Lanka, Thailand, Tunisia, Turkey, Uruguay, and Venezuela.

Developed countries: Australia, Austria, Belgium, Canada, Denmark, Finland, France, Germany, Greece, Ireland, Italy, Japan, Netherlands, New Zealand, Norway, Portugal, Spain, Sweden, Switzerland, the United Kingdom, and the United States.

TSCS Model: Time-Series Cross-Section Panel of Fourteen OECD Countries

Countries: Australia, Belgium, Canada, Denmark, Finland, France, Germany, Italy, Japan, The Netherlands, Norway, Sweden, the United Kingdom, and the United States. Years: 1975–1996.

Gravity Model Sample

Recipient countries: Argentina, Brazil, Chile, China, Colombia, Costa Rica, India, Indonesia, Ireland, Korea, Malaysia, Mexico, Panama, Philippines, Russia, South Africa, Taiwan, Thailand, Turkey, and Venezuela.

Source countries: Australia, Austria, Belgium-Luxembourg, Canada, Denmark, Finland, France, Germany, Greece, Iceland, Ireland, Italy, Japan, Korea, Mexico, Netherlands, New Zealand, Norway, Portugal, Spain, Sweden, Switzerland, Turkey, the United Kingdom, the United States. Years: 1980–2000.

Table 4.6. *Investment policy orientation index – gravity estimates (1980–2005)*

Country	1980	1985	1990	1995	2000
Australia	1.45	1.31	0.54	−0.31	0.11
Austria	−1.10	−1.48	−0.36	−0.36	−1.03
Belgium	1.20	−0.02	1.09	0.67	1.42
Canada	0.38	0.27	0.41	−0.26	0.20
Denmark	−1.04	−1.78	0.07	0.42	0.53
Finland	−0.81	−1.96	−0.70	−0.08	−0.49
France	0.70	−0.59	−0.40	−0.10	−1.16
Germany	−0.02	−1.05	0.21	−0.63	−0.27
Greece	0.63	−0.19	0.98	0.15	−0.92
Hungary		−2.79	−0.29	1.02	−0.61
Iceland		−0.15	−0.38	−0.21	−0.11
Ireland	1.38	−0.54	−1.92	−2.28	0.12
Italy	−0.42	−0.84	−0.65	−2.04	−1.17
Japan	−0.02	−0.56	0.13	−1.52	−1.23
Korea	2.01	0.45	0.22	−0.58	−0.63
Mexico	1.80	2.01	1.20	1.50	−0.34
Netherlands	0.75	0.79	1.62	0.49	0.91
New Zealand	2.04	0.44	1.43	0.91	0.01
Norway	−0.04	0.56	1.03	0.46	−1.29
Poland		−3.91	−2.29	0.91	0.38
Portugal	0.48	0.20	1.17	0.02	−0.10
Spain	0.05	0.03	0.74	−0.24	−0.08
Sweden	0.33	−1.45	−0.52	−0.09	0.40
Switzerland	1.49	0.75	0.88	0.00	0.62
Turkey	0.57	−0.68	−0.25	−0.97	−1.70
United Kingdom	0.92	0.07	1.17	0.08	0.01
United States	0.94	0.71	0.46	0.17	0.41

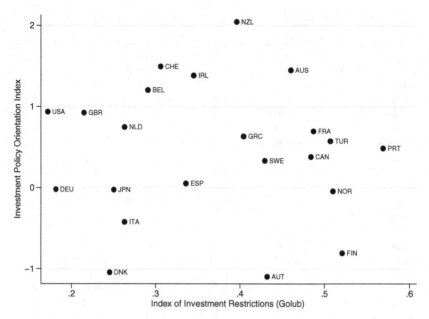

Figure 4.7. Scatter plot investment orientation indices (1980).

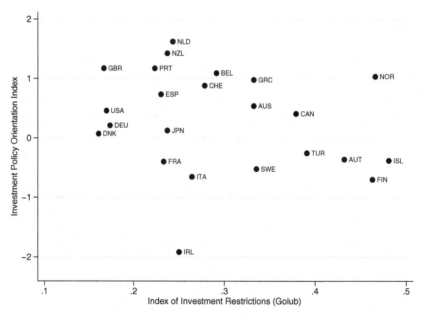

Figure 4.8. Scatter plot investment orientation indices (1990).

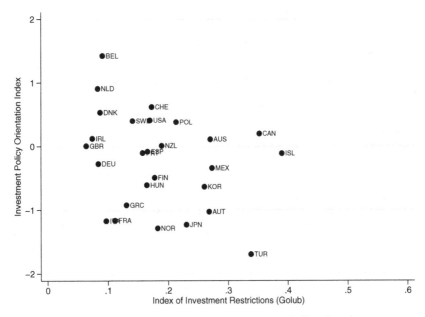

Figure 4.9. Scatter plot investment orientation indices (2000).

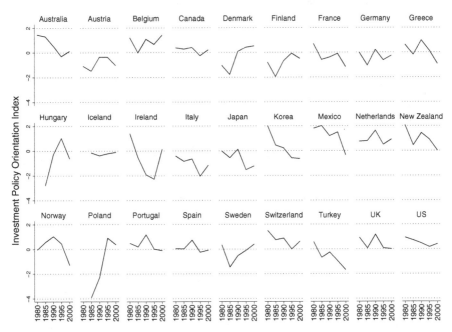

Figure 4.10. Investment policy orientation index by country.

Table 4.7. *Descriptive statistics*

Model 1 in Table 4.3 (1972–2002)

Variable	Unit	Obs	Mean	Std. Dev.	Min	Max
FDI/GDP	%	2267	1.92	3.69	−12.21	92.67
Left	Dummy	2267	0.29	0.45	0	1
Center	Dummy	2267	0.07	0.26	0	1
Political constraints	Index	2267	0.30	0.21	0	0.71
Real GDP/capita	(PPP thousand)	2267	8.30	7.58	0.51	34.36
Trade/GDP	%	2267	63.38	33.81	6.32	368.7
Savings/GDP	%	2267	18.43	10.35	−28.24	80.48
GDP	US$ (Billions)	2267	222	786	0.27	10418
Govt Expt/GDP	%	2267	21.45	8.52	2.46	80.50
Natural resources exports	% Total Exports	2267	22.81	26.77	0	99.78
Political rights	Index	2267	3.25	2.07	1	7

Model 2 in Table 4.3: Emerging markets (1972–2002)

Variable	Unit	Obs	Mean	Std. Dev.	Min	Max
FDI/GDP	%	938	1.45	2.17	−2.76	26.46
Left	Dummy	938	0.23	0.42	0	1
Center	Dummy	938	0.10	0.30	0	1
Political constraints	Index	938	0.28	0.21	0	0.69
Real GDP/capita	(PPP thousand)	938	4.99	3.19	0.73	27.22
Trade/GDP	%	938	57.45	32.05	7.83	220.41
Savings/GDP	%	938	19	9	−20.50	49
GDP	US$ (Billions)	938	69.73	117.97	0.80	871.20
Govt Expt/GDP (%)	%	938	20.19	8.26	9.46	72.43
Natural resources exports	% Total Exports	938	26.32	28.29	0	99
Political rights	Index	938	3.52	1.74	1	7

Model 3 in Table 4.3: OECD sample (1972–2002)

Variable	Unit	Obs	Mean	Std. Dev.	Min	Max
FDI/GDP	%	572	2.14	5.40	−0.66	92.67
Left share of cabinet	Dummy	572	36.57	39.64	0	100.00
Center share of cabinet	Dummy	572	15.05	27.14	0	100.00
Political constraints	Index	572	0.46	0.09	0.15	0.71
Real GDP/capita	(PPP thousand)	572	19570	4848	9175	34365
Savings/GDP	%	572	62.16	30.48	11.83	184.40
Trade/GDP	%	572	22.92	5.33	−8.55	39.55
GDP	US$ (Billions)	572	725.75	1438.77	12.63	10417.60
Govt Expt/GDP	%	572	18.10	3.97	7.67	28.89
Natural resources exports	% Total Exports	572	11.39	13.06	0.93	69.97
Political rights	Index	572	1.05	0.22	1	2

Table 4.8. *Descriptive statistics (cont.)*

Models in Table 4.4: OECD 14 (1975–2000)

Variable	Unit	Obs	Mean	Std. Dev.	Min	Max
FDI Net Inflows	US$ Millions	308	6,348	12,387	−1,038	10,6035
Left	Dummy	308	0.38	0.49	0	1
GDP (PPP)	US$ (Billions)	308	839	1350	27	8,150
GDP per Capita	US$ (1995)	308	23,550	5,841	12,718	43,483
Trade/GDP	%	308	59.06	30.47	15.92	149.41
Savings/GDP	%	293	23.63	4.42	14.84	35.74
Political Constraints	0-1	308	0.49	0.10	0.23	0.74

Models in Table 4.5: Emerging and developing countries (1980–2000)

Variable	Unit	Obs	Mean	Std. Dev.	Min	Max
FDI_{ij}/GDP_i	%	10,066	0.04	0.32	0.00	10.48
Arable Land$_j$	Square km	10,066	163,885	356,790	60	1,769,511
Arable Land$_i$	Square km	10,066	279,692	451,363	2,234	1,615,929
Population$_j$	Thousands	10,066	39,194	53,621	228	275,423
Population$_i$	Thousands	10,066	147,970	295,717	1,950	1,258,821
Real GDP per capita$_j$	Constant prices	10,066	17,737	5,445	4,272	33,293
Real GDP per capita$_i$	Constant prices	10,066	6,484	3,559	1,069	26,381
Distance$_{ij}$	Km	10,066	8,912	3,482	496	19,402
Left$_i$	Dummy	10,066	0.23	0.42	0	1
Average Years of School$_j$	Years	2,380	8.51	2.13	2.80	12.25
Average Years of School$_i$	Years	2,380	5.91	1.86	2.72	10.49

j = Source country; i = Recipient country.

FIVE

Labor and Business Influence, Investment Regimes, and Foreign Investment in Argentina

5.1 Introduction

In previous chapters, I argue that foreign direct investment has differential effects on the demand for workers and business services in recipient countries, and that these distributive motivations are at the core of the politics of regulating FDI. The evidence from cross-national statistical analyses suggest that pro-labor governments, usually those on the left side of the political spectrum, are more likely to regulate inward FDI more favorably, and to consequently receive larger FDI inflows, than are their right-leaning counterparts, who are usually associated with the advancement of the interests of domestic businesses. The policy effect is strongest when a pro-labor government is able to enact the policy preferred by its core constituency, which occurs when the pro-labor government is unconstrained institutionally or politically. In this chapter, I analyze the relationship between constituency links, which can be attributed to partisan alignments, and foreign investment in Argentina in the postwar era.

Argentina's post-war history offers an exceptional background to explore this relationship in more depth. The dramatic movements in the country's governance from democratic to autocratic rule and back has resulted in the alternation of coalitions representing disparate socioeconomic actors in power. The institutional structure provides the permissive environment for the emergence of diverse coalitions of workers, industrialists, agricultural producers, financiers, and consumers. The ascension to power of opposing coalitions, which resulted from electoral turnover or coups is reflected in the diverging foreign economic policies adopted over time. The aim of this chapter is to analyze whether the changing leanings of the ruling coalitions in Argentina can explain the changes in the regulatory environment offered to foreign investors.

Focusing on an individual country over time allows for a richer within-country comparison of the effects of changes in the degree of labor and business influence in politics. Comparing and contrasting Argentina with the South Korean case presented in the following chapter provides a more nuanced understanding of how changes in political institutions affect the degree of workers' and business owners' influence in politics, which in turn can explain changes in FDI policies and outcomes in line with the predictions of the partisan theory of investment.

The evidence presented in this chapter suggests that changes in the political environment in post-war Argentina are indeed associated with changes in foreign investment policy. Changes in the orientation of the incumbent government also seem to have affected the disposition of foreign investors to flow in or out of the country. Movements toward democratic governance are positively correlated with higher FDI inflows, yet the effect is much weaker once the ruling coalition's political leaning is accounted for: after controlling for the determinants of foreign investment identified in the literature, FDI inflows are shown to have been larger under governments that catered to labor interests, and lower when domestic capital owners were more influential.

5.2 Background

For over fifty years since the military coup that overthrew President Hipólito Yrigoyen on September 6, 1930, Argentina has alternated between authoritarian and democratic rule. Political leaders have experimented with development strategies ranging from import substitution industrialization to global integration centered around the country's pattern of comparative advantage. Further, the coalitions ruling the country over time have espoused stances spanning the entire ideological spectrum, from populist to conservative. One peculiarity of the Argentine case is that the different developmental strategies or ideological stances are not the exclusive domain of a particular set of leaders, either autocrats or democrats. Elected conservative leaders, and their autocratic brethren, have adopted import substitution, while others have denounced these policies; some populist leaders have both been the champions of import substitution and government intervention or alternately embraced economic liberalization and orthodox macroeconomic policies as they deemed fit. Yet, irrespective of their choice of developmental strategies and government programs, there is a key feature that differentiates political leaders in post-war Argentina: the changing pattern of political influence by workers, industrialists, and agricultural producers is reflected in the composition of the ruling coalition. While agricultural interests and some industrialists have fared better under military rule, workers' political influence has been strong under democratically elected governments, and has been strongest when the Peronist Party has been in power. As predicted by the partisan theory of investment, the composition and orientation of the ruling coalition can in turn be linked to the different policy regimes adopted vis-à-vis foreign capital.

The analysis begins with the political realignments occurring in the postwar era, which led to Colonel Juan Perón's ascension to power and to the incorporation of organized labor into Argentine politics (Collier and Collier, 1991). The advent of the Peronist movement had a dramatic impact on Argentine politics for years to come, an impact that has been punctuated by the succession of military coups and the reinstatement of democratic rule. In this chapter, I focus on how changing political alignments have affected one particular area of foreign economic policy: the regulation of foreign direct investment.

The evolution of the Argentine economy in the twentieth century, prior to Perón's ascent to power, presents two distinct stages, which have been associated with starkly different patterns of integration with the global economy through commerce and capital flows: first, the outward oriented stage running through the Great Depression and second, the import-substituting stage that followed (Taylor, 1994, 1998a). At the turn of the century and through the first World War, Argentina was fully integrated with global markets through trade. This period has been dubbed the *Belle Époque* or the *agro-exporting* phase of Argentine development (Díaz-Alejandro, 1970; Azpiazu et al., 1986; Taylor, 1994). A large endowment of natural resources and the secure access to foreign markets for Argentine exports steered the country toward specializing in the production of primary products. The strict adherence to the Gold Standard allowed Argentina to enjoy a steady flow of capital from the United Kingdom and mass migration from the Old World. Most of the capital took the form of financial flows, but direct investment also played an important role in sustaining the infrastructure, including railways, ports, and commercial services, that allowed for the steady flow of primary products to Europe (Azpiazu et al., 1986; Taylor, 1994).

The disruptions created by the first Great War followed by the responses to the Great Depression had negative effects on international markets and, subsequently, on Argentina. Trade volumes declined and Argentina's terms of trade took a sharp nosedive while sources of foreign capital began to dry up simultaneously (Taylor, 1994). The interwar period arguably forced

Argentina off of the outward-oriented development path.[1] Limited access to markets for Argentina's primary products and disruptions in the supply of manufacturing imports led to an inward-looking strategy where the scarce resources were funneled into the production of substitutes for Argentina's imports in order to attain self-sufficiency in manufacturing. This new pattern of specialization ultimately changed the politics of economic policy-making in Argentina for years to come. The inward looking strategy of the interwar era was pervasive throughout Latin America (Díaz-Alejandro, 1970; Taylor, 1994, 1998b). Foreign capital inflows remained low throughout the period, partly driven by conditions external to Argentina, but also by policy decisions of the leaders of that time. There was a trickle of direct investment from the United States, which steadily replaced the United Kingdom as the source of capital in the region, into the nascent manufacturing in Argentina (Azpiazu et al., 1986; Twomey, 1998).

By the time that Perón was elected in 1946, the Argentine economy had already undergone close to two decades of an inward-looking development strategy. This strategy created vested interests among the urban producers of import-substituting manufacturers that demanded sustained protection from foreign competition in product and factor markets. A 1943 coup, led by Generals Arturo Rawson, Pedro Ramírez, Edelmiro Farrell, and the United Officers' Group (or GOU, the Spanish acronym for Grupo de Oficiales Unidos), a group of fascist-leaning army commanders that opposed Argentina's involvement in World War II, supported by a coalition of urban industrialists. This coalition had risen to economic power in the shadow of the forced import-substitution era that had resulted from the closure of the economy to foreign manufactured goods during the Great Depression and the sharp drop in world trade during the interwar period. The industrialists were concerned about the rising influence of the provincial aristocracies under the Infamous Decade of Conservative rule, and the impending opening of the Argentine economy. A young and rising army officer named Juan

---

[1] It is worth noting that the period of export-led growth in Argentina, as in the rest of Latin America, occurred under a high level of protectionism, as persuasively shown by Coatsworth and Williamson (2004): "Apparently, the famous export-led growth spurt in Latin America was consistent with extremely high tariffs (even though the region might have done better without them). Latin American tariffs were still the world's highest in the 1920s, although the gap between Latin America and the rest of the world shrunk considerably" (Coatsworth and Williamson, 2004, p. 212). Tariff rates were initially set at the level that would maximize revenue across all sectors of the economy. The introduction of alternative sources of fiscal revenue led to the a new form of protectionism where tariffs and non-tariff barriers were use primarily as a system aimed at protecting import competing interests, which had steadily become vocal politically (Taylor, 1998b; Coatsworth and Williamson, 2004).

Domingo Perón, a prominent figure of this military regime, held appointments as Secretary of Labor under Ramírez, and the Vice-Presidency and Secretary of War under Farrell. Perón played a key role in broadening the support base of the ruling coalitions by a direct appeal to urban workers. Perón's rising popularity among workers and organized labor presented a threat to his military colleagues in government leading to his forced resignation on October 9, 1945, and imprisonment until a massive uprising of workers, culminating in a march to Plaza de Mayo in Buenos Aires, demanding that he be released. The strong bond between Perón and labor was cemented by these events.

In popular accounts Peronism is portrayed as synonymous with anti-business but particularly inimical to foreign investment. During the early years of Perón's first mandate, the government expropriated the railway system, phone companies and other public utilities, and opportunistically seized a handful of firms belonging to German interests. Most historiographical accounts point to these early years as defining the Peronist stance toward foreign investors. Yet, the evidence presented in this chapter, which draws on primary and secondary sources, suggests that the downturn in direct investment flows and the adoption of anti-foreign investment regulations and policies predate Perón (Figure 5.1). Moreover, toward the end of his first Presidency, it was Perón himself who put an end to the wave of nationalization which had been started by the Ramírez-Farrell regime. Under Perón's guidance, the Central Bank adopted the first comprehensive foreign investment regime as early as 1948, which aimed at reassuring investors who planned on entering the country. Immediately after his second term inauguration, Perón sent to Congress the Second Five-Year Plan, which reserved a central role for foreign investment in the manufacturing and oil sectors. The aim of these provisions was to promote the development of domestic production and to reduce the dependence of the country on imports of oil, gas, and intermediate goods, thus saving on hard currency. These provisions were supplemented with a new investment promotion regime that was sent to Congress for approval in 1953. The contentious changes in investment policy resonated in the heated Parliamentary debates of the time where opposition forces challenged Perón's initiatives. I argue that the precursor to the changing attitude toward foreign investors at this time can be found in the steady estrangement between Perón and the industrialists who had been prominent members of the urban coalition that had been Perón's early supporters. Contrary to conventional wisdom, the new investment regime was successful in attracting new investment. After Congress passed the investment statute, investors flocked into the manufacturing sector and into the oil industry.

Under the *Revolución Libertadora*, the military government that overthrew Perón in 1955, the policy toward foreign investors took a restrictive turn and FDI inflows dropped. The change in policy is unsurprising given that the regime found its core support in agricultural producers and other domestic business interests that had been affected under Perón, as well as the middle classes employed in the service sector. The military government also removed Peronist loyalists from the national leadership board of trade unions, confiscated unions' property, and repressed labor activity. FDI resumed during the early years of the reformist administration led by Frondizi to fall again in the 1960s. Though the affiliates of MNCs steadily gained a significant share of economic activity in manufacturing during this period, FDI flows overall were highly volatile for the next two decades. In the 1990s, another Peronist administration with strong support from organized labor, especially in manufacturing, adopted an open regime toward foreign investment. Counter to these trends, the orthodox policies of trade and current account liberalization adopted by Martínez de Hoz during in 1976 failed to lure inflows of FDI. On the contrary, several of the most prominent MNCs left the country in the mid-1970s, which is also predictable based on the constituency of the military in power.

Tables 5.11 and 5.12 present a summary of the main characteristics of the governments ruling Argentina from 1938 to date, as well as their trade and FDI policies in schematic form. As is shown in the ensuing sections, pro-labor governments have on average offered better conditions to foreign investors and have received higher levels of investment flows, a pattern that is consistent with the predictions from the partisan model of investment and that cannot be fully accounted for by alternative explanations.

5.3 Labor Influence and Investment Regimes

In earlier chapters, I argued that the politics of investment is driven by the differential demand for workers and business services created by inward inflows of FDI; I identified the source of this differential demand as the technology that allows foreign investment to either complement or substitute for labor or capital in production. The resulting distributive consequences of foreign investment have the potential to mobilize the actors who are affected by investment flows to demand policies aimed at regulating investment flows and the activity of MNCs. The logic is further developed in Pinto and Pinto (2007, 2008, 2011) and Jensen et al. (2012), where the effects of FDI are allowed to vary across sectors of the economy. It has been shown in the Argentine case, however, that FDI does not create backward linkages in the economy and that it competes with domestic firms for local resources (Chudnovsky and López, 2007). Moreover, inward FDI is on average associated with higher wages, labor costs, and employment, supporting the assumption that as FDI increases labor demand it creates a cleavage between workers who support it and business owners who are opposed. We should thus expect that governments that cater to workers promote inward investment that increases relative labor demand and creates employment, unlike their counterparts, which place a higher value on the support of domestic business owners. As a result, inflows of foreign direct investment are larger under pro-labor governments than under pro-capital governments, all else equal.

These predictions are based on explicit and straightforward assumptions about the effect of direct investment flows on the demand for labor, the constituency links between socio-economic actors and political parties, and the interactions between governments and investors. The main assumption is that when FDI is a complement to labor in production, workers' interests converge with those of foreign investors. The interests of domestic businesses on the impact of the investment regime, on the other hand, are likely to clash with foreign investors' preferences.[2] Even when labor values higher taxes or government spending, the level of taxes offered to foreign investors is lower than when capital owners are more influential on government, even though capital owners, by assumption, do not place any value on the extra revenue obtained from taxing foreign capital. The responsiveness of governments to foreign investors, and the disposition of foreign investors to flow into and to reinvest in the country, are a function of the relative power of labor and of the receptiveness of politicians to labors' demands. This argument runs counter to conventional wisdom and to the traditional predictions proposed by the dependency school.[3]

The results from the statistical analyses presented in Chapter 4 suggest that the partisan investment hypothesis is plausible: movements of government

[2] The underlying condition for this convergence of interests results from the choice of a functional form where labor and capital are complements. We could alternatively look at whether factors are complements or substitutes in different sectors of the economy, and make predictions about the sectoral allocation of FDI under governments of different partisan orientations. The analysis of sectoral data for OECD countries suggests that there are indeed partisan cycles in both the amounts and sectoral allocation of FDI, and that FDI inflows are likely to increase wages, labor costs, and employment, particularly under left-leaning governments. See Pinto and Pinto (2007, 2008, 2011).

[3] See, among others, Evans (1979), Evans and Gereffi (1982), Gereffi (1983).

orientation along the left-right dimension are associated with higher levels of FDI inflows. In that chapter, I proxied government orientation along the pro-business/pro-labor dimension with the partisanship orientation of the chief executive in the sample of host countries.[4] I identified pro-labor with the left and pro-capital with the political right. But the ideological orientation of a government may not capture the relationship of governments to workers and capital owners. In the Argentine case, for instance, the Peronist party has been the party of labor. Equating pro-labor with Peronism should not be controversial because time and again Peronist governments have received the support of labor and Peronist leaders have tended to be closer to organized labor, whereas their military or civilian counterparts, even those that have tried to appease organized labor, have systematically clashed with trade unions. Therefore, we should expect higher levels of foreign direct investment in Argentina when the pro-labor Peronists are in power.[5] In the ensuing sections, I conduct a series of statistical analyses of the amount of FDI inflows under Argentine governments of different orientations and constituency bases. The within-country design allows for a better identification of the different governments along the pro-labor/pro-capital dimension than the left-right variable used in the cross-country analyses.

5.3.1 FDI Performance Under Alternating Coalitions

The difference in performance of pro-labor and pro-capital governments can be seen in a simple comparison of the average level of investment flows under different regimes.[6] The data is presented graphically in Figures 5.1 and 5.2. The first set of statistical tests is performed on data from Argentina broken down into two periods, 1912–75 and 1950–2005, respectively,

---

[4] The ability of the incumbent to enact policies does not depend exclusively on her own preferences, particularly other actors' acquiescence is required to pass policy. In the empirical applications in Chapter 4, I use two different measures of the orientation of the government: first, the cabinet share of the left-leaning party in a subsample of OECD countries, and second, a combination of whether the party of the left controls the executive with a measure of institutional constraints developed by Henisz (2002).

[5] In contrast, in the South Korean case we should expect to find increasing foreign investment inflows when the chaebols lose political clout.

[6] The FDI series for the period 1912–75 were obtained from CEPAL (1986); the data for the 1976–2004 period are from UNCTAD (2010). For data sources and description, see Appendix 5.1.

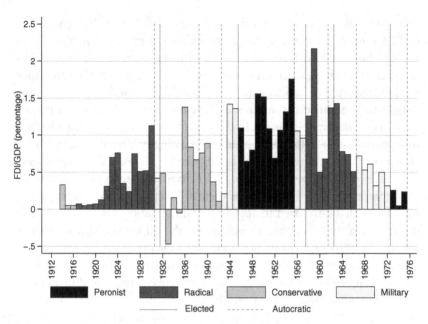

Figure 5.1. Argentina FDI/GDP (1914–75).

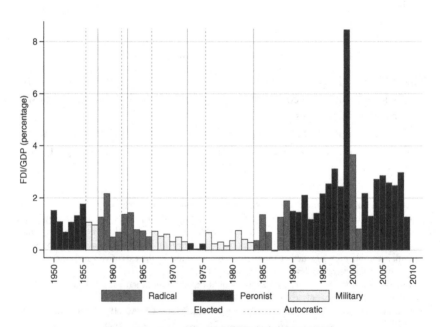

Figure 5.2. Argentina FDI/GDP (%) (1950–2009).

Table 5.1. *Mean FDI/GDP (%) by incumbent (1938–2007)*

Group	Mean	Std. Err.	Obs.
(A) Peronist	1.81 (1.24, 2.39)	0.28	29
(B) Other	0.82 (0.60, 1.03)	0.10	41
(C) Democratic	1.47 (1.10, 1.84)	0.18	51
(D) Military	0.59 (0.41, 0.77)	0.09	19
(E) Other Dem.	1.01 (0.65, 1.37)	0.17	22

Differences in mean FDI/GDP

$Mean_i - Mean_j$	Difference	Std. Err.	$t - stat$, d.f.	p value
(A) – (B) Peronist–Other	1.00 (0.47, 1.53)	0.27	3.73, 68	0.00
(C) – (D) Democ.–Military	0.88 (0.26, 1.49)	0.31	2.86, 68	0.01
(A) – (E) Peronist–Other Dem.	0.80 (0.09, 1.52)	0.36	2.25, 49	0.03
(E) – (D) Other Dem. – Military	0.42 (0.01, 0.83)	0.20	2.09, 39	0.04

95% confidence intervals in parentheses.

to better reflect the differences across incumbents in historical perspective. Table 5.1, which reproduces the results of these tests, shows that there is indeed a systematic difference in the average level of FDI inflows (measured in constant dollars) under pro-labor governments (Juan Perón 1946–55; Héctor Cámpora-Juan Perón-Isabel Perón, 1973–75; Carlos Menem, 1990–98; Eduardo Duhalde, 2002–03; Nestor Kirchner, 2003–2007) than under any other democratic or autocratic governments in this period.

The annual average level of FDI inflows under pro-labor governments is U.S.$4.17 billions (an average 1.81 percent of GDP), whereas under other regimes it is U.S.$1.39 billion (or 0.82 percent of GDP). Figures 5.1 and 5.2 convey this information graphically. The differences are statistically significant as shown by the results of the t-statistics and the confidence intervals reproduced in the tables and in Figure 5.4.[7] There is also a systematic

---

[7] While the results are stronger for the last three decades of the century, where yearly FDI flows represent 2.16 percent of domestic output under Peronist governments compared to

Table 5.2. *Mean FDI/GDP (%) by incumbent (1938–70)*

Group	Mean	Std. Err.	Obs.
(A) Peronist	1.16	0.10	10
	(0.88, 1.43)		
(B) Other	0.84	0.12	23
	(0.64, 1.05)		
(C) Democratic	0.99	0.10	24
	(0.79, 1.2)		
(D) Military	0.80	0.14	9
	(0.47, 1.13)		
(E) Other Dem.	0.87	0.14	14
	(0.57, 1.18)		
	Differences in mean FDI/GDP		
$Mean_i - Mean_j$	Difference	Std. Err.	$t - stat$, d.f.	p value
(A) – (B)	0.31	0.17	1.80, 31	0.08
Peronist–Other	(−0.04, 0.66)			
(C) – (D)	0.19	0.18	1.05, 31	0.33
Democ.–Military	(−0.18, 0.57)			
(A) – (E)	0.28	0.20	1.44, 22	0.16
Peronist–Other Dem.	(−0.12, 0.69)			
(E) – (D)	0.08	0.21	0.36, 21	0.72
Other Dem. – Military	(−0.36, 0.51)			

95% confidence intervals in parentheses.

difference between the annual amount of FDI received under democratic rule: the average is U.S.$3.09 billion (1.47 percent of GDP), compared with U.S.$0.88 billion under military governments (0.59 percent of GDP).[8]

The differences in mean values of FDI inflows under different administrations provide a baseline comparison. While these differences are strong

0.75 percent under other administrations, there are stark differences as well for the earlier period: before 1970, FDI inflows were on average 1.16 percent in years under Peronist administrations, and 0.85 percent under governments of different orientations, democratic and autocratic alike. These differences are statistically significant beyond the 99 percent confidence level. In alternative tests, I have used different transformations of the dependent variable, such as net FDI inflows in levels, natural logs, or as a ratio of world flows, producing identical results. In all cases, the tests show that the means remain statistically different beyond conventional levels of confidence.

[8] Additionally, Figure 5.3 shows that there is a systematic rise in the level of reinvested earnings starting in the early 1950s, an outcome preferred by workers over profit repatriation, as particularly under Perón and Frondizi organized labor became a pivotal political player. Unfortunately, the data on dividends is incomplete and these series are not available for more recent years and thus cannot be used for systematic statistical analysis.

Table 5.3. *Mean FDI/GDP (%) by incumbent (1971–2007)*

Group	Mean	Std. Err.	Obs.
(A) Peronist	2.07 (1.04, 3.10)	0.48	16
(B) Other	0.78 (0.35, 1.21)	0.20	18
(C) Democratic	1.80 (1.07, 2.53)	0.35	24
(D) Military	0.40 (0.27, 0.54)	0.06	10
(E) Other Dem.	1.25 (0.29, 2.21)	0.40	8

	Differences in mean FDI/GDP			
$Mean_i - Mean_j$	Difference	Std. Err.	$t - stat$, d.f.	p value
(A) – (B) Peronist–Other	1.29 (0.27, 2.32)	0.50	2.57, 32	0.02
(C) – (D) Democ.–Military	1.40 (0.27, 2.52)	0.55	2.52, 32	0.02
(A) – (E) Peronist–Other Dem.	0.82 (−0.72, 2.37)	0.75	1.10, 22	0.28
(E) – (D) Other Dem. – Military	0.85 (0.07, 1.62)	0.37	2.32, 16	0.03

95% confidence intervals in parentheses.

and of the expected direction, the absence of controls and other confounders may render these comparisons suspicious. Ideally, governments' ability to attract FDI should be compared once the conditions that affect government-investor interactions have been accounted for; further, those determinants of FDI activity identified in the literature should be controlled for. Economic performance, GDP growth, macroeconomic management, trade liberalization, or simply international capital mobility measured by higher global FDI flows in the 1990s may be driving the apparent difference in performance over the different administrations. I control for those conditions in a multivariate regression setup using time series data.

5.3.2 Regression Analysis

As discussed in Section 4.3.1 in the previous chapter, there is no overwhelming consensus on the factors that should be considered as determinants of

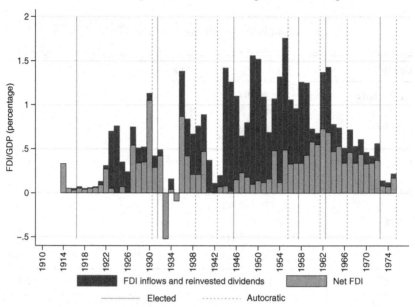

Figure 5.3. Argentina FDI net flows and reinvested dividends (1912–75).

foreign investment in the empirical literature, or even on the direction of the effects attributed to these factors (Chakrabarti, 1997, 2001). In the statistical tests performed in this chapter, I include variables that proxy for the conditions identified in the model presented in Chapter 2, such as government spending, relative endowment of capital (GDP per capita or GDP per worker), trade orientation (openness as a percentage of GDP), domestic savings, and international capital mobility (world FDI flows). At the same time, these variables serve as control for the determinants of FDI that stand out in the literature.[9] One of the central assumptions in the model is that foreign capital is an imperfect substitute for domestic capital. To control for this substitution effect, I add savings in the host country as one of the regressors. To control for market size, I transform the dependent variable, FDI net inflows, into a ratio of GDP.[10] In order to account for the opportunity costs of investing in the host country, I use two different variables:

[9] Other variables used in the empirical literature include competitiveness, domestic investment, growth, government intervention, infrastructure, privatization, and trade balance (Wheeler and Mody, 1992).

[10] Identical results are obtained when using alternative transformations of the dependent variable and when controlling for market size on the right-hand side of the estimating equation. These transformations include using the volume of net inward FDI, in constant dollars, as well as its natural log.

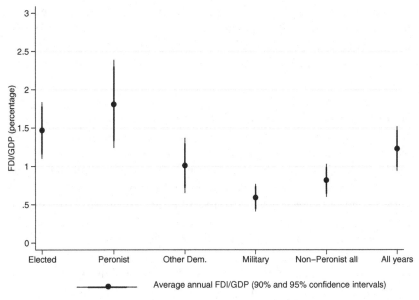

Figure 5.4. Mean FDI/GDP (%) (1938–2007).

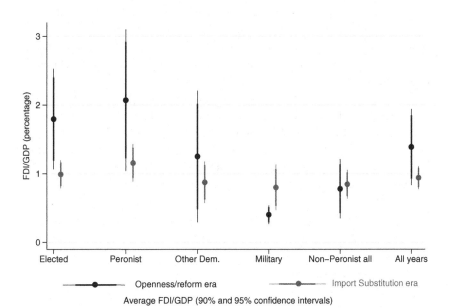

Figure 5.5. Mean FDI/GDP (%) by government.

first, I include the long-term interest rate in the United States and second, the total amount of world direct investment flows. The expected sign for these two variables are opposite: inward FDI should be lower when the cost of capital is higher and should be higher when capital mobility is higher.

Data and Methodology

Due to limited data availability for FDI Net inflows and the relevant covariates, the empirical analysis is limited to a seventy-year span, which is relatively short for time-series analysis. There is an additional methodological problem, which is frequently present when dealing with economic data: the series are likely to be non-stationary. Non-stationarity renders the estimates inefficient and underestimates the standard errors. Diagnostic tests suggest that that we cannot reject the null hypothesis that FDI Net inflows in levels, natural log form, and as a ratio of GDP are indeed non-stationary. There is reason to believe that these series are integrated of the first order: first-differencing the dependent variable makes the series stationary. The control variables also appear to be integrated of the same order. Modeling the dependent and independent variables in differences also makes it more difficult to interpret the substantive effect of the coefficients. Data availability for the independent variables, first differencing variables and introducing lags in the different model specifications further reduces the number of observations available to conduct the tests. Bearing these caveats in mind, I proceed to describe the results, which by no means can be considered conclusive.

In Table 5.4, I reproduce the results of the tests using the first difference of the ratio of FDI to GDP as the dependent variable.[11] Model 1 in Table 5.4 suggests that the ratio of FDI to GDP is positively related to the dummy variable that indicates years under a pro-labor government. The coefficient is statistically different from zero beyond the 95 percent level of confidence.[12] Models 2, 3, and 4 include additional control variables: the first of these

---

[11] Post-diagnostic checks suggest that the relationship is not spurious. Breusch-Godfrey LM tests suggest that there is no residual autocorrelation in all models (Greene, 2003). In alternative specifications, I fit ordinary least squares models with the dependent and control variables entering as first-differences. These results are identical to the the Prais-Winsten correction for autocorrelated errors reported in Tables 5.4 and 5.5.

[12] In alternative specifications not reproduced here but available upon request, I have included a dummy for the two years of the Isabel Perón administration (July 1974 to March 1976). Including this dummy makes the coefficient on Peronist larger and significant beyond the 99 percent level. The coefficient on the Isabel dummy is, on the contrary, always negative while its significance varies according to which variables are included in the different specifications. In the qualitative section, I explain these results.

Table 5.4. *Time series results*

Variables	(1)	(2)	(3)	(4)	(5)	(6)	(7)	(8)
					Dependent variable: ΔFDI/GDP			
FDI/GDP$_{t-1}$	−0.430^c	−0.566^c	−0.515^c	−0.511^c	−0.471^c	−0.497^c	−0.506^c	−0.495^c
	(0.101)	(0.121)	(0.116)	(0.105)	(0.108)	(0.042)	(0.104)	(0.041)
Peronist	0.661^c	0.797^b	0.760^b	1.154^a	1.097^a	1.042^c	1.157^a	1.022^c
	(0.218)	(0.324)	(0.309)	(0.584)	(0.557)	(0.272)	(0.581)	(0.277)
ΔPolitical Constraints		0.145	0.415	−0.428	0.568	−0.412	−0.471	−0.065
		(0.436)	(0.306)	(0.912)	(0.555)	(0.626)	(0.897)	(0.891)
Peronist x ΔPol. Con.			−1.24		−3.107^a		1.157^a	−0.758
			(1.163)		(1.581)		(0.581)	(1.760)
ΔGDP/capita (1,000 constant dollars)		−0.731	−0.668	−0.818	−0.657	−1.217^b	−0.814	−1.163^b
		(0.562)	(0.544)	(0.815)	(0.760)	(0.476)	(0.827)	(0.475)
ΔTrade/GDP (%)		0.019	0.023	0.015	0.035	0.157^c	0.0141	0.158^c
		(0.025)	(0.025)	(0.067)	(0.064)	(0.036)	(0.067)	(0.038)
ΔPublic Spending/GDP (%)		11.25	13.45	8.084	15.31	−18.61^b	7.355	−15.72
		(9.902)	(10.740)	(16.770)	(19.640)	(8.827)	(18.460)	(11.060)
ΔSavings/GDP (%)				−0.042	−0.047	−0.164^c	−0.0403	−0.152^b
				(0.029)	(0.032)	(0.048)	(0.030)	(0.065)
ΔWorld FDI flows (billion dollars)						6.877^c		6.813^c
						(1.343)		(1.314)
ΔUS interest rate								0.0182
								(0.092)
Constant	0.263^c	0.412^c	0.370^c	0.286^b	0.274^b	0.008	0.280^b	0.024
	(0.099)	(0.123)	(0.115)	(0.111)	(0.101)	(0.091)	(0.108)	(0.096)
N	78	69	69	44	44	34	44	34
Years	1930–2007	1936–2004	1936–2004	1961–2004	1961–2004	1971–2004	1961–2004	1971–2004
R^2	0.272	0.405	0.374	0.402	0.386	0.801	0.400	0.803
Adj. R^2	0.253	0.347	0.302	0.285	0.245	0.738	0.262	0.728
DW *stat* (transformed)	2.029	1.952	1.953	1.977	2.034	2.477	1.978	2.462
DW *stat* (original)	2.084	1.941	1.966	2.012	2.077	2.614	2.015	2.593
ρ	−0.142	0.039	−0.0519	−0.0821	−0.204	−0.742	−0.090	−0.744

Prais–Winsten AR(1) regression; semi-robust standard errors in parentheses.

^{a} $p < 0.1$, ^{b} $p < 0.05$, ^{c} $p < 0.01$.

157

controls tries to capture the effect that an increase in international capital mobility may have on the inflows received by Argentina, irrespective of any internal conditions in the country.[13] The coefficient on this variable is positive and significant beyond the 99 percent level of confidence. Another control is trade openness. This variable returns a positive coefficient but is not significant in any specification.

Savings enters negatively into the equation, whereas relative endowment of capital (proxied for by GDP per worker) is also negative. None of these variables, however, are significant at conventional levels of confidence, which is unsurprising based on the limited number of observations available and the short time-series structure of the data.[14] The sign and significance of the pro-labor variable remains robust to changes in model specification.

Next, I include an index of political constraints, a proxy for institutional and partisan veto gates constructed by Henisz (2002).[15] Model 4 also includes an interactive term of this variable with the pro-labor dummy to capture the fact that the strength of the executive is an inverse fraction of how divided government is, or whether the party holding the presidency needs to muster a coalition of votes in the legislature from other parties. When the interactive term is included on the right-hand side of the equation, the pro-labor dummy remains positive. Both the index of political constraints and the interaction between pro-labor orientation of government and political constraints are negative, but neither is significantly different from zero.[16]

These findings suggest that there is a systematic relationship between the years under governments with pro-labor orientation and the inflow of FDI to Argentina.[17] These results seem to support the labor influence

---

[13] I proxy international capital mobility by the total amount of world FDI outflows in that year. The variable World FDI and Ln World FDI appear to be I(1); their first differences are stationary: $Z(t) = -5.358$ and $Z(t) = -4.368$, respectively, with MacKinnon approximate p-value for $Z(t) = 0.00$ in both cases.

[14] The ratio of government consumption to GDP is negative in Model 3, flips sign in Model 4, and does not seem to belong in the model.

[15] As discussed in Chapter 4, Polcon is an index of how constrained the chief executive is in her choice of policies derived from a spatial model of political interactions. It is a measure of the likelihood of policy change given the structure of political institutions (the number of veto points) and the preferences of the actors that hold each of these points (the partisan alignment of various veto points and the heterogeneity or homogeneity of the preferences within each institutional branch).

[16] Similar results are obtained when using the natural log of FDI and Argentina's share of World FDI as the dependent variables.

[17] Tests using quarterly data available for the period 1977–2003 yield similar results (not reproduced here). These results also make apparent that not only did Peronist governments perform better than the military in government, but so did all democratic regimes.

Table 5.5. *Time series results: Import substitution era*

Variables	(9)	(10)	(11)	(12)	(13)	(14)
			Dependent variable: ΔFDI/GDP			
FDI/GDP_{t-1}	-0.828^c	-0.426^c	-0.778^c	-1.135^c	-1.116^c	-0.597^c
	(0.171)	(0.102)	(0.178)	(0.157)	(0.154)	(0.195)
Peronist	0.339^a	0.963^c		0.340		
	(0.174)	(0.349)		(0.213)		
Peron (1946–1951)			0.206		0.123	0.16
			(0.192)		(0.206)	(0.203)
Peron (1952–1955)			0.590^c		0.774^c	0.532^c
			(0.178)		(0.273)	(0.174)
GOU						0.329
						(0.304)
Military not GOU						−0.192
						(0.190)
ΔPolitical Constraints				0.730^a	0.794^a	
				(0.426)	(0.403)	
ΔGDP/capita (1,000 constant dollars)				-0.610^a	-0.692^b	
				(0.320)	(0.292)	
ΔTrade/GDP (%)				0.010	0.011	
				(0.017)	(0.018)	
ΔPublic Spending/GDP (%)				0.676	1.515	
				(4.687)	(4.552)	
Constant	0.621^c	0.168	0.583^c	1.040^c	1.037^c	0.434^b
	(0.170)	(0.136)	(0.172)	(0.212)	(0.215)	(0.169)
N	41	38	41	35	35	41
Variables	1930–70	1970–2007	1930–70	1930–70	1930–70	1930–70
R^2	0.422	0.311	0.42	0.665	0.71	0.389
Adj. R^2	0.391	0.271	0.373	0.593	0.635	0.302
DW *stat* (transformed)	1.925	2.052	1.937	1.687	1.643	1.969
DW *stat* (original)	1.881	2.128	1.895	1.612	1.634	1.982
ρ	0.178	−0.176	0.136	0.39	0.421	−0.0314

Prais-Winsten AR(1) regression; semi-robust standard errors in parentheses.
[a] $p < 0.1$, [b] $p < 0.05$, [c] $p < 0.01$.

hypothesis, but also appear to refute the institutional constraints hypothesis. The negative sign on the proxy for veto gates may indicate that once we control for the partisan orientation of government, political constraints do indeed affect the probability that policy will change. Inflows of FDI are larger in years under pro-labor administrations, but when pro-labor executives are constrained by the presence of multiple veto players, inflows tend to be lower because in order to introduce policy amendments the pro-labor executive needs to obtain the approval of a political actor that may prefer the status quo.

The results are of substantive impact: a movement toward a pro-labor government results in a change of close to one standard deviation of the dependent variable in first difference form. Note that the aggregate level of the data does not allow to fully test the potential of the theory, which as previously developed is more likely be at play at the sectoral level. In Argentina, the change of relative endowment of capital may have a more immediate effect at the industry level. In addition, unions and business associations are organized at the industry level. However, there is no reliable source of sectoral data on foreign direct investment in Argentina that would allow for a comparison of the pre- and post-Menem era.[18] The limited data on sectoral inward FDI available for the period 1991 to 2005 suggests that foreign investment in manufacturing goes up under Peronist leaders, yet there is also evidence of sizable variance even among Peronist administrations with the Carlos Menem's and Nestor Kirchner's administrations receiving higher investment than Eduardo Duhalde's (see Figure 5.7 and Tables 5.7 and 5.8). These results are far from conclusive because there is only one non-Peronist administration, the short-lived reign of the Alianza under Fernando de la Rúa, and the period includes the economic collapse of 2001 to 2003, which affected all economic activity. Yet note that under Duhalde the drop in the ratio of FDI to aggregate output is not consistent across sectors.

5.4 Labor Influence in Argentina

The statistical tests discussed in the previous section cover over five decades of the country's history. Much like other forms of capital flows, the larger amount of inflows received by Argentina throughout the period under

---

[18]   The government agency in charge of collecting this data, Dirección Nacional de Cuentas Internacionales, only holds data for the 1992–2002. Argentine experts on multinational corporations and foreign investment have indicated that the archival data on FDI for previous years has been destroyed. Interview with Daniel Azpiazu, FLACSO Argentina, August 13, 2005.

analysis could be attributed to either push or pull factors (Calvo et al., 1993; Fernández-Arias, 1996). The main push factor leading to higher inflows is the increase in international capital mobility that resulted from changes in the strategies of MNCs and in the liberalization of trade and investment regimes.[19] The data suggests that the presence of MNCs in manufacturing has increased since the 1950s, but dramatically picked up in the 1980s (see Figure 5.7). Toward the end of the century, we also observe increasing MNC activity in other sectors, including finance, utilities, and mining. To the naked eye, the pattern of FDI flows has been highly volatile throughout the period. This volatility can be partly explained by external factors and by economic activity in Argentina. The drop in FDI in the interwar era could be attributed to the closing of the trading system and the war effort, as much as it could result from the subsidence of the developmental model based on agricultural exports. The volatility observed in the 1980s, predating and post-dating the debt crisis, could be explained by external factors, such as international interest rates and liquidity, and domestic factors, such as social unrest, economic and political instability, and successive attempts to reform Argentina's economy. Pull factors that could have led to higher levels of inflows in the 1990s include structural reforms, including the privatization of utilities and SOEs; price and exchange rate stability, and the balancing of fiscal accounts, increasing the creditworthiness of the Argentine government; trade liberalization, regional integration, and the formation of MERCOSUR; and an overall improvement in economic performance. However, the time-series statistical analysis suggests that, once we account for the determinants of FDI, the political orientation of the incumbent has played an important role: throughout the post-war era, we observe that FDI tends to be higher when the Peronist Party held power; and the Peronist Party is, with no doubt, the party of organized labor in Argentina.

It could be argued that it was not labor support that brought about the dramatic increase in foreign investment, but instead Menem's embrace of orthodox economic policies, an alleged departure from the stance traditionally associated with the Peronist party. In this section, I try to show that there is no such departure: once we account for changes in the external

---

[19] A fall in interest rates in capital exporting countries may "push" capital to emerging markets; "pull" factors are associated with domestic developments in the recipient economies, in which case larger inflows would be associated with changes in the macroeconomic performance and creditworthiness of the recipient economy. In the extant literature on international capital flows whether pull factors dominate push factors or conversely whether international factors dominate is contested.

and domestic conditions that the Peronist leaders have had to confront, we find a remarkable similarity in the policies adopted by Perón in the 1950s, Menem in the 1990s, and the Kirchners in the 2000s. Both Menem's close relationship to the Confederación General del Trabajo (CGT) and organized labor and Perón's relationship to industrialists in his earlier years in office have been understated in extant accounts of Argentina's political economy in the postwar era. I also show that these constituency links played a key role in the regulation of FDI, confirming that the pattern that arises from the statistical analyses is not just happenstance.

There are alternative explanations to the trend in FDI inflows observed in this period. One explanation is completely unrelated to politics and domestic coalitions: ISI and the nature of economic performance should have created a disincentive to invest in the country. Post-war economic performance in Argentina was characterized by stop-go cycles. Under a strategy of import substitution industrialization, the economic authorities had to balance the demands from the agricultural exporting sector, and the import-competing manufacturing sector. Leaders would usually yield to the needs of the latter, because they were a more politically influential cluster. A combination of poorly designed policy programs that comprised tariffs and tax incentives, differential exchange rates, price freezes, and financial repression created allocation mechanisms divorced from price incentives (Taylor, 1998a).[20]

The import competing sector was dependent on intermediate inputs and capital goods that could only be procured overseas. Increasing domestic demand for agricultural products from a burgeoning urban population, disincentives to invest and produce in the exporting sector because of to policy discrimination against agriculture, and declining international prices for the country's exports led to cyclical foreign exchange crises. The corrective package adopted by different administrations always included a devaluation of the peso to correct for the distortions in relative prices in order to boost exports and to discourage imports. Devaluations, however, usually exacerbate inflationary pressures and the orthodox policies enacted to tame this inflation have recessive consequences on output and ultimately affect

---

[20] According to Taylor, this phenomenon, which persisted until the aftermath of the debt crisis, was not privy to Argentina: "only recently have economic reforms began to undo the price distortions that have been built into the Latin American economies since the generalized interwar autarky and specific policy reactions of the 1930s. Prior to those reforms the region remained unattractive to foreign investors not only because of its low levels of technology (low productivity) but also because unfortunate price twists lowered the realizable rate of return on capital" (Taylor, 2003, p. 28).

income distribution. Cycles of expansion and contraction of the economy and price distortions created by the ISI strategy deter all forms of investment. As FDI is particularly elastic to these disincentives, it becomes volatile and would increase rapidly when the economic authority tried to correct these distortions. If this argument were correct, we should expect FDI to be at its lowest level under Perón, particularly during his first term in office. Perón's bouts of expropriation of the railway system and other public utilities, his lackluster record in managing the economy and his attachment to organized labor should have deterred rather than encouraged inward investment flows. In reality, investment activity picked up under Perón.[21]

A second alternative explanation would expect a negative correlation between FDI inflows and labor influence. The surge in flows in the 1990s could be explained by Menem's ability to weaken unions. A first look at union density data seems to support this argument (see Table 5.6), yet in the 1990s and even after the 2001 crisis foreign investment flowed into the formal sector where unions remained strong, remarkably so when compared to other countries.

In sum, it is true that poorly designed policy instruments and recurring economic crises throughout the post-war era might have affected the incentives to invest in Argentina. Still, different governments adopted distinctively divergent combinations of policy instruments to fight macroeconomic instability and declining economic performance.[22] In some instances, these packages included built-in incentives to lure FDI into the country, whereas in other instances investors were purposefully left out. In the end it becomes apparent that that politics has played an important role in determining the level of foreign investment received. It is indeed likely that the adoption of unsustainable policies and poor management of macroeconomic aggregates could discourage investment. However, it should be no surprise that the level of inward investment flows would peak under pro-labor governments that enact sound monetary, exchange rate and fiscal policies. In the Southern Cone, there are a number of examples that seem to corroborate this pattern, including Brazil under the PT, Chile under the Concertación, and Uruguay under the Frente Amplio. In the following sections, I produce further evidence to support the predictions from the model and hypotheses derived from it. I review patterns of labor influence in Argentine politics

---

[21] One feature that remains constant across Peronist leaders is their strong link to organized labor. See Table 5.11 for a classification of the different governments according to their support base, ideology, and form of access to power.

[22] See Ardanaz et al. (2010) on the effect of distributive conflict on pro-cyclical spending.

and map these patterns onto changes in the regulation of foreign direct investment.

5.4.1 Labor Organization and Influence

A series of social, cultural, political, and economic conditions have made Argentina a propitious environment for the emergence of a strong labor movement.[23] In the post-war era, unionization in Argentina has been among the highest across developing countries and compares to the rates found in industrialized societies.[24] Reforms to labor market statutes introduced by Perón in the late 1940s that strengthened the position of organized labor in the marketplace helped shape one of the strongest labor movements in Latin America (Collier and Collier, 1991).[25] These institutions outlived Perón and made labor one of the central actors in Argentine politics for years to come. Organized labor has since become a central political force to be reckoned.[26] Blue-collar workers have maintained their loyalty to unions and to the Peronist party. Governments with weak links to organized labor have either attempted to appease unions, whereas others, particularly autocratic rulers, have resorted to sheer repression of workers and their representatives. Under non-Peronist democratic governments, including those led by Arturo Frondizi, Arturo Illia, Raúl Alfonsín, and Fernando de la Rúa, the CGT leadership faced internal pressure from the rank-and-file, and they have usually responded by militant behavior against the government, forcing their internal opposition to take a stance. Military regimes have been

---

[23] Among these conditions, we find a high rate of urbanization; immigration from industrial nations in the late 19th and early 20th centuries; a large internal market; a relatively small and highly skilled labor force; and the virtual absence of surplus labor (Ranis, 1994).

[24] See Table 5.6. In the early 1990s, close to 50 percent of Argentine workers were unionized. Within the industrial sector the figure reached 65 percent of the workers (ILO, 1997; Ranis, 1994).

[25] In the 1946–1954 period, union membership in Argentina increased roughly sixfold, from 500,000 to 3,000,000 workers.

[26] During his first years in office, Perón succeeded in placing the union movement under government control using tactics such as political favoritism, bribery and the imprisonment of union leaders that opposed government initiatives. Jose L. Figuerola, one of Perón's closest aides who had a central position in drafting the five-year plan, labor reforms and other initiatives aimed at holding sway over the labor movement, had helped Primo Rivera gain control over unions in Spain. In terms of ideology, the Argentine labor movement under Perón has been characterized as fascist. Latin America labor unions had opposed to the Argentine unions' participation in ILO conferences until September 1946 (29th Conference), when they decided to court them. The pro-Perón Confederacion General del Trabajo (CGT) has systematically clashed with the continental labor organization (ORIT) affiliated with the International Confederation of Free Trade Unions. Perón created his own Latin American grouping of unions (ATLAS) to oppose ORIT.

Table 5.6. *Union density (1985–2007)*

Country	Union membership as a percentage of:						
	Non-agricultural workers		Wage and salary earners			Formal sector	
	1985	1995	1985	1995	2000s	1995	2000s
Argentina	48.7	25.4	67.4	38.7	37.6[c]	65.6	–
Bolivia	–	16.4	–	–	–	59.7	–
Brazil	–	32.1	–	43.5	20.9[d]	66.0	27.9[a]
Chile	11.6	15.9	–	–	11.5[d]	33.0	11.0[d]
Colombia	11.2	7.0	–	–	28.7[c]	17.0	–
Costa Rica	22.9	13.1	29.1	16.6	9.5[b]	27.3	13.9[b]
Dominican Rep.	18.9	17.3	–	–	–	–	–
Ecuador	–	9.8	–	–	–	22.4	–
Paraguay	–	9.3	–	–	–	50.1	–
Peru	–	7.5	–	–	–	18.3	–
Canada	31.2	31.0	36.7	37.4	31.4[d]	–	29.7[d]
Mexico	54.1	31.0	59.6	42.8	16.8[d]	72.9	–
United States	15.0	12.7	18.0	14.2	11.4[d]	–	12.1[d]
Uruguay	19.9	11.6	–	–	19.0[c]	20.2	–
Venezuela	25.9	14.9	29.8	17.1	–	32.6	–
Americas (Average)	23.0	15.9	39.7	35.4	40.4	–	–
Asia (Average)	22.0	16.6	27.7	19.5	–	–	–
Africa (Average)	24.2	14.0	30.2	32.8	–	–	–
Europe (Average)	53.4	41.3	58.1	47.0	–	–	–

Source: International Labour Office (1997, 2011); Johnson (2004); Lawrence and Ishikawa (2005); Hayter and Valentina (2008); OECD.stat.
[a] Value is for 2001.
[b] Value is for 2004.
[c] Value is for 2006.
[d] Value is for 2007.

blatantly anti-labor.[27] Under the 1976–83 regime, for instance, direct repression and disappearance of labor activists had an obvious effect on union activity, which remained low until late 1981.

The consolidation of democratic rule in last two decades of the 20th century brought about changes in union behavior. In the past, union militancy against weak democratic governments at times paved the way for military intervention or led to an authoritarian regime with the decisive support

---

[27] The Onganiato is a special case and is discussed in more detail in the section titled MNC activity under Organia.

from organized labor, as in the case of the fall of Illia in 1966. During Alfonsín's 1983–89 tenure, organized labor played multiple roles, blocking the government's agenda early on, later participating in the Cabinet, and undermining the government's ability to adopt a program of economic reform. Yet, unions seemed to be more conscientious about the need to strike a balance between opposing government policies to advance the Peronist partisan agenda without debilitating democratic life. In the years of structural reform under Menem, unions were forced to go beyond income redistribution and pursued a broader range of policy issues, such as investment policies, restructuring of the state, and even union leaders' personal and political agendas.[28] Resorting to general strikes and belligerency became ineffectual in pursuit of those objectives. The evolution of the statutes regulating union activity is quite informative of the position of the different administrations toward labor.

The internal organization of trade unions and their activity in Argentina is regulated under the Professional Associations Act (*Ley de Asociaciones Profesionales* or LAP). The first LAP was passed in 1945 during Perón's tenure in the Ministry of Labor and Social Welfare.[29] The exclusive right to represent workers granted to the government-recognized unions and their right to bargain collectively were instituted on October 1953 (Ley 14,250 de Convenciones Colectivas de Trabajo).[30] Collective bargaining was suspended not only under military regimes but under democratic governments as well.[31] The legal framework was formally revised on four occasions, none of which have had a substantial effect on the overall makeup of the system.[32]

---

[28] On union behavior at times of structural adjustment, see (Murillo, 2001).

[29] Decreto-Ley 23,852, October 2, 1945.

[30] Similar rights were granted to employer associations. These associations were regulated by the Ley 14295 de Asociones Profesionales de Empleadores (Employers' Associations Act), passed in 1953. This regime was abrogated in 1955, and there has been no attempt at regulating the organization of employers' associations since.

[31] During Perón's second government, a social pact suspended collective bargaining until 1975; under Alfonsín collective bargaining was banned until 1988 because it would disrupt the Plan Austral (stabilization plan passed in 1985), at which point it was formally reinstated under a new regulatory regime (Ley 23,545 de Convenciones Colectivas de Trabajo).

[32] The first reform took place in 1958 under Frondizi (Ley 14,455, August 8, 1958), basically reinstating the provisions of the 1945 law, which had been suspended by the military regime of 1955 to 1958. The next reform to the system came under Perón in 1973 (Ley 20,615, November 20, 1973), followed by the 1979 reform by the military junta (Ley 22,105, November 15, 1979). The last reform, resulting from a compromise between the Radical President and a Peronist in Congress, came under Alfonsín in 1988 (Ley 23,551, March 3, 1988). See Fernández Madrid and Caubet (1994), Brumat Decker (2001), Vázquez Vialard (1981), Krotoschin (1972), and Krotoschin and Ratti (1983).

However, the direction of the amendments of labor union regulations at the margins may indicate labor's relative political strength and influence.

Appendix 5.2 presents a simple comparison of the main provisions of the different Acts.[33] This comparison shows that the original regime and the amendments introduced by Perón in 1973 have tended to strengthen unions vis-à-vis employers and the position of union leaders over rank and file workers. Frondizi yielded to labor demands, in fulfillment of an agreement with Perón that brought him into office, but was troubled by the overwhelming political clout of union leaders and their limited account- ability to workers. All democratic Presidents not elected under the Peronist Party ticket shared this concern. Frondizi restored the 1945 LAP regime that had been suspended by the Revolución Libertadora, but introduced sev- eral amendments that have been less favorable to union leaders. The 1958 LAP reduced their term of appointment, promoted electoral competition within unions, sanctioned the right of rank-and-file workers to call for a congress, and amended the system of grievances upon which the contract of a union leader could be terminated. But all these amendments were sug- arcoated with a major concession that Frondizi made to labor: the creation of the welfare fund system (obras sociales).[34] The 1979 LAP sanctioned by the military government removed these contributions from union control, following the practice started by the 1966–73 authoritarian regime.

Alfonsín adopted a confrontational stance towards the Peronist unions: he believed that in a democratic society it was political parties, not interest groups, that should be responsible for political intermediation. Soon after his inauguration in 1983, Alfonsín tried to get Congress approval of a new LAP regime aimed at decentralizing union power, known as the *Ley Mucci* after Alfonsín's first Minister of Labor Affairs. The main objective of this regime was to democratize unions and to force their atomization in order to reduce their influence in politics. Ultimately, the Mucci initiative was stalled in Congress by the opposition. But the relationship between Alfonsín and organized labor never healed despite his conciliatory moves in successive years, which even led to the appointment of Carlos Alderete, a prominent union leader, to the Ministry of Labor Affairs in 1987. In 1988, the Alfonsín administration caved to union pressure and Congress passed a new LAP,

---

[33] The table was constructed by the author using data from Ranis (1994) as well as the original statutes.

[34] The 1958 LAP which mandated employer contributions to fund welfare and retirement pro- grams; these earmarked funds were managed by the government-accredited union in each sector.

which was identical in substance to the 1973 legislation.[35] Under this statute, unions regained the monopoly of representation of workers in their sector and control of social welfare organizations, but were deprived of the right of collective bargaining on wage related issues, particularly during the years of the Plan Austral, which froze prices and wages to control inflation.

Another indication of the link between the party in office and interest groups is the fate of legislation aimed at reforming labor contracts. Wage bargaining in Argentina is conducted at the industry level, with low levels of coordination when compared to other countries with similar labor market institutions. In the early 1990s, roughly 40 percent of Argentine workers belonged to a labor union and close to 90 percent of workers were covered by an industry-wide union negotiated agreements signed over two decades earlier, given that from 1976 through 1988 collective bargaining was outlawed for various reasons. These labor market institutions have been criticized by businesses for allegedly stifling job creation, and created a wedge between those employed, who are represented by unions, and the unemployed, who had no functional representation.[36] Organized labor's political influence during the Menem administration is undoubtedly reflected in its ability to block labor reform (Etchemendy and Palermo, 1998; Etchemendy, 2001). Menem's reluctance to force these reforms through legislative decree powers, which he used (and probably abused) in other policy areas, further shows labor's influence.

A partial reform of labor market institutions was finally passed in 1995 amidst a recessionary economy facing the spillover effects of the Tequila crisis.[37] But in 1998, the government, with the conspicuous support of labor, backpedaled, eliminating the temporary and fixed term contracts as well as several of the limited reforms introduced earlier.[38] It is noteworthy

---

[35] The 1988 reform decreed that the government would grant this right to a union only if at least 20 percent of the workers in the sector favored collective bargaining. Delegate lists needed support by 3 percent of the union's members to be acknowledged by the Ministry of Labor.

[36] In the late 1990s, the unemployed organized politically, forming groups that blocked public roads and highways to demand unemployment insurance, government subsidies, and access to government social programs. They came to be known as the *piqueteros* and their protest played a major role in the fall of de la Rúa.

[37] Congress passed a labor reform act, which had been negotiated by the recently appointed Minister of Labor Armando Mera Figueroa on behalf of the administration, the UIA in representation of business groups and organized labor, represented by the CGT. Yet two years after this piece of legislation was passed, introducing more flexible labor contract conditions, 46 percent of the labor agreements in force had been signed before 1975 (Etchemendy, 2001).

[38] Major changes to labor market institutions were introduced under the de la Rúa administration as part of the notorious Labor Reform Act of 2000. This legislation eliminated the ultra-activity clause of labor agreements, under which the conditions negotiated in a pre-existing agreement

that while organized labor at the national level lobbied Menem and Congress to keep the labor reform legislation from passing, unions in different sectors negotiated flexible conditions to encourage foreign investment.

In conclusion, the analysis of the changes introduced to the legislation that regulates labor unions and labor market institutions in Argentina suggests that "Peronist-sponsored governments tended to be most generous in their defense of trade unions' organizational and bargaining strengths vis-à-vis employers" (Ranis, 1994, p. 45). Therefore, it is fairly uncontroversial to classify the Peronist as the party of labor.

5.4.2 Labor Influence and Foreign Direct Investment

Governments' reliance on the support from labor or business described in the previous sections could be mapped onto investment policies and investment outcomes in the postwar era. Table 6.5 in the Appendix presents a summary of the different statutes that have regulated foreign investment in Argentina since 1946. While some of these statutes seem to have had a direct impact on the amount of foreign investment received by the country following their issuance, others were inconsequential. There are two reasons why we find this dissimilar effect of the regulatory environment on investment outcomes: the first reason, which will become apparent in the following section, is that all of these statutes have delegated the authority to decide which investors will receive preferential treatment and which type of investment are promoted or restricted to a government agency. The choice to delegate this authority is political and more often than not these agencies are permeable to the pressure of interest groups and lobbies. Second, there are multiple other policy instruments that affect the decision of potential foreign investors to enter or not, as well as what form of entry to take. It is the combination of these multiple policy instruments determine how friendly or hostile the investment climate is to foreign investors.

---

become the reversionary point. It also reduced labor taxes, instituted a longer probation period, and made labor contracts more flexible. This was presented to the public as a major piece of legislation, a stepping stone for the de la Rúa administration upon which the government would claim that it was capable of advancing a reform package that Menem had failed to deliver. However, the legislative process that led to the passage of this law was smeared with accusations that the government had bribed Senators to change their vote. The labor reform act became de la Rúa's worst nightmare: the allegations of corruption led to the disintegration of the coalition of parties that had brought him to power to eliminate the corruptive practices that were rampant under Menem. Vice-President Carlos Alvarez resigned in disapproval of the events.

5.4.3 The Advent of Peronism and Organized Labor

Until the onset of military mobilization and war in Europe, Argentina enjoyed a privileged relation with the United Kingdom. Britain was Argentina's main trading partner and source of capital. Foreign investment from the United Kingdom took the form of financial loans to the Argentinian government and private sector, and the investment regime was designed to support the export of primary products. The privileged economic relationship between the two countries came to an official end in 1947, the year when the British Parliament declared that the government would no longer honor the convertibility of the sterling pound. Though the declaration of inconvertibility of the pound was the final nail in the coffin, the relationship had been steadily deteriorating during the previous two decades.

The Great Depression had a huge impact on global demand and forced countries to become more inward looking. Gloomy economic conditions in the United States and Europe in the 1930s resulted in trade restrictions and dried up foreign financial capital sources available to developing countries. The Smoot-Hawley Act in the United States and the preference system the British Commonwealth adopted at the Ottawa Convention in 1932 negatively affected Argentina's trade. The Argentine government adopted a series of reactive economic policies, including the institution of capital controls and multiple exchange regimes, as did many other governments in Latin America and elsewhere.[39] The Argentine government at the time represented a conservative coalition of the landed elite comprised of exporters of high quality chilled-beef, represented by the Sociedad Rural Argentina (SRA), and a burgeoning industrial bourgeoisie, represented by the Union Industrial Argentina (UIA). The rural elite of beef exporters that had been a prominent component of the military regime that toppled Hipólito Yrigoyen in 1930. Having secured access to the British market under the 1933 Roca-Runciman agreement, the ruralists tolerated a limited form of industrialization through import substitution and selective government intervention in order to preserve the level of economic activity enjoyed by the country in the pre-depression era. Substituting for imports was virtually a necessity at a time when global trade had been restricted as a consequence of the protectionist stance adopted by the global power houses in North America and Europe. The other sector of lower quality

---

[39] Capital controls were used extensively between 1931 and 1936, an era of Conservative rule in Argentina.

meat producers, who had been left out of the trade agreement with the United Kingdom, promoted free trade. They lined up with the opposition led by the deposed Radical party (Halperín Donghi, 1964, 1980; Murmis and Portantiero, 1971).

Argentina was among a handful of countries that did not default in the 1930s, behavior that was duly rewarded by international financial markets. However, policy innovations introduced to address the drop in aggregate demand brought about by the the Great Depression became the orthodoxy in Argentina, and in Latin America, for years to come. Economic dirigisme and the promotion of a larger role for the public sector became the dominant developmental strategy in the region (Taylor, 2003). The result was a high black market premium, distortions in relative capital prices, and periodic depreciation of the exchange rate in response to competitive pressures. These distortions explain the low investment rates in Argentina, as in the rest of Latin America, that led to slow economic growth (Taylor, 1998a). The sharp fall in foreign investment inflows follows naturally. While in the pre-war era foreign capital filled the gap between domestic savings and investment, the artificially higher costs of capital depressed the demand for investment in these countries, reducing the need to borrow abroad.[40]

The onset of World War II and the imposition of restrictions on exports of military technology to Argentina by the U.S. government increased the interest of the military in domestic industrialization. In the wake of the military coup of 1943, the coalition of beef exporters and industrialists that had ruled since the deposition of Yrigoyen started to crumble.[41] What had been conceived of by the elites as an effort to industrialize the country as a response to the external crisis eventually backfired. Industrialization brought forth a class that would become highly influential in Argentine politics: organized labor (Escudé, 1983, 1988; Waisman, 1987; Collier and Collier, 1991). From his position in the Secretary of Labor, Juan Domingo Perón made a clear effort at incorporating this rising social actor into Argentine politics; yet Perón conceived incorporating labor in a coalition with urban capital.[42]

---

[40] Taylor (1994) argues that two conditions led to these inter-generational transfers from the core to the New World: immigration and frontier expansion; see Taylor and Williamson (1997) and Taylor (2003).

[41] On the evolution of political coalitions in Argentina in the post-war era, see Waisman (1987).

[42] In 1945, before being elected to the Presidency, Perón promised industrialists that he would preserve import substitution as the central developmental strategy of the government; one key component of this strategy was wooing workers to join the coalition with urban business interests. The losing side of the Union Democrática ticket received support from an ideologically

Perón is traditionally depicted as a hardcore nationalist and a populist with a penchant for anti-business discourse. At first sight, Perón's first government should be a "hard case" for the partisan investment hypothesis. The nationalization of railways, electricity and telecommunications during his first years in office is a central precedent in traditional historiographic accounts. Yet, on closer inspection, Perón's stance towards foreign direct investment seems to fit the theory about the link between labor support and foreign investment. The data suggests that the decline in foreign investment attributed to Perón clearly precedes his election to office. The ruling coalition under the Ramírez-Farrell regime was built around industrial interests; Perón's role within that regime was to tame a radical unionism dominated by anarchist and socialist leaders. He managed to muster the support of workers, whose votes became critical in the 1946 polls that brought Perón to power. Perón found workers and organized labor to be a formidable resource, and as economic and social policies slowly but steadily shifted in their preferred direction, so did the foreign investment regime. Perón's initial stance towards foreign capital is reflected in his October 21, 1946, speech before Congress introducing his Five-year Plan (Plan Quinquenal), a body of legislative initiatives aimed at regulating economic activity in the country. According to Perón, (international) financial capital is an instrument of exploitation. Productive (patrimonial) capital, on the other hand, could be an instrument of national well-being. To the extent that it is tolerated, foreign capital should take a subsidiary role to domestic capital.[43]

Yet, the Peronist administration paid lip service to industrialists by revoking the subsidiary status of foreign investment to local capital in its investment promotion regimes. As early as 1948, the Peronist administration adopted a series of Central Bank resolutions that had a clear intent of promoting inward flows of FDI despite regulating the amount of dividends that could be repatriated. The combination of the promotion of inward flows and restrictions on dividend repatriation is optimal for workers. The efficacy of the regime in attracting investors is reflected in the reversal of the earlier trend of divestment, as new investment began to flow into the manufacturing sector, as well as in the sharp increase in the amount of reinvested dividends (Figure 5.3). Even before the turn of the decade the urban coalition

diverse spectrum of interests ranging from landowners, stock-breeders, and the upper classes close to Jose Tamborini, former Interior Minister of President Marcelo T. de Alvear, on the right, to the Communist and Socialist parties on the political left.

[43] La Nación, October 22, 1946, cover and page 6: "El Jefe de Estado expuso ayer el Plan Quinquenal. En la Cámara de Diputados y ante crecida concurrencia se desarrolló la exposición."

of industrialists and workers that brought Perón to office started to show signs of estrangement. Perón reformed the foreign investment regime in 1952, formally putting an end to the wave of nationalization started by the previous military regime. The explanation of this reversal is probably found in the fact that Perón's support base changed over time. The coalition that voted Perón into office in 1952 for a second term represented two different regionally based constituencies: In rural and peripheral areas Perón's party incorporated conservative leaders and his appeal was broader, or populist in Mora y Araujo's words (Mora y Araujo, 1980). In central and urban areas his appeal was class-based. By 1954 Perón came to represent labor almost exclusively.[44] After his re-election in 1952, opposition to Perón came from the Catholic Church, probably a strawman hand-picked by the leader himself to divert attention from excruciating economic hardship, as well as from a fraction of the armed forces, intellectuals, and university students. By the end of his term, disparate groups of nationalists and capitalists, including businessmen, bankers, and landowners, joined the ranks of the opposition. At this time, Perón turned away from capital to openly favor labor.[45] Unionized workers and the *descamisados* were the only groups that remained loyal to Perón until his fall in September 1955.[46]

5.4.4 Foreign Investment Regimes in Argentina

Perón's First Presidency
In 1948, an executive decree (3347/48) signed by Perón established a regulatory framework for foreign investment and created a government agency,

---

[44] On the debate about the origins and support base of the Peronist party see, Mora y Araujo (1980), Smith (1980), Llorente (1980), Germani (1980), Halperín Donghi (1980), and Kenworthy (1980).

[45] In 1955, the Confederación General Económica (CGE), an association of businessmen created by Perón to counterbalance the influence of the Union Industrial Argentina (UIA), made a final attempt to bring the multi-class coalition back together by summoning a Productivity Congress. This came at a time when, according to Torre (1974), foreign exchange shortages affected domestic businesses such that they could no longer import the supplies and raw materials needed to keep their factories running. Torre (1974) reports that business leaders, in both the UIA and the CGE, opposed several policy initiatives adopted by the government to overcome the crisis. Among these initiatives were the negotiation of oil contracts, the establishment of Kaiser in Cordoba, the change in domestic prices in favor of agriculture, the application of anti-inflationary policies and the government's disposition to respond to the demands of international credit institutions (Torre, 1974). These tensions are reflected in the Congressional debates on the passage of the legislation adopting Perón's second Five-year Plan in 1952 and in the debates on the adoption of the foreign investment statute in 1953.

[46] To curb the imminent threat from disgruntled army officials, in a massive rally held on August 31, 1955, Perón publicly threatened to arm the *descamisados* in defense of his government.

the Comisión Nacional de Radicación de Industrias (CNRI), to oversee foreign investment initiatives. The regime, and consequently the agency, would promote the selective location of foreign investment projects, especially in the manufacturing sector.

In 1951, Perón unveiled a new plan for the economy. One of the key elements of this plan was the deepening import substitution and the encouragement of export promotion by courting foreign investors. By 1953, the government had already realized the importance of creating an environment conducive to better investment conditions that would boost economic performance (Altamir et al., 1967). For the first time in Argentine history, the government adopted a comprehensive regime that would unambiguously regulate and promote foreign investment. The regime, established by Congress under Law 14,222, created a National Registry of Foreign Investment (*Registro Nacional de Inversiones Extranjeras*) and granted certain privileges in the form of tax breaks and preferential access to foreign exchange to foreign investment projects that received government approval, but limited annual remittances to an 8 percent of the total amount invested in the country (Altamir et al., 1967). These restrictions on dividend remittances are in line with the level of dividends paid at the time and even more permissive than the prevailing provisions in other countries in Latin America and even Europe. The motivation for the new investment regime was to increase employment in manufacturing, reduce the pressure on the hard currency reserves created by the import of foreign oil, capital and intermediate goods needed to sustain import substitution.

Concurrently with the adoption of a regime to promote foreign investment, Perón's government decided to place higher controls on imports by domestic companies and threatened to expropriate their equipment, machinery, and intermediate goods. This anti-business rhetoric by Perón, who had earlier nationalized public utilities and built a reputation for lack of restraint vis-à-vis the private sector, would make the prospect of investing in Argentina hardly appealing at all. Yet, foreign investment position in the country remained stable throughout his tenure, and by 1953 there was a net inflow of FDI, reversing the negative trend of disinvestment and expropriations that had characterized the previous two decades: After 1934, net flows of investment had been negative following a wave of nationalizations, but by the early 1950s inflows turned positive again, rising to U.S.$58 million in 1953 (Altamir et al., 1967). Tables 5.1 and 5.2 and Figures 5.1 to 5.3 reflect this pattern. Moreover, note that the decrease in foreign capital stock between 1945 and 1949 corresponds to the amounts paid by the Argentine government for the formerly British owned railways, a solution for which the British had been lobbying since the early 1940s.[47] All other forms of investment in the country increased during this period.[48] The end result was a return of foreign investment into manufacturing and, particularly, the oil industry, which would help save foreign exchange and improve the government's fiscal position. As reflected in Figure 5.3, returns to foreign investors increased dramatically, yet investors opted to reinvest their dividends in Argentina, a result that the government sought in designing the investment regime.

Ensuing Perón's fall, the political arena became unstable and fluid. In the absence of any form of institutionalized political intermediation, interest groups used all of the resources at their disposal in their quest for political influence. During a quarter of a century of import substitution industrialization, economic groups became more heterogeneous and so did their interests. An emerging industrialist class fought for political influence with the landed elite. And even within the industrialists, the wedge between big and small business widened. Industrialists, both big and small, as well as agricultural producers had to face a new political actor, which Perón helped take a prominent role in the political scene: organized labor. Coalitions became transient and the content of economic policies varied dramatically as political leaders, authoritarian, and democratic alike, searched for support in their quest for survival.

Foreign Investment Under the Revolución Libertadora

Despite the overall liberal outlook of the economic program adopted during the 1955–58 tenure of the Revolución Libertadora, there was little prospect that the government could induce foreign investment due to the regime's support base. The government appointed Raul Prebisch as its main economic advisor. Prebisch designed an economic program that would reduce trade deficit by promoting traditional exports. The currency was devalued and the multiple exchange rate system eliminated: the official rates for one U.S. dollar went from $5, $7.5, and $15 to a single value of $18, and the market rate reached $36. The government reduced barriers to

---

[47] It is worth noting that when seizing foreign assets, Perón made use of the expropriation provisions in the Argentine Constitution. In most cases, he made sure that the settlement was equitable, and in many circumstances, such as for railways, telephone and shipping interests, the outcome was overtly favorable to the previous owners of the expropriated assets. Expropriation of assets that belonged to German nationals after the late declaration of war with the Axis was an exception. These expropriations are probably better characterized as targets of opportunity.

[48] See Altamir et al. (1967).

trade and eliminated capital controls. The Central Bank was given independence. In 1956, the country joined the Bretton Woods institutions and soon after that successfully renegotiated the country's foreign debt with the Western European economies. Trade liberalization had a negative impact on the manufacturing sector, which was not competitive by international standards.[49] Devaluation had an impact on domestic prices, affecting the real income of wage earners in particular. The program resulted in transfers that contrasted sharply to those under Perón: from the city to the countryside and from labor to capital (Rapoport, 2000). The government removed union leaders from office and banned all forms of union activity. In September 1956, a series of strikes brought economic activity to a virtual standstill. These outbursts of union militancy were brutally repressed. Despite labor repression, the liberal outlook of the economic program, and the repeal of the restrictions to repatriate capital and dividends, the government of the Revolución Libertadora failed to attract foreign capital (Rapoport, 2000). Several of the policies adopted by the government signaled the regime's negative disposition toward foreign investors: not only did the government annul oil contracts and stall the negotiations with oil producers initiated by Perón, but it also modified the investment statue issued by Perón in 1953. The new conditions established by a 1955 Central Bank resolution required that new investment projects obtain government approval. Among the conditions for approval investors had to persuade the government that their project did not hurt domestic businesses, that it would be established in "convenient" locations, that the project would reduce foreign exchange and increase exports, and it was compatible with the government's developmental priorities. The vagueness of the powers granted to the regulatory authority ultimately restricted the inflow of investment capital, resulting in approximately U.S.$17 million for the period.[50] A Cabinet crisis in March 1958, two months before the inauguration of President elect Arturo Frondizi (elections were held in Februay 23, 1958), may reflect the government's position regarding foreign investment: Julio Cesar Cueto Rúa, Minister of Industry and Commerce in Aramburu's Cabinet, made public an initiative to allow foreign investment in the oil industry, which was forbidden by legislation of the time. The debate led to the resignation of the Minister of the Interior, Carlos Alconada Aramburu, and the Minister of Education,

---

[49] One of the sectors where the impacts was very stark was the auto industry: car imports doubled between 1955 and 1957, while the import of auto parts and chassis increased three-fold and eight-fold, respectively (Rapoport, 2000).

[50] In 1957, the auto manufacturer Kaiser Industries Corp launched production in Córdoba under conditions negotiated with the previous administration.

Acdeel Salas, both figures affiliated with Balbín's Unión Cívica Radical del Pueblo (UCRP), which lost to Frondizi in the presidential elections.

Frondizi and Developmental Capitalism

Arturo Frondizi took office on May 1, 1958, and due to the proscription of the Peronist Party, his Unión Cívica Radical Intransigente (UCRI) party was able to control both houses of Congress. Frondizi, a leader of the Radical Party, was one of the most prominent nationalists in Argentine politics before taking office. He had fervently opposed Perón's opening to foreign capital in the mid-1950s. The Radical Party formally split in 1957 along the lines of its main factions: the left-leaning element of the party led by Frondizi clashed with party leader Balbín over support for the Revolución Libertadora.[51] Frondizi and his followers left the party and founded the UCRI.[52] The differences between the two groups deepened with Frondizi's about face when he took office. The new party soon reversed the policy position that had led Frondizi to vehemently oppose Perón's opening to foreign capital in 1952.[53]

From his exile in Venezuela, Perón asked his followers to support Frondizi's bid for the Presidency; allegedly the two leaders signed a secret agreement that would grant Frondizi the votes of the core Peronist constituency, organized labor, in exchange for a package of measures related to labor market regulations, normalization of unions and several economic initiatives. Soon after his inauguration, Frondizi began to fulfill his side of the bargain:

---

[51] The excuse for the split was the call for a congress to reform the Constitution in 1957 under the military government, which the Frondizi-led faction opposed. But as much as this division was based on their different attitude toward the military regime, Balbín and Frondizi disagreed over Perón and his economic program.

[52] ArturoFrondizi recruited Rogelio Frigerio, a businessman and editor of *Qué*, an influential magazine founded by Frigerio to propagate his desarrollista (developmentalist) program. Frondizi also joined forces with a group of intellectuals from the left, including socialists, such as Marcos Merchensky and Bruno Strobino, Juan José Real and his communist followers, Arturo Jauretche and Raul Scalabrini Ortiz, from FORJA, Isidro Odena and Ramon Prieto, formerly Peronists, and a group of nationalists imbued with the Catholic Church's values such as Oscar Camilion and Arnaldo Musich (Rapoport, 2000).

[53] The change has been explained by Frondizi himself in the following terms: "Se dice que la política petrolera del presidente era todo lo contrario de lo que había sostenido el ciudadano Frondizi en su libro *Petróleo y Política*. Me complace recoger este cargo. No vacilo en reconocer que la doctrina de dicho libro no corresponde enteramente a la política practicada por mi gobierno." Arturo Frondizi, public address of February 15, 1962 (Clarín, February 16, 1962). *It has been said that the policy for the oil sector of the President was the opposite to that which Frondizi upheld as a citizen in his book* Oil and Politics. *I am pleased to respond to this charge. I do not hesitate in acknowledging that the doctrine in the book does not exactly correspond to the one enacted by my government.* (Author's translation.)

on August 8, 1958, the Senate gave final approval to a law initiated by the President to regulate the activity of labor unions (LAP), which Frondizi soon signed. The new regime reinstated Peronist loyalists, who had been banned from participating in union elections by the military government of Aramburu and Lonardi, at the head of the CGT, restored the monopoly of representation to a single union per sector certified by the Ministry of Labor, and returned union assets and facilities seized in 1955 by the Revolución Libertadora. The union certified by the Labor Ministry would also control the union members' compulsory dues collected by employers.

There is a link between Frondizi's policy toward foreign investment and his quest to secure labor's support.[54] Campaigning for the Presidency in 1958, Frondizi affirmed that the main hindrance to Argentina's development was its dependence on the export of agricultural products at a time when agriculture faced ever declining international prices, leading to a systematic decline in the country's terms of trade. The previous attempts at industrial development under ISI failed because of its emphasis on light industry, which strained the country's external balance. Therefore, the desarrollistas (or developmentalists) promoted the development of basic sectors such as oil and energy, steel, chemicals, machinery, mechanics, transportation, and automobiles. The success of the developmentalist program purportedly depended on the government's ability to channel investment toward priority sectors. Frondizi and his allies believed that there were two alternative ways of setting the country on a developmental path: either by encouraging the development and consolidation of domestic capital or by promoting the inflow of foreign investment. The latter option was considered preferable to the former because it was deemed to have a less negative effect on income distribution and would expose the country to new technologies needed to break the development gap (Rapoport, 2000). As a result, Frondizi's economic program combined ISI with the selective opening to foreign direct investment in these sectors.

In order to attract foreign investment, Frondizi proposed a major overhaul of the country's investment regime. The key legislation was the foreign investment act of 1958 (Ley 14,780 de Inversiones Extranjeras), which established that foreign capital should play a subsidiary role to domestic business while simultaneously granting national treatment to foreign investors. This legislation was complemented by a series of subsidies and policies aimed at promoting industrial and regional development, an investment insurance

---

[54] Frigerio, a key advisor to Frondizi on economic and labor issues, was both a decisive figure in preparing the program to attract foreign investment and Frondizi's liaison with the Peronist labor unions.

mechanism, tariff exemptions for the import of capital goods, and selective trade protection.[55] Investment licenses were granted by the Executive branch on a selective basis, following the recommendation of the Advisory Commission on Foreign Investment created by executive decree in 1958.[56] Domestic industrialists opposed the selective incentives provided to foreign businesses because they would result in higher competition in product and factor markets. Moreover, conservative and nationalist elements in Argentine politics vehemently denounced Frondizi's oil program for exposing the country to foreign dominance of a critical resource.

FDI resumed its pre-coup trend during the first half of Frondizi's tenure, flowing largely into manufacturing and concentrating in a handful of sectors: chemicals and petrochemicals, autos, and auto parts, and steel and machinery received 90 percent of the inflows (Azpiazu, 1995). Frondizi hoped that foreign investment would result in higher levels of economic activity and employment that would help him court Perón and obtain the support of the Peronists. Organized labor did not reciprocate the UCRI's effort at courting workers as the union's willingness to cooperate soon dwindled was replaced with a combative stance. Frondizi was closely checked by the Armed Forces, who would ultimately force him to revise his economic plan.

In mid-1959, the administration faced an economic crisis which further eroded the administration's support. While domestic businessmen neither trusted the President nor shared his views, they found that the Conservative Party, which began reorganizing at the national level, better represented them. Peronist union leaders fought back to regain control of the country's politics and felt betrayed by Frondizi who, responding to pressure from the military, kept the party outlawed, violating the pre-electoral agreement that had brought Frondizi to power. Perón revealed the 1958 secret agreement with Frondizi and ordered union leaders to cease any form of collaboration with the government. By that time, Congress had voted to remove Cordoba governor Alfredo Zanichelli in June 1960 amidst allegations that he was overprotective of terrorists in order to gain support of Peronist leaders. It was clear that the Frondizi administration had become fully accountable to the military.

Illia's Repeal of Oil Contracts

Frondizi was forced to resign in March 28, 1962. Jose Maria Guido became interim President and called for elections, which were held in July of 1963.

---

[55] See ECLAC and UNCTAD (2002).
[56] Decreto 1594/58.

As the Peronist party was proscribed, it could not participate in the elections. Arturo Illia, representing the Union Cívica Radical del Pueblo (UCRP), obtained 25 percent of the votes, a sufficient amount for election in the Electoral College. He was inaugurated on October 12, 1963.[57] Illia adopted a stance that was clearly opposed to foreign investors as he annulled the oil contracts signed by Frondizi, adopted restrictive rules for licensing investors and imposed foreign currency controls. But policy was not the only determinant of the low levels of FDI inflows in the Illia administration. The position of the radical government matched that of the party's support base, comprising middle class workers and white-collar professionals who appeared to systematically despise all things foreign in general and foreign investment in particular. Why this group would hate foreign investment is a puzzle for any theory that is based on the material preferences of socio-economic actors. Economic conditions also served to lower investment inflows: the excess demand that had drawn FDI in under Frondizi had virtually disappeared by the time that the MNCs's subsidiaries reached full production capacity.

MNC Activity Under Onganía

At first sight, the Onganiato – the military regime led by General Juan Carlos Onganía – appears to disprove the partisan theory of investment, as it was a conservative regime supported by domestic capital that received larger inflows than did its democratic predecessor.

On closer scrutiny, however, we find that the junta's erratic relationship with labor might have played a role in shaping both the conditions offered to investors and investors' behavior. Unions had played a major role in debilitating Illia, welcomed the military coup, and thrown their support behind Onganía. The appointment of Adalbert Krieger Vasena to the Ministry of Finance in December 1966 deepened the pre-existing rift between two groups within organized labor. In 1957, a group of sixty-two unions that remained loyal to Perón united as the "62 organizaciones Peronistas" in order to coordinate their political activity. The group, however, split in 1966 into the "62 Organizaciones de pie junto a Perón," led by José Alonso, and the "62 organizaciones leales a Perón," headed by Augusto Vandor. In 1968, organized labor split along the lines of this schism. One group aligned behind Vandor, a neo-Peronist leader and the head of the UOM (Union of Steel Industry Workers) who had political ambitions of

---

[57] In the 1963 election, 22 percent of blank votes were cast in protest for the proscription of the Solano Lima-Berni ticket, which had been supported by Perón from the exile.

his own. The other founded the combative CGT de los Argentinos.[58] The Vandor group adopted a conciliatory approach toward Onganía and his economic policies. The Ministry of Finance, headed by Adalbert Krieger Vasena, adopted a series of economic measures to control inflation, which included a sharp devaluation of the currency (the peso lost 40 percent of its value), reduction of public employment, abrogation of labor contract conditions agreed upon under collective bargaining, and salary and price freezes. The freezes were unevenly applied, however: while wages were frozen at their pre-crisis levels, prices were adjusted upwards before the freeze. Any form of protest was harshly repressed. Under Krieger, Vasena macroeconomic conditions improved and so did the investment climate. By 1968, the economy was operating at close to full capacity and after a drastic fall in wages in the prior two years, real salaries recovered. Catering to public sector contractors, the government adopted a massive public works program.

FDI inflows were larger under Onganía's tenure than under Illia's; yet as a percentage of output, the level of FDI activity was on par with or even lower than it was under Illia (Figure 5.2). Incumbent domestic firms opposed these inflows, as did foreign firms whose projects were financed by inflows that had taken place under Frondizi and were already up and running. During yet another economic crisis that forced Onganía to revise his economic program, the more combative group of organized labor, the CGT de los Argentinos headed by Raimundo Ongaro, gained a more prominent political role. In May 1969, university students and workers converged in a massive protest in Cordoba, which was brutally repressed by the military. This protest, which came to be known as the Cordobazo, soon became a symbol of the combative faction of the labor movement. The group adopted a hostile rhetoric and attitude toward foreign investors at a time when Argentine public opinion was particularly sensitized to the issue because of the negative publicity associated with several instances of abuse by MNEs, particularly the fraudulent bankruptcy of Swift and the government's response to factory occupancies of auto assembly lines in Cordoba (Lewis, 1992; McGuire, 1997; Guillen, 2000). Ongania was deposed on July 8, 1970, amidst widespread violence to be succeeded by Roberto M. Levingston.

---

[58] Augusto Vandor, leader of the UOM, was the most prominent representative of a group of Peronist union leaders who decided to part ways with their leader in exile. The group took political initiative in their own hands, following a strategy that came to be known as "Peronism without Perón." The CGT formally split after its general congress elected Raimundo Ongaro as Secretary General in 1968. Ongaro became the head of the CGT de los Argentinos.

Levingston appointed Aldo Ferrer to the Ministry of Finance, and adopted a more nationalist economic policy. This administration restricted the conditions for investing in Argentina: foreign investors were encouraged to establish joint-ventures with domestic capital, were only able to buy non-voting shares in national companies, and were given limited access to credit. In due course, licenses were granted by executive decree, which determined the amounts of and conditions for profit and capital repatriation. Prior to obtaining an investment license, projects had to be approved by a government office. Levingston's tenure was short lived: in March 1971, he was replaced by another military leader, General Alejandro A. Lanusse, who oversaw the transition to democracy.

Cámpora and the Tumultuous Second Perón Presidency

The 1973–6 Peronist government is a fairly atypical case. Perón could not participate in the March 11, 1973, presidential elections, as Lanusse had set a residency requirement for candidates, which Perón did not satisfy due to his eighteen years in exile. The Peronist ticket Cámpora-Solano Lima handily won the election. After Cámpora's inauguration, Perón returned to Argentina. Political pressure mounted, ultimately forcing Cámpora to resign in June 1973. Raul Lastiri, Speaker of the House of Representatives and Cámpora's son-in-law, became interim President and oversaw the September 23, 1973, elections. The elections were won in a landslide by the ticket led by Juan Perón and his wife, Isable Martínez de Perón. Returning to power in 1973, Perón sought to represent a broader political coalition than both the one he had helped to build in 1946 and the one that supported him at the time he was overthrown by the Revolución Libertadora. Perón appointed Jose Ber Gelbard as his Minister of Finance. Gelbard was a businessman and former chairperson of the CGE during Perón's previous government. Forsaking the anti-establishment, populist and nationalistic stance he had held in the mid-1940s, Perón adopted a more conciliatory position aimed at consolidating a moderate form of welfare capitalism with greater union participation. The key instrument of the new economic policy was a broad social contract (*Gran Paritaria Nacional*) between government, business, and labor.[59] The CGT and other Peronist leaders successfully removed the

---

[59] The ambivalent position toward foreign investment adopted by Perón in 1973 is evident in his effort to appeal to labor and business. His discourse to the National Congress of the Peronist Party held on May 24, 1974, is more than eloquent: "... hay algunos que quieren expulsar a todas las compañías que hasta ahora han sido multinacionales. Mientras tanto, en otro sector vecino se sostiene que no hacemos inversiones y que los extranjeros no invierten aquí. Entonces, pregunto: a cuál de estos dos les hacemos caso? Creo que a ninguno de los dos, máxime que en

leftist factions that supported Cámpora from government. These groups, however, failed to stay together after Perón's death. The coalition eventually collapsed from within amidst escalating political violence in an institutional environment characterized by a lack of political leadership.[60]

During Cámpora's administration, the nationalist left's influence had a marked effect on vast sectors of the labor movement; unions' demands became more political and symbolic, and less related to conditions in the marketplace. In only one year under Cámpora and Perón, wages recovered and industrial employment grew by 10 percent (Ranis, 1994). Under the Isabel Perón, who took power after her husband's death in July 1974, the social pact agreed upon under Perón fell apart. Unions became more militant as a reaction the government's determination to contain inflation at the expense of wages. The government devalued the currency in June 1975, leading to a sharp outburst of inflation marked by a staggering 350 percent increase of the consumer price index that year. Soon after, the government announced that collective bargaining, which was to resume by mid-1975, was suspended until further notice. On July 7 and 8, 1975, the CGT called a general strike, the first one against a Peronist government. This is a remarkable event: "For the first time in over thirty years of Peronist history, labor was pitted against Peronist political leadership" (Ranis, 1994, p. 35).

In 1973, Congress passed a new foreign investment statute and adopted measures that discriminated against firms where foreign investors held a controlling interest (above 50 percent of the firm's shares), by limiting their access to industrial promotion regimes. FDI subsequently fell slightly in 1974 and remained low throughout the period. This result cannot be wholly attributed to the change in policy as MNCs at the time were adopting new strategies in response to the uncertainty created by the oil crisis and as the

---

lo que se refiere a esas compaías extranjeras, nosotros tenemos el poder de decisión. Vale decir, si ellas están de acuerdo con las leyes que ya se han dictado, deben hacer lo que decimos nosotros. Para ello, no necesitamos expropiarías ni echarlas del país, en virtud de que constituyen factores de desarrollo indispensables. Los que quieren inversionistas de este tipo, ya no tienen lugar en nuestro país porque ahora los que invertimos somos nosotros. Y si algunos extranjeros quieren invertir, ellos serán bienvenidos siempre que obedezcan las disposiciones que nosotros tomemos respecto a su producción." *There are people who would like to drive multinational firms out of the country. Others claim that we should not expect foreigners to invest here if we ourselves are not willing to do it. Then, I ask myself, whom should we listen to? I think we should listen to none, especially regarding foreign companies, where we have the power to decide. That is, they should do what we tell them to do if they are willing to comply with domestic regulations. And because they are essential to our development, we need not expropriate their assets or force them out of the country. And if some foreign investors would like to invest (in our country), they will be welcome as long as they obey the resolutions regarding their production.* (Author's translation.)

[60] See Di Tella (1983), Godio (1981), and Ranis (1994).

contemporaneous domestic environment was characterized by political and economic instability. The restrictions imposed on foreign investment are probably also the result of a nationalist reaction against the growing role of MNCs in manufacturing at the expense of domestic business and the willingness of multinationals to take advantage of their market power.

Cámpora's and Perón's presidencies were short lived. Cámpora's support came from the left-wing base in the Peronist party, formed mostly by intellectuals and university activists who had become militantly belligerent while fighting the repression of the previous military regime. As soon as Perón placed foot on Argentine soil, however, Cámpora was forced to step down. Perón proved ready to distance himself from the left and tried to reconstitute the old urban coalition. He raised export taxes, imports tariffs, and wages and increased employment, especially in the public sector. These policies in combination with increased government intervention in the economy distorted prices and once again created strong incentives for consumption at the expense of savings and investment (Taylor, 1998b). After Perón's death, the administration led by his wife Isabel shifted policies and demanded more sacrifices from labor (wage controls were reinstated) while courting capital (Monteon, 1987). Yet, Isabel Perón could hardly control the government: her right-wing lieutenant José López Rega, who was appointed to the Ministry of Welfare, was the one in charge. The year and a half under Isabel was a period characterized by economic chaos, political and social unrest, resulting in high level of labor conflict and all-out violence between the left and right wings of the Peronist party. FDI was one among the many victims of these tumultuous times.

Open Borders Under the Juntas

Under the guidance of a Chicago-trained group of economists and lawyers led by José Alfredo, Martinez de Hoz as Minister of Finance came to power. Martinez de Hoz had extensive links with Argentina's business elite: he was a member of a wealthy landowning family and had held positions in business and government. The economic program of the military government aimed at controlling inflation and restructuring the Argentine economy in favor of the most internationally competitive business groups. To that end, the government reformed the financial sector, reduced tariffs, and eliminated subsidies.[61] They did not, however, privatize public utilities or state owned enterprises, which became an important political resource used

---

[61] Key elements of the price strategy included restricting the money supply, liberalizing trade, and adjusting wages below inflation levels. Between 1976–8 export taxes were cut, for example

to benefit domestic business groups. The program had a drastic effect on the manufacturing sector, reducing output and employment. The adoption of this program was possible due to the overt repression of labor and of other groups that might resist the loss of jobs and wage declines caused by trade liberalization. To ease balance of payments constraints, the government relied heavily on foreign borrowing (Haslam, 2002).

At first glance, the investment regime adopted in 1976 looks liberal and permissive. The final version of the foreign investment statute (*Ley de Inversiones Extranjeras No. 21,382*) passed by the Military Junta in 1976, however, was more restrictive than the original version prepared by the Ministry of Finance under the supervision of Minister José Alfredo Martínez de Hoz. In practice, the government created an agency that had the discretionary power to approve which projects would be admitted and granted preferential treatment. Few of the foreign investment projects approved under this regime received investment promotion benefits. The government relied little on foreign direct investment. In fact, the program led to the departure of several of the most emblematic MNCs of the ISI era: General Motors, Citroen, Fiat, and Renault are prominent examples. The decision to leave the country made economic sense for these MNCs, as trade liberalization made it easier to supply the Argentine market from abroad. Additionally, though foreign investors were not discriminated against on paper, they were in practice. As a result, the main beneficiaries of the investment promotion regime were domestic business groups (Azpiazu and Basualdo, 1989). Moreover, the combination of liberalized trade and the new foreign investment regimes forced some MNCs to associate with domestic firms under non-competitive terms, just like in South Korea in the 1980s, as discussed in the next chapter.

Foreign Investment Under Democratic Rule

The defeat in the Malvinas/Falkland war and poor economic conditions accelerated the fall of the military regime. The military left the nascent democratic regime an overwhelming legacy: the country was in deep recession, inflation was rampant at over 400 percent, unemployment was rising, the Central Bank had no reserves left in its coffers, and the external debt accounted for 70 percent of the domestic product and five times the amount

---

from 64 percent to 13 percent on wheat and from 36 percent to 22 percent on meat. Further, manufacturing import tariffs fell 40 percentage points on average, from 90 percent to 50 percent (Kosacoff, 1993).

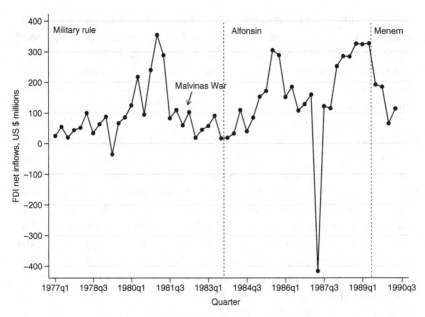

Figure 5.6. Net FDI inflows, quarterly (1977–89).

of the country's exports (Rapoport, 2000). The Alfonsín government, inaugurated on December 10, 1983, had to steer a heavily indebted Argentine economy through the rough years of the debt crisis with limited domestic support and in the face of the threat of capital flight. Alfonsín's Unión Cívica Radical (UCR) government did not have control over Congress, and periodically clashed with organizations representing labor and capital in agriculture and manufacturing alike. Political conflict and erratic economic policies including the introduction of capital controls in 1984 worsened economic conditions and had a negative impact on overall FDI flows.[62] Alfonsín's government did not change the investment regime setup by the military, but instead through Central Bank regulations used the prerogative to restrict the repatriation of dividends. Despite the negative outlook of the economy and political instability and conflict, inflows of FDI reversed the negative trend of the previous three years, and in 1985 were already higher than they were in 1981, the year in which they reached their apex under the military regime. As reflected in Figure 5.6, FDI fell in 1986 and

---

[62] The Alfonsín administration failed systematically in its attempts to pass legislation that would authorize several investment projects by foreign manufacturing firms. The most prominent of these failed initiatives was one by Honda which involved constructing an assembly factory in Cordoba.

1987 but then regained momentum in 1988 and 1989 largely as a result of three successive debt swap schemes devised to reduce the public sector's exposure to rising international interest rates (Azpiazu, 1995).

The Alfonsín government systematically clashed with labor unions, which were playing out the political strategy of the Peronist Party to regain control of the executive, and with the agricultural lobby, which resented the preferential treatment given to manufacturing. Lacking political support from other interest groups, Alfonsín sought support from a grouping of industrialists and government contractors known as the *Grupo María*. This group demanded protection for the domestic market in general and manufacturing in particular, and favored the expansion of government activities that would grant them access to government contracts. The adoption of policies catering toward this group may also explain why the level of inflows under Alfonsín was slightly higher but still very close to that under the military once we control for international trends and domestic conditions. In 1985, Alfonsín approached a pragmatic union group, known as the *Grupo de los 15*, and appointed one of its leaders, Carlos Alderete, as Labor Minister in order to placate organized labor. The irreconcilable differences between the union leaders and the traditional support base of the radicals had deleterious effects on economic policy making in the last two years of Alfonsín's tenure. Yet, the period coincides with Alfonsín's rapprochement with and courting of foreign capital, which included the Plan Houston for investment in the oil sector and attempts to promote foreign participation in transportation, the service sector, and manufacturing.

Alfonsín was succeeded in 1989 by Carlos Saúl Menem, the colorful Peronist leader from La Rioja. The Menem administration was responsible for the major transformation experienced by the Argentine economy in the 1990s. Pressed by hyperinflation, a staggering foreign debt, sagging investment, and a collapsed public sector, Menem had to take immediate action to reform Argentina's economy. Menem's early reform package, aimed at reining in inflation, placed special emphasis on reforming the state through retrenchment, balancing government accounts, privatizing inefficient state enterprises and utilities, reducing subsidies to businesses and linking wage increases to productivity. The State Reform Law and the Law of Economic Emergency were the key pieces of legislation that enabled Menem to implement his reform plan. Another important tool was the Convertibility Law of March 1991, which instituted the currency board that would peg the national currency to the dollar for over a decade. As a whole, the reform package was multidimensional; Menem was undeniably clever in maintaining a broad coalition of diverse interests that made reform possible.

According to received wisdom, this market reform was possible because of the relative autonomy of the executive vis-à-vis interest groups. This autonomy allowed Menem to unilaterally put in practice an orthodox economic plan that would have been impossible under his politically weak predecessor who was beholden to the Peronist majority in Congress, to the pressure of labor and business interests, and to the demands of the military (Smith and Acuña, 1994). An alternative explanation states that reform resulted from the pressure exerted by the most highly concentrated and internationalized part of the capitalist class (Azpiazu and Nochteff, 1994; Margheritis, 1999). Yet another alternative explanation that challenges these two views seems more plausible. Support for economic reform came from formal and informal bargains by a broad coalition of interest groups, specifically labor and business in manufacturing (Etchemendy, 2001), which were anchored in the old ISI model. Those who received preferential government treatment were not necessarily the more competitive sectors, or those in need, but instead politically influential actors. Menem was able to pick the pieces of the puzzle that better allowed him to secure political support.[63]

Menem and Alfonsín shared a view of what a viable economic program demanded: macroeconomic stability, including price stability, fiscal balance, and debt rescheduling; export orientation and exchange rate stability; and higher savings and investment rates to increase output. While most of Alfonsín's attempts at reform failed, the political alignment of labor with Menem played a major role in making some of those changes possible. In the times of Alfonsín, organized labor opposed, while under Menem it had no chance but to acquiesce as domestic and international conditions had changed significantly.

Moreover, Menem is usually depicted as having established a liberal foreign investment regime in 1991. Yet, there were no major changes in the investment regime that had been passed by the military in 1976. His major point of departure was closing down the National Registry of Foreign Investment in 1993, thus abolishing the licensing requirement to conduct business in Argentina and eliminating the tax on "excessive profits" regulated under the previous regime. This regime granted investors the right to remit dividends and to repatriate the principal without restrictions.[64]

---

[63] See Murillo (1997), Gibson (1997), Schamis (1999), and Etchemendy (2001).

[64] An administrative decree issued by the Menem administration in 1993 (Decreto Reglamentario 1,853/93) altered the text of the 1976 investment law. The main amendment introduced by this

Earlier legal instruments used by the Menem administration to reform the public sector, such as the Reform of the State Act and the Economic Emergency Act of 1989, had provisions regarding the participation of foreign investors in the privatization process. Foreign firms associated with banks and domestic capital participated extensively in the privatization of public utilities and state-owned enterprises.

The Menem administration did not open all sectors to foreign investors. In fact, several restrictions tended to protect entrenched domestic business interests, including the oil (especially in administrations' earlier years) and steel industries, at the expense of international capital. Most incentives granted to foreign investors were also at the sectoral level; the auto industry is the most prominent example.

The sectoral pattern of protection and investment promotion observed in Argentina under Menem seems to replicate the economy's pattern of factor mobility. Factor mobility, or the ease with which factors move to a different use in the economy, may affect the pattern of adjustment to increasing exposure to trade. When sectoral mobility is limited, the effect of rising imports is felt at the industry level (Hiscox, 2002). Similarly, when there are costs associated with moving to a different industry due to asset specificity or a lack of training or qualifications, we may also expect that the inflow of investment capital primarily affects the return to factors employed in the recipient industry, increasing the return to labor but hurting capital there. However, these effects are also felt by capital in other sectors of the economy as well. An inflow of capital may release capital from the industry or compete for labor from other sectors. Restrictions to mobility usually lead labor and capital in the sector to organize and become politically vocal. In the auto industry, for example, union leaders lobbied the government to promote the entry of foreign investment into the sector and, on their own part, offered foreign investors a better labor contract than the one offered to the domestic firms operating in the sector under the license of foreign producers.[65] Unions and representatives of foreign businesses called on the government to sign sectoral agreements that included items such as

---

decree was the elimination of the licensing process prior to entry such that foreign investors would be on similar grounds to their domestic counterparts. However, the requirement of a license or government approval was left intact for many activities. Investors were also granted exemptions on import tariffs and value added taxes for the import of capital goods and turnkey plans.

[65] Interview with SMATA leaders Pignanelli and Manrique, August 23, 2006.

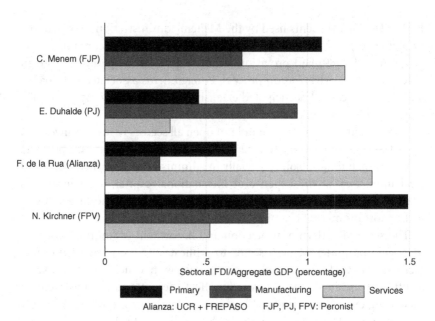

Figure 5.7. FDI/GDP by sector (1992–2004).

provisions on wages, training, employment, strikes, automobile taxes, and tariffs (Catalano and Novick, 1998; Tuman and Morris, 1998).

Unions remained a central constituency in the coalition that supported Menem's reformist program. Organized labor pressed for initiatives that would shield it from some of the negative effects of the adopted structural reform program. On many policy dimensions, unions got their way, but in many other instances it was strong businesses that received the benefits and labor was duly compensated. This pattern is compatible with the finding of Etchemendy (2001) that even though unions were key in shaping the form that reform took place, not all unions got their preferred policies.

The sectoral allocation of FDI under Néstor Kirchner confirms the predictions from the partisan investment model. When technology is allowed to vary across sectors, we should expect FDI to be larger into sectors where investment has a stronger impact on labor demand. Further, the composition of FDI flows should reflect either differences in relative demand for labor in different sectors of the economy or revenue motivations. The pattern that manufacturing sectors receive more FDI inflows under parties that cater to labor, apparent in OECD countries (Jensen et al., 2012), seems to exist in the Argentine case as well. See Tables 5.7, 5.8 and Figure 5.7.

Table 5.7. *Net FDI inflows by sector (1992–2004)*

Sector	1992	1993	1994	1995	1996	1997	1998	1999	2000	2001	2002	2003	2004[a]
Oil and Gas	1,222	277	502	436	1,046	105	1,313	17,830	2,689	796	995	−272	2,067
Mining	4	−6	17	140	682	72	11	15	48	103	138	−6	198
Manufacturing	634	858	1,798	2,186	2,776	3,308	1,147	1,950	1,487	49	988	1,145	1,221
Food, beverages, and tobacco	384	338	1,014	793	405	360	256	1,192	476	6	−133	268	419
Textiles and leather	0	39	−18	80	15	36	−5	−49	−12	−37	36	16	−18
Paper	−102	27	31	119	375	335	89	15	91	−195	78	41	91
Chemical, plastics, and rubber	217	350	325	792	937	770	232	762	695	395	171	538	−51
Cement and ceramics	33	47	26	33	20	51	306	0	−25	−35	12	55	2
Metals and manuf. metals	−120	26	245	−31	86	569	96	−18	74	−20	819	246	122
Machinery and equipment	−152	−32	60	8	165	106	111	360	−64	−47	−75	−62	51
Auto and transp. equipment	373	64	116	392	774	1,082	65	−313	253	−17	80	42	606
Electricity, gas and water	2,119	1,116	124	1,111	681	1,527	932	951	446	197	109	50	170
Commerce and services	82	42	339	318	523	150	699	742	51	662	−23	79	−3
Transportation and comm.	36	−19	245	634	145	845	260	714	3,870	167	−538	−39	−202
Baking	191	418	160	512	747	2,366	1,757	746	382	235	−9	448	158
Other	143	106	452	272	350	788	1,173	1,038	1,445	−42	489	246	665
Total	4,432	2,793	3,637	5,610	6,951	9,161	7,292	23,986	10,418	2,166	2,149	1,652	4,274

Net direct investment inflows by sector in current U.S. dollars.

[a] Provisional results.

Source: Dirección Nacional de Cuentas Internacionales, Ministerio de Economía y Producción, Republica Argentina.

Table 5.8. *FDI/GDP by sector (population average results)*

	Dependent variable: FDI_{jt}/GDP_t		
	(1) Primary	(2) Manufacturing	(3) Services
GDP per Capita	2.839	−0.026	0.15
(thousands)	(3.010)	(0.070)	(0.122)
Openness	−0.314	0.015	0.026
	(0.355)	(0.015)	(0.030)
Investment/GDP	−0.637	0.003	−0.044[c]
	(0.661)	(0.013)	(0.014)
Population	0.001	−0.020	−0.083[b]
(thousands)	(0.035)	(0.012)	(0.038)
Peronist	0.441	0.037[c]	−0.0071
	(0.419)	(0.008)	(0.105)
Constant	−15.316	0.702	1.695
	(17.219)	(0.697)	(1.865)
N	26	104	65
Group	2	8	5
Wald χ^2 (5)	18.07	93.03	56.22
Prob > χ^2	0.000	0.000	0.003

GEE population-averaged model
Cluster Adjusted Robust St. Errors in parentheses
[a, b, c] significant at 10 percent, 5 percent, 1 percent, respectively.

Scholars and pundits alike tend to conclude that both Menem and Perón betrayed labor, trumped its followers, or simply bought off its leaders (Fuchs, 1965, 1981; Monteon, 1987; Murillo, 2001) in courting foreign capital. Yet, Perón in the 1950s, Menen in the 1990s, and the Kirchners today retained a substantial level of support from workers, especially those in industries that received high levels of investment, and counted the unions as one of their most important political organizations.[66] Moreover,

---

[66] "The Menem multiclass appeal rests easily within the ideological framework of the early and mature Peronism, each obeying the pragmatic dictates of the time. But the Menem coalition is broader even than the Perón coalitions of 1945 and 1973, subsuming as it does almost every societal sector and interest. In 1945, Perón initiated an anti-oligarchic, national sectoral alliance, in 1973 an anti-military, multiclass alliance. In the 1990s Menem has mounted another multiclass alliance against public and private bureaucracies and a corporate-protectionist economy" (Ranis, 1994, p. xii).

the foreign investment regime established by the military in 1976, led to lower levels of FDI inflows and encouraged extant MNCs to leave the country. The evidence, therefore, seems to support an alternative explanation, one where attaining labor support and courting foreign investors are congruent. In fact, one of the main challenges of the CGT leadership was to understand the liberal-democratic disposition of the Argentine working class, which an intuitive Menem was apt at capturing (Ranis, 1994).[67] The link becomes apparent at the macro level, which most explanations have ignored.

5.5 Conclusion

In this chapter, I explore the link between politics and foreign direct investment flows. I assess whether the conditions described in the model presented in Chapters 2 and 3 help explain changing patterns of FDI inflows in Argentina. I conduct a series of simple tests on the hypothesis that parties that cater to labor are more likely to attract higher levels of FDI, finding preliminary evidence that supports the core hypothesis.

The findings in the sample of the past three decades of Argentina's history are consistent with the predictions derived from proposition 2 in the formal model, namely that pro-labor/Peronist governments attract more FDI. These results cannot be taken as conclusive evidence. The theory is about preferences of domestic actors derived from their position in the economy and policy outcomes that are assumed rather than tested. I use measures of variables that do not fully map onto the main concepts in the theory, whereas several of the relevant political and economic variables are only measured indirectly. However, the evidence seems to capture a relationship between partisan orientation of government and foreign investment, in the direction predicted by the theory.

Caveats notwithstanding, the results presented suggest that the theory advanced in previous chapters is plausible. When governments are linked to a group of core constituents who are positively affected by FDI inflows,

---

[67] "What has not been significantly emphasized, however, is that the Argentine working class . . . has been predisposed to many of the Menem initiatives, certainly since the onset of democracy, and they have clearly committed to a democratic capitalist culture, even though their union leaders were at first much more ambivalent" (Ranis, 1994, p. x).

they need not be institutionally constrained in order to attract foreign direct investment. This solution brings forth the "mutual exchange of hostages" analogy introduced in Chapter 3. Investment is secure when a government's attempt to opportunistically target investors hurts domestic actors that the government cannot afford to ignore, namely when investors can take a pivotal domestic actor hostage. Preferential treatment given to foreign investors is ransom that political leaders are usually willing to pay in order to prevent pivotal domestic actors from being harmed. What kind of hostages do investors take? It is likely that they choose those actors that have the motive and opportunity to affect government behavior. They must be influential and they must benefit from FDI inflows. When domestic and foreign capital are substitutes, labor's interests become congruent to those of foreign capital allowing the pro-labor government to credibly commit to foreign investors.

The results from the statistical tests seem to be supported by anecdotal evidence from post-war Argentina. The partisan theory of investment helps explains Perón's changing attitude toward foreign investment precisely at a time when he seemingly moved away from domestic capital while still maintaining the overwhelming support of labor. In the last stretch of Perón's government, the trend of FDI flowing out of the country that had been the rule in previous years switched to an inflows; it is precisely the link between Peronist administrations and organized labor that helps explain this change.

The pattern of FDI regulation would arguably have been different had domestic capital owners would have been more influential politically, which appears to be the case in South Korea. In South Korea, labor was repressed and politics was dominated by a ruling coalition centered around the chaebols. Facing similar external constraints to those of Argentina under Perón in the form of balance-of-payment crises policy toward foreign investment in South Korea was restrictive. The outcome was hardly any foreign investment at all, especially when compared to Latin American countries such as Mexico and Brazil, or even other Asian NIEs (Haggard, 1990). More recently, South Korea started to open up to foreign investment, especially after the 1997 financial crisis (Yun, 2003). It is likely that democratization and the collapse of the chaebols opened the door to this liberalization. I explore these events in the following chapter.

APPENDIX 5.1

Table 5.9. *Robustness tests*

	DV: ΔFDI/GDP	
	(15)	(16)
FDI/GDP$_{t-1}$	-1.481^c	-0.518^c
	(0.265)	(0.049)
Peronist$_{t-1}$	1.965^b	1.048^c
	(0.786)	(0.284)
Political Constraints$_{t-1}$	-0.217	
	(0.631)	
Peronist$_{t-1}$ × ΔPol. Con.$_{t-1}$	-1.393	
	(2.074)	
ΔPolitical Constraints		-0.190
		(0.900)
Peronist$_{t-1}$ × ΔPol. Con.$_{t-1}$		-0.353
		(1.597)
GDP/capita$_{t-1}$	0.180	
	(0.332)	
ΔGDP/capita	-1.069^c	-1.300^b
	(0.317)	(0.549)
Trade/GDP$_{t-1}$	-0.0713^a	
	(0.036)	
ΔTrade/GDP (%)	0.154^c	0.156^c
	(0.040)	(0.042)
Public Spending/GDP$_{t-1}$	-17.45^c	
	(5.787)	
ΔPublic Spending/GDP (%)	-38.64^b	-12.960
	(14.270)	(12.360)
Savings/GDP$_{t-1}$	-0.003	
	(0.025)	
ΔSavings/GDP (%)	-0.323^c	-0.171^b
	(0.074)	(0.066)
World FDI flows$_{t-1}$	4.813^b	
	(1.779)	
ΔWorld FDI flows	9.137^c	7.045^c
	(1.528)	(1.429)
ΔUS interest rate		-0.092
		(0.092)
Constant	2.360	0.023
	(2.609)	(0.111)
N	34	34
Years	1971–2004	1971–2004
R^2	0.9330	0.8120
Adj. R^2	0.884	0.731
DW *stat* (transformed)	2.75	2.432
DW *stat* (original)	2.452	2.556
ρ	-0.805	-0.737

Prais-Winsten AR(1) regression; semi-robust standard errors in parentheses.
$^a p < 0.1$, $^b p < 0.05$, $^c p < 0.01$.

Table 5.10. *Labor bargaining conditions under different LAPs*

	1945 D.-Ley 23,852/45	1958 Ley 14,455	1973 Ley 20,615	1979 Ley 22,105	1988[a] Ley 23,551
Term of appointment of delegates	4 years	2 years	4 years	3 years	4 years
Re-election	No limit	No limit		1 term	No limit
Voting	Plurality	Plurality	Plurality	Over 20% of valid votes; at least 50% participation.	Plurality
Number of delegates	No provision	No provision	5-15: 1 16-40: 2 71+: 3 + 2%	Less than 1%	10-50: 1 51-100: 2 100+: 2 + 1%
Demand for extraordinary meeting		10% of union members	20% of union members	5% of union members	15% of union members
Union participation in politics	No restriction; decided by general assembly or congress	No provision	Allowed to take positions and support political parties	Banned	No provision
Taxation and contributions (on union property and activities)			Exempted	Exempted	Exempted
Intervention in local unions	No provision	No provision	According to the federation's statute	Banned	According to union's statutes; decided at the highest union level (national congress)
Grievances	List of illegal actions by employers; decided by Consejo Nacional de Asociaciones Profesionales (CNAP).	Adds conditions for termination by employers due to workers' actions; due process in CNAP decisions.	List of illegal actions by employers only; renames CNAP.	Reinstates illegal worker behavior; no special jurisdiction.	Decision requires a judicial proceeding.
Social welfare funds	No mandatory fund	Union controlled	Union controlled	Government controlled (Ley 18,610)	Union controlled

[a] In 1984, Congress passed legislation (Law 23,071) that regulated elections in order to normalize unions by ridding them of bureaucratized leaders and all vestiges of the military intervention of the previous years.

196

Table 5.11. *Argentina: Government orientation*

President	Tenure	Party	Regime	Support base
J. A. Roca	1898–1904	PAN	Dem	Agric. producers
M. Quintana	1904–06	PAN	Dem	Agric. producers
J. Figueroa Alcorta	1906–10	PAN	Dem	Agric. producers
R. Saenz Peña	1910–14	Union Nacional	Dem	Agric. producers
V. De la Plaza	1914–16	PC	Dem	Agric. producers
H. Yrigoyen	1916–22	UCR	Dem[a]	Middle class
M. T. de Alvear	1922–8	UCR	Dem	Middle class
H. Yrigoyen	1928–30	UCR	Dem	Middle class
J. F. Uriburu	1930–2	MILITARY	Aut[c]	Agric. producers
A. P. Justo	1932–8	National Dem	Dem[c]	Agr.producers (industrialists)
R. M. Ortiz	1938–42	National Coal.	Dem[c]	Agric. producers (industrialists)
R. S. Castillo	1942–3	National Coal.	Dem[c]	Agric. producers (industrialists)
A. Rawson	1943	MILITARY	Aut	Industrialists
P. Ramirez	1943–4	MILITARY	Aut	Industrialists
E. J. Farrell	1944–6	MILITARY	Aut	Industrialists (urban workers)
J. D. Perón	1946–55	PJ	Dem[b]	Urban workers (industrialists)
E. Lonardi	1955	MILITARY	Aut	Agric. producers
P. Aramburu	1955–8	MILITARY	Aut	Agric. producers
A. Frondizi	1958–62	UCRI	Dem[d]	Middle class (industrialists)
J. M. Guido	1962–3	UCRI	Aut	Agric. producers (industrialists, service)
A. Illia	1963–6	UCRP	Dem[d]	Middle class (service)
J. C. Ongania	1966–70	MILITARY	Aut	Industrialists (agric. producers)
R. Levingston	1970–71	MILITARY	Aut	Agric. producers (industrialists)
A. Lanuse	1971–3	MILITARY	Aut	Agric. producers (industrialists)
H. Cámpora	1973	PJ	Dem	Urban workers (industrialists)
R. Lastiri	1973	PJ	Dem	Urban workers (industrialists)
J.D. Perón	1973–4	PJ	Dem	Urban workers (industrialists)
I. M. de Perón	1974–6	PJ	Dem	Industrialists (urban workers)
J. Videla	1976–81	MILITARY	Aut	Agric. producers (contractors, finance, service)
R. Viola	1981	MILITARY	Aut	Agric. producers (contractors, finance, service)
L. Galtieri	1981–2	MILITARY	Aut	Agric. producers (contractors, finance, service)
R. Bignone	1982–3	MILITARY	Aut	Agric. producers (contractors, finance, service)
R. Alfonsin	1983–8	UCR	Dem	Middle class (industrialists, workers)
C. Menem	1989–99	PJ	Dem	Workers (finance, service, contractors)
F. de la Rúa	1999–2001	UCR-Alliance	Dem	Middle class (industrialists)
E. Duhalde	2002	PJ	Dem	Urban workers (unemployed, industrialists)
N. Kirchner	2003–07	PJ	Dem	Urban workers (unemployed, industrialists)
C. F. de Kirchner	2007–	PJ	Dem	Urban workers (unemployed, industrialists)

Source: Mollinelli et al 1999; Ardanaz, Pinto and Pinto 2010.

Support base: Main (secondary)

References: Military: follows a coup; PJ = Peronists; UCR = Radicals; UCRI = UCR Intransigente; UCRP = UCR del Pueblo.

[a] First presidential election under universal, mandatory and secret ballot (Ley Saenz Peña of 1912).

[b] Female suffrage instituted in 1947. The first Presidential election with female suffrage was 1952.

[c] The UCR was proscribed and banned from the 1931 election; pervasive electoral fraud through 1942.

[d] The Peronist party was proscribed and banned from the 1958 and 1963 elections.

Table 5.12. *Argentina: Trade and investment regimes*

President	Tenure	Trade regime	Dev. Ideology	FDI policy	Statute	Content
R. M. Ortiz	1938–42	open	agro-exp	neutral		
R. S. Castillo	1942–3	open	agro-exp	neutral		
A. Rawson	1943	closed	ISI	restrict		
P Ramirez	1943–4	closed	ISI	restrict		discourage invest. in utilities
E.J. Farrell	1944–6	closed	ISI	restrict		discourage invest. in utilities
J. D. Perón	1946–55	closed	ISI	promote	1948; 1953	promote manuf./oil
E Lonardi	1955	closed	ISI	restrict		
P Aramburu	1955–8	closed	ISI	restrict	1955; 1957	repeal 1953 law; subsidiary to dom. invest
A. Frondizi	1958–62	closed	ISI	promote	1958; 1961	promote manuf./oil
J. M. Guido	1962–3	closed	ISI	promote		
A. Illia	1963–6	closed	ISI	selective	1963	repeal oil contracts
J. C. Ongania	1966–70	closed	ISI	restrict	1967 (2); 1970	subsidiary to dom. invest.
F. Levingston	1970–71	closed	ISI	restrict	1970	discourage; subsidiary to dom. invest.
A. Lanuse	1971–3	closed	ISI	restrict	1971	subsidiary to dom. invest.
H. Cámpora	1973	closed	ISI	selective		
F. Lastiri	1973	closed	ISI	selective		
J D. Perón	1973–4	closed	ISI	selective	1973	negative list
I M. de Perón	1974–6	closed	ISI	selective		
J Videla	1976–81	open	reform	open/selective	1976; 1980	national treatment; discourage
E. Viola	1981	open	reform	open/selective	1981	technology transfer; selective
L. Galtieri	1981–2	open	reform	open/selective		
E. Bignone	1982–3	open	reform	open/selective		
R. Alfonsin	1983–8	partial	mixed	selective	1984; 1987	debt-equity swaps
C. Menem	1989–99	open	reform	promote	1989; 1993	promote; privatization
E de la Rúa	1999–2001	open	reform	open		promote utilities; oil
E. Duhalde	2002	partial	mixed	selective		promote manuf.
N. Kirchner	2003–07	partial	mixed	selective		promote manuf.
C. F. de Kirchner	2007–	partial	mixed	selective		promote manuf.

Source: Mollinelli et al., 1999 and Ardanaz, Pinto, and Pinto 2012; see Table 5.11 for references.

Table 5.13. *Foreign investment statutes (1940–2005)*

Year	Instrument	Provisions
1948	Decreto 3347/48	*Establishes Comisión Nacional de Radicación de Industrias (Commission for Promotion of Foreign Industries)* – Offers selective incentives for investment in manufacturing. – No regulation on contributions of capital.
1953	Ley 14.222 (Dec. Regl. 19.111/53)	*Foreign Investment Statute of 1953* Regulatory regime for foreign investment promotion: – Grants national treatment to foreign investors. – Allows investment in equipment, intangible assets, or capital. – Creates the Registro Nacional de Inversiones Extranjeras (National Registry of Foreign Investment) – Government license required prior to investment; projects evaluated by the Comisión Interministerial de Inversiones Extranjeras (Inter-Ministerial Commission for Foreign Investment). – Allows repatriation of dividends (up to 8 percent/year) and principal, with 10-year wait period, 10 to 20 percent/year thereafter. – Grants benefits to foreign investors on case by case basis: access to credit, preferential access to foreign exchange, tax holidays for import of capital goods and inputs.
1955	Resolución 986/55 (Ministry of Finance)	*Free disposition of foreign exchange* (libre disposición de divisas) – Frees exchange rate market; eliminates multi-tier system – Repeals restriction on profit repatriation – Central Bank gradually releases currency for repatriation of dividends and capital.
1955	Circular 2324/55 (BCRA)	*Foreign Investment Regime* (Régimen de Inversiones Extranjeras) Conditions for approval: – License granted to projects that do not negatively affect domestic businesses and that settle in "convenient" locations. – Preference for investment that promotes economic development, reduces foreign exchange and is compatible with government priorities. – Allows investment of new machinery in industries that substitute for imports or increase exports. Domestic firms granted free access to foreign currency to import similar equipment or can request that these imports be treated as foreign investment.

(*continued*)

Table 5.13 *(continued)*

Year	Instrument	Provisions
1956	Circular 2881/56 (BCRA)	*Industrial re-equipment promotion regime* (Régimen de re-equipamiento industrial): – Compensates domestic firms affected by the import of machinery with preferential access to foreign exchange to purchase foreign equipment.
1957	Decreto-Ley 16.640/57	*Repeal of Law 14,222* (Radicación de capitales extranjeros; derogación de la ley 14,222) – Repeals investment regime of 1953.
1958	Decreto 1594/58	*Procedure for foreign investment petition* (Trámite de gestiones de inversiones extranjeras) – Investment project needs prior Executive Branch approval.
1958	Decreto 2483/58	*Advisory Commission on Foreign Investment* (Crea Comisión Asesora de Inversiones Extranjeras) – Establishes a commission for promotion of foreign investment under the Secretariat for Economic and Social Relations.
1958	Ley 14.780	*Regime for investment of foreign capital* (Régimen de inversión de capitales extranjeros) – Grants national treatment to foreign investors. – Preference given to projects that develop natural resources for use in manufacturing; produce capital or intermediate goods; promote local development of the hinterland. – Special treatment conferred to investments that enter in joint ventures with local firms or that promote technology transfers. – Promotes reinvestment of dividends. – The Executive Branch may confer tax and tariff breaks to selected investment projects. – Regulates repatriation of profits and capital, with restrictions. – Preferential access to credit, energy supplies and public utilities. (Additional conditions established in Ley 14.781 de Promoción Industrial.)
1961	Ley 15.803	*Ratifies the US-Argentina Treaty on investment insurance* (Ratificación de un acuerdo con los Estados Unidos de Norte América sobre garantía de inversiones) – Grants US investors access to OPIC investment insurance. – Protection is granted to those projects approved by the Executive Branch.
1963	Decretos 744/63 & 745/63	*Annulment of Oil Contracts* – Annuls oil contracts signed under the Frondizi administration.

Year	Instrument	Provisions
1967	Decreto 5364/67	*Creates Foreign Investment Promotion Service* (Creación del Servicio de Promoción de Inversiones Extranjeras dependiente del Ministerio de Economía y Trabajo) – Creates National Service for Investment Promotion in charge of assessing the viability of the investment program. – Establishes a new foreign investment regime. – Foreign investment plays a subsidiary role to domestic investment. – Domestic firms may challenge concessions and benefits.
1967	Decreto-Ley 17.319	*Hydrocarbons Act* (Ley de Hidrocarburos) – Compensates investors for annulment of contracts under Illia. – Grants concessions to private firms. – Exports permitted after domestic demand is covered; exports pay a 55 percent tax.
1970	Decreto 182	*Renames Investment Promotion Service* (Nueva denominación del Servicio de Promoción de Inversiones Externas) – Investment promotion authority transferred to Secretary of Foreign Trade. – Promotes specific investment projects and outward investment. – Domestic firms may challenge concessions and benefits offered to foreign investors.
1970	Decreto-Ley 18,587	*Industrial Promotion* (Industria – Promoción) – Promotes development of domestic firms in the manufacturing sector. – Foreign firms may only receive industrial promotion benefits when entering in joint ventures with domestic firms.
1971	Decreto-Ley 19,151	*Investment of foreign capital* (Inversiones de capitales extranjeros) – Projects subject to prior study by Secretary of Planning and Government Action. – Investment licenses approved by Executive decree, which would define the conditions for repatriation of profits and capital on case-by-case basis. – Promotes joint ventures and other forms of association with domestic firms. – Foreign investors can only buy non-voting shares. – Limits access to domestic credit. – Over 85 percent of management and technical personnel must be Argentine nationals.

(*continued*)

Table 5.13 *(continued)*

Year	Instrument	Provisions
1973	Ley 20.557	*Foreign Investment Statute of 1973* (Ley de radicación de capitales extranjeros) – Investors sign an investment contract; contract conditions need Executive or Legislative approval depending on the sector. – Promotes investment that leads to higher employment and development of local resources; is not funded locally; employs local technology – Does not allow investment in sectors associated with defense and national security; banking and finance; television, radio, publishing and other media; retail commerce; sectors reserved for state companies or local firms; agriculture, fishing, and forestry – Limits on dividend repatriation (12.5 percent or 4 points over long-term deposits; principal can be remitted after 5 years, and no more that 20 percent/year of original investment value. – Excludes foreign investors from investment promotion incentives.
1976	Decreto-Ley 21.382	*Foreign Investment Statute of 1976* (Ley de Inversiones Extranjeras) – Broad definition of investment. Includes capital, intangible assets, and capital goods. – National treatment; access to short-term credit in local markets (long-term credit is restricted, and requires government approval). – Access to industrial promotion incentives (Decreto-Ley 21.608/77). – Free repatriation of capital (after 3 years) and dividends in "normal times." Banned when Central Bank declares "state of foreign exchange emergency" (can be exchanged for government bonds denominated in foreign currency). – Dividends exceeding 12 percent of investment subject to excess profits tax. – Negative list of sectors where investment is banned. – Approval required for investment in: public utilities (including telecommunications, electricity, gas, transportation, postal services), media, education, energy, financial services, and insurance. – Approval required for projects that exceed U.S.$ 5 million; denationalize local firms; require investment promotion. – Subsidiaries are treated as independent legal entity from parent firm.

Year	Instrument	Provisions
1980	Decreto-Ley 22,208 (Decreto Regl. 1031/81)	*Foreign investment* (Inversiones extranjeras – Modificación de la Ley 21,382) – Streamlines licensing process. – Eliminates prior approval requirement for investments in banking and transportation. – Approval required for projects that denationalize firms with assets worth U.S.$10 million and for all projects over US$ 20 million.
1981	Decreto-Ley 22,426 (Decreto Regl. 580/81)	*Technology Transfer Law* (Ley de transferencia de tecnología) – All technology transfer contracts need to be filed with the INTI (National Institute for Industrial Technology). – Limits royalty payments to 5 percent of net value of product sales. – No royalties to be paid for use of brand name.
1984	Decreto 1506/84	*Suspension of dividend and investment repatriation* (Suspensión del derecho a transferir utilidades y repatriar inversiones) – Aims at preserving level of reserves. – Bans right to repatriate dividends and principal (through 1987). – Investors are compensated with foreign currency denominated Government bonds.
1987	Res. 520 (Min. Econ); Com. A1035, A1056, and A1059 (BCRA)	*Program for debt equity swaps* (Programa de Conversión de la Deuda Externa en Inversiones del Sector Privado) – Regulates debt-equity swap program to promote investment.
1989	Ley 23,696 (Decreto Regl. 1105/89)	*Public Sector Reform Act* (Ley de Reforma del Estado) – Authorizes privatization of public utilities. – Allows foreign investor participation in the privatization process.
1989	Ley 23,697 (Decreto Regl. 1225/89)	*Economic Emergency Act* (Ley de Emergencia Económica) – Suspends industrial promotion regimes that affect the fiscal position of the federal government – Excludes prior benefits granted to foreign investors already operating in the country
1993	Decreto Regl. 1,853/93	*Foreign Investment Statute of 1993* (Ley de Inversiones Extranjeras – Texto Ordenado) Regulates the 1976 Foreign Investment Act: – No need to obtain license prior to investing. – Right to remit dividends and principal without restrictions. – No tax on "excessive profits." – Exemption of import tariffs and value added tax on imports of capital goods and turnkey plants (suspended in 1996 by Executive Decree 937/96).

Data Sources

FDI net inflows (current US$): See description in Chapter 4. Source: UNCTAD, Division on Investment and Enterprise.

Political Constraints: Institutional constraints on policy making (institutional and partisan veto gates) (Henisz, 2002).

GDP per worker (constant price entry): See definition in Chapter 4. (Heston et al., 2002, 2011; PWT 6.2, PWT 7.0).

Savings (% of GDP): See definition in Chapter 4. (Heston et al., 2002, 2011; PWT 6.2, PWT 7.0).

Government Share of GDP: Government consumption as a share of GDP. See description in Chapter 4. (Heston et al., 2002, 2011; PWT 6.2, PWT 7.0).

Trade/GDP (%): Trade is the sum of exports and imports as a share of GDP. (Heston et al., 2002, 2011; PWT 6.2, PWT 7.0).

FDI World Outflows: Foreign direct investment outflows in U.S. dollars at current prices and current exchange rates in millions. FDI includes the three following components: equity capital, reinvested earnings, and intracompany loans. Source: UNCTAD, Division on Investment and Enterprise, UNCTADstat, Inward and outward foreign direct investment flows, annual, 1970–2010.

Business Influence, Politics, and Foreign Direct Investment in South Korea

6.1 Introduction

The statistical evidence presented in Chapter 4, albeit tentative, suggests that the predictions from the partisan theory of FDI are plausible: when pro-labor/left-leaning governments are in power, FDI inflows increase more often than not. In the longitudinal analysis presented in the previous chapter, I discuss the evolution of investment regimes and FDI performance in Argentina in the post-war era. The evidence from the Argentine case provides additional support to the partisan hypothesis by exploring changing patters of the political influence of labor and business: pro-labor and pro-capital coalitions that have alternated in power since the 1930s have treated foreign capital differently. In the Argentine case, I focus on the varying influence of organized labor, which results from institutional and other political conditions, including movements to and from democratic rule as well as partisan cycles. From Juan Perón, through the different military regimes, Radical and Desarrollista governments, to Carlos Menem and Néstor Kirchner, we observe that incumbents received varying degrees of support from workers, industrialists, and agricultural producers. Further, these governments assumed very different pro- or anti-labor stances, which in turn seem to reflect the preferences of their core supporters. As discussed in the previous chapter, changes in labor influence or in the pro-labor or pro-business orientation of the ruling coalition seem to have had an effect on the type of investment regimes adopted and on the degree of openness to FDI. The Argentine case makes apparent that it is the pro-labor nature of the ruling coalition rather than the governments' ideological placement on the left-right dimension that appears to affect the adoption of more favorable investment conditions and to bring larger FDI inflows.

In this chapter, I provide additional evidence from the Korean experience, a country initially ruled by a pro-business coalition, which lost power over time as a function of institutional changes and of the erosion of the economic and political influence of the *chaebols*, the family-controlled business conglomerates that grew in the shadow of the developmental state. In the early post-war era, Korea adopted a highly restrictive investment regime, and received low levels of FDI, a pattern that is quite similar to that of Japan. The Economic Planning Board, which is credited for having played a critical role in Korea's economic policy making (Eriksson, 2005), acted as the gatekeeper in the protection of the chaebols by restricting competition in product and factor markets while promoting technology transfers (Nicolas, 2003). In times of crisis or savings shortcomings most foreign capital took the form of loans whose allocation was administered by the government. Conditions reversed in the late 1990s as the consequence of three processes: democratization, which moved the center of political gravity away from owners of capital and toward owners of labor; the financial crisis of 1997, which eroded the political clout of the chaebols; and the ascent to power of a left-leaning coalition, which aimed at reducing the degree of influence of the concentrated business groups. The end result was a dramatic change in the investment regime, which ultimately led to larger inflows of FDI.

After a short attempt at substituting imports, South Korea embraced an export-oriented development strategy in the early 1960s,[1] much like the rest if the East Asian NIEs at that time. But unlike other NIEs, South Korea has been known for its negative attitude toward foreign investors (Korhonen, 2001; Eriksson, 2005).[2] In this dimension, Korea looks similar to Japan: financially integrated business conglomerates, the chaebol in South Korea, and the *zaibatsu* and *keiretsu* groups in pre-war and post-war Japan, respectively, received preferential treatment by the government and had great influence over policy. In both countries, governments discriminated against foreign investors. As Haggard (1990) puts it: "In Korea, by contrast, a closer alliance between business and the manufacturing sector combined with nationalist fears of Japan to keep policy toward foreign investment

---

[1] South Korea looks deceptively poor in the 1950s in per capita terms due to the destruction of capital stock during the war and the separation from the manufacturing centers located in the North (Noland, 2007; Noland and Pack, 2003).

[2] The difference between South Korea and the other NIEs on this dimension is probably of low magnitude as the claim that foreign investors have dominated the growth of the East Asian NIEs is exaggerated: "In all cases, except Singapore, export-led growth favored the development of local firms. Export-led growth in Korea and Taiwan was accompanied by a secular decline in dependence on total foreign savings, even though Korea borrowed heavily" (Haggard, 1990, p. 193).

restrictive. Foreign direct investment constituted a smaller share of total capital inflows in Korea than in the other Asian NICs" (Haggard, 1990, p. 194). In Korea, as in Japan, outflows of direct investment outpaced inflows throughout the postwar era as both countries have been net exporters of capital. Moreover, even when domestic businesses demanded access to foreign technology, the Korean and Japanese governments alike chose to restrict direct investment flows while promoting licensing instead to shelter domestic firms (Nicolas, 2003; Amsden, 1992; Kim, 1997; Noland, 2007; Westphal et al., 1981, 1985).

The remarkable economic performance of South Korea is usually attributed to the policy choices made during the reconstruction era (Nicolas, 2003). A major event occurred between 1948–1950: while the country was still embarked in the war effort, the government enacted extensive land reform, which removed the old landlord class. During the reconstruction period, the government also seized Japanese enterprises, which together with former state-owned companies were granted to local entrepreneurs. This process would eventually lead to the emergence of a local capitalist class built around family-controlled business conglomerates, which started in labor-intensive manufacturing and gradually diversified and moved up the technology ladder with the support and encouragement of the state (Koo and Kim, 1992; Eriksson, 2005).

The strong relationship between the state and the chaebols was reflected in the orientation of the investment regime offered to foreigners, which despite many reformulations on paper remained highly restrictive in practice until the late 1990s. The instruments of choice were curbs on the sectors in which foreign investors could operate, limits on equity ownership, mandated technology transfer, and export performance and local content requirements. The objective was to preserve the privileged position of domestic firms. In the early 1960s, for instance, the government enacted a restrictive licensing regime that granted virtually all bargaining power to Korean licensees (Kim, 1997). Altogether theses regulations and restrictions made South Korea an unattractive destination for foreign investors despite its phenomenal economic performance (Kwon, 2004).

The negative disposition toward foreign investors in South Korea reversed in the 1990s when investment policy was liberalized. Further, FDI inflows to Korea increased dramatically in the aftermath of the 1997 financial crisis (Yun, 2003). This trend can be observed in the number of cases and amount of inward foreign investment reproduced in Figure 6.1. The deregulation of economic activity and liberalization of Korea's investment regime in the early 1990s has been attributed to foreign pressure and Korea's quest to

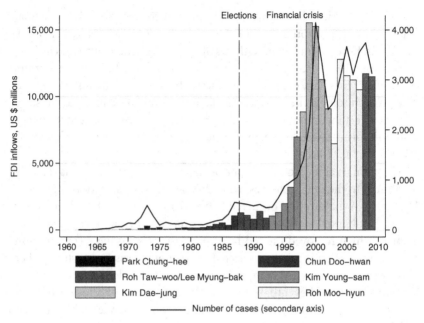

Figure 6.1. Number of FDI cases and amounts, 1962–2009.

become an OECD member (Sachwald, 2001). I find more compelling an alternative explanation rooted in changing domestic political coalitions. I argue that the sudden surge of FDI inflows in the late 1990s is explained by the convergence of two conditions that affected the conduct of politics in South Korea: democratization, which led to a more competitive political system and consequently to the rise of labor; and the financial collapse of the chaebols in the aftermath of the Asian financial crisis, which weakened their relative influence in politics (Mo and Moon, 1999; Moon and Mo, 1999). Furthermore, the left-leaning administrations led by Kim Dae-jung first and subsequently by Roh Moo-hyun pushed a political agenda aimed at reining in the chaebols, as documented in this chapter. The effort resulted in a higher penetration of foreign investors, as predicted by the partisan hypothesis.

In this chapter, I map political changes, including democratization, the decline of political influence by the business conglomerates, and the rise of the left onto differences in the ability of the South Korean governments to attract foreign investment. In the first section, I present the main hypotheses analyzed in this chapter derived from the partisan theory of investment, namely that FDI inflows affect negatively the returns to capital, and that openness to foreign investment is a function of the ability of workers and capitalists to influence government policies. The following section presents quantitative evidence that suggests that the theory is plausible. Next, I introduce qualitative evidence to support the statistical results: foreign investment flows into South Korea rose when politics became more competitive, the chaebols weakened, and workers became more influential. The fact that in comparative perspective South Korea received low levels of FDI can be attributed to the changing influence of the domestic business conglomerates in the pre- and post-crisis eras.

6.2 Government Orientation and Investment Performance

The partisan theory of investment is based on the observation that on average direct foreign investment is likely to increase the demand for labor and at the same time negatively affect the return to domestic capital owners by increasing competition in product and factor markets in the recipient country.[3] Incumbent business owners in the host country are likely to oppose the entry of foreign investment, whereas labor supports policies that attract it. Changing patterns of political influence by labor and business interests should thus be reflected in policy outcomes: investment policies are more restrictive when domestic owners of capital are politically influential, whereas the reverse occur, when labor is relatively more influential. The orientation of the ruling coalition, whether pro-labor or pro-capital, affect, the amount of FDI received by the host government.

In the Argentine case, I have described how the relationship between workers and the pro-labor Peronist party, regardless of its ideological leanings, was instrumental in explaining the content of foreign investment regimes. Military governments have been catalogued as being on the ideological right and radical governments have been traditionally characterized as centrists whereas Peronist governments have been coded as left, center, or right-leaning. Yet, it is clear that irrespective of their ideology and penchant for import substituting or export promoting strategies, governments led by Peronist leaders were supported by workers and have been closer to organized labor. The strong support of labor for Peronist governments becomes particularly clear when their support base is contrasted with that of other political parties under democratic rule and with the coalition that historically supported military rulers, rendering the ideological dimension less relevant.

---

[3] FDI could have a positive effect on the demand for business services through forward and backward linkages or spillover effects. Yet, profuse evidence suggests that these effects are likely to arise under more limited conditions and depend on the existence of absorptive capacities in the host; see Blömstrom et al. (1994), Easterly et al. (1994), Borensztein et al. (1998), and Carcovic and Levine (2005).

An alternative route for assessing the disposition of governments to respond to the demands of labor and capital is to look at the ideological orientation of the party in government. This was the strategy I adopted in Chapter 4. The reasoning is the following: right-leaning governments tend to be more business-oriented, assign high priority to price and stability, and usually clash with labor on issues such as unemployment and income distribution. Governments on the left side of the political spectrum tend to cater to labor for political support, and place more emphasis on issues such as unemployment and income distribution.

Post-war South Korea until democratization and the 1997 crisis was a case where government has had close links to domestic businesses and adopted policies aimed at benefiting the chaebols (Lee, 1997, 2005; Nicolas, 2003). We should expect investment policy to change in tandem with changes in the political regime, such as democratization, and with changes in the orientation of the chief executive, empowerment of workers and consumers, and a gradual movement to the left of the political spectrum. To the extent that income distribution is skewed, the median voter is likely to be relatively more endowed with labor than with capital. Hence, when facing electoral competition of the *Downsian* type, politicians are more likely to respond to labor's interests and/or to react more favorably to labor's demands. Therefore, democratization is likely to affect the content of the policies adopted by the Korean government. This movement is associated with more favorable investment conditions and larger foreign direct investment inflows. Yet even under democratic rule businesses are likely to organize politically to resist policy changes that hurt their interests Lindblom (1977). Business influence in politics is likely to covary with the emergence of countervailing interests in the polity, be it consumers, who traditionally face a collective action problem, or workers organized as unions. In the South Korean case, we should expect swings in the environment regulating economic activity as workers become more influential and incumbent businesses are weakened at the turn of the century. The evidence presented in this chapter suggests that the precipitous change in the balance of political influence was indeed reflected in the regulation of foreign investment in line with the predictions derived from the partisan model of FDI. I next present evidence that to support this claim.

6.2.1 Openness to FDI Under Different Coalitions

Until the wake of the 1997 financial crisis onward FDI into South Korea remained remarkably low (Sakong, 1993; Nicolas, 2003). Given South Korea's disposition toward foreign investors, the *Far Eastern Economic*

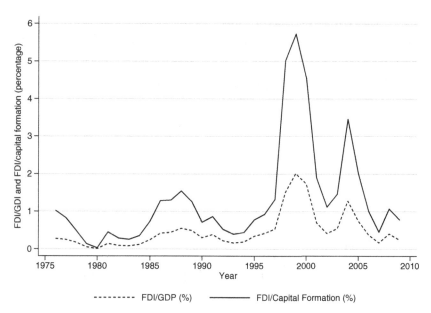

Figure 6.2. Trends in FDI inflows to South Korea, 1975–2009.

Review had labeled the country as the "worst place to invest among Asian countries" (Kwon, 2004). Figure 6.1 presents the degree of openness to FDI for the period 1962–2009, for which reliable data is readily available from the South Korean Ministry of Knowledge Economy.[4] In this forty-eight year span, the average yearly inflow of FDI to South Korea was 3.34 billion U.S. dollars. However, there is ample variance in the average annual flow during clearly distinguishable periods (see Figure 6.2). Table 6.1 reproduces the results of difference-in-means analyses of annual inflows received by South Korea under different political regimes, administrations, and the ideological orientation of the chief executive.[5] In years under elected governments, the average annual FDI inflows were $7.08 billion, or 1.20 percent of aggregate output, roughly two-and-a-quarter times higher than the average share of FDI to GDP under authoritarian rule. This difference is not only substantive but also statistically significant.[6]

---

[4] The source of the data is *Foreign Investment Statistics*, Ministry of Knowledge Economy, Republic of Korea. Accessed on April 26. 2011. http://www.mke.go.kr/info/foreigner/sumTotal.jsp.

[5] Table 6.1 reproduces the results for FDI net inflows as a percentage of GDP. Identical results are obtained when a natural log transformation of FDI net inflows, inflows as shares of investment, or Korea's share of world FDI flows are used instead.

[6] The differences remain substantively and statistically significant when FDI is measured in levels, natural logs, or as a share of world FDI flows.

Table 6.1. *Korea: Mean FDI/GDP (%) by incumbent (1962–2009)*

Group	Mean	Std. Err.	Obs.
(1) Elected	1.21 (0.82, 1.60)	0.19	22
(2) Autocrat	0.53 (0.35, 0.72)	0.09	26
(3) Left	1.88 (1.30, 2.47)	0.26	10
(4) Right All	0.57 (0.40, 0.73)	0.08	33
(5) Center	0.57 (0.04, 1.10)	0.19	5
(6) Elected Right	0.70 (0.27, 1.13)	0.18	7
(7) Left + Center	1.45 (0.92, 1.97)	0.24	15
All years	0.84 (0.62, 1.06)	0.11	48

Autocrat: Park Chung-hee (1962–79), Chun Doo-hwan (1980–87); Elected: Roh Tae-woo (DJP-Right), Kim Youn-sam (DLP-Center), Kim Dae-jung (MDP-Left), Roh Moo-hyun (Uri-Left), Lee Myung-bak (GNP-Right).

Differences in mean FDI/GDP

$Mean_i - Mean_j$	Difference	Std. Err.	$t - stat$, d.f.	p-value
(1) – (2) Elected – Autocrat	0.68 (0.28, 1.08)	0.20	3.41, 46	0.00
(3) – (4) Left – Right (All)	1.32 (0.91, 1.72)	0.20	6.54, 41	0.00
(3) – (5) Left – Center	1.31 (0.46, 2.16)	0.39	3.32, 13	0.01
(3) – (6) Left – Elected Right	1.18 (0.45, 1.92)	0.34	3.44, 15	0.00
(6) – (5) Elected Right – Center	0.13 (−0.46, 0.71)	0.26	0.48, 10	0.64

95% confidence intervals in parentheses.

The data show stark differences across four distinctive patterns in FDI performance that roughly correspond to the developmental policies adopted by Korea over time.[7] During the first period (1961–1971), characterized by the movement from light import substitution to export promotion and the emergence of the local industrial conglomerates, the percentage of FDI to output was 0.43.

FDI inflows go up in the second period (1972–81) when export-led growth and the development of the heavy industries took priority: the average level of FDI/GDP rises to 0.67 percent, yet it remains low when compared to Asian and Latin American countries in a similar position. The strategy to develop heavy industries demanded resources that were covered by retained earnings from the diversified conglomerates that grew stronger under the protection provided by the government, or by external borrowing rather than by FDI (Nicolas, 2003). The third period (1981–97) starts soon after the 1980 crisis, and is characterized by a steady movement toward economic deregulation and liberalization, driven by Korea's bid to become an OECD member, the *chaebols'* venturing into foreign markets, and by political opening (Chung and Wang, 2000; Nicolas, 2003). Yet, inward FDI dropped to o.49 percent of GDP, a level comparable to that of the 1960s. The Korean Development Bank continued its policy of intervention in financial markets in favor of the chaebols (Haggard and Mo, 2000; Nicolas, 2003). It was only after the 1997 financial crisis that FDI took off. The average FDI for this period increased a four-fold to 1.79 percent of GDP.

Note that the political orientation of democratically elected leaders varies dramatically: under Roh Tae-woo, who inherited the coalition that had been built by Park Chung-hee and sustained by Chun Doo-hwan, the chaebols remained influential despite the fact that his government was subject to external pressure to liberalize the Korean economy. Roh was succeeded by Kim Young-Sam and his Democratic Liberal Party, representing a more centrist coalition. The next two administrations led by Kim Dae-jung and Roh Moo-hyun, with different levels of support in the legislature, had closer links to labor and took a more confrontational stance toward the chaebols. Their leanings are also likely to be reflected in the differential ability among different democratic administrations to attract foreign investment.

Table 6.1 indeed suggests that there is a significant difference in the degree of openness to FDI when the chief executive moves toward the left of the political spectrum. The yearly average net inflows under Roh Tae-woo were $1.9 billion (0.44 percent of GDP). Under Kim Young-Sam they reached

---

[7] On the different developmental regimes, see Nicolas (2003).

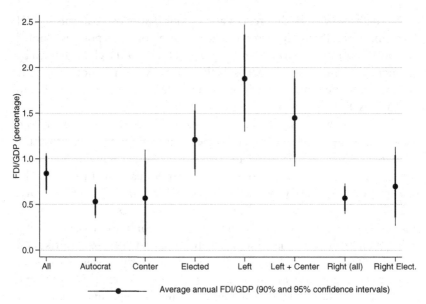

Figure 6.3. Mean FDI/GDP (%) by incumbent orientation.

$2.9 billion per year on average (roughly 0.57 percent of GDP). In the post-crisis era, average FDI flows rise to $12.0 billion under Kim Dae-jung and $10.5 billion under Roh Moo-hyun, representing 2.5 and 1.27 percent of GDP, respectively. The difference between the average FDI/GDP during the Kim Dae-jung and Roh Moo-hyun administrations, and that during their predecessors, democratically elected and authoritarian alike, is statistically significant beyond conventional levels, as shown in the confidence interval around the difference of the mean values of the two groups and in the value of the t-statistic for that difference reported in Table 6.1 and Figure 6.3.[8] The differences in the mean level of FDI/GDP in the Kim Dae-jung and Roh Moo-hyun administrations, on the other hand, are not.

South Korea's share of world FDI flows is also larger under democratic administrations, and even higher under governments located on the left of the political spectrum, suggesting that the relationship is not driven by supply factors alone. In the next section, I conduct additional tests of the differences in FDI openness using time-series data and control for other factors identified in the model and in the empirical literature on the determinants of FDI discussed in Chapter 4.

---

[8] The means remain statistically different beyond conventional levels of confidence for different transformations of FDI inflows.

6.2.2 Time Series Analysis

In this section, I conduct a series of statistical analyses, which allow for economic factors such as market size (GDP), relative endowment of capital (GDP per capita or GDP per worker), and trade orientation (openness as a percentage of GDP) to be controlled for. The change over time of these variables may affect the attractiveness of the Korean economy to foreign investors, and thus affect the level of FDI inflows to South Korea.

One important test is identifying whether movements toward democratic rule are associated with the existence of institutional constraints. This association, as proposed by the extant literature, follows from the assumption that autocratic leaders are unconstrained (North and Weingast, 1989; Jensen, 2006; Li and Resnick, 2003). Yet, democratically elected administrations in South Korea vary in terms of the constraints they face: whereas Kim Young-sam's DLP (and his New Korea Party after 1997) controlled a majority in the National Assembly, neither Kim Dae-jung nor Roh Moo-hyun did during his entire mandate or in his first two years in office, respectively. Kim Dae-jung had to rely on the United Liberal Party to secure passage of his reform agenda. Roh, on the other hand, gained control of the National Assembly in 2005.[9] Therefore, in the econometric analysis I test the partisan orientation hypothesis side by side with the institutional constraints hypothesis, namely that as the number of veto players increases, so should FDI inflows.

I use the yearly data from the Ministry of Knowledge Economy for the 1962–2007 period. The ratio of FDI flows to GDP and several of the control variables are integrated for the first degree, meaning that their first differences are stationary, as was the case with the Argentine sample. For the reasons discussed in the previous chapter, the dependent variable and main independent variables enter the estimating equation in first-differences.

The results from the Prais-Winsten models reported in Table 6.2 confirm the difference-in-means tests. After controlling for GDP per worker, domestic savings, world FDI flows, openness and government spending, the positive relationship between the ideology of the chief executive and the ratio of FDI/GDP in South Korea remains. Governments of the right, democratic and authoritarian alike, are less open to FDI. The difference is of approximately one-half of a standard deviation, and is statistically different from zero beyond the 95 percent level of confidence in all specifications.[10]

---

[9] See Table 6.4.

[10] The substantive and statistical significance of the coefficient on the orientation of the chief executive is stronger when lagged one period.

Table 6.2. *Time series results*

Variables	(1)	(2)	(3)	(4)	(5)	(6)	(7)	(8)	(9)	(10)
FDI/GDP$_{t-1}$	-0.877^c	-1.019^c	-1.027^c	-1.068^c	-0.056	-0.053	-0.095	0.153	0.109	-0.097
	(0.250)	(0.209)	(0.212)	(0.218)	(0.233)	(0.209)	(0.229)	(0.254)	(0.250)	(0.236)
Left	1.099^b	1.276^b	1.260^b	1.334^b	1.368^b	1.325^b	1.417^b	1.115^b	1.121^b	1.418^b
	(0.424)	(0.513)	(0.518)	(0.525)	(0.563)	(0.516)	(0.562)	(0.518)	(0.535)	(0.570)
Center			-0.059							
			(0.300)							
Δ Political Constraints		-0.512	-0.553	-0.402	0.335	-0.454	0.374	1.314	1.549	0.391
		(1.522)	(1.629)	(1.550)	(3.017)	(1.516)	(2.995)	(2.883)	(3.265)	(3.162)
Left × ΔPol. Const.				-1.534					-4.581	-0.255
				(8.318)					(9.303)	(8.642)
ΔGDP per Worker (US$ 1,000)		0.017	0.022	0.031	-0.058	0.028	-0.048	-0.054	-0.043	-0.048
		(0.132)	(0.137)	(0.129)	(0.120)	(0.127)	(0.116)	(0.120)	(0.126)	(0.122)
ΔTrade/GDP (%)		0.016	0.017	0.015	0.010	0.011	0.005	-0.016	-0.007	0.005
		(0.030)	(0.030)	(0.034)	(0.031)	(0.029)	(0.032)	(0.035)	(0.037)	(0.035)
Δ Fedfunds rate				0.017		0.017	0.018			0.018
				(0.028)		(0.028)	(0.032)			(0.032)
ΔGovt. Consumption/GDP (%)		-0.155	-0.150	-0.122	-0.498	-0.127	-0.478	-0.358	-0.331	-0.476
		(0.277)	(0.278)	(0.263)	(0.354)	(0.261)	(0.348)	(0.373)	(0.399)	(0.367)
ΔSavings/GDP (%)					-0.019		-0.021	-0.005	-0.005	-0.021
					(0.050)		(0.051)	(0.052)	(0.057)	(0.053)
ΔLn(FDI World flows)								0.533^a	0.563^a	
								(0.305)	(0.326)	
Constant	0.465^c	0.456^b	0.468^b	0.463^b	0.527^b	0.469^b	0.551^b	0.408^a	0.397^a	0.549^b
	(0.134)	(0.200)	(0.204)	(0.224)	(0.223)	(0.218)	(0.254)	(0.211)	(0.227)	(0.254)
N	45	45	45	45	37	45	37	37	37	37
Years	1963–2007	1963–2007	1963–2007	1963–2007	1971–2007	1963–2007	1971–2007	1971–2007	1971–2007	1971–2007
R²	0.448	0.525	0.529	0.541	0.332	0.271	0.331	0.430	0.412	0.330
Adj. R²	0.422	0.450	0.439	0.440	0.171	0.133	0.139	0.267	0.216	0.107
DW *stat* (transformed)	2.048	1.971	1.972	1.972	1.851	1.995	1.883	2.074	2.029	1.879
DW *stat* (original)	1.603	1.732	1.814	1.799	1.696	1.744	1.765	1.807	1.805	1.775
ρ	0.525	0.636	0.643	0.667	0.680	0.656	0.699	0.585	0.628	0.700

Dependent Variable: ΔFDI/GDP.

Prais-Winsten AR(1) regression; semi-robust standard errors in parentheses.

^{a} $p < 0.1$, ^{b} $p < 0.05$, ^{c} $p < 0.01$.

The variable measuring political constraints is also positive, but not significant in model 4. The first difference of the ratio of FDI/GDP is positively associated with differences in international capital mobility (proxied for by world FDI outflows), capital endowment (proxied for by GDP per worker) and openness, although GDP per worker and openness are not statistically different from zero. FDI/GDP is negatively correlated with domestic savings and government consumption. The sign on the political constraints variable reverses when specified as levels rather than as a first-difference, suggesting that institutional constraints cannot account for the massive reaction of foreign investors to changing policy environments and political conditions. Differences in levels of institutional constraints cannot explain the difference in the ability of Kim Young-sam, Kim Dae-jung, and Roh Moo-hyun to enact regulatory changes toward FDI either, as discussed in the next section.[11]

The effects captured by the previous tests are consistent with the predictions from the theory: democratization requires that political leaders compete for support, and so governments are more likely to become accountable to the median voter, who is more likely to be endowed with labor rather than capital given that income and wealth distribution are skewed. Political competition push political influence away from domestic business interests and closer to those of labor, an assumption that appears to be justified in the South Korean case where democratic governments, particularly those led by Kim Youn-sam, Kim Dae-jung, and Roh Moo-hyun, have denounced business–government links and cronyism and have been better predisposed towards workers.

6.2.3 Organized Labor in South Korea

In sharp contrast to Argentina, organized labor in South Korea was relatively weak and, more often than not, off the radar screens of political leaders in the developmental era. The organized labor movement, established in the 1960s and heavily repressed by Park and Chun, was unable to exert political influence until the mid to late 1980s.[12] Bargaining is also decentralized and

---

[11] Additional tests using the sectoral allocation of FDI, available for the 1985–2008 period, yield results consistent with those reported in Pinto and Pinto (2008) and Jensen et al. (2012) that there is a large variation in the composition of FDI in the different periods. In the aggregate, however, FDI flows are larger under left-leaning governments.

[12] Labor organization is based on the principle of freedom of association, yet only 12 percent of the South Korean labor force is unionized, a low figure when compared to similar countries in South America (see Table 5.6 in Chapter 4). Union density is highest in large companies: in

conducted at the firm level.[13] Employers oppose collective bargaining above the firm level. Collectively bargained agreements apply to unionized workers and employers participating in the negotiations. Yet, as labor in the bigger firms is unionized and these firms tend to enjoy overwhelming market power over their suppliers, the conditions established in these collective agreements are likely to affect mid- and small-sized firms as well.

Under authoritarian regimes, union leaders were persecuted and union activity was repressed. The Great Workers' Struggle of 1987 under the presidency of Roh Tae-Woo marks the start of the era when organized labor became more vocal. This outburst of labor activism coincides with the emergence of the democratic movement in South Korea (Kihl, 2005). The attempts by the Kim Young-sam's DLP party at incorporating labor into the political arena were mild and short lived. Initially, the Kim Young-sam administration could not disregard the union movement, an emerging actor that had gained strength with industrialization and political visibility with democratization. His government committed to a policy of non-intervention in labor market disputes, in stark contrast to the preceding administrations that usually intervened in favor of business interests. The clash with business was inevitable: "while organized labor attempted to gain political and social acceptance as a legitimate social partner of government and business, the chaebol also demanded new powers to discipline labor and make the rules of labor market more flexible" (Kihl, 2005, p. 105). Over time, and as some of the chaebol recovered, the Kim Young-sam administration took a more pro-business stance, which is consistent with its centrist political orientation. By 1997, a series of ill-managed labor disputes fatally wounded the relationship between organized labor the Kim Young-sam

---

manufacturing firms with over 15,000 employees, the rate is 76 percent (You and Lee, 1999). In comparison, the rate of unionization for companies with 30 to 99 employees is 5.4 percent and only 0.9 percent for companies with 10 to 29 employees (You and Lee, 1999).

[13] Though most unionized workers belong to a union organized at the enterprise level, there is a recent trend toward affiliation with industry level unions, a development favored by unions but disliked by business. There are two major unions at the national level: the Korean Confederation of Trade Unions (KCTU) and the Federation of Korean Trade Unions (FKTU). The KCTU is the more radical of the two groups and has systematically clashed with business and government. In 2000 the KCTU participated in the foundation of the Democratic Labor Party of Korea, which received 13 percent of the popular vote in the April 2004 elections for the National Assembly. With ten representatives (two elected in single member districts and eight by proportional representation) the DLP became the third largest party in the Assembly behind the pro-government Uri Party and the conservative Grand National Party. Of the two major union groups the percentage of members affiliated with sectoral unions is larger for the KCTU (42.9 percent, compared to 15.6 percent for FKTU). On the side of business, the peak-level associations have limited influence on their affiliates, and there's no organization at the sectoral level.

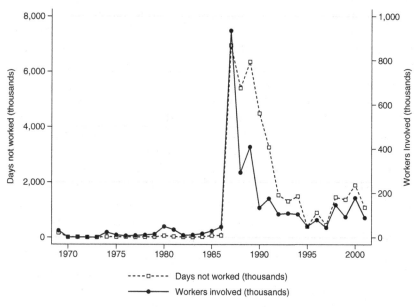

Figure 6.4. Labor disputes, 1969–2001.

administration.[14] A few years earlier, President Kim Young-sam himself had already backed down from his harsh anti-chaebol rhetoric that resonated positively with the Korean voters during his presidential campaign (Kihl 2005, 111).

The Kim Dae-jung administration, in contrast, made a genuine effort to engage organized labor as an equal partner in the structural reform of the economy. Recognition of union organization rights appeared to be one of the top priorities of the government. The effect of this policy is evident in the lower number of days lost to and number of employees participating in strikes (Figure 6.4). The creation of the Korea Tripartite Commission (KTC) on January 15, 1998, regulation on redundancy dismissals and the stress on fair burden sharing in public speeches reflected a rather corporatist stance by the new administration. However, the crisis made the social compromise short lived, as organized labor withdrew from the tripartite commission in February 1999 (Gills and Gills, 2000; Koo, 2001).

Moreover, the tests suggest that the substantive effects brought about by democratization in this policy area are minor, which is not surprising given that domestic businesses still play a major role in Korean politics

---

[14] "Kim's pledges to undertake labor reforms in favor of workers were altered to accommodate business demands, which ultimately failed to satisfy either group" (Kihl, 2005, p. 173).

despite its weakened position. Changes in policy orientation had been gradual and policy reversals were not uncommon. Kim Young-sam's efforts to dismantle business–government links through deregulation, liberalization, and reform, reflected in his campaign rhetoric and early government program, failed, as he caved into business pressure.[15] The policy orientation of his government remained fairly conservative (Lee, 2005). The left-of center coalition led by Kim Dae-jung, on the other hand, faced a retreating business class whose reputation was further tarnished as the financial crisis unfolded. As is discussed in the following section, these changes are reflected in the Korean government's disposition toward foreign investors and in its ability to lure foreign investors into the country. Despite the efforts by both Kim Young-sam and Kim Dae-jung to curb the political clout of the chaebols, political practices and policy outcomes still reflect the overwhelming influence of these groups on this policy dimension as well.

Kim Dae-jung was succeeded by another leader from the Millennium Democratic Party (MDP), Roh Moo-hyun, who espoused a more leftist political orientation than his predecessor, adopted a chaebol-bashing rhetoric, and aspired to promote competition in the marketplace (Lee, 2005). Roh embarked on an FDI-promotion strategy that revolved around the Foreign Investment Promotion Act, which liberalized the investment regime, granted incentives to foreign investors, and created the Korea Trade and Investment Promotion Agency (KOTRA). Under the new regime, foreign investors enjoyed greater privileges than domestic firms (Nicolas, 2003). The end result was a sharp increase in FDI, which remained high even during the 2001 global downturn.

6.3 Explaining South Korea's FDI Performance

South Korea has been characterized as one of the most prominent cases of crony capitalism (Kang, 2002). From this perspective, the Korean government used state-derived rents to prop up the domestic conglomerates, and the support of these congloerates was central to the incumbents' efforts

---

[15] The quid-pro-quo relationship between business and government during the Kim Young-sam administration, for instance, was more than apparent. As Haggard and Mo (2000, 202) recount, when launching the business specialization policy' that would force chaebol to concentrate in one industrial sector and phase out their presence in other sectors, Kim Young-sam offered exemptions in credit and investment controls in exchange. Concessions to the politically influential domestic business sector, lax monetary policy, and expansionary measures aimed at reactivating the economy all led to over-investment. This over-investment, combined with poor monitoring of the financial sector, created a moral hazard problem that lies at the center of all explanations of the 1997 financial crisis.

of building and sustaining political power (Jones and SaKong, 1980; Woo-Cumings, 1991; Noland, 2007). The high level of business influence in politics makes Korea remarkably similar to the Japan, a country that South Korean planners aspired to emulate in the design of their economic program. Under authoritarian rulers, but particularly under Park, labor was repressed. Further, the Korean government systematically discouraged foreign investment, both direct and portfolio. Capital stocks were financed by domestic sources and supplemented with short-term trade credit and long-term loans under strict control from the Bank of Korea (Westphal et al., 1981, 1985; Stoever, 2002; Eriksson, 2005; Noland, 2007). Compared to Latin American countries such as Brazil and Mexico, FDI played a minor role in the early stages of Korea's industrialization (Haggard, 1990; Amsden, 1992; Haggard and Mo, 2000; Nicolas, 2003). Throughout most of the post-war era, and until the late 1990s, inward FDI into South Korea was negligible.[16]

One interpretation of the selective nature of the regulatory regime toward FDI adopted by South Korea holds that this regime was functional to the government's developmental program: when deemed necessary to its industrial strategy, the Economic Planning Board would allow foreign investment, but only in those sectors that needed technological assistance from abroad (Mardon, 1990; Sachwald, 2001). But a different interpretation is also plausible: restrictions on foreign ownership and MNC activity were aimed at promoting and protecting the interests of politically strong domestic business groups. These groups lobbied the government to preserve their prominent status in the Korean economy and the government responded by adopting severe barriers to the activity of multinationals in the country.

The government also opened selectively to international financial markets. The difference between domestic savings and investment was covered by American aid early on, and later by foreign borrowing which was directed by the government to a limited number of firms and sectors (Noland, 2007).[17] It should not be surprising that the sectors that received preferential treatment were those where the chaebol were strongest (Haggard and Mo, 2000). In the following section, I discuss the evolution of the regulatory regime and its link to changing political conditions. Table 6.5 in the Appendix presents the different statutes aimed at regulating FDI in South Korea.

---

[16] The only exception is 1974 as the oil crisis was particularly painful in South Korea, causing FDI and portfolio investment to spike in terms of GDP in that year (Noland, 2007).

[17] American aid covered more than half of the value of imports in the 1950–1953 period (Cho, 1994; Noland, 2007).

6.3.1 Regulation of Foreign Investment

Immediately after the war, Korea remained closed to FDI, as the colonial experience made South Koreans equate foreign investment with Japanese domination (Kwon, 2004). During the reconstruction era, South Korea adopted a liberal policy toward FDI, yet investors stayed out (Eriksson, 2005). That South Korea failed to attract foreign investment despite its liberal statutes should not be surprising: openness to foreign investment is a matter of government pronouncements as well as practices, which in the South Korean case remained fairly restrictive due to historical, cultural, and political legacies (Stoever, 2002).

In 1960, the National Assembly passed Foreign Capital Inducement Act promoted by the government of Rhee Syng-man. This statute was revised in 1961 under the military government of Park Chung-hee, following the spirit of the developmental strategy of the early Park regime where foreign capital played a minor and subsidiary role.

As discussed in Section 6.2.1, the industrial and development policies adopted by South Korea since the 1960s can be classified into three distinct periods. In the first period (1961–71), import substitution of non-durable consumer and intermediate goods was combined with export promotion. Following the normalization of relations with Japan in 1965, Japanese investment started trickling back into South Korea (Stoever, 2002). Japanese investment was concentrated in labor-intensive manufacturing, and gradually entered in competition with domestic firms. The Japanese presence in the sector eventually led to a political backlash that resulted in more stringent investment regulations.

The second period (1972–81), which starts with Park's reelection for a third term, was aimed at deepening industrialization through the expansion of the heavy and chemical industries (the *heavy and chemical industry drive*); this strategy required access to external markets to make up for low domestic savings. The emphasis on heavy industry was accompanied by a move away from import substitution and into export promotion. The government sheltered incumbent firms from competition, allowing them to accumulate retained earnings, and encouraged them to diversify (Sakong, 1993; Noland, 2007). The development of heavy industry put extra financial strain on the Korean economy and domestic savings, and retained earnings soon proved to be insufficient. The shortfall was covered with foreign debt rather than investment. The preferred sources of finance were long-term loans administered under the strict guidance of the Bank of Korea: capital was channeled to the conglomerates by a regulated system of financial repression

(Pyo, 1990; Lee, 1993; Yoo, 1994; Noland, 2007). During this period, the Korean government did allow for some forms of foreign investment, albeit under very specific and restrictive terms. Under the regulatory framework in place at the time the government would screen potential investors and would either steer them into specific sectors where their competitive pressure on domestic firms would be limited or would force them to enter into a joint venture with a local firm. The restrictive conditions for entry granted domestic firms enough leverage to squeeze their partners' claims over profits (Amsden, 1992; Stoever, 2002). In addition, stock market investment by non-residents remained prohibited until 1982 (Noland, 2007).

The next period (1982–97) is associated with a gradual liberalization and opening of the economy. Yet, domestic liberalization proved difficult for the Korea government: the previous strategies, aimed at invigorating domestic industrial conglomerates, transformed the chaebol into strong domestic actors that the government could not afford to ignore (Haggard, 1990; Haggard and Mo, 2000; Nicolas, 2003). The regime was based on a positive list system that restricted the number of sectors where foreign investment was admitted. The authority to control foreign investment was granted to the *Foreign Capital Deliberation Committee*, an agency created within the Economic Planning Board. Though the chaebol controlled the Federation of Korean Industry, the Korean private sector had direct access to the EPB, and thus secured a voice in the economic planning process, allowing it to block any project that would hurt them.

In 1973, the government made the investment regime more restrictive: it revised the list of sectors where investment was authorized and further excluded projects by companies that competed with exports of Korean firms that disrupted the local demand and supply of raw materials or that offered limited technological spillovers. Joint ventures were given priority, yet even where allowed there was a cap of 50 percent of equity in the hands of foreigners. That year, the government enacted the *Engineering Service Promotion Act*, which mandated that engineering projects be granted to Korean firms as major contractors, with foreign firms participating as minority partners whenever their know-how was essential (Eriksson, 2005). Additionally, foreign investment was admitted into the Export Processing Zones (EPZ) under the condition that all resulting output be exported and all inputs be procured in the domestic market.[18] These initiatives were unambiguously

---

[18] EPZs were established under the *Free Export Zone Establishment Act* of January 1970. The EPZs are specially designated areas where firms can process raw materials and imported inputs tax-free. Production from these assembly facilities has to be exported in full (Eriksson, 2005).

aimed at limiting competition with domestic firms (Haggard, 1990). The result, reflected in the data presented in previous sections, was low levels of direct investment inflows (Korea Exchange Bank, 1987).

On September 25, 1980, the Chun Doo-hwan government announced a *Foreign Investment Promotion Plan* aimed at liberalizing and internationalizing economic activity through diversifying the sources of foreign investment and expanding the range of sectors open to foreign investors.[19] The government opened up the food, pharmaceutical, and logistics industries as well as some business services to foreign investors. Additionally, the minimum amount of foreign investment was reduced from U.S.$20 million to $10 million.[20]

In 1981, the government increased the number of sectors open to foreign investment. In total, foreign investment was allowed in 427 manufacturing sectors, comprising 50 percent of the products in the KICS classification (Nicolas, 2003). Response from foreign investors was limited nonetheless. The *Foreign Capital Inducement Act* was revised in 1984. The amendments included switching from a positive to a negative list of sectors where investment would be admitted, eliminating restrictions on the repatriation of capital and dividends and allowing foreigners complete ownership of domestic firms. (Nicolas, 2003). The government also eased the foreign investment approval system. Foreign investment, satisfying certain rules, would be automatically approved. The system of tax reductions to selectively promote foreign investment was also revised: foreign investments contributing to the improvement of the balance of international payments, bringing advanced technology, or setting up shop in a Free Economic Zone would be eligible for tax breaks. However, the new policy reduced the period for which the tax breaks were granted to five years. Before this change, foreign investment in approved activities would enjoy tax breaks for five years at the full level and 50 percent of the tax benefit for an additional three year-interval.[21]

Despite this veneer of liberalization, the investment regime kept its restrictive outlook: it required mandatory technology transfers to local firms and

---

[19] Park was assassinated on October 26, 1979; he was succeeded by then Prime Minister Choi Kyu-hah, who served as Acting President until December 1979 when he was elected to the Presidency. Choi served for less than a year, and was subject to strong pressure by military commanders led by Chun Doo-hwan. Chun was appointed President by the electoral college on August 27, 1980, and inaugurated on September 1, 1980.

[20] National Archives of the Republic of Korea: "Foreign Investment Promotion Plan." http://contents.archives.go.kr/next/content/listSubjectDescription.do?id=006742.

[21] National Archives of the Republic of Korea: "Amendment to the Foreign Capital Inducement Act." http://contents.archives.go.kr/next/content/listSubjectDescription.do?id=006743.

included local procurement clauses that foreign-owned projects had to satisfy. The response from foreign firms was tepid, as the investment and technology transfer regime created an environment that was only conducive for the transfer of mature technologies, which could be otherwise acquired through the purchase of turnkey plants, patents, and licenses or the import of capital goods. In the end, technological progress resulted from the reverse engineering of these mature technologies rather than from technology transfers by foreign firms (Kim and Kim, 1985; Eriksson, 2005). Additional liberalizing measures were adopted in 1989 ensuing a U.S. threat to label South Korea as a Priority Foreign Country for its discriminatory practices, but actual opening to FDI was gradual (Nicolas, 2003).

By 1989, the four largest chaebols, *Samsung, Hyundai, Lucky-Goldstar,* and *Daewoo,* were estimated to account for about half the country's GNP (Sakong, 1993; Noland, 2007). Proponents of democratization in Korea demanded the dispersal of economics as well as political power. When the Roh Tae-woo government sought to undertake political reform, the chaebol served as popular targets in political discourse, which ultimately permeated into regulatory and legislative activity. For instance, the public outcry over land prices was followed by a government decree ordering the chaebol to sell property. Additionally, the Roh government ordered banks to grant 35 percent of their loans to small and middle-sized businesses, in part to deflect the growing public resentment of the influential business conglomerates. Despite its efforts to distance itself from the chaebols, the Roh administration was forced to rely on the conglomerates' economic prowess to pull the country out of a slump as export performance deteriorated. The nuanced stance toward economic groups is reflected in a statement by the Minister of Trade and Industry in February of 1989: "[it is not the government's] intent to restrict the growth of the chaebol; [on the contrary] we aim at sustaining small and medium-sized industries so that the imbalances can be redressed" (Bedeski, 1994).

In 1993, the Kim Young-sam administration adopted a globalization program, the New Economic Policy (NEP), known in Korean as *segyehwa,* which comprised measures to liberalize investment practices as well.[22] His

---

[22] In one of his *Segyehwa* speeches, Kim Young-sam actively criticized previous regimes for having been "so obsessed with growth that they ignored the serious implications of the increasing concentration of economic power in the hands of a few business tycoons, the worsening income distribution, and the intensifying strife among different regions and classes." Globalization vision and strategy (*Segyehwa ui pichon kwa chonryak*), Seoul: Presidential Segyehwa Promotion Commission, August 1995:10.

government was relatively unconstrained as his party had a clear majority in the unicameral National Assembly (Haggard and Mo, 2000).

The government's NEP aimed at relaxing government regulation and creating an environment conducive for the growth of an autonomous market. The anti-chaebol measures already in place, including the fair trade system, mainline business system, and loan and payment guarantee management system, were weakened, and a more radical corporate governance policy aimed at protecting the rights of minority shareholders was abrogated. In addition, with mounting pressure for deregulation from the business community itself and from a ruling coalition that relied on it for political support, Korea's Fair Trade Commission failed to implement the Fifth Amendment of the Fair Trade Act of December 1996, which mandated that the chaebol entirely liquidate the payment guarantees between affiliates by 2001 (Lee, 2005).

In terms of foreign investment, the government announced its plan to open up industries to foreign firms. As of 1993, 244 sectors were closed to foreign investments. The government planned to open up 133 of those sectors by 1997.[23] Moreover, while in 1993, foreign firms were required to collaborate with their domestic counterparts in 50 sectors of the economy, the government planned to open 43 of these sectors to foreigners by 1997 as well.[24] The conservatively inclined government of the Democratic Liberal Party also argued for the need to relax regulations that restricted the ability of big businesses seeking to expand their direct investment overseas.

The reform movement ultimately collapsed, in part because the Kim Young-sam administration failed to break the links between government, big business, and the financial sector (Gills and Gills, 2000).[25] The chaebols continued receiving preferential treatment from the government including regulation of market access and subsidized loans, leading to over-investment in productive capacity and subsequently to business failures in times of

---

[23] The government also planned to create a foreign investment zone where foreign investors would be exempt from regulations related to foreign exchange management, restrictions on land acquisition, and other liberalization measures. *The ChosunIlbo* January 28, 1994.

[24] National Archives of the Republic of Korea; "Five-Year Plan for Foreign Investment Opening." http://contents.archives.go.kr/next/content/listSubjectDescription.do?id=006745.

[25] The permission granted to *Samsung* in December 1994 to build an auto factory in Pusan marks a turning point in the Kim Young-sam government (Haggard and Mo, 2000). The subsequent period is characterized by policy reversals: reform efforts lost momentum and appeal, plans for eliminating barriers to entry were scrapped and deregulation virtually stalled (Haggard and Mo, 2000).

financial stress. In the first quarter of 1997, *Hanbo Steel* and *Sammi Steel* declared bankruptcy, whereas the country's third car manufacturer *Kia* was in deep financial trouble. These failures, the first of leading Korean conglomerates in a decade, were linked to the financial crisis of 1997 (Kihl, 2005).

Major policy changes in the regulation of FDI inflows in the late 1990s coincided with the election in 1997 of Kim Dae-jung, who won the presidency in his fourth attempt with strong support from the left and labor, two of the core constituents of the Millennium Democratic Party. Kim Dae-jung, like Menem in Argentina, was regarded as a populist leader and his administration faced staggeringly difficult economic conditions. Under these circumstances he embraced reform and made clearly identifiable attempts to ease the concerns of economic actors and the international community about his reputation. Moreover, Kim Dae-jung regarded foreign investment rather than loans and other forms of financial capital as necessary for long-term financial stabilization and economic growth.

Prior to the crisis, Kim Young-sam announced his intention to abolish the Foreign Capital Inducement Act of 1966 and promoted the liberalization of the investment regime. There is a major change in the principles under which FICA and the new investment regime were conceived: while FICA focused on regulating FDI, the new regime was allegedly based on the principle of FDI liberalization. In that spirit, the Ministry of Trade Industry and Energy relaxed a provision, which prevented foreign investors from importing capital goods and production machinery; the prior regime demanded that foreign investors procure these machines from Korean sources.[26] Yet, Kim Young-sam was unable to pass the proposed legislation during his mandate. The Foreign Investment Promotion Act (FIPA) was eventually enacted under the stewardship of Kim Dae-jung. FIPA entered in effect on November 17, 1998.

FIPA created new procedures for the establishment of foreign investment in Korea, eliminating restrictions on the foreign control of domestic business and granting tax and other investment promotion incentives including tax cuts for foreign investment projects valued at over U.S.$100 million, rent reductions for government-owned land and access to financial markets.[27] The government had previously allowed foreign investors to engage in

---

[26] *The ChosunIlbo*, March 13, 1996; *The ChosunIlbo*, January 25, 1996.
[27] *The ChosunIlbo*, November 15, 1998.

hostile takeovers and to purchase domestic stocks without any limits.[28] FIPA also led to the establishment of the Office of the Investment Ombudsman under the orbit of the Korea Trade and Investment Agency (KOTRA) and the Korea Investment Service Center (Nicolas, 2003; Sachwald, 2003).

Compared to its predecessors, the Kim Dae-jung administration was successful in attracting FDI: South Korea received U.S.$31.5 billion in the 1997–2001 period, equivalent to three quarters of Korea's FDI inflows between the 1960s to date (UNCTAD, 2003). In 2002, the Ministry of Finance and Economics announced the expansion of tax cuts for foreign investors, lowering the minimum size for eligibility in manufacturing to U.S.$50 million from U.S.$100 million. The Ministry also expanded the list of industries covered by the cuts beyond manufacturing to the logistics and travel industries.[29] In November 2002, the government enacted the controversial *Free Economic Zone Act*, which granted foreign investors operating in the Zone additional tax cuts and exemptions from labor regulations, against strong opposition from unions.[30]

The Kim Dae-jung government was no friend of the conglomerates and criticized the crony capitalist system that sustained them. Yet during its first eighteen months in office, Kim's administration chose not to impose any additional constraints on the enfeebled chaebols. As economic recovery took hold, however, the government adopted a more aggressive agenda. Kim Dae-jung pushed through the Assembly a series of amendments to the Fair Trade Act (FTA) aimed at regulating the activity of the conglomerates, protecting small and medium-sized companies, and promoting competition. The fifth FTA amendment of 1996, passed under Kim Young-sam, stipulated that the chaebol should clear their payment guarantees by March 2000. In February 1999, the National Assembly passed the seventh amendment to the FTA aimed at reinforcing the regulation of cartels by strengthening a ban on joint action. The ninth amendment, enacted in June 2001, extended the ban for an extra year and granted the FTC the authority to demand information from the Office of the National Tax Administration, in order to enforce the provisions of the FTA (Lee, 2005). The overhaul of the financial system was also instrumental in severing the ties between government-controlled banks and the chaebol that characterized the era of crony capitalism in South Korea. This policy also served as an indirect method of

---

[28] *The ChosunIlbo*, April 24, 1998.

[29] *The ChosunIlbo*, January 21, 2002.

[30] *The ChosunIlbo*, November 14, 2002; to promote foreign investment, the government will reduce taxes for foreigners from 2003, *The ChosunIlbo*, December 20, 2002.

coercing the business conglomerates to become self-supporting and to abandon their excessive dependence on government support and protection (Lee, 2005).

Kim Dae-jung was succeeded by Roh Moo-hyun and the Uri party, a splinter from the Millennium Democratic Party. Roh Moo-hyun had a more liberal and more decisively anti-chaebol agenda than his predecessor. Roh's Uri party gained control over the National Assembly in the April 2004 election, after a tumultuous campaign season that resulted in Roh's impeachment by the National Assembly and suspension from the Presidency office. Roh was reinstated after the election by the Constitutional Court, overturning the Assembly's decision.

In an effort to reform the family-owned large conglomerates, the Roh Moo-hyun government decided to enact reforms to the corporate governance regime, allowing minority shareholders to file class-action suits against chaebol firms. The initiative received strong objections from the business community. The Fair Trade Commission planned to force the chaebol to reduce their control over financial entities, placing a limit on the conglomerates' ownership of shares with voting rights in financial institutions including securities, insurance, and investment trust management firms, and banning chaebol takeovers of state-owned enterprises (Lee, 2005).

In 2004, FIPA was amended once again to allow the government to subsidize select foreign investment projects depending on their technological characteristics and the number of jobs created. The Roh government further eased the criteria for designating the foreign investment zones where investors could enjoy the special benefits provided in the law and reduced the minimum amount of investment required to U.S.$30 million from U.S.$50 million to be eligible for the benefits granted by the law to manufacturing firms, while in logistics the amount was reduced to U.S.$10 million from U.S.$30 million. In 2005, the government extended the authority to local governments to grant subsidies as well.[31] In November 2007, the National Assembly introduced the Korean version of the "Exon-Florio Amendment" aimed at preventing hostile takeovers. The government had been opposed to its introduction, but succumbed to pressure from the business sector.[32]

Lee Myung-bak and his Grand National Party regained control of the Presidency in 2008 and a decisive majority of the National Assembly in the

---

[31] Korea Trade and Investment Promotion Agency (2007), *White Paper on Foreign Direct Investment Promotion*.

[32] *The ChosunIlbo*, November 20, 2007.

2009 election. Most regulations on corporate governance and chaebol activity that had been introduced by Kim Dae-jung and Roh Moo-hyun were relaxed under Lee; the Fair Trade Commission shifted its focus towards supporting the "market-friendly" environment demanded by the chaebols.[33] The government also lifted regulations pertaining to the cross-ownership of stocks by major conglomerates enacted during the reform era.[34] The restructured chaebols, those that were able to weather the financial crisis and survived the squeeze from the left, regained a central role in Korean politics. These political changes would eventually be reflected in the regulatory environment offered to foreign investors and in Korea's openness to FDI. Soon after Lee Myun-bak took office, South Korea was once more perceived as becoming less friendly to foreign investors.[35]

6.3.2 Investment Performance

In 1960, the government of Rhee Syng-man designed a foreign investment regime that aimed at opening up the light manufacturing export sector. Korea received its first inflow of foreign investment in 1962. But implementation of the policy remained restrictive, and while the presence of foreign corporations was tolerated, the instruments adopted were carefully designed to the specific case at hand. The Rhee government was deposed by a military uprising led by Park Chung-hee in 1961. Park Chung-hee, South Korea's military president from 1961 to 1979, pursued a nationalist development program pivoting around the public sector and domestic conglomerates. The investment liberalization initiative launched by Rhee was amended under Park; by the early 1970s the original liberal outlook was completely reversed not only in practice but on paper as well. The chaebols developed vested interests in preserving their privileged position in the economy and in minimizing domestic competition. To the extent that they needed access to foreign technology, the chaebol preferred licensing agreements or joint ventures. Foreign investors were banned from holding a controlling stake in Korean firms and could only enter as minority shareholders in a joint venture with local partners. Once the Korean partner had sufficiently benefited from the transfer of technology from its foreign

---

[33] *The ChosunIlbo*, January 7, 2008.

[34] *The ChosunIlbo*, March 4, 2009.

[35] *The Korea Times*, May 5, 2008. Kim Jae-Kyoung, "Foreign Investors Turn Away from Korea. Foreign Direct Investment falls for the first time in one and a half years."

counterpart, the government financially supported initiatives to buy off the foreign partner (Mardon, 1990; Haggard, 1990; Amsden, 1992; Stoever, 2002; Eriksson, 2005). This pattern was not only visible in the oil refining and chemical sectors, but in banking and services as well. As a result, the level of foreign ownership in Korea was low. In 1980, for instance, 14 percent of the firms operating in Korea were foreign-owned, of which only 12 percent were majority foreign-owned (Mardon, 1990). Outward FDI, on the other hand, was liberalized in the 1980s, helping Korean businesses in labor-intensive industries to move abroad (Sachwald, 2003).

Between 1962 and 1973, Korea was relatively open to foreign investment, but still far less so than other countries in a similar position (Haggard, 1990). The steady penetration of Japanese firms in low-tech manufacturing, which came to dominate the sector, led to an overt reaction by local firms, who felt that they could be running the sectors themselves (Stoever, 2002). After 1974 and through 1981, inflows of FDI to South Korea were minimal: according to balance of payment statistics published by the Bank of Korea, the total stock of foreign investment by the end of this twenty-year span was U.S.\$ 1,356 million; by 1981, annual inflows represented 0.1 per cent of the country's GDP, and the ratio of FDI stock to GDP was barely 1.8 percent of GDP (UNCTAD, 2001; Nicolas, 2001, 2003; Stoever, 2002).

At the onset of the heavy industry development phase, FDI played an important role in developing some sectors such as the pharmaceutical, petrochemical, and heavy industries. Yet, as the Korean conglomerates continued their diversification drive in the early 1980s, they started facing a technological bottleneck (Noland, 2007). In their quest to approach the technological frontier, the conglomerates demanded government authorization to team up with foreign companies. The Korean government responded to this demand by reforming the investment regime to encourage joint ventures in technologically advanced sectors, but implementation got caught in a quagmire of bureaucratic red tape and lethargy (Kim and Kim, 1985; Stoever, 2002; Sachwald, 2003; Eriksson, 2005). In the electronics sector, for instance, the government prohibited the presence of fully-owned subsidiaries of MNCs, but encouraged joint ventures between foreign and domestic firms, granting control to the latter (Amsden, 1992). Joint ventures with foreign MNCs and technology transfer agreements helped domestic firms such as Samsung and Lucky Goldstar (now LG) become global players in the electronics and semi-conductor industries (Nicolas, 2003). Throughout the 1980s, the government drove investment into manufacturing, which accounted for roughly 70 percent of all direct investment. By and large, FDI inflows remained low (Figure 6.2) and flowed only into a limited number of sectors permitted by local regulations, mostly consumer goods where brand names were important (see Tables 6.6 and 6.8 and Nicolas [2001, 2003]). The strategy of selective opening to foreign investment was congruent with the chaebols' interests and reflects the influence of these industrial conglomerates (Nicolas, 2001, 2003; Stoever, 2002).

The Kim Young-sam (1993–8) and Kim Dae-jung (1998–2003) administrations abandoned the state-centric model of economic development adopted by their predecessors Chun Doo-hwan and Roh Tae-woo and moved toward a market-oriented economic regime. Both of them condemned the rampant collusion between government officials and chaebol leaders in designing the country's industrial policy, and hoped that introducing competition in the marketplace would erode the influence of the chaebol in politics (Kihl, 2005). Major changes in the foreign investment regime were introduced in the 1990s, as Korea's bid to join the Organization for Economic Co-operation and Development (OECD) and the World Trade Organization (WTO). Both required deregulation and market opening (Sachwald, 2003; Stoever, 2002). Consumer pressure for lower prices also played an important role in the liberalization process, particularly for democratically elected officials who were more responsive to voters' demands. Despite these regulatory changes, enforcement was lax; FDI inflows would only pick up momentum in the aftermath of the financial crisis.

Current explanations of the sudden increase of FDI inflows in the late 1990s point to the combination of two factors: the evolution of firms' valuation (Krugman, 2000) and liberalization of the FDI regime (Sachwald, 2003). That the evolution of firms' valuation played a major role is granted by the amount of mergers and acquisitions, which account for a large share of inflows in recent years.[36] The sudden interest in Korean firms was most likely encouraged by what Krugman (2000) calls a *fire sale condition* resulting from the fall of the dollar denominated value of assets in light of the stark devaluation of the won when the financial crisis hit the Korean economy. Fire sales occur when the purchase of assets result from the financial situation of the targets rather than the technological or managerial advantages of the buyer. The massive purchase of Korean companies in different sectors by foreign investors may indicate that this phenomenon was taking place.[37]

---

[36] Cross-border M&A flows in Korea were $7.3 billion dollars in 1998, $19.6 billion in 1999, $9.7 billion in 2000, and $11.4 billion in 2001 (see UNCTAD, 2000 and Sachwald, 2001).

[37] According to Krugman (2000), Korean assets had on average lost 70 percent of their dollar value due to devaluation in 1997, while pre-crisis prices might have been overvalued. Chari et al. (2004), on the other hand, find no evidence of a fire-sale, and instead argue that the

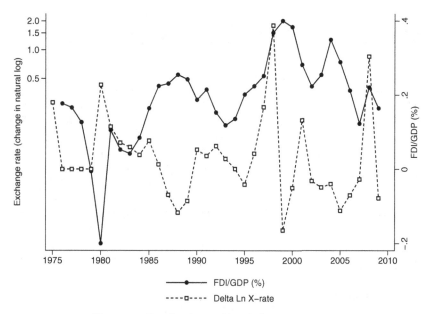

Figure 6.5. Devaluation and FDI inflows, 1976–2002.

However, devaluation seems to have had the opposite effect in previous episodes. Figure 6.5 shows that there is a sharp contrast between the post-crisis era and the previous instances of devaluation, particularly during the 1980 crisis when FDI dropped significantly.[38] From 1970 through 1996, the FDI/GDP series runs counter to the difference in the natural log of the exchange rate series. After the crisis, the sign of the relationship appears to reverse initially.

Table 6.3 reproduces the results of a test that also suggests that devaluation alone cannot explain the difference in FDI performance. I regress the first difference of the natural log of the annual FDI inflows to South Korea in the 1962–2007 period (or 1970–2007 depending on the availability of covariates), on the first difference of the natural log of the exchange rate,

outcome is more likely the result of foreign partners already active in South Korea buying off their counterparts. In any event, the sharp devaluation of 1997 resulted in a major influx of direct investment from abroad, in sharp contrast with earlier episodes in South Korean history.

[38] In February 1980, the Chun government decreed a 20 percent devaluation of the won and the currency remained depreciated throughout most of the decade. It was only revalued after intense United States pressure in 1988, which labeled South Korea as a "currency manipulator" under the provisions of the Trade Act of that year (Kim, 1993; Noland, 2007).

Table 6.3. *FDI inflows and devaluation*

	DV: ΔLn FDI inflows (MKE)					
Variables	(1)	(2)	(3)	(4)	(5)	(6)
Ln FDI inflows$_{t-1}$	−0.103	−0.417[b]	−0.926[c]	−0.967[c]	−0.891[c]	−0.959[c]
	(0.077)	(0.200)	(0.260)	(0.187)	(0.268)	(0.205)
ΔLn Xrate	−1.505	−4.018	−3.542[a]	−1.122	−0.239	−0.163
(Right=1, Dev. =1)	(1.697)	(2.553)	(1.831)	(1.672)	(0.480)	(0.297)
Left		1.179[a]	1.334[b]	1.895[c]	1.242[a]	1.869[c]
(Left=1, Dev.=0)		(0.651)	(0.589)	(0.448)	(0.707)	(0.446)
Left x ΔLn Xrate		3.305	3.368[a]	1.084	1.456[b]	1.897[c]
(Left =1, Dev.=1)		(2.589)	(1.854)	(1.716)	(0.678)	(0.471)
Center		0.654[b]	0.537	0.737[b]	0.532	0.739[a]
(Center=1, Dev.=0)		(0.314)	(0.343)	(0.335)	(0.349)	(0.369)
Center ΔLn Xrate		7.079[b]	7.424[c]	5.910[c]	1.272[c]	1.573[c]
(Center=1, Dev.=1)		(2.944)	(2.206)	(1.740)	(0.375)	(0.276)
Political Constraints		5.540	6.008[b]	8.217[b]	4.453	7.569[a]
		(3.337)	(2.938)	(3.258)	(2.667)	(3.725)
Ln GDP/capita			0.287	−1.159	−0.0313	−1.211
			(0.938)	(1.141)	(0.880)	(1.128)
Ln Trade/GDP (%)			1.591[b]	0.126	1.766	0.0446
			(0.667)	(0.618)	(1.061)	(0.704)
Ln Public spending/GDP (%)			0.790	−3.874	−0.382	−3.920[a]
			(2.674)	(2.707)	(3.282)	(2.227)
Ln Savings/GDP (%)				−1.335		−1.205
				(1.067)		(1.177)
Ln FDI World Outflows				0.645[b]		0.693[b]
($ billion)				(0.249)		(0.267)
Constant	0.859	0.370	−6.307	26.83	−1.204	27.55[a]
	(0.525)	(0.610)	(12.32)	(16.41)	(14.11)	(14.92)
N	45	45	45	38	45	38
R^2	0.105	0.374	0.580	0.595	0.462	0.586
Adj. R^2	0.062	0.256	0.457	0.400	0.303	0.388
$Z(t) =$ (D-F unit root test resids.)	−9.63	−8.56	−6.12	−5.89	−6.34	−5.73
MacKinnon appr. *p*-value	0.00	0.00	0.00	0.00	0.00	0.00
DW *d*-statistic	2.72	2.46	1.82	1.97	1.95	1.93

Dev.: Devaluation = 1 if Δ Ln Xrate ≥ .10 in Models (5) and (6).
Robust standard error in parentheses.
Significance levels: [a] $p < 0.10$; [b] $p < 0.05$; [c] $p < 0.01$.

where higher values indicate depreciation of the won. In a model specification with no political variables on the right-hand side of the equation, the coefficient on changes in the exchange rate is negative but does not attain statistical significance (see Table 6.3, model 1). Model 2 includes variables capturing the orientation of the executive. Center is used for the Kim Young-sam administration and Left for the administrations led by Kim Dae-jung and Roh Moo-hyun. The omitted category is Right, both elected and autocratic. The periods under Center and Left rule, but particularly the last year of the KYS and two years under the KDJ, are of special interest because they comprise the period where the chaebols were in distress and the democratically elected governments had an incentive to restrain the political influence of business in response to demands from their constituencies. Model 2 includes a term that interacts the change in the log of the exchange rate with Center and Left dummies. This model returns a negative coefficient on changes in the exchange rate; a positive and significant coefficient on the interactive term between the exchange rate and the Center dummy; and a positive albeit insignificant coefficient on the interaction term of the change in the exchange rate and the Left dummy. The net effect of changes in the exchange rate and FDI is positive and significant for the Center government, whereas the net effect is not significantly different from zero for the Left-leaning governments. The coefficients on the Left and the Center dummies are also positive and statistically significant beyond the 90 and 95 percent levels, respectively. The findings are robust to the addition of controls as shown by models 3 and 4.

In order to test more directly the *fire sale* hypothesis, I identify six episodes of sharp devaluation of the won (depreciations greater than 10 percent in one year) in the sample: 1964–5, 1971–2, 1975, 1980–1, 1997–8, and 2001. These episodes occur under different economic and political conditions, as previously discussed. I thus interact each of the episodes with the political orientation of the different Korean governments. The expectation is that Right-leaning governments are more protective of domestic businesses and thus associated with lower FDI inflows; these governments will be particularly sensitive to the interests of domestic businesses at times of sharp devaluations as previously discussed. Devaluations would be associated with lower inflows under the Right. Under the Left, on the other hand, we should expect higher inflows and no major effect from devaluations. The results are presented in models 5 and 6. Consistent with the results from the time series analysis presented in Section 6.2.2, I find that the Left is associated with higher FDI inflows than the Right, both under normal times and when the exchange rate depreciates sharply, and the Centrist governments.

There is no difference for devaluations under the Left. The Center government, on the other hand, is associated with higher inflows than the Right during times of devaluation, but lower levels than the Left in normal times. Altogether these results suggest that the Left-leaning governments are associated with higher levels of FDI than their Center and Right-leaning counterparts, irrespective of the value of the exchange rate. When the exchange rate depreciates, FDI flows drop during the non-democratic and Right-leaning administrations. Yet, the effect of devaluation on FDI reverses when Centrist parties are in power. The explanation for this differential effect of devaluation in the two periods is likely to be found in the changing pattern of influence in Korean politics. While devaluation has made assets cheaper, the adoption of a more favorable investment regime under Kim Dae-jung and Roh Moo-hyun has contributed to the exponential increase in FDI inflows to South Korea. Foreign capital was allowed to acquire full ownership over Korean affiliates, and even take control in those cases where it had been operating in joint ventures with domestic counterparts (Sachwald, 2001).

FDI fell sharply in 2001, the last episode of devaluation identified in the sample, but this could be attributed to a decline in foreign investment flows worldwide. A similar pattern can be observed in 2008. However, these declines could also reflect the recovery of the Korean business sector. In recent years, potential investors have complained that South Korea's inward FDI environment remains burdened by the continuing complexities of registration, notification, licensing, and approval requirements. This parallels multiple Korean governments' partial success in their efforts to restructure the corporate sector. A clear example is the fate of the corporate reform agenda pushed by the Millennium Party, which resonated positively with the public immediately after the 1997 crisis. After his inauguration, Kim Dae-jung's administration forced a reform package on the chaebols. This package involved changes in corporate governance regulations, financial restructuring and the elimination of subsidies and preferential treatment for domestic business groups. Changes in corporate governance, such as the requirement that chaebols produce consolidated accounts, would lead to greater corporate transparency and better protection of shareholder rights. The implementation of this package contributed to the collapse of ten of the top thirty conglomerates and placed Daewoo close to bankruptcy. A handful of the largest chaebols survived the crisis, regained their position as major political players, and ultimately forced the Korean government to postpone the deadline for liquidation of crossholdings (Gourevitch and Shinn, 2005).

6.4 Business, Workers, and the Politics of FDI

South Korea is a case where the government has had close links to domestic businesses and has adopted policies aimed at benefiting them. The theory expects that South Korea is closed to FDI. We should expect that democratization and changes in the orientation of the chief executive would be associated with changes in the regime regulating investment and in the conditions offered to foreign investors. The evidence presented in the previous sections seems to support these predictions. The Korean government has systematically discriminated against foreign investors in a clear attempt to cushion domestic businesses from competition from abroad. These groups would lobby the government to preserve their prominent status in the Korean economy and the government responded by restricting inflows of FDI and the activity of MNCs. According to Yoo (1999), the Korean government established a system of protection of domestic firms that is based on the principle of "survival of the fattest."

Democratization of Korean politics has made political leaders less receptive to the demands of the chaebols and more sensitive to those of labor. This movement is associated with more favorable investment conditions and larger foreign direct investment inflows. Until the 1997 financial crisis, the chaebols remained politically influential and were able to stall most initiatives aimed at reforming the Korean economy and opening up the country to foreign investment (Noland, 2007). Eventually, the restrictive investment regime created its own demands for perpetuation, as chaebol leaders exploited their access to government agencies to keep investors out. The 1997 crisis, which affected the ability of the chaebols to survive in the marketplace, undermined their ability to effect favorable conditions in the political marketplace (Moon and Mo, 2000; Gills and Gills, 2000).

The analysis presented in this chapter reveals important differences between the Argentine and South Korean cases. In the Argentine case, I tracked foreign investment policy and performance to the changing pattern of labor influence and support. In this chapter, I show that changes in FDI policy and performance in South Korea appear to be driven by the preferences of capital owners and their political influence. In the South Korean case, labor seems to have played a minor role for reasons related to labor's preferences on this issue dimension, ranging from utter opposition of foreign investment in the post-war years to tolerance toward the end of the century, and to its limited influence in Korean politics.

In terms of preferences, received wisdom has it that organized labor in South Korea has been hostile to multinationals (Guillen, 2000). In the period following World War II, this tension probably resulted from the repressive labor relations conditions that existed under the Japanese colonial rule (Sakong, 1993). Later in the 1960s and 1970s, the few foreign firms that operated in the country had a reputation of exploiting labor. In that period, the main disputes with the foreign owned plants operating in the export-processing zones were no different than those in the plants owned by domestic firms outside of them and pivoted around unionization and working conditions. These conflicts lasted until the late 1970s and criticism of multinationals remained high until the late 1980s. Tension became lower when higher wages eroded the advantage of export-processing activities in Korea. Facing the likely scenario of unemployment and lower wages, the FKTU expressed its support to the Park government initiative to lure MNCs to the EPZs. In the 1990s, organized labor adopted a more positive stance toward multinationals and accepted foreign investment as a necessary evil (Guillen, 2000).

Democratic governments, particularly those with a leftist orientation like Kim Dae-jung and Roh Moo-hyun's administrations, have taken a more positive approach towards labor by trying to ease the level of conflict in the workplace and encouraging peaceful dispute resolution. Despite recent developments that have raised the political status of workers and organized labor, the explanation of South Korea's regulation of FDI is found in the evolution of the relationship between business and government. In times when labor was repressed and politics dominated by a ruling coalition centered around domestic capital interests, policy toward foreign investment was restrictive. The demise of the crony capitalists during the crisis and the ascent of a progressive coalition led to liberalization of the investment regime and the inflow of foreign investment into South Korea. These findings are consistent with the predictions from the partisan theory of investment.

It is worth noting that even though the chaebols have in general lost the overwhelming political clout they once wielded, the groups that survived the crisis still make their presence felt in Korean politics. While the fall of FDI inflows during 2001 and 2008 may be a response to supply factors related to global trends, it is also possible that the remaining restrictions on foreign investment that potential investors complain about is associated with the re-emergence of the chaebol influence felt in this as well as in corporate governance and financial deregulation, particularly under Lee and the GNP.[39]

---

[39] Restrictions on foreign investment remain, especially in the IT sector where foreigners cannot own more than 49 percent of a firm, though restrictions on individual ownership have been lifted.

APPENDIX 6.1

Table 6.4. *South Korea: Government orientation*

Tenure	President	Party	Regime	Assembly, period		Main Party, seats (%)	Opposition, seats (%)	
1963–79	Park Chung-hee	DRP	Auth.	6th	1963–7	DRP	110/175 (62.9%)	
				7th	1968–70	DRP	129/175 (73.7%)	
				8th	1971–2	DRP	113/204 (55.4%)	
				9th	1973–9	DRP (73); app'ed (73)	146/204 (66.7%)	
				10th	1979–80	DRP (68); app'ed (73)	141/231 (61%)	
1980–88	Chun Doo-hwan	DJP	Auth.	11th	1981–4	DJP	151/276 (54.7%)	
				12th	1985–8	DJP	148/276 (53.6%)	
1988–93	Roh Tae-woo	DJP	Dem.	13th	1989–92	DJP	125/299 (41.8%)	PfPD	70/299 (23.4%)
1993–8	Kim Young-sam	DLP	Dem.	14th	1993–6	DLP	148/299 (49.5%)	DP	98/299 (32.8%)
				15th	1997–2000	NKP	139/299 (46.5%)	NCNP	79/299 (26.4%)
1998–2003	Kim Dae-jung	MDP	Dem.	16th	2001–04	GNP	133/273 (48.7%)	MDP	115/273 (42.7%)
2003–08	Roh Moo-hyun	Uri	Dem.	17th	2005–08	Uri	152/299 (50.8%)	GNP	122/299 (40.8%)
2008–	Lee Myung-bak	GNP	Dem.	18th	2009–	GNP	153/299 (51.8%)	DP	81/299 (27.1%)

app'ed = appointed by Park; DJP = Democratic Justice Party; DLP = Democratic Liberal Party; DP = Democratic Party.
DRP = Democratic Republican Party; GNP = Grand National Party; MDP = Millenium Democratic Party.
NCNP = National Congress for New Politics; NKP = New Korea Party; PfPD = Party for Peace and Democracy; Uri = Uri Party.

Table 6.5. *Foreign investment statutes (1960–2007)*

Year	Instrument	Provisions
1960	Act 532	*Foreign Capital Inducement/Promotion Act* – Establishes a positive list system. – Introduces tax incentives for selected investments.
1961	Act 678	First Amendment of *Foreign Capital Inducement/Promotion Act* – Allows foreign investment in agriculture, fisheries, livestock, electricity, tourism industry, and service sector.
1961	Act 778	Second Amendment of *Foreign Capital Inducement/Promotion Act* – Expands the list of countries from which foreign investment is allowed (from countries that signed a *Treaty of Friendship and Commerce* to countries that have diplomatic relations with South Korea).
1966	Act 1802	*Foreign Capital Inducement Act* – Tax reduction (income tax, corporate tax, property tax, acquisition tax).
1973	Act 2598	First Amendment of *Foreign Capital Inducement Act* – Revises the list of sectors where investment is authorized and excludes projects by companies that compete with exports of Korean firms. – Foreign investment allowed in the export processing zones only under the condition that all its output is exported.
1981	Act 3518	Third Amendment of *Foreign Capital Inducement Act* – Relaxes the requirement of foreign investment (the minimum amount is reduced from 200 thousand to 100 thousand U.S. dollars).
1983	Act 3691	Fourth Amendment of *Foreign Capital Inducement Act* – Switches from a positive to a negative list system. – Eliminates restrictions on repatriation of capital, dividends, and on the percentage of the firms foreigners could own.
1991	Act 4316	Sixth Amendment of *Foreign Capital Inducement Act* – Simplifies the foreign investment procedure. – Removes the article on the penalty surcharge that was previously imposed on foreign investors who did not comply with their contracts to export all or part of their output.
1992	Act 4519	Eighth Amendment of *Foreign Capital Inducement Act* – Shifts from authorization/approval system to report/acceptance system.
1993	Act 4584	Ninth Amendment of *Foreign Capital Inducement Act* – Abolishes the Foreign Capital Inducement Review Council.

Year	Instrument	Provisions
1994	Act 4814	Tenth Amendment of *Foreign Capital Inducement Act* – Establishes the Korea Investment Service Center.
1997	Act 5256	*Foreign Investment and Foreign Capital Inducement Act* – Changes the name of relevant law. – Reduction of or exemption from fees on rents of land and facilities owned by the State located in an exclusive zone for foreign enterprises or situated in the national industrial complexes.
1998	Act 5523	First Amendment of *Foreign Investment and Foreign Capital Inducement Act* – Allows acquisition of stocks through merger (M&A)(up to 1/3) without the consent of the board and simplifies the procedure.
1998	Act 5538	Second Amendment of *Foreign Investment and Foreign Capital Inducement Act* – Allows acquisition of stocks through merger (M&A)(more than 1/3) without the consent of the board and simplifies the procedure.
1998	Act 5559	*Foreign Investment Promotion Act* – Increases tax exemption and reduction period to 10 years (previously 8 years; corporate tax, acquisition tax, property tax, aggregate land tax). – Introduces registration tax reduction and exemption (8–15 years). – Tax incentives granted for industry-supporting service businesses. – Allows the Mayor/*Do* governor to designate and develop the foreign investment zone where support for facilities such as harbors, roads, water-supply facilities, railways and electric facilities is provided. – Establishes Foreign Investment Support Center.
2000	Act 6317	First Amendment of *Foreign Investment Promotion Act* – Foreign investment allowed in intellectual property rights, real estate, and stock market as prescribed by a Presidential Decree. – Relaxes the requirement for designation of the foreign investment zone. (The region where two or more foreign investors in relevant industries intend to invest can be designated as the foreign investment zone).

(*continued*)

Table 6.5 *(continued)*

Year	Instrument	Provisions
2001	Presidential Decree 17474	Fifth Amendment of *Enforcement Decree of the Foreign Investment Promotion Act* – Relaxes the requirement for designation of the foreign investment zone; the minimum amount of foreign investment is reduced from 100 million to 50 million U.S. dollars in manufacturing, from 30 million to 20 million U.S. dollars in tourism. – Relaxes the requirement for the reduction or exemption of the rental payments for land owned by the State. (The minimum amount of foreign investment is reduced from 10 million to 5 million U.S. dollars.)
2002	Presidential Decree 17851	Sixth Amendment of *Enforcement Decree of the Foreign Investment Promotion Act* – Designation of the foreign investment zone allowed for facilities engaging in research and development activities. – Relaxes the requirement for designation of a foreign investment zone for firms with advanced technology; the minimum amount of foreign investment is reduced from 50 million to 30 million U.S. dollars.
2003	Act 7039	Second Amendment of *Foreign Investment Promotion Act* – Cash grant for foreign investors depending on whether the relevant foreign investment accompanies high technology, the effect of technology transfer, and the size of job creation.
2004	Presidential Decree 18222	Seventh Amendment of *Enforcement Decree of the Foreign Investment Promotion Act* – Relaxes the requirement for designation of a foreign investment zone; the minimum amount of investment is reduced from 50 million to 30 million U.S. dollars for manufacturing industry and from 30 million to 10 million U.S. dollars for activities in logistics.
2004	Act 7281	Third Amendment of *Foreign Investment Promotion Act* – Allows local governments to provide cash grants.
2007	Act 8401	Fourth Amendment of *Foreign Investment Promotion Act* – Relaxes requirement for cash grant and tax exemption and reduction for foreign investment in R&D industries.

Table 6.6. *Sectoral distribution of FDI inflows*

Year	Total	Primary	Manufacturing	Services	Utilities
1962	3.58	–	3.58	–	–
1963	5.74	–	5.74	–	–
1964	0.65	0.03	0.62	–	–
1965	21.82	0.03	10.80	11.00	–
1966	15.62	0.37	11.67	3.58	–
1967	28.27	–	21.43	6.84	–
1968	25.63	0.16	19.30	2.38	3.78
1969	48.58	–	44.98	3.52	0.08
1970	75.89	0.71	62.09	7.36	5.73
1971	40.25	0.18	29.10	9.72	1.24
1972	121.97	1.85	109.57	10.46	0.11
1973	318.15	2.62	197.86	101.57	16.10
1974	152.83	1.31	128.14	21.70	1.69
1975	207.32	0.71	169.91	34.80	1.90
1976	79.15	0.75	55.80	21.30	1.31
1977	83.63	0.50	38.77	40.45	3.92
1978	149.43	0.73	61.83	73.33	13.54
1979	191.30	0.71	97.73	69.09	23.77
1980	143.14	–	100.72	36.65	5.77
1981	153.16	1.20	128.27	9.10	14.59
1982	189.03	1.77	115.06	39.12	33.08
1983	269.42	1.50	104.73	147.52	15.68
1984	422.35	0.06	251.87	123.84	46.58
1985	532.20	0.93	174.85	345.61	10.81
1986	354.74	1.69	257.14	93.76	2.14
1987	1,063.85	0.74	660.81	400.24	2.06
1988	1,283.76	6.96	694.88	573.99	7.93
1989	1,090.28	1.61	564.43	512.52	11.71
1990	802.64	0.53	519.72	280.66	1.73
1991	1,396.00	1.17	947.98	441.91	4.94
1992	894.51	1.39	516.02	376.76	0.34
1993	1,044.27	–	391.86	588.94	63.47
1994	1,316.51	28.44	490.75	789.15	8.17
1995	1,970.43	1.59	1,041.43	863.45	63.96
1996	3,205.48	232.84	1,674.81	1,222.38	75.46
1997	6,971.14	4.10	2,507.82	4,361.77	97.44
1998	8,858.00	78.43	5,835.31	2,591.01	353.24
1999	15,544.62	8.26	8,368.70	6,783.78	383.87
2000	15,264.88	3.65	6,876.97	8,129.38	254.88
2001	11,287.63	6.75	2,911.34	7,230.98	1,138.56
2002	9,095.33	16.06	2,337.22	5,124.12	1,617.93
2003	6,470.55	5.79	1,699.22	4,132.34	633.20
2004	12,795.59	0.64	6,216.95	6,144.63	433.38
2005	11,565.53	3.01	3,078.03	8,300.96	183.53
2006	11,247.44	1.83	4,252.71	6,627.00	365.90
2007	10,515.63	3.19	2,692.35	7,613.06	207.02
2008	11,711.87	0.94	3,007.32	8,387.87	315.74
2009	11,484.14	15.88	3,724.86	7,594.55	148.85

Table 6.7. *Sectoral distribution of FDI inflows (%)*

Year	Primary	Manufacturing	Services	Utilities
1962	0.0	100.0	0.0	0.0
1963	0.0	100.0	0.0	0.0
1964	4.7	95.3	0.0	0.0
1965	0.1	49.5	50.4	0.0
1966	2.4	74.7	22.9	0.0
1967	0.0	75.8	24.2	0.0
1968	0.6	75.3	9.3	14.7
1969	0.0	92.6	7.3	0.2
1970	0.9	81.8	9.7	7.6
1971	0.4	72.3	24.2	3.1
1972	1.5	89.8	8.6	0.1
1973	0.8	62.2	31.9	5.1
1974	0.9	83.8	14.2	1.1
1975	0.3	82.0	16.8	0.9
1976	0.9	70.5	26.9	1.7
1977	0.6	46.4	48.4	4.7
1978	0.5	41.4	49.1	9.1
1979	0.4	51.1	36.1	12.4
1980	0.0	70.4	25.6	4.0
1981	0.8	83.8	5.9	9.5
1982	0.9	60.9	20.7	17.5
1983	0.6	38.9	54.8	5.8
1984	0.0	59.6	29.3	11.0
1985	0.2	32.9	64.9	2.0
1986	0.5	72.5	26.4	0.6
1987	0.1	62.1	37.6	0.2
1988	0.5	54.1	44.7	0.6
1989	0.1	51.8	47.0	1.1
1990	0.1	64.8	35.0	0.2
1991	0.1	67.9	31.7	0.4
1992	0.2	57.7	42.1	0.0
1993	0.0	37.5	56.4	6.1
1994	2.2	37.3	59.9	0.6
1995	0.1	52.9	43.8	3.2
1996	7.3	52.2	38.1	2.4
1997	0.1	36.0	62.6	1.4
1998	0.9	65.9	29.3	4.0
1999	0.1	53.8	43.6	2.5
2000	0.0	45.1	53.3	1.7
2001	0.1	25.8	64.1	10.1
2002	0.2	25.7	56.3	17.8
2003	0.1	26.3	63.9	9.8
2004	0.0	48.6	48.0	3.4
2005	0.0	26.6	71.8	1.6
2006	0.0	37.8	58.9	3.3
2007	0.0	25.6	72.4	2.0
2008	0.0	25.7	71.6	2.7
2009	0.1	32.4	66.1	1.3

Table 6.8. *Sectoral FDI inflows*

FDI inflows (million dollars)	1985	1990	1995	2000	2005	2009
Total	236.1	759.2	1,246.9	8,643.1	6,065.8	6,586.3
Primary sector	0.9	0.7	0.8	−0.1	2.9	38.4
Agriculture and fishing	0.3	−0.1	0.8	3.2	0.5	11.0
Mining and quarrying	0.6	0.8	0.0	−3.3	2.4	27.4
Petroleum and natural gas	0.0	0.0	0.0	0.0	0.0	0.6
Manufacturing	167.7	367.8	493.6	3,223.1	512.3	708.1
Food products	4.2	28.1	11.8	78.1	−134.6	−1,660.0
Textiles, apparel, wood	5.0	18.8	56.2	110.4	64.9	115.7
Refined petroleum, chemical, rubber, and plastics	28.8	79.3	225.4	319.9	−461.3	618.2
Metal and mechanical	9.4	74.8	135.5	1,647.9	36.9	564.6
Office, computers, radio and TV	37.9	7.5	−0.7	143.9	294.8	144.7
Medical, precision, and optical instruments	0.0	5.7	8.5	2.7	12.7	16.4
Vehicles and transportation equipment	79.2	153.6	56.8	920.3	699.0	871.8
Electricity, gas, and water	0.0	0.0	0.0	149.2	14.6	67.2
Construction	19.8	0.2	9.4	10.6	47.1	4.9
Service sector	46.8	342.8	618.2	3,035.0	6,075.8	4,086.8
Trade and repairs	14.3	79.2	178.2	23.5	667.5	1,192.2
Hotels and restaurants	10.2	65.7	97.7	94.1	18.7	107.9
Transportation, storage, and communications	0.0	5.2	5.3	125.7	1,142.0	257.3
Financial Intermediation	19.9	173.6	328.6	1,630.7	3,096.4	1,237.1
Real estate and other business activities	0.0	15.0	7.9	1,112.8	1,021.5	1,210.7
Other services	2.5	4.0	0.6	48.3	129.9	81.5
Unallocated	0.9	47.7	124.9	2,225.3	−586.9	1,680.9

Source: Source OECD (Online Resource).

Table 6.9. *Sectoral FDI outflows*

FDI outflows (million dollars)	1985	1990	1995	2000	2004	2009
Total	115.6	958.9	2,758.7	3,476.9	5,964.7	20,259.7
Primary sector	76.8	185.4	17.1	40.8	341.0	5,118.1
Agriculture and fishing	5.4	33.4	−8.0	14.2	34.5	49.6
Mining and quarrying	71.4	152.0	25.1	26.5	306.5	5,068.5
Petroleum and natural gas	0.0	0.0	51.1	24.7	249.5	4,106.1
Manufacturing	20.7	482.4	1,860.3	971.8	3,388.7	7,047.2
Food products	2.4	65.0	67.3	46.2	162.9	270.4
Textiles, apparel, wood	1.5	0.0	246.2	55.8	346.4	375.6
Refined petroleum, chemical, rubber, and plastics	6.7	78.7	118.0	187.7	379.1	647.9
Metal and mechanical	0.6	206.2	287.5	105.9	482.8	1,748.9
Office, computers, radio, and TV	0.0	0.0	708.3	309.9	1,245.1	1,042.5
Medical, precision, and optical instruments	0.0	0.0	0.0	0.0	60.2	78.2
Vehicles and transportation equipment	0.0	0.0	226.5	13.2	402.3	1,545.5
Electricity, gas, and water	0.0	0.0	0.0	1.3	0.0	489.0
Construction	1.6	4.9	77.5	47.7	77.0	284.8
Service sector	16.5	286.2	774.7	2,399.7	2,158.0	7,320.6
Trade and repairs	11.1	229.8	251.9	487.4	1,153.0	1,866.4
Hotels and restaurants	0.0	0.0	56.1	15.7	109.2	104.8
Transportation, storage, and communications	0.0	1.7	332.8	57.0	101.4	323.1
Financial Intermediation	0.0	0.0	0.0	9.1	4.0	1,523.6
Real estate and other business activities	2.8	0.0	130.1	1,807.9	586.4	3,275.4
Other services	2.6	54.7	3.9	22.6	204.0	227.4
Unallocated	−0.1	0.0	29.1	15.6	0.0	0.0

Source: Source OECD (Online Resource).

Data Description and Sources

FDI net inflows (current U.S.$): Foreign direct investment is net inflows of investment, as defined in previous chapters. Data are in current U.S. dollars. Source: *Foreign Investment Statistics*, Ministry of Knowledge Economy, Republic of Korea. Accessed on April 26. 2011. http://www.mke.go.kr/info/foreigner/sumTotal.jsp.

Political Constraints: See definition in Chapter 4. Source: Henisz (2000a), 2010 release.

GDP per worker (constant price entry): GDP per worker is gross domestic product divided by the economically active population. Source: Heston et al., 2002, 2011; PWT 7.0.

Savings (% of GDP): See definition in Chapter 4. Heston et al., 2002, 2011; PWT 6.2, PWT 7.0.

Government Share of GDP: Government consumption as a share of GDP. Source: Heston et al., 2002, 2011; PWT 7.0.

Trade/GDP (%): Trade is the sum of exports and imports as a share of GDP. Heston et al., 2002, 2011; PWT 6.2, PWT 7.0.

Exchange rate: Exchange Rate to U.S.$ (national currency units per U.S. dollar). Source: Heston et al., 2002, 2011; PWT 7.0.

FDI World Outflows: Source: UNCTAD, Division on Investment and Enterprise, UNCTADstat, Inward and outward foreign direct investment flows, annual, 1970–2010.

SEVEN

Conclusion

The broad paradigms that dominate the study of internationalization of the world economy suffer from a great weakness: they tend to neglect the interests of political actors or assume away their political strength. This book aims at overcoming this neglect. I develop a *partisan theory of investment* aimed at explaining why countries adopt different regimes toward foreign direct investment (FDI) and how these investment regimes change over time. Contrary to received wisdom, I argue that labor-based governments welcome foreign investment, whereas governments catering to domestic business interests oppose it.

My predictions are derived from a formal model that parallels the intuition from the political economy of trade. I build the model around the expected distributional consequences of investment flows, namely that inward FDI is likely to have a differential effect on the return to labor and capital in the receiving country. FDI can affect the relative demand for labor and business services: in general, FDI inflows are likely to decrease the return to capital and increase the return to labor. This prediction is the flip-side to the uncontroversial argument that outsourcing has a negative effect on wages and employment in the sending country. Workers and business owners are likely to organize politically in defense of their sources of income and support parties that better represent their interests. I predict that the party representing domestic capital opposes FDI, whereas the party of labor promotes inward investment flows. Therefore, partisan governments seek out investors that are likely to contribute to the well-being of the core constituents of their party or coalition and investors choose forms of production that are tailored to the specific political conditions in host countries, particularly the partisan orientation of the incumbent government. The main predictions from the partisan theory of investment run counter to conventional wisdom in the political science literature, which predicts that labor hates FDI and that FDI hates labor. I have argued that this conventional wisdom in the discipline is likely to be theoretically inconsistent and empirically flawed.

The plausibility of this argument is assessed using a variety of statistical models and qualitative evidence. The quantitative analyses are conducted on data from developing and developed countries using different statistical techniques. The qualitative analysis is based on a structured comparison of Argentina and South Korea in the post-war era until the end of the twentieth century. These two cases are chosen based on variation on the patterns of labor and capital influence in politics over time. Moreover, they present some interesting puzzles that elude received wisdom on the politics of FDI, such as Perón's about face adoption of a pro-investor statute in the early 1950s, the anti-foreign business stance of the military regime in 1976 Argentina, which repressed labor and liberalized the economy, and the anti-investor stance adopted by the South Korean regime through the late 1990s.

The predictions from the theory seem to be consistent with the evidence produced in the empirical section of the book: polities where labor is more influential politically are likely to adopt investment regimes that are more favorable to foreign investors. The combination of the quantitative and country analyses provides strong support to the partisan theory of FDI. The corollary is that countries with labor-based coalitions receive more foreign direct investment than those countries whose ruling coalitions are built around domestic capital. In sum, there is good reason to believe that in the globalized economy the Left loves FDI and FDI loves the Left.

This political theory of FDI can be located in the political economy tradition, side by side with debates about the role of interest groups and their preferences. Specifying preferences is a stepping stone that allows theories to identify political cleavages and the behavior of political actors. However, the theory presented here represents an improvement over simple coalitional models as per Rogowski (1987, 1989). I not only look at political alignments as in the coalitional explanations, but also develop a theory of outcomes, both political and economic. As preferences alone do not suffice to predict outcomes, it is important to incorporate into the analysis the mechanisms that determine how preferences are aggregated. In that sense, the theory is constructed in similar terms to those described by Rodrik as the demand and supply conditions in the political economy of trade policy (Rodrik, 1995). On the demand side of politics, political institutions play an important role in the process of preference aggregation. Institutions also affect the supply side of politics as they determine the incentives politicians face in their relationship to voters and other relevant political actors, as well as how policies are enacted and enforced. For these reasons, I have included institutions as intervening variables bridging the gap between preferences, coalitions, and policy and economic outcomes.

7.1 The Role of Partisanship in the Politics of FDI

The central contribution of the partisan theory of FDI is the emphasis placed on the expected distributive effects of foreign investment on the wages and the return to capital in factor markets, a motivation in regulating FDI that has been neglected in the literature. We should expect domestic actors to organize politically in response to the distributive consequences of FDI inflows: those who benefit from investment inflows mobilize to promote FDI and those who hurt from FDI activity would try to keep investors out. Under most general conditions, we should expect FDI to increase the demand for labor and to add competitive pressure on domestic businesses in product and factor markets. Thus, workers and their representatives are more likely to push for policies to encourage FDI inflows. Domestic business owners are likely to hurt from these types of foreign investment inflows, in which case capital owners would act politically to restrict inflows. The assumption that labor benefits and domestic capital hurts from investment inflows can be relaxed to allow different types of FDI to have different effects on the relative demand for labor and capital. Yet, irrespective of the motivation to enter a host country, FDI is likely to increase labor demand as suggested by the positive correlation between inward FDI and wages, particularly under the Left, as found in Pinto and Pinto (2008) and Jensen et al. (2012). The predictions and findings presented in this book seem to contradict traditional accounts in the extant literature, which predict that foreign and domestic investors would coalesce under the auspices of authoritarian rulers to exploit the popular sectors in host countries. I show that these predictions only hold under very restrictive assumptions, which can be subsumed as a special case of the partisan theory of FDI; moreover, the empirical content of the *Triple Alliance* hypothesis is scant as is persuasively shown by Dominguez (1982).

The regulation of foreign investment affects individuals' well-being in the marketplace, as lowering FDI inflows creates a trade-off at the expense of the consumption of government services financed by the taxes levied on foreign capital. The relative weights placed on the income derived from participation in the market and the utility from consuming these government services (or from receiving a direct transfer from the government) will be reflected in the choice of policies adopted by host governments of different partisan types. These motivations suggest that there are different shades of left: some parties of the Left prefer lowering taxes on MNCs to magnify labor market effects, whereas for others, revenue incentives dominate. For most pro-business governments, on the other hand, the regulation of FDI is dominated by factor market effects: if FDI competes with domestic businesses in product and factor markets, these governments are more likely to adopt a *prohibitive tax*, one that would keep investors out.

By focusing on the constraints and opportunities created by strong contemporary increases in globalization of production through foreign direct investment, I am able to analyze in a rigorous manner the interaction between global economic forces and politics. The conclusions from this analysis provide stronger support to the divergence school, whereas shedding some light on central debates in political science about the role of political institutions and preferences in foreign economic policy making.

7.2 Political Risk, Political Institutions, and Credible Commitments

Investment by MNCs is not a one-off endeavor. Investors usually enter a host country with the expectation that they are able to reap the fruits of their effort over time. They are thus exposed to the risk that these benefits might never materialize because of unforeseen circumstances, both economic and political. On the political side, investors are likely to be subject to the whim of host governments once they have deployed their assets. The host government could potentially target these assets, which become hostage to the government's opportunistic behavior. Adding a dynamic dimension to the investor–government interaction makes the relationship more complex. To the extent that relocating their assets in response to changing conditions is costly, investors are exposed to a well-known hold-up problem which is not privy to business government relations.[1] Received wisdom on the politics of FDI is built around this time inconsistency problem, which is usually described as political risk.

In the literature on capital taxation, the hold-up problem is defined in the following fashion: governments have an incentive to tax capital more heavily once investment decisions have been made, given that the elasticity of capital to taxation becomes zero. This problem is at the core of one of the most influential contributions in the literature on the political economy of direct

---

[1] See Henisz (2000b, 2002) for an excellent discussion of the private and public sources of risk that MNCs face.

foreign investment: the *obsolescing bargain* proposition. This proposition states that when the return from an investment occurs over time, the *ex-ante* bargaining leverage enjoyed by an investor over a host government gradually obsolesces as the investment sinks in. It thus becomes optimal for the host to choose *ex-post* the highest possible tax rates on that investment. This incentive to act opportunistically is present even for governments that had promised to maintain tax rates at the ex-ante optimal level (Kindleberger, 1969; Vernon, 1971). Institutional constraints on policy makers are usually touted as a solution to this commitment problem. When the hands of government are tied, or when the incumbent's ability to move the status quo is subject to delays by institutions constraints, their ex-ante promises are more likely to be honored (North and Thomas, 1973; North and Weingast, 1989; Henisz, 2000b).

Yet, tying the government's hands is equivalent to adopting an inflexible policy, a departure from the first-best or optimal practices that would have been chosen in a complete contract environment or adopted by a welfare-maximizing social planner (Spiller and Tommasi, 2003). Moreover, the argument assumes away the distributive consequences of inward FDI flows which, as has been demonstrated, either exacerbate or mitigate the commitment problem faced by host governments. Additionally, the literature on capital taxation has persuasively shown that even in the absence of institutional constraints capital tax rates are not set at confiscatory levels (Chari and Kehoe, 1990; Klein and Ríos-Rull, 2003). Institutions may also constrain government activity and determine how hard it is to change the status quo (Cox and McCubbins, 2001; Tsebelis, 2002). To the extent that institutional design constrains governments and provides for stable outcomes, it is at the core of the transaction costs explanations of investment (Williamson, 1979; Henisz and Williamson, 1999; Henisz, 2000b, 2002). Investment risk can be mitigated when the government is institutionally constrained and thus cannot change policy at will. These institutional constraints, in turn, result in stable and inflexible policy, which may not be an optimal solution for investors and governments.

I have discussed in previous chapters that as much as investors worry about the possibility of opportunistic behavior, they also need to worry about other forms of risk. Moreover, theoretical explanations of MNCs have persuasively shown that the interaction between political and contractual risk, the one derived from potential opportunistic behavior by other private actors, determines the choice of investing with control. Investment in risky environments is thus more likely to occur under direct control, and risky environments are likely to be populated by firms that are able at coping with the risk. Firms that are organized as multinationals in order to protect their proprietary assets are also likely to enjoy an exit option, and, as is the case for most economic agents, they would not reject a stable policy environment. In the face of economic shocks affecting their profitability, however, MNCs are more likely to tolerate some degree of flexibility than their less internationally mobile counterparts. MNCs can preempt opportunistic attempts from host governments by threatening to leave. What is key for MNCs is finding political allies who hold congruent preferences and have access to policy-makers.

In addition, the argument that the presence of multiple veto players eliminates the time inconsistency problem is incomplete: veto players' preferences are only fixed along a policy space when the realizations of the different parameters that enter into their objective function are held constant. Yet the time inconsistency property of sequential policy making is built around the principle of ex-post heterogeneity (Drazen, 2000). In the case of taxing mobile capital, for instance, an increase in the costs of relocation, which are usually associated with the existence of sequential returns to an investment, affects a key parameter in the objective function of all veto players. The veto players all have an ex-post incentive to tax investors more heavily in the period when the investors cannot move their investment. Institutional constraints would indeed restrict the ability of any actor to move the policy away from the status quo as long as the status quo dominates any other option. Yet, the drop in the elasticity of investment to taxation would move the optimal policy space for all veto players at once. Therefore, increasing the number of veto players alone would not suffice to prevent opportunistic behavior. Institutional constraints still matter, but their impact is a function of the preferences of those holding veto power.

The corollary is that, depending on their type, governments are indeed able to commit to investors even in a dynamic setting. Partisan preferences resulting from the internalization of the well-being of workers or business owners may aggravate or mitigate the incentives of governments to act opportunistically. This is my main point of departure with institutional explanations of commitment. Institutions are not necessary to reassure foreign investors, as when governments are partisan, they need not be institutionally constrained to attract foreign direct investment. Moreover, partisan links could provide guarantees to investors even when institutional constraints are ineffective. I argue that investments could be secure when a government's attempts to take advantage of investors may indirectly hurt the government's constituents. Hence, I append the analogy upon which the obsolescence bargaining hypothesis is built.

In a dynamic setting, the relative political influence of labor works as a reassurance to foreign investors, whereas the influence of owners of capital may increase the risk of opportunism against them. The interaction between foreign investors and domestic governments results in a mutual exchange of hostages where partisanship acts as a commitment mechanism to investors over time. The prediction is that governments are more likely to commit (renege) on the policies that they offer to foreign investors when they are constrained by a constituency base that is positively (negatively) affected by flows of foreign investment. One of the propositions introduced in Chapter 3 is that political motivations can be binding even when institutional constraints are not. The risk of losing the support of core constituents may force partisan governments to hold their promises to foreign investors even when facing incentives to act opportunistically. For this reason, pro-labor governments receive more foreign investment and pro-capital governments receive less. In the partisan theory of investment, institutions do play a role and are likely to indirectly affect outcomes as they determine who is enfranchised and who is more likely to be accounted for in the policy-making process.

The solution provided by partisanship is analogous to a mutual exchange of hostages between governments and foreign investors (Williamson, 1979, 1983a,b). While investors expose their assets to opportunistic government behavior, governments expose one of their core constituents to the possibility of being harmed by foreign investors who have the ability to leave the country if mistreated. The potential to harm each other keeps investors and host governments honest in their interactions. Following the assumption of the effect of FDI inflows on the returns to labor and capital, I argue that government alignment with labor, whose interests are congruent with those of foreign investors, may act as a commitment mechanism that makes pro-labor governments more reliable to foreign investors. Foreign investment is attracted to countries with pro-labor governments and turns away from countries governed by pro-business coalitions.

The "*mutual exchange of hostages*" analogy helps explain why Perón, usually portrayed as a bully of foreign investors, was able to lure investment back into Argentina, the early 1950s. A counter example is found in South Korea where labor was repressed and politics was dominated by a business-centered coalition. Through the mid-1990s South Korea received almost no foreign investment at all, especially when compared to other Asian NIEs. The South Korean case shows that when domestic business interests are influential governments will adopt policies that limit investment opportunities to foreign capital. When business interests weakened and politics became competitive, the investment policy orientation of the Korean government moved toward the more open end of the spectrum.

7.3 Evidence

In the empirical section of the book. I produce evidence from statistical analyses and from two historical narratives. While the statistical analyses are conducted on data from developing and developed countries, the qualitative evidence comes from South Korea and Argentina in the post-war era.

The results in the quantitative section provide support for the partisan/ pro-labor hypothesis. The coefficient on government partisanship is always positive, statistically significant, and substantively important. The tests find weaker evidence for the veto-gates hypothesis once partisan constraints are accounted for. The coefficient on the variable measuring political constraints is positive, but not significant at conventional levels. The evidence presented suggests that pro-labor governments are likely to receive larger inflows of foreign direct investment. But the evidence is far from conclusive. The theory is about the preferences of domestic actors that are derived from their position in the economy and these preferences are assumed rather than tested. Additionally, there is probably measurement error in the cross-country measures used, especially in the dependent variable as discussed by Lipsey (2001), and several of the relevant political and economic variables are only measured indirectly. However, the fact that the results capture a direct and systematic relationship between the partisan orientation of government and foreign investment using aggregate data and a coarse measure of the main explanatory variable is quite noteworthy. The results from the statistical tests seem to be supported by primary and secondary sources from Argentina and South Korea.

Chapter 5 identifies clear instances when FDI inflows to Argentina increased dramatically. FDI inflows were larger at times when either the ruling coalition was built around labor or under governments that tried to construct a coalition with large labor participation. On the other hand, FDI fell under governments that catered to domestic businesses. The theory seems to take us a long way in explaining why Perón courted FDI in the 1950s, and why the legislative debates on this issue were so controversial. Changes in political alignments and in the administration's political support base correlate with changes in the statutes that regulate FDI in a manner that is in line with the predictions of the theory: Perón's coalition changed over time, from an urban labor-capital coalition to a labor based one, and so did the regulatory framework on foreign investment. The theory also explains why the Revolución Libertadora (1955–8) and the Proceso de Reorganización Nacional (1976–83) pushed investors out. The theory is also compatible with the pattern of political and economic changes occurring the end of the century, especially Frondizi's about face in 1958, the contrast between the consequences of opening up the economy under the military in the 1970s or under Menem in the 1990s, and even the surprisingly high level of FDI in the auto and other manufacturing industries under Kirchner.

Labeling Peronist administrations as pro-labor is relatively uncontroversial: the Peronist party has been *the* party of labor, and Peronist leaders have tended to be closer to organized labor, while their military and civilian counterparts, even those that have tried to attract workers to their coalition, have systematically clashed with labor. The evolution of the statutes regulating union activity or the fate of legislation aimed at reforming labor contracts discussed in Chapter 5 supports this claim. The relationship between Frondizi's disposition to foreign investment and his quest to secure the support of labor is quite apparent. Explaining the Radical governments is more problematic, especially when contrasted to military administrations. Political competition should have led Radical Presidents to pay more attention to workers' demands, but instead they all had a hostile relationship with organized labor. The stance adopted by the radical government is probably aligned with the preferences of white-collar middle-class workers and professionals who have become the core of the support base of the party. Survey data suggests that these groups have systematically opposed foreign investment (Ranis, 1994). The partisan theory of FDI presented here, which is based on preferences rooted in the material rather than ideological preferences of actors, cannot explain the position of these groups. The position adopted by the *Onganiato* in its early years could be linked to the relationship between an important sector of organized labor with the leaders of the military revolt that overthrew Illia. The poor FDI performance under the 1973–6 Peronist governments seems to disprove the theory. This was a period of economic chaos and political and social unrest that resulted in a high level of labor conflict and all-out violence between the left and right wings of the Peronist party. The fact that FDI inflows were low could be also attributed to the strategies adopted by MNCs to respond to the uncertainty created by the oil crisis in addition to the prevailing environment characterized by political and economic instability.

South Korea, much like Japan, is a case where the government has had close links to domestic businesses and has adopted policies aimed at benefiting the large business conglomerates called chaebols. The theory expects

South Korea to be closed to FDI. The key determinant of the move toward an investment regime that was friendlier to foreign investors there is the waning influence of domestic business. From the early 1960s onward Korea adopted a restrictive foreign investment regime. Restrictions on foreign investment were aimed at protecting the chaebols, which lobbied relentlessly to preserve their prominent status in the economy. The government, through the Economic Planning Board, responded to business demands and set up barriers to the activity of multinationals in the country. This situation partially reversed in the late 1990s, especially in the aftermath of the 1997 financial crisis, when the chaebols seemed to be losing their political grip. Comparing two episodes in Korea's economic history, the 1981 and 1997 crises, underscores the importance of two political factors: democratization and the collapse of the chaebols. The analysis suggests that democratization, which forced politicians to move their attention away from the interests capital owners, in addition to the erosion of the political clout of domestic businesses resulted in dramatic changes in the regulation of foreign investment, ultimately leading to higher levels of FDI inflows under Kim Dae-jung and Roh Moo-hyun. The level of FDI received by South Korea remains low when compared with countries in similar positions, which suggests that the influence of the domestic business conglomerates remains high despite being dampened by the financial crisis.

7.4 Partisanship and the Politics of Globalization

Changes in global production spearheaded by multinational corporations are a central characteristic of the current globalization era (Bordo et al., 1999). Yet, while there is profuse literature on the political economy of trade and financial flows, research on the politics of direct investment flows and the regulation of the activity of multinationals is scant. We live in a world of globalized markets where goods, services, capital, and workers move across national borders with ease, albeit with different degrees of latitude, depending on the type of flow. The transforming effects of this rapid process of global economic integration are subject to heated debates among scholars, pundits, and journalists. As discussed in the introduction, the debate centers on whether technological innovation and changes in the pattern of production at the global level lead to the convergence or divergence of regulatory policy. Globalization pessimists conclude that politics do not matter any more, if they ever did. On the opposing side of the debate, optimists point to the systematic patterns of divergence, which depend on the preferences of the actors as they react to the constraints and opportunities created by global forces (Cameron, 1978; Rodrik, 1997). Scholars subscribing to this tradition argue that governments have ample room to maneuver and make policy choices that are a clear reflection of their types (Swank, 1998; Hall and Soskice, 2001; Garrett and Mitchell, 2001; Swank and Steinmo, 2002). The heated debate on the consequences of globalization, present in politics, journalism, and academics, is far from settled. The argument and evidence presented in this book are closer to the optimists' camp. The theory is built around the strategic interaction between investors and host governments, and predicts that despite the pressure created by competition for foreign investment, divergence in regulatory standards is more likely to attain. An important determinant of this divergence is the partisan orientation of the ruling coalition as persuasively argued in Geoffrey Garrett's *Partisan Politics in the Global Economy*, Carles Boix's *Political Parties, Growth, and Equality* and Torben Iversen's *Contested Economic Institutions* (Garrett, 1998b; Boix, 1998; Iversen, 1999). Political parties represent different groups in the polity and they translate these groups' preferences into policies. Preferences for FDI are derived from the consequences of FDI flows on the well-being of different socio-economic actors in the host country. When governments are partisan, they tend to respond to the preferences of the members of their coalition by adopting regulatory regimes that are more or less favorable to foreign investment. Policy choices depend on the partisan allegiances of the incumbent or whether workers or business owners are part of the core of their coalition. The partisan theory of FDI thus predicts that government partisanship affects FDI policy and the level of foreign investment flowing into host countries, and hence policy divergence in the globalized economy.

7.5 The Role of Institutions in the PE of FDI

The existing scholarship on the politics of investment in political science has debated how political regimes affect FDI. In many cases, scholars cite work by Nathan Jensen in contrast to Li and Resnick (Jensen, 2003, 2006; Li and Resnick, 2003). As discussed in depth throughout the book, this literature emphasizes the role of investment risk in impacting investors' choice of location but fails to account for their search for higher returns. Moreover, the existence of institutional constraints makes policy inflexible, and inflexible policies are never the optimal response to changing environments. Last, the institutional argument in its current form treats host governments as passive actors in the exchange, which is unreasonable given the salience of foreign investment in policy debates and political campaigns. Contrary to the traditional view presented by work in the *Triple alliance* literature, such as Peter Evans's *Dependent development* or Guillermo O'Donnell's *Bureaucratic authoritarianism* that leftist governments always discourage foreign investment and that pro-business governments always welcome it. I show how partisan governments treat different types of foreign investment differently by building upon both economic theory and political economy models (Evans, 1979; O'Donnell, 1988).

The book makes an important contribution to a broader literature on the role of institutions in the political economy of foreign policy making. In particular, it extends our understanding of the role of ex-ante commitment mechanisms, such as democratic institutions, veto-gates and institutional constraints, on the ability of governments to respond to changes in a swift and resolute manner. Scholarly work on the political economy of FDI has applied this logic to assessing political risk (Jensen, 2003, 2006; Li and Resnick, 2003; Henisz, 2000b, 2002). Pinto and Pinto (2011) show that the hand-tying technology provided by institutions is only optimal under fairly extreme realizations of the parameters that determine how easily investors can relocate and how foreign investment combines with factors of production in the host. Following the logic in Pinto and Pinto (2011), I argue here that there is an alternative commitment mechanism related to the partisan orientation of the ruling coalition. As proposed by Williamson (1983a,b), investment takes place when governments and investors can mutually exchange hostages. Investment will be secure when a government's attempt to target investors hurts domestic actors that the government cannot afford to ignore.

Foreign investors usually have limited electoral voice in the political system of the host government; as a result, more often than not they seek strategic alliances with domestic counterparts that allow them to amplify their political demands. Henisz proposes that political risk increases the incentive choose joint ventures as the mode of market entry (Henisz, 2000b, 2002). Political contributions may buy foreign investors some influence over policy outcomes as persuasively argued by Malesky (2009), but the political clout of multinationals is ultimately enhanced by their ability to harm an influential member of the incumbent coalition when they threaten to exit. What kind of hostages should investors take? As stated earlier, they should choose those that have the motive and opportunity to affect government behavior. The ideal hostage must be influential and must benefit from FDI inflows. To the extent that foreign capital complements labor in production, the two group's interests become congruent. Under pro-labor governments, or when labor can make its influence felt in the political system, investors become politically influential. The reverse pattern of support and opposition is predicted to occur when FDI substitutes for labor in production, lowering labor demand.

The bottom line is that the means through which host governments can offer foreign investors sufficient reassurance that contracts offered to them are duly enforced, but are not limited to institutional constraints that tie the rulers' hands. Investors' ability to take a pivotal political actor in the host country hostage to their investment strategies increases the probability that these contracts will be self-enforcing. Preferential treatment to foreign investors is thus ransom that political leaders are usually willing to pay to prevent pivotal domestic actors from being harmed.

Moreover, different institutional settings result in the empowerment of different groups in the polity, mitigating and mediating conflicts between governments and firms. The argument relates to work by Pinto and Pinto (2007, 2008, 2011), which examines when these conflicts emerge, and when the interests of firms and governments overlap. The key insight is that partisan governments (left or right) will naturally have more similar interests with firms in certain sectors (labor intensive or capital intensive). Enlarging the franchise, for instance, would result in changes in the identity of the median voter and could affect whose preferences are likely to be translated into policy. In the basic setup of the model, we could think that a movement from autocracy to democracy would result in a greater weight placed on the well-being for workers as the median voter is more likely to be a worker than a capital owner. Yet, it is also plausible that democratic governance leads to more hands on the wheel and hence more constraints on the ability of the government to move the status quo policies, implying a lower risk of ex-post opportunism. This is the interpretation of the effect of democracy on FDI in the extant literature. Yet, not all democratic governments are the same and the partisan argument exploits these distinctions. In South Korea, for instance, democratization occurred in 1987, yet changes in policy toward foreign investors did not take place until the late 1990s when a less pro-business government came to power and after the financial crises had eroded the clout of the chaebols. Differences within democratic countries such as Argentina also suggest that the institutional setting is not enough to explain changes in FDI policies and outcomes. This book-length project has allowed me to delve into the nuances of the argument and provide a broader array of evidence in support of these propositions.

7.6 Caveats, Extensions, and Conclusions

The preceding chapters present a political economy model of FDI built around the interaction between partisan governments and foreign investors, and argued that the partisan link has been overlooked in recent empirical literature on the politics of FDI. The theory presented in Chapters 2 and 3, and subsequent findings in the empirical part of the book, capture part of the large variance in the level of foreign investment that countries receive that remains unexplained in the extant literature in economics and political science. I argued that most of the recent empirical work in political science has not been able to fully account for this puzzle largely because it overlooks the distributive consequences associated with the inflows of direct investment.

Investment regimes and aggregate levels of direct investment appear to covary with government partisanship in the host country as defined by the the pro-labor or pro-capital nature of the incumbent domestic coalition. Governments that cater to labor interests tend to be friendlier to foreign investors than those that cater to business interests and countries are more open to FDI when a pro-labor government is able to move policy in its desired direction. These findings stand in stark contrast to the received wisdom in political science that coalitions based on labor should be averse to foreign investment. These predictions also diverge from those in the globalization literature, which neglects the importance of domestic politics. The main weakness of this literature is its built-in assumption that external forces are so compelling that governments have no option but to yield to them. The partisan theory of FDI suggests that these supposedly compelling external forces are actually sifted through domestic processes. This is why we fail to observe full policy convergence: countries look different in terms of the regulatory regimes toward foreign investment they adopt, and FDI performance varies a great deal across countries. External forces alone cannot explain this variance (Kahler and Lake, 2003). The assumption that host governments maximize revenue also sets my argument apart from models in the Grossman and Helpman tradition (Grossman and Helpman, 1994, 2001) that assume that governments maximize aggregate welfare, which they trade-off for political support.

These results should not be taken as conclusive. The Korean case underscores an important condition associated with the definition of FDI. As I discuss in Chapter 2, the link between the left and FDI is built around the assumption that inflows of capital have a positive effect on the return to labor and a negative effect on the return to domestic business owners who compete with foreign investors in product and factor markets. FDI is not only associated with inflows of capital, but with technology trans-fers as well (Pinto and Pinto, 2011). Changes in technology may affect factor income in a different direction: to the extent that it is labor saving, technological change might harm labor and benefit domestic capital. The distinction between types of FDI becomes relevant: the distributive effects of FDI depend on whether FDI is a complement or a substitute of labor and capital. The main assumption in this project is that inflows of capital are complements to labor, and this assumption has taken us a long way in predicting outcomes. We could also think of different forms of FDI that fall on a technology-capital continuum. That conceptualization could allow us to derive the preferences of domestic capital and labor toward the inflow of different forms of FDI. Labor would prefer FDI inflows that fall on the capital extreme of the continuum, whereas domestic capital would pre-fer a flow of technology that would not affect relative endowments in the host economy. Therefore, labor is likely to prefer FDI to licensing, whereas capital would prefer licensing to FDI. These differences in preferences are reflected in the regulation of modes of entry, which seems to be granted by the evidence drawn from the Korean case: when domestic businesses demand access to foreign technology, governments restrict inflows of FDI and promoted licensing rather than direct investment. The partisan theory of FDI could be extended to this analysis, where domestic actors would pro-mote some forms of FDI but not others. The corollary is a large variance in sectoral regulation of FDI and the existence of partisan cycles in the sectoral allocation of investment (Pinto and Pinto, 2008; Jensen et al. 2012).

Inflows of capital may result in an increase of production in sectors that employ capital more intensively as shown by Rybczynski (1955). Whether wages change depends on the size of the country. This runs counter to the assumptions around which the theory presented in this book is built. Moreover, the positive effects of capital inflows on the return to labor may not attain if the *factor price insensitivity* (FPI) theorem holds, that is, if shifts in factor demand match shifts in economy wide change in factor supply.[2] To the extent that either the Rybczynski or the FPI theorems are at play we should not expect a regulatory environment more favorable to FDI to be associated with pro-labor governments. If FPI were at play, we would expect the null hypothesis of no partisan effects to attain, yet I am able to identify a systematic relationship even with aggregate data.[3]

---

[2] See Leamer and Levinsohn (1995) for a review of this literature.

[3] In any event, the model can be augmented to allow for at least one factor to be sectorally immobile yielding substantively similar predictions on the emergence of a cleavage around the politics of investment; see Pinto and Pinto (2011) and the discussion in Chapters 1 and 2.

Lastly, note that I have abstracted away from bargaining issues, which may move returns away from the level determined by factors' marginal contribution to production. This method of determination results from assumptions about the production function used in the model presented in Chapter 2. Labor market institutions and the relative strength of labor and capital may determine a different distribution in labor or capital share, irrespective of the distributive effects of inflows on marginal productivity. But suppose that capital owners take advantage of their position in the market to extract from labor in the host country. An inflow of FDI that affects market structure in a way that increases competition is likely to weaken the influential position of capital owners to the benefit of labor. Additional research on the political economy of FDI should pay more attention to this variance in labor market institutions and labor share that is not granted by technology.

The results presented in previous chapters suggest that the partisan theory of investment is plausible. Caveats notwithstanding, the fact that I have been able to capture a relationship between partisan orientation of government and foreign investment performance using a coarse measure of the main explanatory variable and aggregate data on FDI, which would result in a low ratio of signal to noise, is quite noteworthy.

Bibliography

Adserà, A., and C. Boix. (2002). Trade, democracy, and the size of the public sector: The political underpinnings of openness. *International Organization 56*(2), 229–62.

Aitken, B., G. H. Hanson, and A. E. Harrison. (1997). Spillovers, foreign investment, and export behavior. *Journal of International Economics 43*(1–2), 103–32.

Aitken, B., A. Harrison, and R. E. Lipsey. (1996). Wages and foreign ownership a comparative study of Mexico, Venezuela, and the United States. *Journal of International Economics 40*(3–4), 345–71.

Aitken, B. J., and A. E. Harrison. (1999). Do domestic firms benefit from direct foreign investment? Evidence from Venezuela. *The American Economic Review 89*(3), 605–18.

Aitken, N. D. (1973). The effect of the EEC and EFTA on European trade: A temporal cross-section analysis. *The American Economic Review 63*(5), 881–92.

Alesina, A. (1987). Macroeconomic policy in a two-party system as a repeated game. *The Quarterly Journal of Economics 102*(3), 651–78.

Alesina, A. (1988). Macroeconomics and politics. *National Bureau of Economic Research Macroeconomics Annual 3*(1), 13–36.

Alesina, A., V. Grilli, and G. M. Milesi-Ferretti. (1994). The political economy of capital controls. In L. Leiderman and A. Razin (Eds.), *Capital mobility: the impact on consumption, investment, and growth*, pp. 289–321. Cambridge University Press.

Alesina, A. and H. Rosenthal. (1995). *Partisan politics, divided government, and the economy*. Political Economy of Institutions and Decisions. Cambridge, England: Cambridge University Press.

Alesina, A. and G. E. Tabellini. (1989). External debt, capital flight and political risk. *Journal of International Economics 27*(3–4), 199–220.

Alfaro, L. (2004). Capital controls: a political economy approach. *Review of International Economics 12*(4), 571–90.

Alt, J. E. (1985). Political parties, world demand, and unemployment: Domestic and international sources of economic activity. *American Political Science Review 79*(4), 1016–40.

Alt, J. E., F. Carlsen, P. Heum, and K. Johansen. (1999). Asset specificity and the political behavior of firms: Lobbying for subsidies in Norway. *International Organization 53*(1), 99–116.

Altamir, O., H. Santamaría, and J. V. Sourrouille. (1967). Los instrumentos de promoción industrial en la postguerra. la participación extranjera en el proceso de indutrialización. *Dearrollo Economico – Revista de Ciencias Sociales 7*(27), 361–76.

Alvarez, R. M., G. Garrett, and P. Lange. (1991). Government partisanship, labor organization, and macroeconomic performance. *The American Political Science Review 85*(2), 539–56.

Amsden, A. H. (1992). *Asia's next giant: South Korea and late industrialization.* New York, N.Y.: Oxford University Press.

Anderson, J. E., and E. van Wincoop. (2004). Trade costs. *Journal of Economic Literature 42*(3), 691–751.

Ardanaz, M. J., P. M. Pinto, and S. M. Pinto. (2012). Fiscal policy in good times and bad times: Endogenous time horizons and pro-cyclical spending in Argentina. Paper prepared for presentation at the annual meeting of the American Political Science Assosciation, New Orleans, LA, August 30–September 2, 2012.

Arellano, M. (2003). *Panel Data Econometrics.* Oxford England: Oxford University Press.

Arellano, M., and S. Bond. (1991). Some tests of specification for panel data: Monte carlo evidence and an application to employment equations. *The Review of Economic Studies 58*(2), 277–97.

Arellano, M., and O. Bover. (1995). Another look at the instrumental variable estimation of error-components models. *Journal of Econometrics 68*(1), 29–51.

Azpiazu, D. (1995). *Las empresas transnacionales de una economia en transicion: la experiencia argentina en los años ochenta* (1 ed.). Santiago de Chile: Naciones Unidas Comision Economica para America Latina y el Caribe.

Azpiazu, D., and E. M. Basualdo. (1989). *Cara y contracara de los grupos económicos: estado y promoción industrial en la Argentina.* Colección Bajo la lupa. San Martín, Buenos Aires: Cántaro Editores.

Azpiazu, D., E. M. Basualdo, and B. P. Kosacoff. (1986). Las empresas transnacionales en la Argentina, 1976–1983. *Revista de la CEPAL 28*(6), 99–130.

Azpiazu, D., and H. Nochteff. (1994). *El desarrollo ausente* (1 ed.). Buenos Aires: Tesis Grupo Editorial Norma.

Baier, S. L., and J. H. Bergstrand. (2001). The growth of world trade: tariffs, transport costs, and income similarity. *Journal of International Economics 53*(1), 1–27.

Barro, R. J., and J.-W. Lee. (2001). International data on educational attainment: Updates and implications. *Oxford economic papers 53*(3), 541–63.

Beamish, P. W. (1988). *Multinational joint ventures in developing countries.* London, England: Routledge.

Beck, N., and J. N. Katz. (1995). What to do (and not to do) with time-series cross-section data. *The American Political Science Review 89*(3), 634–47.

Beck, N., and J. N. Katz. (1996). Nuisance vs. substance: Specifying and estimating timeseries-cross-section models. *Political Analysis 6*(1), 1–36.

Beck, T., G. Clarke, A. Groff, P. Keefer, and P. Walsh. (2000). New tools and new tests in comparative political economy: the Database of Political Institutions: The World Bank Policy Research Working Paper No. 2283, Washington DC: The World Bank.

Bedeski, R. E. (1994). *The transformation of South Korea: reform and reconstitution in the sixth republic under Roe Tae Woo, 1987–1992* (1st Edition ed.). New York, N.Y.: Routledge.

Berger, S., and R. P. Dore. (1996). *National diversity and global capitalism.* Ithaca, N.Y.: Cornell University Press.

Bhagwati, J. N., E. Dinopoulos, and K.-y. Wong. (1992). Quid pro quo foreign investment. *The American Economic Review 82*(2), 186–90.

Blömstrom, M., and A. Kokko. (1998). Multinational corporations and spillovers. *Journal of Economic Surveys 12*(3), 247–77.

Blömstrom, M., R. E. Lipsey, and M. C. Zejan. (1994). What explains developing country growth? In W. J. Baumol, R. R. Nelson, and E. N. Wolff (Eds.), *Convergence of Productivity: Cross-National and Historical Evidence*, Chapter What Explains Developing Country Growth?, pp. 243–62. New York, NY: Oxford University Press.

Blonigen, B. A., and R. B. Davies. (2002). *Do bilateral tax treaties promote foreign direct investment?* NBER Working Paper Series No. 8834. Cambridge, MA: National Bureau of Economic Research.

Blonigen, B. A., and R. B. Davies (2004). The effects of bilateral tax treaties on U.S. FDI activity. *International Tax and Public Finance 11*(5), 601–22.

Blonigen, B. A., and R. C. Feenstra. (1997). Protectionist threats and foreign direct investment. In R. C. Feenstra (Ed.), *The Effects of U.S. Trade Protection and Promotion Policies*, pp. 55–80. Chicago, IL: University of Chicago Press.

Blonigen, B. A., and M. G. Wang. (2005). Inappropriate pooling of wealthy and poor countries in empirical fdi studies. In T. H. Moran, E. M. Graham, and M. Blömstrom (Eds.), *Does foreign direct investment promote development?*, pp. 221–44. Washington, D.C.: Institute for International Economics.

Boix, C. (1997). Political parties and the supply side of the economy: The provision of physical and human capital in advanced economies, 1960–90. *American Journal of Political Science 41*(3), 814–45.

Boix, C. (1998). *Political parties, growth and equality: conservative and social democratic economic strategies in the world economy.* Cambridge Studies in Comparative Politics. Cambridge, England: Cambridge University Press.

Boix, C. (2003). *Democracy and redistribution.* Cambridge Studies in Comparative Politics. Cambridge, England: Cambridge University Press.

Bordo, M. D., B. Eichengreen, J. Frankel, D. A. Irwin, and A. M. Taylor. (1999). Is globalization today really different from globalization a hundred years ago? *Brookings Trade Forum 1999*, 1–72.

Borensztein, E., J. De Gregorio, and J.-W. Lee. (1998). How does Foreign Direct Investment affect economic growth? *Journal of International Economics 45*(1), 115–35.

Brainard, S. L. (1993a). *An empirical assessment of the factor proportions explanation of multinational sales.* NBER Working Paper Series No. 4583. Cambridge, MA: National Bureau of Economic Research.

Brainard, S. L. (1993b). *A simple theory of multinational corporations and trade with a trade-off between proximity and concentration.* NBER Working Paper Series No. 4269. Cambridge, MA: National Bureau of Economic Research.

Brainard, S. L. (1997). An empirical assessment of the proximity-concentration trade-off between multinational sales and trade. *The American Economic Review 87*(4), 520–44.

Brown, D. K., A. Deardorff, and R. Stern. (2004). The effects of multinational productionon wages and working conditions in developing countries. In R. E. Baldwin and L. A. Winters (Eds.), *Challenges to globalization: analyzing the economics*, National

Bureau of Economic Research conference report, pp. 279–330. Chicago, IL: University of Chicago Press.

Brumat Decker, N. (2001). *Sindicatos en la Argentina: legislación y razón de equilibrio social.* Buenos Aires: Ediciones Ciccus.

Calvo, G. A. (1978). On the time consistency of optimal policy in a monetary economy. *Econometrica: Journal of the Econometric Society 46*(6), 1411–28.

Calvo, G. A., L. Leiderman, and C. M. Reinhart. (1993). Capital inflows and real exchange-rate appreciation in latin-america – the role of external factors. *International Monetary Fund Staff Papers 40*(1), 108–51.

Calvo, G. A., L. Leiderman, and C. M. Reinhart. (1996). Inflows of capital to developing countries in the 1990s. *The Journal of Economic Perspectives 10*(2), 123–39.

Cameron, D. R. (1978). The expansion of the public economy: A comparative analysis. *The American Political Science Review 72*(4), 1243–61.

Carcovic, M. and R. Levine. (2005). Does foreign direct investment accelerate economic growth? In T. H. Moran, E. M. Graham, and M. Blömstrom (Eds.), *Does foreign direct investment promote development?*, pp. 195–220. Washington, D.C.: Institute for International Economics.

Carr, D. L., J. R. Markusen, and K. E. Maskus. (2001). Estimating the knowledge-capital model of the multinational enterprise. *The American Economic Review 91*(3), 693–708.

Carr, D. L., J. R. Markusen, and K. E. Maskus. (2003). Estimating the knowledge-capital model of the multinational enterprise: Reply. *The American Economic Review 93*(3), 995–1001.

Catalano, A. M., and M. S. Novick. (1998). The Argentine automotive industry: redefining production strategies, markets, and labor relations. In J. P. Tuman and J. T. Morris (Eds.), *Transforming the Latin American automobile industry: unions, workers, and the politics of restructuring*, pp. 26–76. Armonk, N.Y.: M.E. Sharpe.

Caves, R. E. (1974). Multinational firms, competition, and productivity in host-country markets. *Economica 41*(162), 176–93.

Caves, R. E. (1996). *Multinational enterprise and economic analysis* (2nd ed.). Cambridge, England: Cambridge University Press.

CEPAL. (1986). *Las Empresas transnacionales en la Argentina.* Estudios e informes de la CEPAL, 56. Santiago, Chile: Unidad Conjunta CEPAL/CET sobre Empresas Transnacionales, Naciones Unidas.

Chakrabarti, A. (1997). The distribution of foreign direct investment and the excluded economies. Working Papers 397, Research Seminar in International Economics, University of Michigan.

Chakrabarti, A. (2001). The determinants of foreign direct investment: Sensitivity analyses of cross-country regressions. *Kyklos 54*(1), 89–113.

Chari, A., P. P. Ouimet, and L. L. Tesar. (2004). *Acquiring Control in Emerging Markets: Evidence from the Stock Market.* NBER Working Paper Series No. 10872. Cambridge, MA: National Bureau of Economic Research.

Chari, V. V., and P. J. Kehoe. (1990). Sustainable plans. *The Journal of political economy 98*(4), 783–802.

Cho, S. (1994). *The dynamics of Korean economic development.* Washington, D.C.: Institute for Internationsl Economics.

Chudnovsky, D., and A. López. (2007). Foreign direct investment and development: The Mercosur experience. *CEPAL Review 92*, 7–23.

Chung, K. S., and Y. K. Wang. (2000). Republic of Korea. In J. Zhuang, D. Edwards, D. Webb, and M. V. Capulong (Eds.), *Corporate governance and finance in East Asia: a study of Indonesia, Republic of Korea, Malaysia, Philippines, and Thailand*, Volume 1, pp. 53–152. Manila, Philippines: Asian Development Bank.

Coatsworth, J. H., and J. G. Williamson. (2004). Always protectionist? Latin American tariffs from independence to Great Depression. *Journal of Latin American Studies 36*(2), 205–32.

Collier, R. B., and D. Collier. (1991). *Shaping the political arena: critical junctures, the labor movement, and regime dynamics in Latin America*. Princeton, N.J.: Princeton University Press.

Cox, G. W., and M. D. McCubbins. (2001). The institutional determinants of economic policy outcomes. In M. D. McCubbins and S. Haggard (Eds.), *Presidents, parliaments, and policy. Political economy of institutions and decisions*, pp. 21–63. Cambridge, England: Cambridge University Press.

Delios, A., P. W. Beamish, and D. Xu. (2008). Within-country product diversification and foreign subsidiary performance. *Journal of international business studies 39*(4), 706–24.

Delios, A. and W. J. Henisz. (2003). Political hazards, experience, and sequential entry strategies: The international expansion of japanese firms, 1980–1998. *Strategic Management Journal 24*(11), 1153–64.

Desai, M. A., C. F. Foley, and J. R. H., Jr. (2002). Chains of ownership, regional tax competition, and foreign direct investment. NBER Working Paper Series No. 9224. Cambridge, MA: National Bureau of Economic Research.

Di Tella, G. (1983). *Argentina under Perón, 1973–76: the nation's experience with a labour-based government*. New York, N.Y.: St. Martin's Press.

Díaz-Alejandro, C. F. (1970). *Essays on the Economic History of the Argentine Republic*. New Heaven, CT: Yale University Press.

Dixit, A. K. and R. S. Pindyck. (1994). *Investment under uncertainty*. Princeton, N.J.: Princeton University Press.

Dominguez, J. I. (1982). Business nationalism: Latin American national business attitudes and behavior toward multinational enterprises. In J. I. Dominguez (Ed.), *Economic issues and political conflict: US-Latin American relations*, pp. 16–68. London, UK: Butterworth Scientific.

Drazen, A. (2000). *Political economy in macroeconomics*. Princeton, N.J.: Princeton University Press.

Dunning, J. H. (1977). Trade, location of economic activity and the MNE: a search for an eclectic approach. In B. G. Ohlin, P.-O. Hesselborn, and P. M. Wijkman (Eds.), *The international allocation of economic activity: proceedings of a nobel Symposium held at Stockholm*, pp. 395–418. London, England: Macmillan.

Dunning, J. H. (1993a). *Multinational enterprises and the global economy*. International Business Series. Wokingham, UK: Addison-Wesley.

Dunning, J. H. (1993b). *The theory of transnational corporations*. International business and the world economy; United Nations library on transnational corporations vol. 1. London, UK: United Nations and Routledge.

Dutt, P., and D. Mitra. (2005). Political ideology and endogenous trade policy: An empirical investigation. *The Review of Economics and Statistics 87*(1), 59–72.

Easterly, W., R. King, R. Levine, and S. Rebelo. (1994). *Policy, technology adoption, and growth*. NBER Working Paper Series No. 4681. Cambridge, MA: National Bureau of Economic Research.

ECLAC and UNCTAD (2002). *La inversión extranjera en América Latina y el Caribe: Informe.* ECLAC and UNCTAD and Joint Unit on Transnational Corporations, United Nations.

Edwards, S. (1995). *Crisis and reform in Latin America: from despair to hope.* New York, N.Y.: Oxford University Press.

Eichengreen, B. J. (1990). The capital levy problem in theory and practice. In R. Dornbusch and M. Draghi (Eds.), *Public debt management: theory and history,* pp. 191–220. Cambridge, England: Cambridge University Press.

Eriksson, S. (2005). Innovation policies in South Korea and Taiwan. Vinnova Analysis, VA 2005–03.

Escudé, C. (1983). *Gran Bretaña, Estados Unidos y la declinación Argentina, 1942–1949.* Buenos Aires: Editorial de Belgano.

Escudé, C. (1988). *El boicot norteamericano a la Argentina en la década del 40.* Buenos Aires: Centro Editor de América Latina.

Esping-Andersen, G. (1990). *The Three Worlds of Welfare Capitalism.* Princeton, N.J.: Princeton University Press.

Etchemendy, S. (2001). Constructing reform coalitions: The politics of compensations in Argentina's economic liberalization. *Latin American Politics and Society 43*(3), 1–35.

Etchemendy, S. and V. Palermo. (1998). Conflicto y concertación. Gobierno, Congreso y organizaciones de interés en la reforma laboral del primer gobierno de Menem (1989–1995). *Desarrollo Económico-Revista de Ciencias Sociales 37*(148), 559–90.

Ethier, W. J. and J. R. Markusen. (1996). Multinational firms, technology diffusion and trade. *Journal of International Economics 41*(1–2), 1–28.

Evans, P. B. (1979). *Dependent development: the alliance of multinational, state, and local capital in Brazil.* Princeton, N.J.: Princeton University Press.

Evans, P. B., and G. Gereffi. (1982). Foreign investment and dependent development. In S. A. Hewlett and R. S. Weinert (Eds.), *Brazil and Mexico: patterns in late development,* pp. 111–168. Philadelphia: Institute for the Study of Human Issues.

Feenstra, R. C., and G. H. Hanson. (1997). Foreign direct investment and relative wages: Evidence from Mexico's maquiladoras. *Journal of International Economics 42*(3–4), 371–93.

Feliciano, Z., and R. E. Lipsey. (1999). Foreign ownership and wages in the United States, 1987–1992. NBER Working Paper Series No. 6923. Cambridge, MA: National Bureau of Economic Research.

Fernández-Arias, E. (1996). The new wave of private capital inflows: Push or pull? *Journal of Development Economics 48*(2), 389–418.

Fernández Madrid, J. C., and A. B. Caubet. (1994). *Leyes fundamentales del trabajo: sus reglamentos y anotaciones complementarias* (4. ed.). Buenos Aires: Editorial Pulsar.

Figlio, D. N., and B. A. Blonigen. (2000). The effects of foreign direct investment on local communities. *Journal of Urban Economics 48*(2), 338–63.

Findlay, R. (1978). Relative backwardness, direct foreign investment, and the transfer of technology: A simple dynamic model. *The Quarterly Journal of Economics 92*(1), 1–16.

Frankel, J., E. Stein, and S.-J. Wei. (1995). Trading blocs and the americas: The natural, the unnatural, and the super-natural. *Journal of Development Economics 47*(1), 61–95.

Frankel, J. A., and S.-J. Wei. (1993). *Trade blocs and currency blocs*. NBER Working Paper Series No. 4335. Cambridge, MA: National Bureau of Economic Research.

Franzese, R. J. (2002a). Electoral and partisan cycles in economic policies and outcomes. *Annual Review of Political Science 5*(1), 369–421.

Franzese, R. J. (2002b). *Macroeconomic policies of developed democracies*. Cambridge studies in comparative politics. Cambridge, England: Cambridge University Press.

Freedom House. (2010). Freedom in the world: The annual survey of political rights and civil liberties. New York, N.Y.: Freedom House. Electronic resource.

Freeman, R. B. (1993). Lavor market institutions and policies: Help or hindrance to economic development. In World Bank (Ed.), *Proceedings of the World Bank Annual Conference on Development Economics*, Volume 1993, pp. 117–44. Washington, DC: International Bank for Reconstruction and Development/World Bank.

Frieden, J. A. (1991). Invested interests: The politics of national economic policies in a world of global finance. *International Organization 45*(4), 425–51.

Friedman, T. L. (2007). *The world is flat: a brief history of the twenty-first century*. New York, N.Y.: Farrar, Straus and Giroux.

Frye, T., and P. M. Pinto. (2009). The politics of chinese investment in the US. In K. P. Sauvant (Ed.), *Investing in the United States: Is the US Ready for FDI from China?*, Studies in international investment, pp. 85–121. Cheltenham, UK: Edward Elgar.

Fuchs, J. (1965). *Argentina: su desarrollo capitalista*. Buenos Aires: Editorial Cartago.

Fuchs, J. (1981). *Argentina, actual estructura económico social*. Buenos Aires: Ediciones Estudio.

Garrett, G. (1995). Capital mobility, trade, and the domestic politics of economic policy. *International Organization 49*(4), 657–87.

Garrett, G. (1998a). Global markets and national politics: Collision course or virtuous circle? *International Organization, International Organization at Fifty: Exploration and Contestation in the Study of World Politics 52*(4), 787–824.

Garrett, G. (1998b). *Partisan politics in the global economy*. Cambridge studies in Comparative Politics. Cambridge, England: Cambridge University Press.

Garrett, G. (2000). The causes of globalization. *Comparative Political Studies 33*(6–7), 941–91.

Garrett, G., and D. Mitchell. (2001). Globalization, government spending and taxation in the OECD. *European Journal of Political Research 39*(2), 145–77.

Gereffi, G. (1983). *The pharmaceutical industry and dependency in the Third World*. Princeton, N.J.: Princeton University Press.

Germani, G. (1980). El surgimiento del peronismo: el rol de los obreros y de los migrantes internos. In M. Mora y Araujo and I. Llorente (Eds.), *El Voto Peronista*, pp. 87–163. Buenos Aires: Editorial Sudamericana.

Gibson, E. L. (1997). The populist road to market reform – policy and electoral coalitions in Mexico and Argentina. *World Politics 49*(3), 339–70.

Gills, B. K., and D. S. Gills. (2000). Globalization and strategic choice in South Korea: Economic reform and labor. In S. S. Kim (Ed.), *Korea's globalization*, Cambridge Asia-Pacific studies, pp. 29–53. Cambridge, England: Cambridge University Press.

Glass, A. J., and K. Saggi. (1998). International technology transfer and the technology gap. *Journal of Development Economics 55*(2), 369–98.

Godio, J. (1981). *El último año de Perón* (1a ed.). Bogotá: Universidad Simón Bolívar.

Golub, S. S. (2003). Measures of restrictions on inward foreign direct investment for OECD countries. *OECD Economic Studies 2003*(1), 85–116.

Gourevitch, P. A. (1986). *Politics in hard times: comparative responses to international economic crises.* Cornell Studies in Political Economy. Ithaca: Cornell University Press.

Gourevitch, P. A., and J. Shinn. (2005). *Political power and corporate control: the new global politics of corporate governance.* Princeton, N.J.: Princeton University Press.

Graham, E. M. (1996). *Global corporations and national governments.* Washington, DC: Institute for International Economics.

Greene, W. H. (2003). *Econometric analysis* (5th ed.). Upper Saddle River, N.J.: Prentice Hall.

Grossman, G. M., and E. Helpman. (1994). Protection for sale. *American Economic Review 84*(4), 833–50.

Grossman, G. M., and E. Helpman. (1996). Rent dissipation, free riding, and trade policy. *European Economic Review 40*(3–5), 795–803.

Grossman, G. M., and E. Helpman. (2001). *Special interest politics.* Cambridge, MA: MIT Press.

Guillen, M. F. (2000). Organized labor's images of multinational enterprise: Divergent foreign investment ideologies in Argentina, South Korea, and Spain. *Industrial & Labor Relations Review 53*(3), 419–42.

Haddad, M., and A. Harrison. (1993). Are there positive spillovers from direct foreign investment?: Evidence from panel data for Morocco. *Journal of Development Economics 42*(1), 51–74.

Haggard, S. (1990). *Pathways from the periphery: the politics of growth in the newly industrializing countries.* Ithaca, N.Y.: Cornell University Press.

Haggard, S., and J. Mo. (2000). The political economy of the Korean financial crisis. *Review of International Political Economy 7*(2), 197–218.

Hall, P. A., and D. Soskice. (2001). *Varieties of Capitalism: The Institutional Foundations of Comparative Advantage.* New York, N.Y.: Oxford University Press.

Halperín Donghi, T. (1964). *Argentina en el callejón.* Montevideo, Uruguay: ARCA.

Halperín Donghi, T. (1980). Algunas observaciones sobre Germani, el surgimiento del peronismo y los migrantes internos. In M. Mora y Araujo and I. Llorente (Eds.), *El Voto Peronista*, pp. 219–50. Buenos Aires: Editorial Sudamericana.

Hanson, G. H. (2001). Should countries promote foreign direct investment? *G-24 discussion papers series* no. 9, New York, NY: UNCTAD and Harvard Center for International Development.

Hanson, G. H., J. Mataloni, Raymond J., and M. J. Slaughter. (2001). Expansion strategies of U.S. multinational firms. *Brookings Trade Forum 2001*, 245–82.

Haslam, P. A. (2002). *Transnational development: the changing relationship between the state, transnational corporations, and local firms in Chile and Argentina, 1970–2000.* Ph. D. thesis, Queen's University, Kingston Ontario.

Helpman, E. (1984). A simple theory of international trade with multinational corporations. *The Journal of Political Economy 92*(3), 451.

Helpman, E. (1985). Multinational corporations and trade structure. *The Review of Economic Studies 52*(3), 443–57.

Helpman, E. (2006). Trade, FDI, and the organization of firms. *Journal of Economic Literature 44*(3), 589–630.

Helpman, E. and P. R. Krugman. (1985). *Market structure and foreign trade: increasing returns, imperfect competition, and the international economy*. Cambridge, MA: MIT Press.

Henisz, W. J. (2000a). The institutional environment for economic growth. *Economics & Politics 12*(1), 1–31.

Henisz, W. J. (2000b). The institutional environment for multinational investment. *Journal of Law Economics & Organization 16*(2), 334–64.

Henisz, W. J. (2002). The institutional environment for infrastructure investment. *Industrial and Corporate Change 11*(2), 355–89.

Henisz, W. J., and O. E. Williamson. (1999). Comparative economic organization: within and between countries. *Business and Politics 1*(3), 261–76.

Henisz, W. J., and B. A. Zelner. (2003). The strategic organization of political risks and opportunities. *Strategic Organization 1*(4), 451–60.

Heston, A., R. Summers, and B. Aten. (2002). Penn World Tables version 6.1. Center for International Comparisons of Production, Income and Prices at the University of Pennsylvania.

Heston, A., R. Summers, and B. Aten. (2011). Penn World Tables version 7.0. Center for International Comparisons of Production, Income and Prices at the University of Pennsylvania.

Hibbs, Douglas A. J. (1977). Political parties and macroeconomic policy. *The American Political Science Review 71*(4), 1467–87.

Hibbs, Douglas A., J. (1992). Partisan theory after fifteen years. *European Journal of Political Economy 8*(3), 361.

Hicks, A. M., and D. H. Swank. (1992). Politics, institutions, and welfare spending in industrialized democracies, 1960–82. *American Political Science Review 86*(3), 658–74.

Hillman, A. L. (1982). Declining industries and political-support protectionist motives. *The American Economic Review 72*(5), 1180–87.

Hillman, A. L. (1989). *The political economy of protection*. Chur, Switzerland: Harwood Academic Publishers.

Hines, J. R. (2001). *International taxation and multinational activity*. Chicago: University of Chicago Press.

Hirschman, A. O. (1970). *Exit, voice, and loyalty: responses to decline in firms, organizations, and states*. Cambridge, MA: Harvard University Press.

Hiscox, M. J. (2002). *International trade and political conflict: commerce, coalitions, and mobility*. Princeton, N.J.: Princeton University Press.

Hiscox, M. J., and S. Kastner. (2002). A general measure of trade policy orientations: Gravity-model-based estimates for 82 nations, 1960–1992. Unpublished Manuscript, Harvard University.

Horstmann, I. J. and J. R. Markusen. (1992). Endogenous market structures in international trade (natura facit saltum). *Journal of International Economics 32*(1–2), 109–129.

Hymer, S. (1976a). *The international operations of national firms: a study direct foreign investment*. Ph. D. thesis, MIT, Cambridge, MA.

Hymer, S. (1976b). *The international operations of national firms: a study direct foreign investment*. Cambridge, MA: MIT Press.

ILO. (1997). *World labour report 1997–98: industrial relations, democracy and social stability*. Geneva: International Labour Office.

Iversen, T. (1999). *Contested economic institutions: the politics of macroeconomics and wage bargaining in advanced democracies.* Cambridge Studies in Comparative Politics. Cambridge, England: Cambridge University Press.

Janeba, E. (2001). Attracting FDI in a politically risky world. NBER Working Paper No. 8400. Cambridge, MA: National Bureau of Economic Research.

Jensen, N. M. (2003). Democratic governance and multinational corporations: Political regimes and inflows of foreign direct investment. *International organization 57*(3), 587–616.

Jensen, N. M. (2006). *Nation-states and the multinational corporation: a political economy of foreign direct investment.* Princeton, N.J.: Princeton University Press.

Jensen, N. M., G. Biglaiser, Q. Li, E. Malesky, P. M. Pinto, S. M. Pinto, and J. L. Staats. (2012). *Politics and Foreign Direct Investment.* Ann Arbor, MI: University of Michigan Press.

Jones, L. P., and I. SaKong. (1980). *Government, business, and entrepreneurship in economic development: the Korean case,* Volume 91 of *Studies in the modernization of the Republic of Korea, 1945–1975.* Cambridge, MA: Council on East Asian Studies, Harvard University; Harvard University Press.

Kahler, M. (1998). Modeling races to the bottom. In *Annual Meeting of the American Political Science Association,* Washington, D. C.

Kahler, M. and D. A. Lake. (2003). Globalization and changing patterns of political authority. In M. Kahler and D. A. Lake (Eds.), *Governance in a global economy: political authority in transition,* pp. 412–38. Princeton, N.J.: Princeton University Press.

Kang, D. C. (2002). *Crony capitalism: corruption and development in South Korea and the Philippines.* Cambridge Studies in Comparative Politics. Cambridge, England: Cambridge University Press.

Katz, L. F., and L. H. Summers. (1989). Industry rents: Evidence and implications. *Brookings Papers on Economic Activity. Microeconomics 1989,* 209–90.

Katzenstein, P. J. (1978). *Between power and plenty: foreign economic policies of advanced industrial states.* Madison, WI: University of Wisconsin Press.

Kenworthy, E. (1980). Interpretaciones ortodoxas y revisionistas del apoyo inicial del peronismo. In M. Mora y Araujo and I. Llorente (Eds.), *El Voto Peronista,* Buenos Aires: Editorial Sudamericana.

Kihl, Y. W. (2005). *Transforming Korean politics: democracy, reform, and culture.* Armonk, N.Y.: M.E. Sharpe.

Kim, I.-J. (1993). Fluctuating foreign-exchange rates and price competitiveness. In J. Mo and R. H. Myers (Eds.), *Shaping a new economic relationship: the Republic of Korea and the United States.* Stanford, CA: Hoover Institution Press, Stanford University.

Kim, L. (1997). *Imitation to innovation: the dynamics of Korea's technological learning.* Management of Innovation and Change Series. Boston, MA: Harvard Business School Press.

Kim, L. and Y. Kim. (1985). Innovation in a newly industrializing country: A multiple discriminant analysis. *Management Science 31*(3), 312–22.

Kindleberger, C. P. (1969). *American business abroad: six lectures on direct investment.* New Haven, CT: Yale University Press.

King, G., M. Tomz, and J. Wittenberg. (2000). Making the most of statistical analyses: Improving interpretation and presentation. *American Journal of Political Science 44*(2), 347–61.

Klein, P. and J.-V. Ríos-Rull. (2003). Time-inconsistent optimal fiscal policy. *International Economic Review 44*(4), 1217–45.

Kobrin, S. J. (1987). Testing the bargaining hypothesis in the manufacturing sector in developing countries. *International Organization 41*(4), 609–38.

Kokko, A. (1994). Technology, market characteristics, and spillovers. *Journal of Development Economics 43*(2), 279–93.

Kokko, A., R. Tansini, and M. C. Zejan. (1996). Local technological capability and productivity spillovers from fdi in the uruguayan manufacturing sector. *The Journal of Development Studies 32*(4), 602–11.

Koo, H. (2001). *Korean workers: the culture and politics of class formation.* Ithaca, N.Y.: Cornell University Press.

Koo, H., and E. M. Kim. (1992). The developmental state and capital accumulation in South Korea. In R. P. Appelbaum and J. W. Henderson (Eds.), *States and development in the Asian Pacific Rim*, pp. 121–149. Newbury Park, CA: Sage Publications.

Korea Exchange Bank. (1987). Direct Foreign Investment in Korea. Monthly Review, October 1987. Seoul: Korea Exchange Bank.

Korea Trade and Investment Promotion Agency. (2007). White paper on foreign direct investment promotion: Foreign direct investment for 10 years after the financial crisis. Technical report. Seoul: Korea, Ministry of Commerce, Industry and Energy, Republic of Korea.

Korhonen, K. (2001). *Role of government intervention in foreign direct investment: case of South Korea.* Helsingin Kauppakorkeakoulun julkaisuja. B, 32. Helsinki: Helsinki School of Economics and Business Administration.

Kosacoff, B. P. (1993). *El Desafío de la competitividad: la industria Argentina en transformación.* Buenos Aires: Alianza Editorial.

Kravis, I. B., and R. E. Lipsey. (1982). The location of overseas production and production for export by U.S. multinational firms. *Journal of International Economics 12*(3–4), 201–23.

Kravis, I. B., and R. E. Lipsey. (1993). The effect of multinational firms' operations on their domestic employment. NBER Working Paper No. 2760. Cambridge, MA: National Bureau of Economic Research.

Krotoschin, E. (1972). *Manual de derecho del trabajo.* Buenos Aires: Ediciones Depalma.

Krotoschin, E., and J. A. F. Ratti. (1983). *Código del trabajo anotado: recopilación de leyes nacionales del trabajo, decretos reglamentarios* (7a ed.). Buenos Aires: Depalma.

Krugman, P. R. (2000). *Currency crises.* Chicago, IL: University of Chicago Press.

Kwon, O. Y. (2004). Causes for sluggish foreign direct investment in Korea: A foreign perspective. *The Journal of the Korean Economy 5*(1), 69–96.

Kydland, F. E., and E. C. Prescott. (1977). Rules rather than discretion: The inconsistency of optimal plans. *The Journal of Political Economy 85*(3), 473–92.

Leamer, E. E., and J. Levinsohn. (1995). International trade theory: The evidence. In G. M. Grossman and K. S. Rogoff (Eds.), *Handbook of International Economics*, Volume 3 of *Handbooks in economics*, pp. 1339–94. New York, N.Y.: Elsevier Science Pub. Co.

Lee, C.-P. (1993). Preconditions for a successful liberalization and a feedback process of managing progressive liberalization. *Joint U.S.-Korea Academic Studies 3*, 1–23.

Lee, Y. (1997). *The State, Society, and Big Business in South Korea.* London, England: Routledge.

Lee, Y. (2005). Participatory democracy and chaebol regulation in Korea: State-market relations under the MDP governments, 1997–2003. *Asian Survey 45*(2), 279–301.

Lewis, P. H. (1992). *The crisis of Argentine capitalism.* Chapel Hill, NC: University of North Carolina Press.

Li, Q., and A. Resnick. (2003). Reversal of fortunes: Democratic institutions and foreign direct investment inflows to developing countries. *International organization 57*(1), 175–211.

Lin, P., and K. Saggi. (2005). Multinational firms and backward linkages: A critical survey and a simple model. In T. H. Moran, E. M. Graham, and M. Blömstrom (Eds.), *Does foreign direct investment promote development?*, pp. 159–74. Washington, D.C.: Institute for International Economics.

Lindblom, C. E. (1977). *Politics and markets: the world's political economic systems.* New York, N.Y.: Basic Books.

Lipsey, R. E. (2001). *Foreign direct investment and the operations of multinational firms: concepts, history, and data.* NBER Working paper series No. 8665. Cambridge, MA: National Bureau of Economic Research.

Lipsey, R. E. (2004). Home- and host-country effects of foreign direct investment. In R. E. Baldwin and L. A. Winters (Eds.), *Challenges to Globalization: Analyzing the Economics*, pp. 333–382. Chicago, IL: University of Chicago Press.

Lipsey, R. E., and I. B. Kravis. (1982). Do multinational firms adapt factor proportions to relative factor prices? In A. O. Krueger (Ed.), *Trade and Employment in Developing Countries, vol. 2: Factor Supply and Substitution*, pp. 215–56. Chicago, IL: University of Chicago Press.

Lipsey, R. E., and F. Sjöholm. (2004). Foreign direct investment, education and wages in indonesian manufacturing. *Journal of Development Economics 73*(1), 415–22.

Lipsey, R. E., and F. Sjöholm. (2005). The impact of inward FDI on host countries: Why such different answers? In T. H. Moran, E. M. Graham, and M. Blömstrom (Eds.), *Does foreign direct investment promote development?*, pp. 23–43. Washington, D.C.: Institute for International Economics.

Llorente, I. (1980). Alianzas políticas en el surgimiento del peronismo: El caso de la provincia de Buenos Aires. In M. Mora y Araujo and I. Llorente (Eds.), *El Voto Peronista*, pp. 269–317. Buenos Aires: Editorial Sudamericana.

Loungani, P., A. Mody, and A. Razin. (2002). The global disconnect: The role of transactional distance and scale economies in gravity equations. *Scottish Journal of Political Economy 49*(5), 526–43.

Lucas, R. E. B. (1993). On the determinants of direct foreign investment: Evidence from East and Southeast Asia. *World Development 21*(3), 391–406.

Malesky, E. J. (2009). Foreign direct investors as agents of economic transition: An instrumental variables analysis. *Quarterly Journal of Political Science 4*(1), 59–85.

Mardon, R. (1990). The state and the effective control of foreign-capital – the case of South-Korea. *World Politics 43*(1), 111–38.

Margheritis, A. (1999). *Ajuste y reforma en Argentina (1989–1995): la economía política de las privatizaciones* (1 ed.). Buenos Aires, Argentina: Grupo Editor Latinoamericano.

Markusen, J. R. (1984). Multinationals, multi-plant economies, and the gains from trade. *Journal of International Economics 16*(3,4), 205–26.

Markusen, J. R. (1995). The boundaries of multinational-enterprises and the theory of international-trade. *Journal of Economic Perspectives 9*(2), 169–89.

Markusen, J. R., and K. E. Maskus. (2001a). *General-equilibrium approaches to the multinational firm: a review of theory and evidence.* NBER Working paper series no. 8334. Cambridge, MA: National Bureau of Economic Research.

Markusen, J. R., and K. E. Maskus. (2001b). Multinational firms: Reconciling theory and evidence. In M. Blömstrom and L. S. Goldberg (Eds.), *Topics in Empirical International Economics: A Festschrift in Honor of Robert E. Lipsey*, pp. 71–98. University of Chicago Press.

Markusen, J. R., and K. E. Maskus. (2001c). *A unified approach to intra-industry trade and direct foreign investment.* NBER Working paper series no. 8335. Cambridge, MA: National Bureau of Economic Research.

Markusen, J. R., and K. E. Maskus. (2002). Discriminating among alternative theories of the multinational enterprise. *Review of International Economics 10*(4), 694–707.

Marvel, H. P., and E. J. Ray. (1983). The Kennedy Round: Evidence on the regulation of international trade in the united states. *The American Economic Review 73*(1), 190–97.

Mayer, W. (1984). Endogenous tariff formation. *The American Economic Review 74*(5), 970–85.

McGuire, J. W. (1997). Peronism without Perón: unions, parties, and democracy in Argentina. Stanford, CA: Stanford University Press.

Milner, H. V. (1988). *Resisting protectionism: global industries and the politics of international trade.* Princeton, N.J.: Princeton University Press.

Milner, H. V., and B. Judkins. (2004). Partisanship, trade policy, and globalization: Is there a left-right divide on trade policy? *International Studies Quarterly 48*(1), 95–120.

Mo, J., and C. I. Moon. (1999). *Democracy and the Korean economy.* Stanford, CA: Hoover Institution Press.

Monteon, M. (1987). Can argentina's democracy survive economic disaster? In M. Peralta-Ramos and C. H. Waisman (Eds.), *From Military Rule to Liberal Democracy in Argentina*, pp. 21–34. Boulder, CO: Westview Press.

Moon, C. I., and J. Mo. (1999). *Democratization and globalization in Korea: assessments and prospects.* Seoul, Korea: Yonsei University Press.

Moon, C.-I., and J. Mo. (2000). Economic crisis and structural reforms in South Korea: Assessments and implications. Washington, D.C.: Economic Strategy Institute.

Mora y Araujo, M. (1980). Introducción: La sociología electoral y la comprensión del peronismo. In M. Mora y Araujo and I. Llorente (Eds.), *El Voto Peronista*, pp. 524. Buenos Aires: Editorial Sudamericana.

Moran, T. H. (1974). *Multinational Corporations and the Politics of Dependence: Copper in Chile.* Princeton, N.J.: Princeton University Press.

Moran, T. H. (1978). Multinational corporations and dependency: A dialogue for dependentistas and non-dependentistas. *International Organization 32*(1), 79–100.

Moran, T. H. (1998). The changing nature of political risk. In T. H. Moran (Ed.), *Managing international political risk*, pp. 7–14. Malden, MA: Blackwell.

Moran, T. H. (1999). Foreign direct investment and good jobs/bad jobs: The impact of outward investment and inward investment on jobs and wages. In A. Fishlow and K. Parker (Eds.), *Growing apart: the causes and consequence of global wage inequality*, pp. 95–117. New York, N.Y.: Council on Foreign Relations.

Moran, T. H. (2002). *Beyond sweatshops: foreign direct investment and globalization in developing countries.* Washington, D.C.: Brookings Institution Press.

Morley, S. A., R. Machado, and S. Pettinato. (1999). *Indexes of structural reform in Latin America*. Serie Reformas Económicas 12. Santiago, Chile: United Nations, Economic Commission for Latin America and the Caribbean.

Mundell, R. A. (1957). International trade and factor mobility. *The American Economic Review 47*(3), 321–35.

Murillo, M. V. (1997). Union politics, market-oriented reforms, and the reshaping of argentine corporatism. In D. A. Chalmers (Ed.), *The new politics of inequality in Latin America: rethinking participation and representation*, pp. 72–94. Oxford, England: Oxford University Press.

Murillo, M. V. (2001). *Labor unions, partisan coalitions and market reforms in Latin America*. Cambridge studies in comparative politics. Cambridge, England: Cambridge University Press.

Murmis, M., and J. C. Portantiero. (1971). *Estudios sobre los orígenes del peronismo*. Buenos Aires: Siglo Vientiuno Argentina Editores.

Nicolas, F. (2001). A case of government-led integration into the world economy. In F. Sachwald (Ed.), *Going multinational: the Korean experience of direct investment*, Volume 9 of *Studies in global competition*, pp. 17–76. New York, N.Y.: Routledge.

Nicolas, F. (2003). FDI as a factor of economic restructuring: the case of South Korea. In A. Bende-Nabende (Ed.), *International trade, capital flows, and economic development in East Asia: the challenge in the 21st century*, pp. 150–82. Aldershof, England: Ashgate.

Noland, M. (2007). *South Korea's Experience with International Capital Flows*, pp. 481–528. Chicago, IL: University of Chicago Press.

Noland, M. and H. Pack. (2003). *Industrial policy in an era of globalization: lessons from Asia*. Policy analyses in international economics. Washington, D.C.: Institute for International Economics.

North, D. C. (1990). Institutions, institutional change, and economic performance. Cambridge, England: Cambridge University Press.

North, D. C., and R. P. Thomas. (1973). *The rise of the Western world: a new economic history*. Cambridge, England: Cambridge University Press.

North, D. C., and B. R. Weingast. (1989). Constitutions and commitment: The evolution of institutional governing public choice in seventeenth-century England. *Journal of Economic History 49*(4), 803–32.

O'Donnell, G. (1988). *Bureaucratic authoritarianism: Argentina, 1966-1973, in comparative perspective*. Berkeley, CA: University of California Press.

OECD. (1998a). *Foreign Direct Investment and Economic Development: Lessons from Six Emerging Economies*. Paris: Organisation for Economic Co-operation and Development.

OECD. (1998b). International Sectoral Database (ISDB). Organization for Economic Cooperation and Development: Online resource.

Ohmae, K. (1995). *The end of the nation state: the rsie of regional economies*. New York, N.Y.: Free Press.

Olson, M. (1971). *The logic of collective action*. Cambridge, MA: Harvard University Press.

Olson, M. (1993). Dictatorship, democracy, and development. *The American Political Science Review 87*(3), 567–76.

Oneal, J. R. (1994). The affinity of foreign investors for authoritarian regimes. *Political Research Quarterly 47*(3), 565–88.

Oneal, J. R. and F. H. Oneal. (1988). Hegemony, imperialism, and the profitability of foreign investments. *International Organization 42*(2), 347–73.

O'Rourke, K. H. and J. G. Williamson. (1999). *Globalization and history: the evolution of a nineteenth-century Atlantic economy.* Cambridge, MA: MIT Press.

Pandya, S. S. (2008). *Trading Spaces: The Politics of Foreign Direct Investment Regulation.* Ph. D. thesis, Government Department, Harvard University, Cambridge, MA.

Peltzman, S. (1976). Towards a more general theory of regulation. *Journal of Law and Economics 19*(2), 211–40.

Persson, T., and G. E., Tabellini. (1994). Representative democracy and capital taxation. *Journal of Public Economics 55*(1), 53–70.

Persson, T., and G. E. Tabellini. (2000). *Political economics: explaining economic policy.* Cambridge, MA: MIT Press.

Pinto, P. M. (2004). *Domestic Coalitions and the Political Economy of Foreign Direct Investment.* Ph. D. thesis, Department of Political Science and IR/PS, University of California San Diego, La Jolla, CA.

Pinto, P. M., and S. M. Pinto. (2007). The politics of investment: Partisan governments, wages and employment. Prepared for presentation at the *International Political Economy Society Annual Conference (November 9-10),* Palo Alto, California.

Pinto, P. M., and S. M. Pinto. (2008). The politics of investment: Partisanship and the sectoral allocation of foreign direct investment. *Economics and Politics 20*(2), 216–54.

Pinto, P. M., and S. M. Pinto. (2011). Partisanship and the allocation of foreign investment under imperfect capital mobility. *Prepared for presentation at the Annual Meeting of the American Political Science Association (September 1–4, 2011),* Seattle, WA.

Pinto, P. M., S. Weymouth, and P. A. Gourevitch. (2010). The politics of stock market development. *Review of international political economy 17*(2), 378–409.

Pinto, P. M., and B. Zhu. (2008). Fortune or Evil? The effects of inward foreign direct investment on corruption. Saltzman Institute of War and Peace Studies, Working Paper No. 10, New York, N.Y.

Polanyi, K. (1957). *The great transformation.* Boston, MA: Beacon Press.

Przeworski, A., M. E. Alvarez, J. A. Cheibub, and F. Limongi. (2000). *Democracy and development: political institutions and well-being in the world, 1950–1990.* Cambridge Studies in the Theory of Democracy. Cambridge, England: Cambridge University Press.

Pyo, H. K. (1990). Export-led growth, domestic distortions, and trade liberalization: The Korean experience during the 1980s. *Journal of Asian Economics 1*(2), 225–47.

Quinn, D. (1997). The correlates of change in international financial regulation. *The American Political Science Review 91*(3), 531–51.

Quinn, D. P., and C. Inclan. (1997). The origins of financial openness: A study of current and capital account liberalization. *American Journal of Political Science 41*(3), 771–813.

Quinn, D. P., and R. Y. Shapiro. (1991). Economic growth strategies – the effects of ideological partisanship on interest rates and business taxation in the United States. *American Journal of Political Science 35*(3), 656–85.

Ranis, P. (1994). *Class, democracy, and labor in contemporary Argentina.* New Brunswick, N.J.: Transaction Publishers.

Rapoport, M. (2000). *Historia Económica, Política y Social de la Argentina (1880–2000).* Buenos Aires: Ediciones Macchi.

Ray, E. J. (1981). The determinants of tariff and nontariff trade restrictions in the United States. *Journal of Political Economy* 89(1), 105–21.

Rock, D. (1987). Political movements in Argentina: A sketch from past and present. In M. Peralta-Ramos and C. H. Waisman (Eds.), *From military rule to liberal democracy in Argentina,* pp. 3–20. Boulder, Colo.: Westview Press.

Rodrik, D. (1995). Political economy of trade policy. In G. M. Grossman and K. S. Rogoff (Eds.), *Handbook of International Economics,* Volume III, pp. 1457–94. New York, N.Y.: Elsevier Science Pub. Co.

Rodrik, D. (1997). *Has globalization gone too far?* Washington, D.C.: Institute for International Economics.

Rodrik, D. (1998). Why do more open economies have bigger governments. *Journal of Political Economy* 106(5), 997–1032.

Rogowski, R. (1987). Political cleavages and changing exposure to trade. *The American Political Science Review* 81(4), 1121–37.

Rogowski, R. (1989). *Commerce and coalitions: how trade affects domestic political alignments.* Princeton, N.J.: Princeton University Press.

Rogowski, R. (2003). International capital mobility and national policy divergence. In M. Kahler and D. A. Lake (Eds.), *Governance in a global economy: political authority in transition,* pp. 255–74. Princeton, N.J.: Princeton University Press.

Rosecrance, R. N. (1999). *The rise of the virtual state: wealth and power in the coming century.* New York, N.Y.: Basic Books.

Rybczynski, T. M. (1955). Factor endowment and relative commodity prices. *Economica* 22(88), 336–41.

Sachwald, F. (2001). Emerging multinationals: The main issues. In F. Sachwald (Ed.), *Going multinational: the Korean experience of direct investment,* Studies in global competition, pp. 1–16. New York, N.Y.: Routledge.

Sachwald, F. (2003). Exporting dynamism: Korea's overseas direct investment. In *Confrontation and innovation on the Korean Peninsula. Part II: Innovation and Reform,* Volume 5, pp. 85–95. Washington, D.C.: The Korea Economic Institute.

Sakong, I. (1993). *Korea in the world economy.* Washington, DC: Institute for International Economics.

Sauvant, K. P., and L. E. Sachs. (2009). BITs, DTTs and FDI flows: An overview. In K. P. Sauvant and L. E. Sachs (Eds.), *The Effect of Treaties on Foreign Direct Investment: Bilateral Investment Treaties, Double Taxation Treaties, and Investment Flows,* pp. xxvii–liv. Oxford, England: Oxford University Press.

Schamis, H. E. (1999). Distributional coalitions and the politics of economic reform in Latin America. *World Politics* 51(2), 236–68.

Scheve, K., and M. J. Slaughter. (2004). Economic insecurity and the globalization of production. *American Journal of Political Science* 48(4), 662–74.

Scheve, K. F., and M. J. Slaughter. (2001a). Labor market competition and individual preferences over immigration policy. *The Review of Economics and Statistics* 83(1), 133.

Scheve, K. F., and M. J. Slaughter. (2001b). What determines individual trade-policy preferences? *Journal of International Economics* 54(2), 267.

Sjöholm, F., and R. E. Lipsey. (2006). Foreign firms and indonesian manufacturing wages: An analysis with panel data. *Economic Development & Cultural Change 55*(1), 201–21.

Smith, P. H. (1980). La base social del peronismo. In M. Mora y Araujo and I. Llorente (Eds.), *El Voto Peronista*, pp. 57–86. Buenos Aires: Editorial Sudamericana.

Smith, W. C., and C. Acuña. (1994). The political economy of structural adjustment: The logic of support and opposition to neoliberal reform. In W. C. Smith, C. Acuña, and E. Gamarra (Eds.), *Latin American political economy in the age of neoliberal reform: theoretical and comparative perspectives for the 1990s*, pp. 17–66. New Brunswick N.J.: Transaction Publishers.

Spiller, P. T., and M. Tommasi. (2003). The institutional foundations of public policy: A transactions approach with application to argentina. *Journal of Law Economics & Organization 19*(2), 281–306.

Srinivasan, T. N. (1998). Trade and human rights. In A. V. Deardorff and R. M. Stern (Eds.), *Constituent interests and U.S. trade policies*, Studies in international economics, pp. 225–54. Ann Arbor, MI: University of Michigan Press.

Stigler, G. J. (1971). The theory of economic regulation. *The Bell Journal of Economics and Management Science 2*(1), 3–21.

Stoever, W. A. (2002 April). Attempting to resolve the attraction-aversion dilemma: a study of FDI policy in the Republic of Korea. *Transnational corporations 2*(1), 49–76.

Stolper, W. F., and P. A. Samuelson. (1941). Protection and real wages. *The Review of Economic Studies 9*(1), 58–73.

Strange, S. (1996). *The Retreat of the state: the diffusion of power in the world economy*. Cambridge, England: Cambridge University Press.

Strange, S. (1998). *Mad money: when markets outgrow governments*. Ann Arbor, MI: University of Michigan Press.

Swank, D. (1998). Funding the welfare state: Globalization and the taxation of business in advanced market economics. *Political Studies 46*(4), 671–92.

Swank, D. (2006). Comparative Parties Data Set. Electronic Resource. http://www.marquette.edu/polisci/faculty/faculty_swank.shtml.

Swank, D., and S. Steinmo. (2002). The new political economy of taxation in advanced capitalist democracies. *American Journal of Political Science 46*(3), 642–55.

Taylor, A. M. (1994). Three phases of argentine economic growth. NBER Working Paper Series on Historical Factors in Long Run Growth no. 60. Cambridge, MA: National Bureau of Economic Research.

Taylor, A. M. (1998a). Argentina and the world capital market: saving, investment, and international capital mobility in the twentieth century. *Journal of Development Economics 57*(1), 147–84.

Taylor, A. M. (1998b). On the costs of inward-looking development: Price distortions, growth, and divergence in latin america. *Journal of Economic History 58*(1), 1–28.

Taylor, A. M. (2003). *Foreign capital in Latin America in the nineteenth and twentieth centuries*. NBER Working paper series No. 9580. Cambridge, MA: National Bureau of Economic Research.

Taylor, A. M., and J. G. Williamson. (1997). Convergence in the age of mass migration. *European Review of Economic History 1*(1), 27–63.

Taylor, C. L., and D. A. Jodice. (1984). World handbook of political and social indicators III, 1948–82. Ann Arbor, MI: Inter-University Consortium for Political and Social Research.

The Heritage Foundation. (2010). *The index of economic freedom*. Washington, D.C.: The Heritage Foundation.

Tiebout, C. M. (1956). A pure theory of local expenditures. *The Journal of Political Economy 64*(5), 416–24.

Tomz, M., J. Wittenberg, and G. King. (2003). Clarify: Software for Interpreting and Presenting Statistical Results. *Journal of Statical Software, 8*(1).

Torre, J. C. (1974). The meaning of current workers' struggles. *Latin American Perspectives 1*(3), 73–81.

Trefler, D. (1993). Trade liberalization and the theory of endogenous protection: An econometric study of U.S. import policy. *Journal of Political Economy 101*(1), 138–60.

Tsebelis, G. (1995). Decision making in political systems: Veto players in presidentialism, parliamentarism, multicameralism and multipartyism. *British Journal of Political Science 25*(3), 289–325.

Tsebelis, G. (2002). *Veto players: how political institutions work*. Princeton, N.J.: Princeton University Press.

Tufte, E. R. (1978). *Political control of the economy*. Princeton, N.J.: Princeton University Press.

Tuman, J. P., and J. T. Morris. (1998). The transformation of the Latin American automobile industry. In J. P. Tuman and J. T. Morris (Eds.), *Transforming the Latin American automobile industry: unions, workers, and the politics of restructuring*, pp. 3–25. Armonk, N.Y.: M.E. Sharpe.

Twomey, M. J. (1998). Patterns of foreign investment in latin america in the twentieth century. In J. H. Coatsworth and A. M. Taylor (Eds.), *Latin America and the World Economy since 1800*, pp. 171–202. Cambridge, MA: David Rockefeller Center for Latina American Studies and Harvard University Press.

UNCTAD. (1992). *World Investment Report: Transnational Corporations as Engines of Growth*, Volume 1992 of *World Investment Report*. New York, N.Y.: United Nations.

UNCTAD. (1999). *World Investment Report: Foreign Direct Investment and the Challenge of Development*, Volume 1999 of *World Investment Report*. New York, N.Y.: United Nations.

UNCTAD. (2000). *World Investment Report: Cross-border mergers and acquisitions and development*, Volume 2000 of *World Investment Report*. New York, N.Y.: United Nations.

UNCTAD. (2001). *World Investment Report: Promoting Linkages*, Volume 2001 of *World investment report*. New York, N.Y.: United Nations.

UNCTAD. (2002). *World Investment Report: Transnational corporations and export competitiveness*, Volume 2002 of *World investment report*. New York, N.Y.: United Nations.

UNCTAD. (2003). *World Investment Report: FDI Policies for Development. National and International Perspectives*, Volume 2003 of *World investment report*. New York, N.Y.: United Nations.

UNCTAD. (2010). *World Investment Report 2010: Investing in a low-carbon economy*, Volume 2010 of *World Investment Report*. New York, N.Y.: United Nations.

UNCTAD, Z. Zimny, and H. El-Kady. (2009). *The role of international investment agreements in attracting foreign direct investment to developing countries.* UNCTAD series on international investment policies for development. New York, NY: United Nations.

Vázquez Vialard, A. L. R. (1981). *El sindicato en el derecho argentino: Formación y funcionamiento. Relaciones internas y externas. Garantías y responsabilidad sindical. Suspensión, retiro, disolución y liquidación del sindicato.* Buenos Aires: Astrea.

Verdier, D. (1998). Domestic responses to capital market internationalization under the gold standard, 1870–1914. *International Organization 52*(1), 1–34.

Vernon, R. (1971). *Sovereignty at bay; the multinational spread of U.S. enterprises.* The Harvard Multinational Enterprise Series. New York, N.Y.: Basic Books.

Vernon, R. (1977). *Storm over the multinationals: the real issues.* Cambridge, MA: Harvard University Press.

Vogel, S. K. (1996). *Freer markets, more rules: regulatory reform in advanced industrial countries.* Ithaca, N.Y.: Cornell University Press.

Waisman, C. H. (1987). *Reversal of development in Argentina: postwar counterrevolutionary policies and their structural consequences.* Princeton, N.J.: Princeton University Press.

Wells, Louis T., J. (1998). God and fair competition: Does the foreign direct investor face still other risks in emerging markets? In T. H. Moran (Ed.), *Managing international political risk,* pp. 15–43. Malden, MA: Blackwell.

Westphal, L. E., L. Kim, and C. Dahlman. (1985). Reflections on Korea's acquisition of technological capability. In N. Rosenberg and C. Frischtak (Eds.), *International technology transfer: concepts, measures, and comparisons,* pp. 167–221. New York, N.Y.: Praeger.

Westphal, L. E., Y. W. Rhee, and G. Pursell. (1981). *Korean industrial competence: where it came from. World Bank staff Working paper* no. 469. Washington, D.C.: World Bank.

Wheeler, D. and A. Mody. (1992). International investment location decision – the case of united-states firms. *Journal of International Economics 33*(1–2), 57–76.

Whiting, V. R. (1992). *The political economy of foreign investment in Mexico: nationalism, liberalism, and constraints on choice.* Baltimore, MD: Johns Hopkins University Press.

Williamson, J. G. (1990). *Latin American Adjustment: How Much Has Happened?* Washington, D.C.: Institute for International Economics.

Williamson, O. E. (1979). Transaction-cost economics: The governance of contractual relations. *Journal of Economic Issues 22*(2), 233.

Williamson, O. E. (1983a). Credible commitments: Using hostages to support exchange. *The American Economic Review 73*(4), 519.

Williamson, O. E. (1983b). *Markets and hierarchies: analysis and antitrust implications: a study in the economics of internal organization* (2nd ed.). New York, N.Y.: Free Press.

Williamson, O. E. (1985). *The economic institutions of capitalism: firms, markets, relational contracting.* New York, N.Y.: Free Press.

Woo-Cumings, M. (1991). *Race to the swift: state and finance in Korean industrialization.* Studies of the East Asian Institute. New York, N.Y.: Columbia University Press.

Wood, A. (1991). *A new-old theoretical view of North-South trade, employment, and wages.* Brighton, England: Institute of Development Studies.

Wood, A. (1994). *North-South trade, employment, and inequality: changing fortunes in a skill-driven world.* Oxford, England: Oxford University Press.

World Bank (2010). World Development Indicators: Database. Computer file. Washington, D.C.: The World Bank.

Yoo, J.-H. (1994). South Korea's manufactured exports and industrial targeting policy. In S. Yang (Ed.), *Manufactured exports of East Asian industrializing economies: possible regional cooperation,* pp. 149–74. Armonk, N.Y.: M.E. Sharpe.

Yoo, S.-M. (1999). Corporate restructuring in South Korea. *Joint U.S.-Korea Academic Studies 9,* 131–99.

You, J.-I. and J.-H. Lee (1999). *Economic and social consequences of globalization: the case of South Korea.* Working paper series No. 9904. Seoul, Korea: School of Public Policy and Management, Korea Development Institute.

Yun, M. (2003). FDI and corporate restructuring In post-crisis korea. in S. Haggard, W. Lim, and E. Kim (Eds.), *Economic crisis and corporate restructuring in Korea: reforming the chaebol,* Cambridge Asia-Pacific studies, pp. 233–64. Cambridge, England: Cambridge University Press.

Index

Printed in the United States
by Baker & Taylor Publisher Services